GEORGE GROVE

1820–1900

GEORGE GROVE

1820–1900

A BIOGRAPHY

Percy M. Young

GROVE'S DICTIONARIES OF MUSIC, INC.

Published 1980 by
GROVE'S DICTIONARIES OF MUSIC, INC.
1283 National Press Building, Washington, D.C. 20045, U.S.A.

Printed in Great Britain by
EBENEZER BAYLIS AND SON LIMITED
The Trinity Press, Worcester, and London

Library of Congress Cataloging in Publication Data

Young, Percy Marshall, 1912–
  George Grove 1820-1900.

  Bibliography: p.
  Includes index.
    1. Grove, George, Sir, 1820-1900. 2. Musicians—
  Great Britain—Biography.
  ML423.G8Y7   780′.92′4 [B]   79-29705
  ISBN 0-333-19602-3

Contents

List of Illustrations

between pages 48 and 49

Preface

'I've liked to imagine the "party" writing the var. him (or her) self. . . ,' said Elgar in respect of the 'Enigma' Variations. Something of that spirit must of necessity underlie the writing of the biography of George Grove, who was himself a master of this craft. Like C. P. Scott, he held that facts were sacred, and he was tireless in searching for them—often in obscure corners. To serve Grove's memory best is to emulate him in these particulars, and in so doing I have done as I believe he would have wished a latter-day biographer to do. He would not, I believe, have wished a biographer at this distance in time from the persons and events which framed his life to turn away from what is documented, least of all from what he himself had put on paper. I take courage from his attitude to his subjects in the three great studies of Beethoven, Schubert and Mendelssohn, which is summed up towards the end of the last of these: 'But let us take the man as we have him.'

C. L. Graves published a Life of Grove in 1903. This has many virtues; but Graves, well acquainted with his subject, decided that he had to describe not the man he knew but the monument he wished to be preserved. He was aware of some of his omissions and—a little ingenuously —acknowledged them. He wished to represent Grove as an Eminent Victorian. Enough time has elapsed since then for us to be able (without belonging to the post-Strachey counter-revolution) to look back at a remarkable age in the history of Britain, and to recognize that among the Victorians there were some whose enterprises defy emulation. Grove was one of them.

His track record is of the legendary order certified by the motto, *labor omnia vincit*. An early school-leaver who had shown no outstanding promise of academic distinction, he went to the top of several professions buoyed up by a combination of faith in the work ethic and an insatiable curiosity. He was a practical man who developed management skills on the shop floor; and he was an idealist who suffered in the internecine quarrels of theologians on the one hand, and on the other in the contest between belief and disbelief in the philosophical arena in which he claimed a place.

He was said by all who knew him to have been unfailingly good company, with a merry quip for any occasion. Men who are so described are rarely what they seem. Grove—however the quality is defined—was in the category of genius, and it is axiomatic that those who belong there invariably suffer. Many areas of Grove's life were invaded by unhappiness and discontent. True to the traditions by which he was most influenced, however, he took pains to disguise the effects of those erosive forces. But now we can see the facts which most of all show him as he was.

There is a comprehensive record of his inner life in the letters which he wrote to his Irish student Edith Oldham—some quarter of a million words spread over seventeen years. There are many other documents to which I have had access, but these letters are of the greatest significance, for in them is to be found the price demanded of this Eminent Victorian.

It is ironic that while it is now conceded that the practical skills required of an engineer have long been set on a level lower than those thought effective in the sphere of the humanities, Grove's humanism flourished because it was nurtured in Clapham and on the Clyde. The boy was the father of the man who changed from engineer into Bible scholar, and thereafter into archaeologist, man of letters, administrator and musician, without losing the essence of any of these functions. By the side of all these functions, however, lay a powerful consciousness of moral frailty. On the personal plane Grove fought many battles, concerning which the most significant evidence has only lately come to light.

Whether it is better to build lighthouses or to inaugurate one of the world's most famous encyclopedias is an open question. It is not one that often needs to be posed. This book is the one context where one may do so. In biblical, archaeological and musical scholarship Grove has long since been overtaken in respect of method, and often controverted in the matter of conclusion. Yet he must seem immeasurably superior to those who have overtaken him: for his concern was less with the parts than the whole.

P.M.Y.

Acknowledgements

For making source material available I am indebted to:

The Royal College of Music, in respect of documents originally belonging to George Grove and letters to Edith Oldham in the care of the Keeper of Portraits; the British Library; the Pierpont Morgan Library, New York; the Public Record Office (British Transport Historical Records); the City of Westminster Archives Department; the Minet Library, Lambeth; the Institution of Civil Engineers; Dr Chalmers Burns; Mr Raymond Monk; and Professor Ian Parrott.

The Librarians and officers of the following institutions have readily put their resources at my disposal:

Bibliothèque Nationale, Paris; the British Association for the Advancement of Science; the Brighton Area Library; the *Daily Telegraph*; the *Guardian*; Gloucestershire County Archives; the House of Commons; Jones Memorial Library, Lynchburg, Va.; the Cities of Liverpool and Manchester; the Mitchell Library and the Museum of Transport, Glasgow; *Punch*; Salisbury Divisional Library; Staatsbibliothek, Berlin; Staffordshire County Archives; *the Strathearn Herald*; the University Libraries of Birmingham (Barber Institute), Glasgow, Halle and Trinity College, Dublin; and Wolverhampton Art Gallery.

For continuing advice and friendly encouragement I am grateful to:

Mr Reginald Allen, Dr Bernd Baselt, Miss Catharine Carver,[1] Mr J. F. Earle, Dr Nigel Fortune, Mr E. G. H. Kempson, Mr Alec Hyatt King, Dr A. G. Marshall, Mrs Rhona Marshall, Dr Edward Pringle, Mr Frank Singleton, Mr E. E. F. Smith, Mrs D. Stevens, Miss Joan Trimble, Mr Terence de Vere White, Mr David R. Young.

At a very late stage in production Mrs Margaret O'Connor of Bath, daughter of the late Walter Grove, identified herself as George Grove's sole surviving grand-daughter, and I wish to thank her for so doing.

While in the United States in November 1979 I was able to consult Mrs Brenda Jean Grove Corbett-Smith, of Los Gatos, California, great-grand-daughter of George Grove Blackwell (see p. 35). The genealogical information communicated by her is of considerable interest, and I am most grateful for the trouble taken by Mrs Corbett-Smith to establish contact with me and in furnishing me with a copy of the birth certificate of George Grove Blackwell and other pertinent family records. If there are others to whom further acknowledgement in respect of copyright material may be due apology is hereby proffered.

I am particularly aware of a twofold debt of gratitude to the Royal College of Music. In the first place I am ever mindful of the influence of my music master of more than fifty years ago — Robert Wilkinson, student at the College from 1892 — from whom I heard directly of the period of Grove's Directorship.

[1] Who lives — coincidentally and appropriately — in *Edith Grove*, London S.W.10.

Secondly, while working on this book the present Director and staff of the College have afforded me much hospitality; Dr Watkins Shaw, Miss Joan Littlejohn and Miss Celia Clarke enabled me to work in comfort in the Parry Room and were always ready to answer questions.

Renée Morris Young has been a constant support throughout the time devoted to this undertaking.

The review of *Beethoven and his Nine Symphonies* (Appendix B) appears by permission of the Society of Authors on behalf of the Bernard Shaw Estate.

P.M.Y.

List of Abbreviations

BL	British Library
E.O.	Edith Oldham (Oldham Letters, Royal College of Music)
Graves	C. L. Graves, *The Life and Letters of Sir George Grove, C.B.* (1903)
Grove 1	*Grove's Dictionary of Music and Musicians*, 1st edn (1879–89), 4 vols.
PICE	*Proceedings of the Institution of Civil Engineers*
PML	Pierpont Morgan Library, New York
RAM	Royal Academy of Music
RCM	Royal College of Music
RIAM	Royal Irish Academy of Music

The place of publication for all sources cited in the footnotes is London unless otherwise indicated. For full data on sources cited in short form in the text, see the Bibliography (p. 315).

CHAPTER ONE

A Comprehensive Education in Clapham

1820–1835

IF George Grove had been the eldest son of his father he would have become a Master Fishmonger rather than a lexicographer. If he had been as academically apt as some of his companions of youth he would have gone to university and might well have developed into a dignitary of the Church. With a more secure temperament and the singlemindedness of his younger brother Edmund he would have remained constant to his first calling of civil engineer. As it was he felt compelled to conduct a lifelong struggle on the battlefield of ambition to satisfy a basic tenet of Victorian philosophy which held that 'God rewardeth every man according to his work'. Certainly, few men ever worked harder than Grove and few were so honoured as he was for achievement in disparate professions. In the end, however, Grove—like Johnson—is a synonym for a dictionary.

The dictionary of which he was the creator came into being out of a combination of industriousness and discontent. George Grove was successful, but his success was borne on a turbulent flood of unhappiness. All his life he was haunted by the prospective fate of sinners, but secretly he came to enjoy contemplation of the more alluring of the sins in the Victorian catalogue of impropriety.

At the beginning of the nineteenth century there was no better place in England to comprehend the theological division between virtue and vice than Clapham, where Grove—missing the reign of George III by only six months—was born on 13 August 1820. He was the third son and eighth child of Thomas and Mary Grove, who were then forty-six and thirty-six years old respectively.[1]

Clapham at that time had an ethos of its own, since its leading residents had become aware of a sense of special responsibility. It was sometimes derisively termed by outsiders the 'holy village'. In 1772 a new Vicar had come to Clapham: John Venn, son of Henry Venn who was one of the

---

[1] The children of Thomas and Mary Grove were: Mary Bithiah (b. 1808), Bithiah Blades (b. 1809), Thomas Blades (b. 1812), Frances Moore (b. 1813), Eliza Jane (b. 1815), Edmund I (b. 1817), all born in the parish of St Martin-in-the-Fields; Kezia (b. 1819), George (b. 1820), Edmund II (b. 1823), Anna (b. 1824), Eleanor (b. 1827), all born in Clapham. Edmund I died on 17 May 1819, Frances Moore on 8 Jan 1833.

leaders of the Evangelical revival in the Church of England and had himself once been a curate at Clapham. The younger Venn continued a friendship his father had had with Henry Thornton, the philanthropist, and also conceived a sense of responsibility for the peoples of Africa whose lands were being increasingly and ruthlessly exploited. In 1797 Venn founded the Church Missionary Society, and a year later he read a paper on the need for educating African children in England, so that they should be able afterwards to return home as missionaries. In 1799 Zachary Macaulay, Governor of Sierra Leone—a colony created for freed slaves—arrived home in Clapham with twenty-one African boys and four girls. On 1 June he wrote to his Quaker fiancée, Selina Mills, that the children 'excited no small admiration among our friends who account them a highly favourable specimen of African youth'. Macaulay's friends, who at that time included, as well as Thornton, William Wilberforce and his brother-in-law James Stephen,[2] became known as the 'Clapham sect', which 'drew the wonder of the worldly, and provoked the scoffing of the proud' as they followed Zachary Macaulay in his high purpose— 'the sweeping from the face of the earth of the wrong and shame of slavery'.

The Venns and the Wilberforces were connected with Yorkshire, and it was agreed that William Greaves, a Yorkshireman, should be the teacher of the African children, accommodated by Macaulay in a house (now 8 Rectory Grove) which he owned near St Paul's Chapel. A well-built man with a ruddy complexion, Greaves provided a sensible curriculum, with English, carpentry, printing, and 'the elements of mechanics', all wrapped by the local clergy in religious dogmatics. The enterprise, however, failed. By 1805 two of the children were dead and all but eight of those who survived had gone home; in this year the African Academy—now in 3–4 Church Buildings—opened its doors to local boys. Thomas Babington Macaulay was a pupil there, and so, somewhat later, was George Grove.

George's father, Thomas, belonged to a farming family (variously known as Grove or Groves) settled in Penn, Buckinghamshire—since Norman times, some of them liked to believe.[3] Born in 1774, Thomas

[2] Others were William Smith, Unitarian Member of Parliament for Norwich; Lord Teignmouth, in whose house the Bible Society was formed; Granville Sharp, one-time supporter of the cause of the American colonists; Thomas Gisborne, moralist and naturalist; Charles Simeon, Evangelical theologian; and Isaac Milner, like Simeon a scholar at Cambridge where he was Professor of Natural Philosophy.

[3] Letter to F. G. Edwards, 5 May 1890; BL, Eg. MS. 3091, f. 18. George's brother Thomas in due course purchased an estate in Penn, on land which had belonged—so it was thought—to former generations of Groves, but had been disposed of by those who were improvident or unlucky, or both. 'Stonehouse, formerly Grove's Plat, the residence of Mr Walter Grove J.P. [son of George; see p. 262], has for many generations belonged to his family'; *Victoria County History of Buckingham*, vol. III (1925), p. 235.

were taken to St James's to hear the Revd Charles Bradley. . . . Though it is forty years ago, I remember perfectly his manner and appearance; the pleasant kindly face, with the iron-grey hair and whiskers, the attractive style, the clear voice, the loving, earnest way of analysing his subject. . . . In those days there was a good deal of Ritualism in the pulpit, though none in the chancel: the adjusting of the gown, unfolding of the pocket-handkerchief, the task of taking off and putting on black or lavender kid gloves,—from mannerisms of this kind Mr Bradley was quite free. The service, too, at his church was, for those days, hearty and congregational.[11]

Evangelistic fervour had a good run, but already in Grove's schooldays it seemed to be diminishing. In 1890 he remembered the Church of England in 1830 as having been 'a mass of deadness and stiff dulness. The Old Wesleyan, Evangelical movement had died down and the clergy were a body without a soul. . . .'[12]

None the less Clapham provided an impressive array of clerisy. Two prelates were comfortably resident there during some part of George's schooldays: John Jebb, until 1833 Bishop of Limerick, and John Bird Sumner, for whom Leveson Lodge, Clapham, was a convenient home from home while in charge of the distant see of Chester and awaiting a call to Canterbury. And there was the Revd Charles Pritchard—the total antidote to 'deadness and stiff dulness'. Pritchard's influence on Grove was as great as, if not greater than, that of any other person, and it was to a school maintained by him that the boy was transferred from Elwell's in 1832. Pritchard was one of the most remarkable men of his generation, and among schoolmasters of his time without peer. He was that *rara avis*, an educationist with an open mind.

At the beginning of the nineteenth century the teaching of mathematics was revitalized by the researches and inventiveness of Robert Woodhouse, Professor of Mathematics and later of Astronomy at Cambridge University. Woodhouse had some brilliant pupils whose influence was to become widespread and of lasting significance. Among the second generation of talented mathematical scholars at Cambridge was Charles Pritchard, who, at the age of seventeen, had published an *Introduction to Arithmetic* and four years later a treatise on the *Theory of Statistical Couples* which was used as a university text book. After four more years he married and was on that account compelled to resign his Fellowship at St John's College. Adrift in the world at the age of twenty-five, he was fortified by extraordinary mathematical skills, a wide knowledge of and competence in humane letters, a conviction that education in general was in need of

[11] From *The Guardian*, 5 Apr 1882, quoted in C. Bradley, *A Selection from the Sermons* . . . (1884).
[12] E.O., Sat. Aug 16 [1890].

thorough reconstruction, and an inextinguishable faith in his own ability
to show how such reconstruction should be undertaken.

It was a period of reform in the general sense (the first Reform Bill
was passed in 1832) and the landed gentry were being relieved of some of
their privileges, with a proportionate increase in those of the middle
class. In education the important changes brought about by Thomas
Arnold, headmaster of Rugby School from 1828 until 1842, were considered spectacular at the time because, recognizing certain deficiencies
in the educational system (as it existed for the well-to-do), Arnold was
able to remedy some of its most palpable defects while retaining the
conventions of morality that were publicly praised if privately abused.
The great 'character-builder' was somewhat suspicious of refinements
which did not have the approval of the majority of his patrons. Charles
Pritchard, on the other hand, was attuned to the broader principles
which had inspired the foundation of King's College, London, in 1828,
where procedures were advocated which would bring education into,
rather than away from, the challenging social, industrial, and economic
conditions of the 1830s.

It was a feature of Pritchard's system—in contrast to that of Arnold—
that contact with the home on the part of the teachers, and participation
by parents in the school organization, were both necessary. Up to a point
it could not have been otherwise. 'Undoubtedly', he said in 1840, 'there
was something cheering and elevating in the thought that the great body
of our middle-classes were dissatisfied with the education which their
children could ordinarily receive. . . .' This dissatisfaction, primarily
with the public schools, led to the setting up of 'proprietary grammar
schools'. Without endowments, these schools were entirely dependent
on fees, and the manner in which fees were disposed was made subject to
scrutiny and confirmation by representative committees of fathers
brought into being for this purpose.

Pritchard's first arena for the exposition of his philosophy was a school
established in Stockwell in connection with King's College. There, as
he said in his inaugural address of August 1833, the plan of education
was 'based upon the study of the Greek and Latin languages', but also
contained 'a considerable infusion of elementary mathematics' and
'beyond all . . . a systematic course of instruction relating to the physical
phenomena in the midst of which we live and move and have our being.'
As the foundation of the whole scheme, Pritchard continued, he 'laid it
down as a maxim, that the main intention of early education should be
the development of *the habit of thinking*, and the exhibition of the right
mode of setting about it'. And in addition he insisted on 'the necessity of
providing "*resources for the leisure hours of maturer life*" '.[13]

At the end of a year, however, Stockwell Grammar School was no

[13] A. Pritchard, *The Life and Work of Charles Pritchard* (1897), pp. 47–8.

more. The Stockwell school committee had presumed to interfere in curricular matters, in particular taking exception to Pritchard's refusal to use the *Eton Latin Grammar*. Apart from that, he was young, idealistic and companionable, and therefore liable to be regarded unfavourably by those who had a different picture of a pedagogue. Fortunately, however, he held the confidence of a substantial group of parents and a new establishment was opened under his direction, in Clapham High Street, in August 1834. George Grove and George Bradley had left Elwell's school for Stockwell and they were among the first group of 65 boys under Pritchard's care in Clapham.

In paying tribute to his old master many years later, Grove wrote:

I had been at two other schools which were considered good of their class, but with Pritchard the atmosphere was very different. The master was younger and more sympathetic, and full of a wider knowledge than I had before dreamed of; also, he had a great power of explanation and illustration, and took constant interest in his boys. One or two things I had not met with before, and they made a great impression on me. First, the mathematics and the natural philosophy. These were taught in a practical and interesting way, and as connected with common life—not with the abstract world—which made them always fresh. Some of his precepts and examples recur to me almost daily.[14]

The broad aim of Clapham Grammar School was 'a complete preparation for the Universities or higher grades of commerce'. Pupils were admitted between the ages of ten and twelve and were able to remain in the school until they were sixteen and a half; parents were advised against removing their sons too soon. Tuition fees, excluding some 'extras', were 20 guineas per annum, and boarding fees were 40 guineas. Classes were held from 9.00 to 12.30, and from 2.30 to 5.00 in summer, but with a shortened afternoon session from 2.30 to 4.00 in winter. A committee of six fathers was elected from among the parents to manage 'pecuniary affairs and general welfare'. Among those who entrusted their sons to Pritchard's care were some of the luminaries in the world of mathematics who had also been pupils of Woodhouse at Cambridge, including George Airy, sometime Astronomer Royal, and John Herschel, President of the Astronomical Society.

There was a classical foundation to the curriculum, but Pritchard treated it in a quite new way. In translating from Latin and Greek, as Grove remembered, he urged his pupils to '*render* the passages as well as *construe* them; and thus we felt that they were about real transactions and people, and reflected the same emotions as our own literature'. In respect of English literature, including the Bible, this was brought to life by the practice of reading aloud on Saturday mornings. Also on Saturday mornings boys found that the history and geography of the biblical lands

[14] ibid., p. 71.

were wonderfully illuminated by exercises in map-drawing. For Grove (who had learned the Hebrew alphabet at Elwell's) an interest was developed which was to grow into later and deeper biblical and archaeological studies.

All boys at Clapham were taught French, while seniors could have German lessons at an extra cost of 10 shillings per quarter. Mathematics included arithmetic, algebra, trigonometry, and extended to optics and light. Experimental Philosophy represented a course of lessons in general science, of which, said Pritchard, 'the utility, especially that of Chemistry, in contributing to the comforts and conveniences of life, must be obvious to all . . .'. It was not long before the school possessed 'a convenient lecture-room, amply provided with chemical and philosophical apparatus', in which Pritchard used to deliver weekly lectures on 'several branches of Natural Philosophy'.

His credentials were formidable, his zest for knowledge unquenchable; after his schoolmaster days he became Savilian Professor of Astronomy at Oxford. The enthusiasms of Pritchard are mirrored in Grove's career at almost every turn, and early experience of astronomy is reflected in a letter written more than sixty years after leaving school: 'A new star—last night—Just think! a *new star*: what can it mean? It's really very thrilling—are you very excited? But the stars excite me always. They are the most mystic things we have to do with. . . .'[15]

Undoubtedly Pritchard's most interesting educational principle concerned the use of leisure, preparation for which, he said in a prospectus of *c.* 1840, 'to be sound and available, must be of a mixed character; if it be exclusive, we shall run the hazard of neglecting to cultivate some of those faculties with which the Creator has endowed us.' The idea that leisure was important was not uncongenial to those who lived in the age of George IV, but its significance as a factor in education was not to be generally acknowledged in the coming Victorian era.

Pritchard's progressive attitudes led him not only to engage a visiting 'drilling master', but to instruct this member of his staff to teach athletic exercises with the aid of 'gymnastic apparatus of the most complete description'. In the course of time a swimming bath was built as one of the school's amenities. (This and the chapel, however, were added after Grove's schooldays.)

Pritchard was no less insistent than Arnold on a Christian education, and a considerable part of one day in each week was devoted to Divinity, or Religious Study. But he was aware that Christian education needed a

---

[15] E.O., Feb 17 [1892]; the 'new star', in the constellation Auriga, was discovered 'by Mr T. D. Anderson of Edinburgh, who was engaged in comparing the sky with a star chart by the aid of a small pocket telescope. . . . It was of a dull orange colour, and of about the fifth magnitude. . . . It increased in brightness till on February 7 it appeared like a star of the fourth magnitude . . .'; *Annual Register*, 1892, p. 125.

pastoral element, and in his prospectus he remarked that he looked on 'his little community as his parish'.

Maintaining that his assistant should hold the highest qualifications, Pritchard appointed Henry Power, a graduate of his own college, as Second Master. The annual examination papers were published, 'to afford the friends of the Clapham Grammar School the means of forming a correct judgment of the nature and extent of the plan of education', and the reports of the external examiners—distinguished scholars—were also published.[16] In every discipline the examination questions bore evidence of the high academic standard set by Pritchard.

George Grove was not recorded as among the more successful pupils at Clapham Grammar School. His friends George Bradley, George Hemming—to become a celebrated mathematician and lawyer—and William Blades, Grove's cousin from Thurlow Cottage, according to the examination results were outstanding. Edmund Grove also made good progress.[17]

A lover of music, with a predilection for the oratorios of Handel and Mendelssohn and for English cathedral music, Pritchard noted that although he had no technical knowledge of music himself, he 'was well aware of what its effect would be on a community of men or boys';[18] later generations of pupils were given the opportunity to share his interest through performances on the organ he had built by J. C. Bishop, one of the best organ-builders of the day, in the chapel erected in 1846. As far as Grove was concerned, the fact of his master's interest was an additional stimulus to his own already deep-seated enthusiasm for music.

Like many other middle-class children the young Groves were acquainted with the music of Handel. Their mother, possessing a Broadwood piano, worked her way through Arnold's edition of *Messiah*, and essayed the choice of excerpts given by William Ayrton's *Musical Library* and *Sacred Minstrelsy*. George's sister Eliza was also a capable pianist. Local influences, apart from Pritchard and Blackburn, included William Beale, formerly a sailor and a Gentleman of the Chapel Royal,

[16] A part of the report by Dr T. H. Silvester, of the College of Physicians, who examined the pupils in Chemistry in 1838, gives a convincing reason for the success of Pritchard's methods: 'The science of "cramming" has made great progress of late years amongst professional students in the schools of the Metropolis. . . . I rejoice to say, and I can say it with perfect truth, that the pupils of the Clapham Grammar School have not been "crammed", but taught.'

[17] In 1837 Mr Merivale, who came from Cambridge to examine the boys in Classics, wrote: 'E. Grove appeared to be the best in the second [class]. . . . Bradley and Hemming acquitted themselves very much to my satisfaction.' Two years later Edmund won prizes for Classics, Mathematics and Natural Philosophy.

[18] A. Pritchard, op. cit., p. 65.

organist of Wandsworth Parish Church from 1821 until 1842 when he
transferred to a similar post in the new church of St John at Clapham
Rise. Beale, whose second wife was one Georgiana Grove (apparently
not a close relative of George Grove), was a neo-madrigalist of considerable charm. Sometimes, with one of his cousins, George went to the
Surrey Chapel in Walworth, where the music of J. S. Bach had been
made familiar through the efforts of the organist, Benjamin Jacob(s), and
Samuel Wesley. 'My cousin Benjamin Palmer was Jacob's pupil,' he
later wrote, 'and I think he always called him Jacob (and my cousin was
not a *singular* man either). I *think* but am not quite sure a propos *we* used
to be called Groves and my other cousins (Blades) often had their S
cut off—Blade.'[19] Grove also remembered across the years his disgust on
his first visit to the Surrey Chapel 'to see Mr Newth (or Nute) the reader
directly he had finished the prayer take off his surplice and hang it over
the side of the reading desk'.[20]

During Grove's youth there was little music to be heard publicly in
Clapham except in church buildings. London was a long way off, and
even there opportunities were scarce. Until 1832 the only choral society
was the Caecilian, which used to meet in the Albion Hall in London Wall.
To perform an oratorio, which was the aim of this valiant body, dedication
and good eyesight as well as musicianship were required, for the members
sang either from manuscript copies made by themselves or their friends,
or from the weighty scores of Randall, Harrison, Arnold or Clarke-
Whitfield. When the Sacred Harmonic Society came into existence in
1832 it met in an inconvenient dissenting house, the Gate Street Chapel,
in Lincoln's Inn.

The great choral occasions were closed-shop affairs. In 1834, for
example, Sir George Smart—then the *pontifex maximus* of London music
—refused offers from amateur singers to give their services for the
Westminster Abbey Handel Festival of that year, on the grounds that the
cathedral lay clerks would be deprived of work. The amateur choralists,
who had given two small-scale concerts in 1833, were not to be put off.
On 7 July 1834 a Festival took place in Exeter Hall, with the encouragement of Methodist ministers who had known him, as a tribute to 'the
late Charles Wesley, Organist of St. Marylebone Church and nephew of
Revd John Wesley'. Excerpts from Handel's *Saul*, *Funeral Anthem* and
Messiah, and Mozart's *Requiem*, as well as Samuel Wesley's noble anthem
'All go unto one Place', were performed. (The last work was 'composed
on the death of his brother and performed at his request on this occasion
for the first time'.) Next year one Robert Bowley became a member of
the committee of the Sacred Harmonic Society, and in 1836 a performance

[19] BL, Eg. MS. 3091, f. 18. Benjamin Palmer was one of the witnesses at the marriage
of Mary Bithiah Grove to James Bennett on 18 Aug 1837 (see p. 29).
[20] ibid.

of *Messiah* with 300 participants, which won the approval of an oratorio-hungry public, finally broke the stranglehold of the lay clerks.

When he came into the inner counsels of the Sacred Harmonic Society, Bowley, son of a boot-maker in Charing Cross, was twenty-one years of age. He quickly made himself indispensable and in 1837 became Librarian of the Society. It was in this year, on 7 March, that the Society achieved its greatest success to date with the first London performance of Mendelssohn's *St Paul*. From the small acorn planted in 1832 grew the mighty oak tree that was English amateur choral music in the Victorian era.

In the reign of William IV the amateur music-lover in England was equally badly off for popular musical literature. In 1818 *The Quarterly Musical Magazine and Review* began publication; ten years later it was extinct, although some of its features founded the basis for later musical literature in England. It had been addressed to a general audience, with emphasis on a felicitous literary style, and had contained some notable contributions, among them, in vol. II, a review of Forkel's biography of Bach, and vol. VII, an account of the Philharmonic Society performance in 1825 of Beethoven's Eighth Symphony. Two years later, in vol. ix, a view of the latter composer was expressed which would now seem to contain a degree of bias: 'The effect which the writings of Beethoven have had on the art', stated the contributor, 'must, I fear, be considered as injurious'. As well as critical essays, the *Quarterly Musical Magazine* also published musical items suitable for domestic use. Between 1823 and 1830 William Ayrton's *Harmonicon* led a similarly useful life. Five years after the demise of this journal, C. H. Purday produced *The Musical Magazine*, a frail infant which hardly survived a year.

On 10 March 1836 *The Musical World* made its appearance, published at first by Alfred Novello. Edited by Charles Cowden Clarke, who assembled a talented team of contributors, this journal provided the impetus required for a new style of music criticism appropriate to a period in which professionals needed to come to terms with informed and often gifted amateurs. Not the least important agent in bringing this about was Alfred Novello, son of Vincent, who continued his father's enterprise in issuing Catholic church music and in 1829 broke new ground with the publication of the first part of his father's edition of *Purcell's Sacred Music*. In 1834 Novello moved from Frith Street to premises at 69 Dean Street, Soho, which were to be a regular port of call for George Grove in his early apprentice years in London.

These began at the end of December 1835 when George was removed from Pritchard's school. Towards the end of his life Grove reflected on his schooldays and his early musical experiences, indicating that could he have ordered them, they would have been otherwise than they were. He regretted that his and his brother's schooling was too brief:

I began music by my mother playing the Messiah to us, out of an old vocal score (voices and figured bass). Then came Bach's 48 and the Sacred Harmonic Society concerts to which we used to walk from home, returning on our feet! But neither I nor my brother ever could play more than a 'psalm tune quick' like Punch's Italian. We were to be engineers and get too soon into the world.[21]

[21] Letter to F. G. Edwards, 14 Aug 1897, from Woodhall Spa; BL, Eg. MS. 3091, f. 203.

CHAPTER TWO

Iron Age Culture

1836–1850

In January 1836 Grove was apprenticed to a Scottish civil engineer, Alexander Gordon, whose office was at 22 Fludyer Street, Westminster.[1] At the start of his apprenticeship Grove walked the three miles from Clapham to work each morning, and home again in the evening. He was thus instructed in frugality by his father who, however, took the coach that plied between Wandsworth and Charing Cross, or—on fine days—varied this practice by going part of the way, from Vauxhall Bridge to Whitehall Stairs, by water.

The son of a distinguished engineer, Alexander Gordon, born in New York in 1802, had been educated at Edinburgh University, after which he worked for a time as assistant to Thomas Telford. Though his special area of research concerned the development of optical apparatus for lighthouses, Gordon became an authority on transport and in 1837 published a treatise on railway locomotion. He was interested in technological education in the wider sense and, anxious to extend opportunity and to raise standards of training, was to be one of those responsible for the establishment in 1838 of the Polytechnic Institution of London.

That Grove was dispatched into technology shows the distinction between education at a proprietary school of progressive character and a public school. It also had something to do with Charles Pritchard's Shropshire family background, for a kinsman of his, Thomas Farnell Pritchard, was the architect commissioned in 1775 to produce designs for an iron bridge to cross the Severn. From T. F. Pritchard's designs Abraham Darby III worked to build the first such bridge in the world—the harbinger of the second great phase of the Industrial Revolution. Confirmed into the new technology by his schoolmaster, who is to be seen as belonging to its apostolic succession, Grove remained associated with it in one way or another throughout his life. At the Annual General Meeting of the Institution of Civil Engineers on 18 January 1842, James Walker, F.R.S., warned parents that engineering was a vocation, observing:

[1] The next street south from Downing Street, Fludyer Street was obliterated when the India Office was built.

if one lad be intended in their minds for Engineering, as the others may be for a profession, or for mercantile pursuits, where the chances of success are numerous, a disappointment will be just as probable as if they had apprenticed the youth to be a musician, a painter, or a poet, who had shown no natural taste for those arts. . . .

Grove's feeling for engineering was that of an artist, while his understanding of the arts owed something to his technological competence.

When Grove was a boy music was expensive, and the first guinea ever given to him, in 1837, was invested in a piano score of *Messiah*. Fifty years later, in a Preface to *A Short History of Cheap Music*, he remarked that the price then for the same score was one shilling. While he worked with Gordon, Grove went to the performances of the Sacred Harmonic Society, and when she was old enough his youngest sister, Eleanor (Ellen), went with him. From his office in Fludyer Street he was able quite often to walk over to Westminster Abbey—of which at that time James Turle was organist—to hear Evensong. He remembered the deep voice of Richard Clark, a famous bass singer, editor of a celebrated collection of words of madrigals and glees, author of pamphlets on Handel and other musical subjects, and a campaigner for the proper conduct of liturgical music. When in later life Grove recalled Purcell's 'They that go down to the sea in ships' it was because of Clark's failure on one occasion to reach one of the four picturesque low D's.

At the beginning of the Victorian era church music was at a very low ebb, and the manner in which services were performed at St Paul's Cathedral—as pointed out by Sydney Smith, Maria Hackett and Samuel Wesley—was to be regarded as a national disgrace. By the sterner moralists the decline was thought symptomatic of a general malaise, for which the permissiveness encouraged in the days of George IV and William IV was primarily responsible. In the secular field, on the other hand, there was a plethora of music. In the 1837 season, for example, there was in London 'the unprecedented number of 135 concerts', of which 4 were given in private houses, 6 in London taverns, 13 in Willis's Rooms, 33 in the Concert Room of the King's Theatre, and 79 in the Hanover Square Rooms. The Philharmonic Society was in full swing, the Antient Concerts still continued, and there were music-making clubs of a semi-private nature, of which the Madrigal Society was the best known.

Grove's apprenticeship to Gordon coincided with the beginning of the railway era and his first instruction was in railway construction, a science as exciting then as aerodynamics in a later age; its dominant personality in the 1830s was George Stephenson's son, Robert. After many difficulties and initial rejection a Parliamentary Bill authorizing the building of a railway between Birmingham and London had been passed in 1833; further authority allowed the extension of the system, by the Grand Junction Railway, to Manchester and Liverpool. Work on the line between

London and Birmingham was impeded by technical difficulties and administrative quibbles, but in the summer of 1838 a single through track was ready. On 27 August a four-carriage train, carrying officials who had breakfasted early, left Curzon Street, Birmingham, for London at 6.30 a.m. The station at Euston Grove was reached in about six hours, after a stop had been made to inspect work on the one-and-a-half-mile-long Kilsby Tunnel—one of Robert Stephenson's great achievements. On 17 September the line was opened to the public.[2]

In the meantime the construction of another railway, between London and Southampton, helped to bring about the marriage of Mary Bithiah Grove—now approaching thirty—with James Bennett, a widower, of Salisbury. The wedding ceremony took place in Clapham on 18 August 1837 and was solemnized by the Revd Charles Bradley. Ten years older than his bride, Bennett was a man of substance. He was a silversmith and owned the *Salisbury Times* (unlike some newspaper proprietors he kept his own affairs out of the headlines). He had been appointed a magistrate by William IV, was Mayor of Salisbury in 1825, Chamberlain in 1826, and Alderman in 1827. As his wife, Mary Bithiah—who bore him six sons as well as looking after the children of his first marriage—held an influential place in Wiltshire society, though she and her husband kept in close touch with the Groves in Clapham.[3]

Not long after the departure of his eldest sister for the West Country, George had the opportunity to accompany his employer to Belgium, where the railway system was the most advanced in Europe. From the outset, through the foresight of King Leopold I, it had been a national enterprise. The Duke of Wellington, Lord Londonderry and George Stephenson, among others, thought that the British railways should also be nationalized. Gordon was negotiating a contract in Malines, and it was here that Grove stayed from 30 November until 17 January 1838, with a fellow pupil and Gordon and his wife.

It was a terrible winter and George noted how three men travelling in an open carriage on the recently opened Ghent–Brussels–Malines–Antwerp line had been found frozen to death. Always impressed by the monumental, whether in architecture or music, and in spite of the weather, Grove was grateful for opportunity to inspect the splendid medieval memorials of Malines—the Metropolitan Cathedral of St Rombaut, the Town Hall, the Court of Busleyden, and the church of Our Lady of Hanswijk, which had been rebuilt in baroque style.

[2] Work continued on the line for some years, however, and from time to time (as Grove once reported) passengers suffered diversion on account of engineering work.

[3] Two of the Bennett sons carried Grove as an additional forename: the first, Edmund Grove Bennett, was born on 25 Apr 1841. Twenty years after the Bennetts' marriage Anna Grove also found a husband in Salisbury—William David Wilkes, a doctor, with whom George Grove was to become very friendly.

Back in London he worked methodically, but kept up his musical interests. A new source of pleasure and instruction became available to him with the opening of the new Reading Room in the north wing of the British Museum, then in Montague House, on 9 January 1838. Grove was an early habitué, and learned to bear with fortitude the incidence of 'Museum headache', as denoted by Carlyle, and the attacks of that hardy parasite the 'Museum flea'. His frequent companion in his early incursions into musicology was a bank clerk, William Pickering Stevens, who is occasionally noted in Grove's commonplace books as a source for some, and the arranger of other, material. In the Preface to *A Short History of Cheap Music* Grove related how he pored over the collections of Burney, Tudway and Needler, learning to interpret notation and to realize figured bass. 'It obliged one', he said, 'to play from score or to write one's own accompaniment—in fact, gave one knowledge against one's will for which the modern student has little or no occasion.'

The first of Grove's commonplace books (RCM 1061, a manuscript book containing musical examples) has items from the Burney, Tudway and Needler Collections. Occasional annotations show the student wrestling with his subject. William Byrd's 'Bow thine ear originally set to Civitas tui' (from *Ne irascaris, Domine*, part II) is augmented with figured bass and solfa, and is described as 'modern' and 'church'; some Gregorian tones are harmonized 'in a modern way'; Orlando Gibbons's 'Hosanna to the Son of David', also supplied with figuring, is remarked as 'the noblest English anthem ever written'; Tallis's *Miserere nostri Domini* is labelled so that its canonic design is clear to the eye. *Grove's Dictionary* may, in a sense, be said to have commenced at this point; for Grove himself ultimately wrote for it the entries on Gibbons and Tallis.

On 26 February 1839 Grove was admitted a graduate of the Institution of Civil Engineers, being deemed by a committee of ten members satisfactorily to have passed through the stage of pupil. At the meeting at which successful members and associates were accredited John Watt read a paper 'On the Economy of Working Expansively in Crank Engines'.

Alexander Gordon was the London agent of the Glasgow marine engineer, Robert Napier, to whom, soon after his graduation from the I.C.E., Grove was seconded for almost two years. The journey to Scotland, on which he was accompanied by his elder brother Tom, was fairly hazardous. After having had to by-pass the Kilsby Tunnel by road the brothers reached Liverpool, whence there was a generally rather rough sea passage to Glasgow. In a ship powered by a Napier-designed engine, however, George was able at once to appreciate the quality of his prospective employer's workmanship.[4]

[4] The sea route to Glasgow was served by *Orion*, *Fire King* and *Commodore*, of the Glasgow and Liverpool Steam Shipping Company, *Princess Royal* of the Glasgow and

In Napier's Glasgow foundry on the Broomielaw—an extension of West Clyde Street fronting the river—Grove was at the very heart of advanced technology. Napier, the son of a blacksmith, was the best engineer on the Clyde and one of the best in the world. In 1839 his 400-horsepower engines took the *British Queen* on her pioneer run to New York, and in the next year the *Britannia* on a record-making voyage to Boston. Grove worked in Napier's pattern and fitting shops, from which experience he later advised young engineers never to be afraid of soiling their hands.

Grove's first commonplace book, which accompanied him to Scotland, was inscribed: 'Geo. Grove, 425 Argylle [*sic*] St., Mrs. Morrison's Lodgings'.[5] Argyle Street, described at that time as 'one of the most crowded thoroughfares in Europe', ran parallel to the Broomielaw. Across the river, eastward, were the crowded misery of the poor lodged in the squalor of the old Baronial Hall—which housed a spirit cellar— and the insanitary housing of Main Street, a sombre clutter of railway yards, Dixon's ironworks with their six blast-furnaces, and Higginbotham's spinning mills. In the river lay the steamers awaiting their engines, and above them towered the great cranes able to lift loads up to 60 tons. George's younger brother Edmund, having left school and followed him to Scotland, was an apprentice in nearby Greenock.

Besides being convenient to Napier's foundry George's rooms were also within easy reach of the Theatre Royal and Stirling's Library. Other libraries within easy access were the Glasgow Public Library and the Robertson Library. Although he worked hard he found time to become acquainted with some of Glasgow's more interesting citizens, among whom particular friends were a clergyman named Symington,[6] and Frederick F. Pellatt, owner of the Clyde Bottle Works. The one helped to broaden his literary tastes—otherwise stimulated by the century-old Literary Society—by introducing him to Coleridge's *Aids to Reflection* and the other to historical works by Henry Hallam.

So far as music was concerned at that time, Glasgow suffered from the strictures of Calvinism, and sacred music was almost non-existent. A long campaign was fought before *Messiah* was performed there for the first time, in 1844. There were occasional concerts in the Trades Hall and

Liverpool Steam Packet Company, and *Admiral* of the City of Glasgow Steam Packet Company. The first-class fare was 15 shillings, with a supplementary steward's fee of 2 shillings.

[5] See p. 30. A No. 425 Argyle Street is shown in the Glasgow Post Office Directory of 1898.

[6] See Graves, p. 20. Symington was probably William Symington, D.D. (1795–1862), a minister and Professor of Divinity in the Reformed Presbyterian Church of Scotland, Glasgow, in 1838. One of a family of ministers, Symington had a reputation as a powerful preacher, and was the author of several theological works. F. F. Pellatt lived at 25 Newton Place, Sauchiehall Street.

the Assembly Rooms, and opera in the Theatre Royal (tickets for boxes being obtainable from Mrs Wright's grocer's shop in Argyle Street). One work which was surprisingly popular was *Der Freischütz*, during performances of which Glasgow audiences were regularly entranced by a display of fireworks, until in 1845 the City Theatre caught ablaze after such a performance and was destroyed.

After his return from Scotland, at the end of 1840, Grove seems to have had a good deal of time at his disposal, and in a second commonplace book (RCM 1062) he noted a variety of pieces, from Tye to Mozart by way of Handel, which he looked at in the British Museum on 15 December. On 31 December he copied Benjamin Rogers's 'Behold now, praise the Lord'; on New Year's Day he turned to Handel's 12 chamber duets; on 2 January 1841 he transcribed an organ voluntary by Maurice Greene; next day he collected Croft's 'Northampton' tune; and on 4 January another voluntary by Greene and Pergolesi's *Propter magnam gloriam*, which was in Vincent Novello's *Sacred Music*. Novello's *Adeste fideles* was also copied into Grove's book, to be followed in January by excerpts from Cesti and Callcott, and Handel's 'How beautiful are the feet', with Mozart's accompaniments. On 11 March 'Ye sons of Israel' from *Esther* was transcribed, and later that year the contents of J. Stevens's 'book of [Handel's] VI fugues'. Apart from further explorations into the sixteenth- and seventeenth-century schools, with extracts from Gibbons (2 October), Nanini, Anerio and Benevoli (progressions from 'chants from the Studii di Palestrina'), Grove worked through Kalkbrenner's exercises in counterpoint and turned to Bach. The fugue with which he had become familiar through John Blackburn's playing at Clapham parish church was subjected to close scrutiny and careful analysis. From the opening movement of Church Cantata no. 80, *Ein' feste Burg*, which he looked at in the Breitkopf & Härtel edition, Grove took this figure at bar 143:

mit Ernst er's jezt meint, mit Ernst

'This subject', he wrote, 'is something like "For the Lord God" in the Hallelujah [*Messiah*] Music'. During this year Grove, who did not hesitate to grade excerpts as 'good', 'very good', and so on, was beginning to establish for himself a scale of critical values. He was also being made aware of new ventures in the sphere of musical scholarship.

On 8 April a letter from Joseph Warren appeared in the *Musical World*, deploring the negligence of the authorities of the British Museum in respect of the care and the cataloguing of important musical manuscripts, and the editor suggested that the matter should be raised in Parliament when the renewal of the Museum's annual grant was debated. At the end of the year the Trustees appointed Thomas Oliphant, a conspicuous member and officer of the Madrigal Society, to take charge of the musical holdings. But the appointment caused some resentment, and commenting on the complaint of a correspondent that it seemed to have been made in secret, the editor of the *Musical World* remarked: 'The appointment . . . was not settled by election, but was entirely a matter of private interest. This gentleman is so completely an *amateur*, even in his antiquarian research, that his qualifications are as questionable as we think his appointment unjust.'[7] An amateur Oliphant may have been, but at the end of 1840 he had resigned as secretary of the Musical Antiquarian Society because his fellow members would not agree to pay him for his work.[8]

Grove had been present at one of the meetings of that newly formed Society (to which John Blackburn of Clapham belonged) when its members were looking forward to the early issue of their first publications:

A very interesting occurrence at Crosby Hall was a meeting of a large number of musicians to read the proof sheets of the Mus. Antiquarian Society publication of Wilbye madrigals. There must have been 200 or more there. We had tea (if I remember) and then sang through the music. I remember most distinctly [George] Macfarren, with the sheet pressed almost against his blind eyes but in those days I knew no one (1840–50).[9]

In the early part of 1841 John Hullah—later to become a friend of Grove—began his music classes for schoolmasters at Exeter Hall. In the summer Joseph Mainzer, once an engineering apprentice in the Saar coalfield, then a priest, and now a political refugee, arrived in England. Making for the industrial regions of England, with his headquarters in Manchester, Mainzer (whose career was written up in due course by Grove in the *Dictionary*) launched his 'singing for the million' campaign, and soon afterwards issued the *National Singing Circular*, which developed into the *Musical Times*. Also during the summer of 1841 a Motett Society was established 'to revive the study and practice of the ancient Choral Music of the Church . . . to the middle 17th century'. Edward Rimbault was managing editor of the Society, which at first met on Monday nights in the All Souls and Trinity National Schools in Langham Place. In Clapham, the Rector of Holy Trinity was the chief inspiration

---

[7] Oliphant notwithstanding remained music librarian, in effect if not in name, in the British Museum until he resigned in 1850 after a row with Anthony Panizzi, Keeper of Printed Books.

[8] *Musical World*, 17 Dec 1840.

[9] Letter to F. G. Edwards, 29 July 1895, referring to Edwards's recently published *Musical Haunts in London*; BL, Eg. MS. 3091, f. 107. Wilbye's *The First Set of Madrigals*, edited by J. Turle, was published by the Musical Antiquarian Society in 1841.

2

of a Literary and Scientific Institution, opened on 9 November 1841 in response to a general urge for more educational opportunity.

But by that time Grove was far away from London. Having collected sufficient music to stand him in good stead if he should be sent to some distant island, he found that that indeed was to be his fate. The development of transport by sea as well as on land during the early years of Victoria's reign brought great opportunities to engineers and merchants alike. But the hazards of ocean transport were great, and the frequent wrecking of valuable ships in dangerous and distant waters led to a thorough consideration of preventive measures. From this came a demand for the erection of lighthouses, about which subject few knew more than Alexander Gordon. He was called to advise on the construction of a lighthouse for Morant Point, Jamaica.

On the 8th March 1841 a meeting of the [Lighthouse] Commissioners took place, at which Admiral Sir Thomas Harvey presided, assisted by Commodore Douglas, when the iron tower recommended by Mr Gordon, in his report of the 31st December 1840, was selected and finally determined on, and instructions were given to Mr Burge[s] forthwith to proceed with the work. These instructions were promptly attended to by Mr Gordon with a zeal and alacrity which enabled that highly talented gentleman to inform the Commissioners in October 1841 (only eight months after the selection of the tower by the commissioners) . . . that the tower was about to be shipped for its place of destination, and that Mr Grove, as clerk of the works, and two labouring engineers who had attended to the execution of the work in England, would be sent out for the purpose of erecting the light-house and the necessary apparatus upon the site which had been selected.[10]

When Grove arrived in Jamaica slavery had officially been abolished, but economic depression made for a hard life for the Jamaicans. The Governor, Sir Charles Metcalfe, was a radical politician who had been sent to Jamaica to ensure better community relations, in which he was much assisted by Christopher Lipscombe, the first Bishop of the island diocese. The route to independence for the former slaves was, however, more clearly shown by the Baptist preachers, particularly James M. Phillippo, pastor of Spanish Town. In 1842 he fulminated against the morals of many of the whites on the island, and in describing the increasing practice of 'myalism'—a form of 'hot revivalism'—gave some indication of the genuine culture of the black workers. On the estates, he noted, 'there were usually found one or more males or females, who, resembling the improvisatori or extempore bards of Italy or ancient Britain, composed lines and sung them on their festive occasions'. Although ethnomusicology as a science lay some distance in the future, at an early stage in his career Grove showed an interest in music of

[10] A. Gordon, *Lighthouses of the British Colonies* . . . (1847); Appendix A, 'The Jamaica (Point Morant) Lighthouse', p. 26.

traditions other than European. No doubt Jamaica was a fascinating introduction to the more exotic forms of folk music.

From a technical angle his work on the island was not difficult. The lighthouse which had been shipped out from England was a typical artefact of the period, of cast-iron. Like some of the churches sent out to the West Indies which were also of this material, it was an early example of prefabrication, and economic in construction.[11] The site on Morant Bay was a good one—the roadsteads were open and the only danger in near approach came from the Galatea Rock. There was a plentiful supply of labour, both black and white, but Grove had early experience of the problems of management, more than once finding himself having to deal with industrial disputes. Work was also interrupted by stormy weather. Nevertheless, a light was shown from the tower on 13 August 1842, Grove's birthday, and from 1 November the lighthouse became fully operational. The cost of the erection, including its trial in London, was £11,608.

On two occasions Grove was in some danger. On the first, while trying to make sure that a light would shine on his birthday, he was momentarily careless, and, losing his footing, fell through the girders. Managing to hold on some 60 feet from the floor of the tower, he was rescued by his black workmen. A few days later while in the lantern he almost fell victim to a lightning flash during a severe storm. In Jamaica Grove established his professional credentials and in later life he reflected on his island experience with pleasure.[12] But he was apparently never able to dispossess himself of one secret, even to his closest confidante. On 22 March 1842 one Elizabeth Blackwell gave birth to a son – named George Grove on his birth certificate – in the Union Workhouse, Stratford-on-Avon. With help from his putative father it is said, in time he too became an engineer.[13] At this point Grove felt himself to have reached maturity:

I went to Jamaica before I was 21, and of course it made a man of me, and when I came back I can well recollect how pleasant was the society of my two eldest sisters, good looking, clever, accomplished women—our family was in two halves, divided by a gap, 4 in the upper half and 4 in the lower, and I had not known the upper half at all—so they were comparative outsiders to me, and very interesting and nice they were.[14]

[11] Morant Point Lighthouse was first erected and tried out in the yards of Cottam and Hallen on the south bank of the Thames. Its 135 cast-iron plates made a tower of 130 feet, rising from a base with a diameter of 24 feet, and tapering to 14 feet up to the bulge which accommodated platform and lamp room. These were reached by a spiral staircase separated from the outer plates by brick and concrete.

[12] Grove was remembered in Jamaica, his portrait being in the *Catalogue of the Portraits in the Jamaica History Gallery of the Institute of Jamaica* (Kingston, 1914).

[13] George Grove Blackwell (1842–1908), professionally active near Liverpool, founded the firm now known as S. & A. Blackwell (St Annes) Ltd.

[14] E.O., June 25 [1893]. There is some confusion here, which was not helped by a

Back in England Grove returned to his musical interests. He bought a spinet for 12 shillings in Holborn.[15] He heard Sainton rehearse the Beethoven Violin Concerto for a Philharmonic concert, 'at a time when Beethoven meant *nothing* to me—far less than Handel (in whose faith I was brought up) . . .'.[16] So far as the family was concerned he was pleased that Edmund and Eleanor in particular were maintaining their musical interests, and that the former was making professional progress.

At this time Grove's sister Bithiah Blades was coming to a momentous decision. Joshua Clarkson Harrison, a Nonconformist minister in Camden Town, was pressing his advances more and more resolutely. With no prospect other than that of a stay-at-home spinster daughter responsible for ageing parents, she accepted his proposal. The marriage took place at Holy Trinity Church, Clapham, on 5 October 1843 and was solemnized by the Revd Charles Bradley, as had been that of Mary Bithiah six years before. George Grove disapproved, and in looking back on the situation he put forth an argument likely to be appreciated by latter-day women's liberationists. Harrison, he said, was

a great man among the Dissenters . . . of immense fame among them, though I never could appreciate him. It was a *pis aller* marriage. She was very clever and brilliant and accomplished and sarcastic, and young Harrison had followed her like a dog for years—and she had always laughed at him and derided him: but at last no one else came and he was persistent and she married him when she was about 30 but she was meant for a different climate—not that she shewed it—she was too sensible for that.[17]

On the whole he was relieved not to have had to attend the wedding. For he had hardly had time to accustom himself to life in England again before he was required to go overseas on another mission. This time the destination was Bermuda.

---

clerical error in the 1841 census which misrepresented Bithiah as 'Bethsabe'. Edmund I and Frances Moore died when George was a boy, and it would appear that Kezia, who spent much of her life 'away from the family' (see p. 202), was mentally subnormal. Thus it can be seen that the eldest four children in Grove's recollection were those who were effective members of the family during his impressionable years. The youngest of the senior four was Eliza, who was five years older than George.

[15] Letter to A. J. Hipkins, 7 Sept [1894?]; BL, Add. MS. 41639, f. 276: 'I have found the Spinet which I bought in Holborn about the year 1842 for 12/–; which I had put into order by old Edwards the tuner; which then after the breaking up of our old house in the Wandsworth Road, on the death of my mother, got put somewhere, I never knew where, and which is now in the garrett [*sic*] of my brother's house at 33 Charing Cross with about ½ a ton of furniture on top of it. . . . As far as I can recollect the name was an English name and the date 1703. . . .' The instrument is now in the Museum of Historical Instruments at the RCM.

[16] E.O., May 20 [1891].

[17] E.O., June 25 [1893].

The discussions which led to Grove's Bermuda trip had begun as early as July 1841 when a meeting had been called in the Town Hall in Hamilton, the capital of the colony, to consider the matter of lighthouses. In the past ten years 37 ships had been stranded on the reefs off the coasts of the island, and since Cunard Line mailboats (powered by Napier engines) had started plying between Southampton and Bermuda it was important that the economic potential of this service should be realized. The erection of a lighthouse at Gibb's Hill, seven miles from Hamilton, became first a subject for acrimonious debate in London and then a classic example of waste of public money. The consultant engineers engaged by Trinity House, not bothering to study local conditions before drawing up grandiose but unrealizable plans, only succeeded in squandering time, money and material. Alexander Gordon was called in by the Treasury to advise, and when he was able to assume control the project went ahead rather more satisfactorily. Even so there were delays and setbacks, and Grove, who was sent out towards the end of 1843 to supervise the work, was kept in Bermuda for nearly three years.

Hamilton was a fine town, and the culture of the colonists refined. A few months before Grove's arrival the first performance of *Messiah*—the orchestra supplied by the 20th Regiment—was given in the Town Hall under the direction of Mr Oliver, the bandmaster. The Governor, Sir William Reid, was of a liberal disposition, and, like Metcalfe in Jamaica, had been sent to usher in a new dispensation after the abolition of slavery. He was a keen educationist, as also was the distinguished and, indeed, heroic Bishop, Edward Feild, a High Churchman and one of a number of old Rugbeians with whom Grove became friendly. The diocese which contained Bermuda had its headquarters in Newfoundland, in which inhospitable land Feild suffered great hardships with saintly fortitude. Grove found both his company and his theology congenial.

When he took up his work at Gibb's Hill, Grove discovered that the labour force had been conscripted from among the able-bodied convicts on the island. About a hundred of these men were lodged on Port's Island. One day four of them made a bid for freedom, setting off in a pilot boat in a strong north-east wind. After a perilous voyage—of 600 miles—they were picked up, in a famished condition, and returned to their captors. Grove had other problems. The military had an interest in the building of this lighthouse, and had insisted that a lieutenant-colonel of the Royal Engineers should be drafted from Ireland, first to learn the engineering details in London and then to go out with Grove, nominally to supervise the scheme. Gordon was furious, as he indicated in his final report, that work which should have been accomplished in twelve months had taken three times as long. The first plate was put in place on 19 December 1844, and the last on 9 October 1845, but Grove was less than satisfied with the work. Trinity House had recommended that a certain kind of light should be used of which Gordon disapproved, and which at times apparently could not be seen even at Hamilton. On 9 May 1846 Grove wrote that he and two assistants had to look for some minutes before he could catch a glimmer of light, during which time a ship could easily run on a reef.[18] But he had done what he had been instructed to do.

Even more than those of Jamaica, memories of Bermuda haunted Grove long after he returned home: 'The most mystic remembrance I have is of a small bay in Bermuda, when I was 23 . . . and where I used to walk at night sometimes, and when the crescent moon and a large planet formed a *slant* line which drew down to the dim dark horizon and made me feel Eternity. But why?'[19] And again:

Why should the sight of the moon and a great star, *slanting down* to the sea line, have made an impression of *eternity* on me? Why should I have—in a way at once quite vague and yet very strong—on my mind a feeling of an after life evoked by the round afternoon shadows creeping over the islands as I watched them one Sunday afternoon in 1845?[20]

During the whole of the period of overseas commitment Grove continued to dedicate himself (and sometimes also his sister Ellen) to further education, within which literature occupied an increasingly significant sector. The interest in the works of Coleridge aroused by Symington in Glasgow had been further stimulated in Jamaica, where Grove met an expatriate doctor named Porter, a former pupil of Coleridge's friend the apothecary Gillman, who possessed autograph items by Coleridge (which Grove copied) as well as 'wonderful stories of the *marginalia* written by Coleridge on the pages of the circulating library books, and returned all unbeknown'. Porter also told entertaining stories of Charles Lamb, in particular of his weekly visits to Coleridge at Highgate. Between the Jamaican and Bermudan interludes Grove had made the acquaintance of William Pickering, the publisher, who in 1842 moved into premises at 122 Piccadilly. Pickering lent Grove a copy of *Omniana*—a joint work by Coleridge and Southey published in 1812 after the last visit of the former to the Lake District—with marginal annotations in Coleridge's own hand. Through such opportunities Grove began to feel himself within the tradition of English poetry, for which his affection was to be deepened by experience. In later periods of isolation he would often turn back to the poetry he had read in youth, and perhaps memorized while shaving, and find in its recollection a form of therapy.

Across these adventurous years Grove pursued his musicological interests with undiminished fervour. Often denied opportunity to hear

[18] Gordon, op. cit.; Appendix B, 'The Bermuda (Gibb's Hill) Lighthouse', pp. 27–9.
[19] E.O., Feb 17 [1892].
[20] E.O., Jan 28 Sat. [1893].

music, he trained himself to comprehend it through his eyes and to appreciate the ordered patterns of sound, which seemed to him to bear some relationship to the engineering structures that were his first concern. Conscious of a mystical influence exercised by distant places, he was also aware of a particular effect produced by distances in time.

During 1842, in Jamaica, Grove had copied pieces—for the most part hymn tunes—into one of his commonplace books (RCM 1062), which had been started on the last day of 1840 with a transcription of Benjamin Rogers's 'Behold now, praise the Lord'. A *Polyhymniae Sacerdotes Liber 1842, Georgii Grove* (RCM 1143) contains an Agnus Dei by Rossini, the Kyrie from Samuel Wesley's *Missa Gregoriana 'Pro Angelis'* (copied by Grove on 14 December 1842), and another setting of the Kyrie from a mass by Giovanni Battista Casali, whose brief biography in the *Dictionary* was ultimately written by Grove. Regarding 'O giorno d'oror' (Scena 7a) from Rossini's *Otello*, Grove noted that it was 'cribbed from Graun'. He had in mind, no doubt, the affecting harmonies of this passage as also those of the Finale of Act I of the opera, which he carefully copied. A continuing interest in Handel is shown in the transcription of the minuet from the Overture to 'Sampson' [*sic*].

Another book of excerpts (RCM 1142), inscribed 'George Grove M.B.L., September 1841' at one end and 'Ellen and George Grove January 1843' at the other, has the 'Alleluia' from *Athalia* (copied on 23 November 1843), an Amen by Benjamin Cooke 'in the manner of the old Italians', and further examples of J. S. Bach. Among these is the fugue on BACH by Johann Christian Bach, published by Peters of Leipzig, *c*. 1820. Grove otherwise at this point was concentrating on chorales and 'Wie schön leuchtet der Morgenstern' and *Puer natus* are respectively annotated 'T.B.S. 23 Sept. 1847' and '25 Sept. 1847'.[21]

Another book (RCM 678), 'Bound in Bermuda, March 17th 1846', contains many home thoughts from abroad, and its compiler's competence in handling technical terminology may be seen to be more assured by now. In Farrant's Service in A minor (culled from Tudway's Collection, BL, Harl. MSS. 7337/13) Grove pencilled notes on the cadences:

X Notice this fine chord

6   7   6

---

[21] On the endpaper of commonplace book RCM 1142 is also written 'Revd J. S. Wiggett, 8 Cavendish Place, Brighton'. James Samuel Wiggett, a native of Wiltshire, was living in Norfolk, aged forty-three, in 1834; in 1841, when he was first known in Brighton, Wiggett was a 'Clergyman, not having the cure of souls'. Possibly Grove met him in the Reading Room of the British Museum.

X This is a curious modulation
from a major key E to the minor
key of the Dominant A.

In Croft's 'Put me not to rebuke' he selected a succulent chord of the dominant minor ninth attached to the word 'chasten' and described it as 'splendid'. Croft's 'good contrary motion' also met with his approval. Grove was in debt to earlier commentators, particularly R. J. S. Stevens and Stafford Smith—both of whom interested him also as composers—and Burney. Grove (or W. P. Stevens on his behalf[22]) ransacked Burney's 'Musical Extracts' (BL, Add. MSS. 11581–2), and sometimes he adopted the patronizing tone which Burney thought proper for barbarous 'Gothic' music such as that of Josquin. Of the *L'homme armé* Mass of this composer Grove wrote: 'No accidental sharps or flats are printed and however a modern eye or ear may want them it is by no means certain that the rigid adherence to Ecclesiastical modes and scales for which Josquin was remarkable would allow them to be used when these masses were first composed.'

Grove was specially interested in the four-note motif which generates the following excerpt from Turini (copied by him from a copy of R. J. S. Stevens and quoted in *Grove 1*, vol. I, p. 190) and which appeared to him to exercise a unifying function throughout musical design.

Chri - ste - e - - - - - - - le - i - son

He passed through works by Morley, Gibbons, Purcell and Handel; Frescobaldi and J. S. Bach—the 'Osanna' from the Mass in B minor capturing his early respect; until arriving at Haydn, passages from whose masses (as issued by Novello) provoked brief expostulations of delight. So, in the fugue ending the Credo of the St Cecilia Mass the first example below is rated 'ingenious'; in the second 'the discords here are excellent'; and the third is simply declared to be 'a famous passage'. It is fair to say that the masses of Haydn were not at that time widely known or appreciated in England.

---

[22] In Grove's commonplace book RCM 667 ('George Grove Mus: Brit: Lect.'), passages from Burney's 'Extracts during his Tours etc.' were 'found out by W.P.S[tevens]'.

After returning from Bermuda Grove went to visit Edmund, who was in Lincoln working on the installation of a new gas system, and the two brothers found time to visit the more notable churches in the area. After he had fulfilled his obligations in Lincoln Edmund joined the staff of C. H. Wild, a principal assistant of Robert Stephenson. Those were the exciting years in railway development, and the achievements of the engineers involved remarkable. By 1844 2234 miles of railway had been built in Britain, and in the next year Parliament authorized the construction of a further 2170 miles, at an estimated cost of £500 million. Thereby was induced the severest attack of 'railway mania' that the country ever had known or was likely to know. George Grove decided that his future, like that of Edmund, lay on the railway.

In 1886 he wrote a waggish letter to his confidante of that period, purporting to be from a fictitious company 'Jobbins and Cheffins', in which he remarked that 'our senior partner Mr Jobbins began business in the lithographic line in the year 1845 [*sic*] when Sir G. Grove was on the staff of Mr Stephenson the eminent engineer, and executed many of the plans of the Birmingham railway.'[23] (It is clear that, forty years on, Grove—as he did in other instances—slipped a year, for he could not have been so employed before the autumn of 1846.)

His immediate chief then was Captain W. S. Moorsom, formerly of the RMC Sandhurst, who as part of his military duties had carried out surveys of Dublin and of Nova Scotia. He resigned his commission and then made detailed surveys of sections of the London and Birmingham Railway, which brought him to the attention of Robert Stephenson; as a result Moorsom became secretary of the vital and developing link with the north-west. A nodal point in the network of communications, Birmingham had thirteen railways running into it in 1845. A necessary exercise in rationalization now undertaken led to designs for the central stations of New Street and Snow Hill, the incorporation of the lines to Derby and to Manchester into the Midland scheme, and in 1846 the amalgamation of the original railways to Liverpool and to London into the London and North Western Railway. One of the main purposes of this railway was to provide rapid connections with Ireland, and in order to realize this objective it was required that there should be an understanding between the existing smaller companies westward from Chester and a new major station complex in Chester.

Already Stephenson's blueprints for a new railway bridge between the mainland and Anglesey—to complement, and architecturally to be worthy of comparison with, Telford's existing road bridge—were coming to life. In May 1846 Frank Foster, Acting Engineer of the Conway and Holyhead Railway, laid the first stone of the Britannia Bridge (so named from the rock on which part of its foundations lay).

[23] E.O., June 1 [1886].

On 22 December a meeting was held in Chester to consider the subject of a 'Joint Station'; the bodies represented were the LNWR, the Chester and Holyhead (taking in the links to Mold and Caernarfon), the Shrewsbury and Chester, the Chester and Birkenhead, and the Birkenhead, Lancashire and Cheshire Junction Companies. Moorsom was present on behalf of the Chester and Holyhead Company. On 2 July 1847 C. H. Wild, Edmund Grove's boss, attended a meeting of the Joint Committee to explain the plans for the station and for a proposed new bridge over the railway. He also reported the progress of negotiations with Thomas Brassey in respect of the construction of these works. The architect was Francis Thompson, who in 1840 had built Derby Station, the model for the Chester work, while R. L. Jones, the secretary and general manager to the Committee, superintended the general scheme and 'suggested' and 'caused such alterations to be made as he deemed necessary for the general comfort and convenience of the public'.[24] George Grove was appointed to act as supervising site engineer.

The Chester project had got off to an unfortunate start in that it was overshadowed by an accident which had resulted in the death of 4 passengers and serious injury to 19 when one of the three spans of a bridge across the Dee, belonging to the vital Chester and Holyhead line, collapsed in May. It was 'the first failure Mr Stephenson had, out of about 100 trussed bridges'.[25]

While inspectors appointed by the Government argued over this disaster (which threatened the continuation of similar schemes) work proceeded fast on the other undertakings and the General Railway Station was officially opened on 1 August 1848. The cost of that station and auxiliary buildings was £220,000, and the whole project had been brought to fruition in a year. It was welcomed as a new companion to the worthiest old buildings of the city, 'admirably adapted to carry on with comfort to the public and with facility to the employees, the immense business that has so suddenly been brought to the city by the convergence of so many railways at this point.'[26]

[24] E. Parry, *The Railway Companies from Chester to Shrewsbury* (1849), pp. 20–1.

[25] *Illustrated London News*, 24 May 1847. In other bridges of this kind the girders were continuous, which was not the case here. See W. Fairbairn, 'On Tubular Girder Bridges', *Proceedings of the Institution of Civil Engineers* [*P.I.C.E.*] IX, 12 Mar 1850, pp. 233ff.

[26] T. Hughes, *The Stranger's Handbook of Chester* . . . (1856), pp. 11–12, where it was further noted: 'The passengers' shed occupies a space of ground nearly a quarter of a mile in length, and presents to the city an elegant façade 1010 feet long, and a frontage, including the house and carriage landings, of 1160 feet. It is built of dark red fire bricks, relieved with copings and facings of Stanton stone. At each end of the Station, and projecting from the main building, there is a shed for cabs and omnibuses awaiting the arrival of trains, each 290 feet long by 24 feet broad, covered with an iron roof.

'On the inner side of the building is the Grand Departure Platform, extending 1010 feet in length by 20 feet in width; this and three lines of rails are covered with an

There were soon to pass through the station 98 passenger trains and 3500 passengers daily, the latter able to linger in the Refreshment Rooms rented to a Mr Hobday where 'the utmost wish of your soul will be incontinently gratified'. The efficient operation of railways demanded total obedience. On 31 August 1848 a carriage inspector, having been absent from duty for part of two days, was 'discharged from the service of the Station Committee' while the next year a workman reported drunk on duty was also dismissed. The engineers were kept on their toes. On 28 September Wild was instructed to plan for coal wharfs and for cattle landings to take livestock from Ireland. At the beginning of the next year both Stephenson and Wild were summoned before the Joint Committee to explain why they had exceeded their estimates.

Grove enjoyed his year in Chester, where he was able to consolidate his reputation as a reliable and competent member of an exacting profession. He remembered those days with pride:

Yes, I lived in Abbey Square. I was then resident Engineer of the Great Station and worked (as I have always done) like a tiger. That was in the year 1847-48. What an age ago, it's almost like looking back to the world before the flood. It was a *warming* time of my life—I was very good and religious. I had already done much in Jamaica and Bermuda—but that was nothing to what was to come after. . . .[27]

Grove, it would seem, lodged in one of the houses on the Abbey Street side of the square, where several widows had rooms to let. In a house near the Abbey Gateway lived W. F. Ayrton, son of William Ayrton, organist of Ripon Minster and nephew of Edmund Ayrton, sometime Master of the Children of the Chapel Royal. W. F. Ayrton was himself briefly organist at Ripon in succession to his father; but after three years, in 1802, he moved to Chester where he practised as a 'Professor of Music'. Off Abbey Street, in Abbey Court, was the house of Frederick Gunton, the young cathedral organist.

In spite of its then generally impoverished appearance (apart from the fine carved choir stalls), Grove found Chester cathedral a continual source of pleasure both to eye and to ear. The organ, which had been built by Gray and Davison in 1844 and was only smaller than that in York Minster, was an outstanding instrument. Gunton, a co-signatory of the 1840 protest with John Blackburn of Clapham, who had, it was said, been credited by Mendelssohn with a 'touch like velvet', was very friendly with Grove. Although it was not a period in which the cathedral

---

exceedingly chaste and elegant iron roof of 60 feet span, designed and carried out by Mr Wild C.E. Behind this shed again, but visible from the general platform through the arches, is the spare carriage shed, 600 feet long by 52 broad.'

[27] E.O., Saturday July 29 [1893].

music was at its best there was one notable ecclesiastical event to stimulate the choristers while Grove was in Chester. A new bishop was en-
throned and the climax of the service was the singing of Beethoven's
'Hallelujah' from *The Mount of Olives*.

Another 'Professor of Music' in the city with whom Grove was
acquainted was the organist of St Bridget's Church, John Owen, later
to be distinguished by his fellow Welshmen as 'Owain Alaw' ('Owen the
Melody'). A year younger than Grove, Owen was busy writing hymn
tunes—'Calfari' was published in 1849—and investigating the traditions
of Welsh music. He helped to arouse interest in the art of pennillion and
to recreate the Eisteddfod. Under the influence of John Hullah he in-
stituted a 'New Singing Class on the Hullah system' in the Mechanics'
Institution, in which a variety of musical events took place. Henry
Phillips, celebrated as a Purcell and Handel singer, and Charles Lockey,
who had not long before been praised by Mendelssohn for his part in
the first performance of *Elijah*, were among the artists to appear there.
While Grove lived in Chester the Literary Improvement Society was
founded, at whose soirées a body of glee singers was always engaged to
perform.

But when the General Station had gone into commission Grove's
work in Chester was ended. However, he did not have to go far for his
next assignment. Stephenson moved his technical assistants from
Chester to the Menai Straits, where there had lately been much rejoicing
over the opening of the Conway Bridge and where the completion of the
railway bridge across the Straits was eagerly awaited. At a Public Dinner
given in Conway on 17 May 1848—at which not only Robert Stephenson
but also his father, George, were guests—the company was entertained
with a fine programme of glees which were interspersed among the
speeches. The association between music and engineering was close at
that time, especially in Wales. This was not surprising, in view of the
almost religious fervour with which the public regarded the achievements
of the great engineers of the age. The Conway Bridge was hailed as a
masterpiece: the 'gigantic undertaking' further down the Straits was to
be an even greater source of pride.

Before joining the team working on the Britannia Bridge as an assistant
site engineer, Grove went with his brother Edmund for a holiday in
France. In recognition of his good work at Chester Grove's expenses
were generously paid by Wild. For George the excursion was timely, as
he later recalled:

. . . So you are reading Carlyle's F[rench] R[evolution]. It's an epoch in your
life. There's no book like it for force and impression—and on the whole, I
believe, for truth. I remember my pleasure was interfered with by the
amount of knowledge it presupposed. I was so puzzled by the 'Oeil de Boeuf'
etc. etc. I went to Paris soon after reading it (in 1848, the Revolution Year)

and was wild to trace everything, and many sites could be traced, now demolished.[28]

Only a few months after the political destiny of France had been fought out in the streets of the capital, with the victims of revolution piled high as in Meissonier's horrific *La Barricade—1848*, and only weeks after Louis Bonaparte's silent departure for England, the Groves and their lawyer friend J. W. Hawkins, having travelled by way of Amiens,[29] entered Paris.

George led the party, and insisted on visiting as many churches as possible. For one with a close knowledge of architecture it was a particularly interesting time. In Paris the churches were beginning to recover from the wounds inflicted during the earlier Revolution of 1789, and to establish a new identity. Notre Dame was in the zealous hands of Viollet-le-Duc; Saint-Germain-des-Prés had just emerged from Baltard's restoration. The cult of the Picturesque was responsible for the Church of Saint-Clotilde, now under construction, and a renewal of Gregorian chant, which George listened to in the draughty nave of Saint-Roch. The nearby Madeleine—a Greek temple intended for the justification of reason—was at last in use as a church.

Across the Seine George went to the complementary palace which was the National Assembly to hear a speech by Lamartine. One afternoon he happened to be with his companions in the Place before the Palais Royal (as it had been), where he accosted a police sergeant who had just dispersed a group of unruly teenagers, and questioned him as to the proper application of the triple concept, *Liberté*, *Egalité*, and *Fraternité*. Not satisfied that this functionary was in any way authoritative in matters of philosophy, George surprised him by demonstrating leap-frog over the back of the obliging Hawkins. After the passage of a few years it was, however, not Grove who was to shock the Parisians but they him. But his respect for the French language was great, and in later life he found it useful for expressions of feeling requiring a delicate touch.

The idea of greatness is implicit in almost every tenet of Victorian thought, and the belief that great works were being produced was one

[28] E.O., New Year's Day [1891].
[29] Late in life Grove related how he and two of his 'then friends went to Abbeville to see Boucher de Perthes and the "flint instruments" which he had discovered and about what all the world was mad' (E.O., Aug 29 [1896]). Although Grove guessed at *c.* 1860—'a very distant year'—it seems that he only went to Abbeville once, and that was in 1848, on the way to Amiens and Paris. Boucher de Perthes, a local customs official and antiquary, had found chipped implements near Abbeville between 1841 and 1847, and his surmise that these were evidence of human handiwork in prehistoric times was duly confirmed in due course by the English scholars John Evans and Joseph Prestwich. Grove's later confusion with 1860 may well have been due to the publication of material concerning the finds of Boucher de Perthes in the journal *Archaeologia* in 1860.

reason why often they were produced. It is not to the prose and poetry of the masters of literature that we look for the realization of the sense of the sublime (one of Grove's favourite words), but to the prose (and poetry) of those whose talents were generally otherwise disposed. It is important to recognize that Grove himself was of this order. He was an engineer whose organizing abilities took him into areas in which such abilities were required and from which literary exercises evolved. His approach to the great masters of literature and of music derived from the optimistic philosophy of those under whom he worked.

In the little town of Bangor—Stephenson's headquarters for the Britannia Bridge operation[30]—Grove was still able to keep in touch with some music, through J. S. Pring, cathedral organist and wit, and John Owen. But the greatest influence on him in the Bangor period was his chief in the work-force, Edwin Clark. Born in Great Marlow in 1814, Clark was educated in Normandy, where he mastered French well enough to produce a translation of a minor work by Scott in that language. Apprenticed to a solicitor uncle, Clark interested himself in mathematics, astronomy, mechanics and chemistry, and in 1834 went up to Cambridge to read Classics. After some years as a mathematics teacher he turned his attention to railways, and when Stephenson made his acquaintance, and recognized his competence, he took him into his Great George Street office as a mathematical analyst. Grove revered Clark—'a great engineer . . . and a most interesting, original person',[31] and in old age attended his funeral.

Elgar likened the Fifth Symphony of Beethoven to the Forth Bridge. For Grove the paradigm was the Britannia Bridge, and the Preface to the first edition of *Grove's Dictionary* is couched in terms similar to those used by Clark in the opening pages of *The Britannia and Conway Tubular Bridges* (1850). In spirited words the 'Young England' to which Grove belonged is exemplified in Clark's faith in the best of all possible worlds:

The present age is remarkably distinguished from all that have gone before it, by the extraordinary energy manifested during it in all regions of thought and action. Other centuries, as the sixteenth and seventeenth, have been characterised by vast activity and vigour, but neither so widely extended nor so intense as in this. Among the Continental nations, the particular directions in which this energy has displayed itself is that of the great political and social questions which, happily for us, were in great measure settled by our forefathers during the former periods; while, among ourselves, progress hitherto has shown itself mainly in a material and mechanical direction. The thirty-five years which have passed since the Peace have seen—not, it is true, the invention, but the almost

[30] Stephenson lodged across the straits in Llanfair P.G. (with 58 letters in the name). Sir Francis Head said that his colleague slept there 'undisturbed by consonants'. See Grove, *The Times*, 8 Jan 1878.
[31] E.O., Monday night [30 Oct 1894].

universal application of machinery and the power of steam to the processes of manufacture and agriculture; whilst the electric telegraph, probably only the commencement of our mastery over this mysterious agent, is a much more recent invention. Of this energy and progress, railroads are at once the most prominent embodiment and the fittest symbol; and it is of the greatest railroad work yet achieved,—offering in itself a striking and interesting specimen of that energy—that in the following pages an explanation and description is attempted.

Stephenson had great problems to solve in designing the Britannia Bridge. It was recognized from the outset that the suspension method so elegantly employed by Telford in 1822 would not serve for heavy railway trains. That a bridge on vast cast-iron arches would answer the requirements was rendered impossible by the insistence of the Admiralty on a height too great to permit this method. So Stephenson arrived at the idea of a huge beam, or tube.

The building of the bridge was a joint effort, with architects and engineers in collaboration. The engineering side was dominated by Stephenson; the great towers, of stone brought by water from Runcorn, were by Francis Thompson, while the monumental lions were the work of John Thomas, whose work for Barry's Houses of Parliament and for the Birmingham and London Railway had brought him into prominence. A great deal of the machinery used by the various contractors was quite new. The magnitude of the undertaking is illustrated by the fact that 26 travelling cranes and 6 steam engines were employed; 2177 vessels brought stone to the site; 5 wharfs and landing stages, 80 wooden cottages for about 500 workers and their families, shops, school, Sunday school, and meeting houses were built. When the work was completed 700 men had been engaged on the stonework, 800 on the ironwork, 700 in the floating operations, and 36 on the delicate task of raising the great tubes of best wrought iron from Staffordshire. There were always in attendance resident clergymen and doctor.

Moorsom was the resident director, Frank Foster the resident engineer. Wild and Clark were assistant engineers, the latter being responsible for the overall floating and lifting operations. Clark put in the first rivets on 10 August 1847. In November 1848 all the four tubes were nearing completion. Clark looked down them with awe: 'the appearance of the interior of the large tubes, as seen from the end, is very striking . . . there is really no very distant resemblance to the "long drawn aisles" of a cathedral'.

On 22 February 1849 the side towers were ready. The directors of the Company, conscious of the money they had raised and still had to raise, urged Stephenson to go faster. Within three months it was generally felt that satisfactory progress had been made, and that a celebration was in order. On Friday, 18 May, the engineering staff arranged a unique concert in the central tube of the bridge. The entrance had been taste-

1   George Grove in 1861
Portrait by Henry Phillips

2   The Spring Well, Clapham Common

3   Cast Iron Lighthouse at Morant Point, Jamaica

4 Robert Stephenson

5 Chester Railway Station

6 Britannia Tubular Bridge,
the Floating of the Second Tube,
July 1850, by G. Hawkins

7 Charles Kingsley

8 F. D. Maurice

9 A. P. Stanley

10 Alexander Macmillan

grew up in a period of restructuring of agriculture, in which his father—
described by George as 'the last Yeoman of the county'—like many
others with insufficient resources to meet change, became impoverished.
After his younger brother John had gone to London he went too, and in
due course he established himself as a 'Fishmonger and Venison Dealer'.
In 1807 he married Mary Blades, sister of Joseph Blades, a principal of
the printing firm of Blades and East, of Abchurch Lane.

Thomas Grove conducted his business in a favourable situation, at 33
Charing Cross, which for some years was the family home, and where in
due course his eldest son, succeeding to the business, also lived for a
time. Grove senior was depicted by Charles Dickens in this unflattering
manner:

I have consulted Mr. Groves [sic] of Charing Cross. His suggestive mind gave
birth to this remarkable expression—'then why not consider this here breast
o' wenson, off—and let me git another prime 'un in good eatin' order for
you, for Sunday week? What'—continued Mr. Groves—'is the hodds to a
day?'
Mr. Groves slapped a piece of venison as he spoke, with the palm of his hand;
and plainly signified, by his manner no less than by his words, that this was
wisdom.[4]

When the time came to separate home and business, shortly before
their son George was born, the Groves moved to Thurlow Lodge,
74 Thurlow Terrace, in the Wandsworth Road, Clapham. The Blades
family later came into the next house, which was named Thurlow Cottage.
The houses were set on a high bank, from which there was a panoramic
view across meadows, Battersea Fields, and the Thames, towards distant
Chelsea. It was an enchanting place to spend one's childhood. Almost a
lifetime later George Grove recollected how

There was a place under the wall of the field at our old house, where I was
born, where a deer used to lie with his horns showing above the docks and
large-leaved plants that grew there; and we children playing in the field used
always to feel a kind of cold dread come over us as we went near that corner
and saw the creature's horns.[5]

Clapham was a large village recommended to city merchants on account
of its rural amenities, its educational facilities—which included Batten's
lending library and reading room—its respectability, and its convenient
two-horse coach service from the Plough Inn to town. At the time of
George Grove's birth there was a population of 7151, and 230 families

[4] Letter to Thomas Beard, 21 July 1842; *The Letters of Charles Dickens, 1842–3*,
Pilgrim Edn, vol. III (Oxford, 1974), p. 276. See also p. 285, where an instruction to
Frederick Dickens reads, 'Don't forget Mister Groves'.
[5] BL, Eg. MS. 3091, f. 107.

were still engaged in agriculture. The Poor Rate, out of which Mr and Mrs Levesque were maintained as Master and Mistress of the Workhouse on a joint salary of 60 guineas a year, was levied at 4s. 9d. in the pound and the annual yield was £4690. But not even Clapham could escape the effects of the licentiousness that prevailed in the age of *Vanity Fair* (Thackeray paid his tribute to the holier Claphamites in *The Newcomes*), and in 1823 the inhabitants were shocked by the brutal murder of an elderly widow, Mrs Elizabeth Richards, as she lay in her bed. Two years later, in response to undiminished anxiety, four constables were appointed to the parish. This was four years before Sir Robert Peel established a police force in London.

So far as education was concerned—apart from Greaves's school, which was for the well-to-do—there was a proliferation of 'dame schools' and little, often one-room, 'academies'. There was also the parochial school, which had been founded in 1648, and had been once considered as a grammar school. By 1810, however, it had been reduced to the rank of a 'national school', providing minimal instruction for the children of the poor.

During George Grove's childhood the former African Academy passed from the care of Greaves to that of one Elwell, a kindly Calvinist who wore a peruke and was familiarly known by his pupils as 'Old Rum Wig'. In the course of time Elwell became in sequence an Irvingite, a bankrupt and an emigrant. But before religious zeal carried him into disorder and disaster he was entrusted with the elementary education of, among others, the sons of Sir Andrew Agnew, a celebrated defender of the Lord's Day; the Revd Charles Bradley, preacher at St James's Chapel, Clapham; Edward Hawke Locker, Civil Commissioner of Greenwich Hospital; and Thomas Grove.

George had been taught the basic elements of literacy by his sister Bithiah, before he went to Elwell as a weekly boarder at the age of eight. He was, however, bewildered by his removal from the comforts of Thurlow Lodge and consignment to the rigours of a male-dominated institution. Being sent to a boarding establishment at a tender age affected him deeply. Even at the age of seventy-three he recalled 'an extraordinary night at school when I was about 9 (at most) when I woke to find myself on the floor and in presence of some dreadful something, or negation of anything—a "horror of great darkness" as it is in the bible somewhere. . . .'[6]

There were about fourteen boys in the school and gradually George discovered its more pleasant aspects. There were 'prisoners' base'—a pastime well known in Elizabethan times—and cricket on the Common, which also afforded walks through 'groves and gorse-wildernesses'. But

---

[6] E.O., Sunday Feb 19 [1893]. Dates of all letters to E.O. are given as Grove wrote them.

from these too came certain phobias: 'When I was a child I remember having a perfect aversion to the smell of gorse (or furze as we called it) and of mountain ash (or rowan).'[7]

An elderly one-eyed barrow boy brought cheer to George and his friends by supplying them with sweets and ginger pop. There was a farmyard on the edge of the Common which, George remembered, was still in use in 1832, while near the Cock Inn were the pound and the stocks—which, however, were not in use. There were ditches across the Common. In one the boys found an iron girder, said to have been a relic from Marc Brunel's work on the Thames Tunnel; in another, bordered by lime trees and leading to the church, little fishes darted.

Life, however, was only thought to continue according to divine ordinance as interpreted in Clapham from the pulpits of Holy Trinity parish church, St Paul's Chapel of Ease, St James's Chapel, and various Nonconformist places of worship. The Grove children, beneficiaries of the broadminded, or politic, attitude of their father, were encouraged to go to the parish church; Thomas himself, preferring a Congregational point of view, often went elsewhere.

Holy Trinity, designed by Kenton Couse in a simple classical style, replacing an older church which had become inadequate to serve an increased population, was consecrated by the Bishop of Lichfield and Coventry on 10 June 1776. John Venn, Vicar until 1813, proved a powerful promoter of good order and—recalling perhaps that Nicholas Brady, the metrical psalmist, had been one of his predecessors—was responsible for the introduction of improved versions and better selections of Psalms and hymns into the service. His successor was W. Dealtry, B.D., F.R.S., whose interests were somewhat wider (if his piety was a little lighter) than those of Venn. The church was a notable centre of charitable intention,[8] and the well-to-do citizens of Clapham were required frequently to put their hands in their pockets. As liturgical decency became a matter for concern they found themselves also with dues to pay for improvements in ecclesiastical music performance. In *Clapham, with its Commons and Environs* (1828) it was stated: 'In the West Gallery is a very superior Organ, which in 1825 was greatly enlarged and improved by [J.C.] Bishop, the expense of which was defrayed by voluntary contributions. The present organist is Mr Blackburn.'

John Blackburn (or Blackbourn), Professor of Music, had once been a

[7] E.O., May 14 [1893].

[8] Some of the causes for which Charity Sermons were arranged during George Grove's childhood serve as index to social and political concerns then in the forefront of consideration. They included the London Society for Promoting Christianity among the Jews; the Hibernian Society; Asylums for the Deaf and Dumb, and for Orphans; the Funds for those in Distress in the Neighbourhood of Hanover, and for the Distressed Irish; the Society for the Propagation of the Gospel; and the Distressed Silk Weavers of Spitalfields.

chorister at St Paul's Cathedral. He deserves special notice because he was among the select band of those in England concerned with propagating the keyboard music of J. S. Bach.[9] George Grove remembered how when young he and his brother Edmund were specially taken with Blackburn's playing of the E major fugue of the Second Book of the 'Forty-eight'.

St Paul's Chapel was on the site of the old parish church, the aisle and transept of which stood until 1814. A modest essay in classical style by a local architect, it was built in 1815. The opening sermon was delivered by Dealtry, but he was soon shown what preaching in the Evangelical manner really was by the minister appointed to the chapelry, William Burrows. A native of Derby, Burrows was thirty-four at the time of his appointment and he remained at St Paul's until his death at the age of seventy. He acquired a great reputation as an apostle of Evangelism, and with his flat northern accent he called sinners to repentance with a fervour and rhetorical virtuosity that brought them to his feet by the carriage-load. His hour-long monologues were a considerable source of pleasure. But the twenty or thirty carriages left in St Paul's Close every Sunday morning gave rise to unprecedented parking problems.

At Elwell's school George's closest friend was George Granville Bradley, son of the Revd Charles Bradley, the incumbent of St James's Chapel.[10] Grove's connection with the Bradley family, thus early formed, was to be lifelong and close—and ultimately calamitous. Charles Bradley published seven volumes of sermons and a number of pedagogic works, but it was the style of his oratory that most compelled attention and lingered in the memory. An anonymous schoolboy of Clapham recollected both Burrows and Bradley, and thus contrasted them:

Mr Burrows, doubtless a very good man in his way, . . . never preached under an hour. He had a stentorian voice, thumped the pulpit, and flung the cushions about wildly. He preached what is called 'high doctrine', but was very unintelligible to juvenile hearers. As a great treat, and on very rare occasions we

[9] Well respected among progressive church musicians, Blackburn was in 1840 one of those, mainly cathedral and collegiate organists, who signed a petition addressed to the Deans of English and Welsh cathedrals on account of their proposing extensive cuts in the budgets of their musical establishments. He was also among the earliest members of the Musical Antiquarian Society.

[10] Charles Bradley was forty years of age when he arrived in Clapham, partly through the recommendation of William Wilberforce, and at the height of his fame as an Evangelical preacher. More or less self-educated, he had acquired a scholar's reputation in early life and during his curacies in Wallingford and High Wycombe eked out his stipend by taking pupils, of whom some became famous. In 1824 he was inducted to the living of Glasbury-on-Wye in Brecknockshire, and five years later he came to Clapham. He held the two livings together, which—however inconvenient for his more distant flock—was necessary for the maintenance of his large family (see p. 54).

11   Grove's House at Sydenham

12   The Crystal Palace

13   Arthur Sullivan, by Sir John Millais   14   August Manns, 'Spy' cartoon

15   Joseph Joachim and Clara Schumann, drawing by Adolf von Menzel

16 Sir Austen Layard

17 The Golden Gateway at Jerusalem

18 The Duke of
Edinburgh
Conducting at a
Liverpool Concert in
Aid of the Royal
College of Music

19 Royal College of
Music Decorated for
the State Opening,
May 1894

20 Edith Oldham, 1898

23   *Toy Symphony*, Andreas Romberg, St James's Hall, May 1880

Back row: John Stainer, Arthur Chappell, William Kuhe, Louis Engel, Charles Santley, Carl Rosa, Francis Burnand, August Manns, Wilhelm Ganz
Second row: Joseph Barnby, F. H. Cowen, Albert Randegger, William Cusins, Viscountess Folkestone, Julius Benedict, Hugo Daubart, Jacques Blumenthal
Seated: Arthur Sullivan, Henry Leslie

24 Sir George Grove, 1890

fully disguised with branches to resemble a 'grove' (his colleagues surely used George's expertise in the faculty of music). About forty singers from Caernarfon and Bangor were assembled by Hayden, organist of St Mary's Church in Caernarfon, and sang a choice programme to an enthusiastic audience of more than 700 local worthies.[32] After the concert 'a couple of flutes, violins, and triangles [sic]' played the music for lancers, quadrilles, polkas and country dances to which the nimble and love-lorn among the engineers and their guests disported themselves until midnight.

The great tubes—each more than a quarter-mile long—had been constructed some 200 feet from the site of the bridge. On 1 June the *Liverpool Mercury* reported: 'A party of jack tars from the Sailors' Home, Liverpool, have reached the locality, and are barracked on the banks of the Menai and these will be under the direction of Captain Claxton, to whom the arduous task of floating the tubes has been confided.'

On 19 June the first attempt to float the first tube into its raising position was made. The banks were lined with spectators—among whom was Grove, inconspicuously writing descriptive notes—and cake-sellers and tricksters, in search respectively of customers and victims, moved through the throng. Stephenson and some of his assistants, with Brunel, Joseph Locke, Captain Claxton and Sir Francis Head, were on the tube. But the first attempt to float it was unsuccessful; so too was the second, early the next morning. However, at 8 o'clock on the evening of 20 June the operation was satisfactorily completed. As the great tube had begun to move on its course, the band in attendance appropriately struck up 'I'm Afloat'.

On the Saturday following, the *Spectator* contained an account of the operation with the introduction: 'A correspondent supplies us with the following as a strictly accurate account of this interesting operation.' That account was the first published piece by George Grove. The same issue of the *Spectator* carried news of the decision of the Common Council of the City of London to petition Parliament to remove the disabilities of Jews from sitting in the Commons; of the presence of the Queen and Prince Albert at a Sacred Harmonic Society performance of Mendelssohn's *Athalie*; of the impact made by Beethoven's 'mysterious posthumous quartet' in B flat (Op. 130) at a Musical Union concert organized by John Ella; of the successful performance of *Elijah* by the pupils of John Hullah's 'upper singing classes' at Exeter Hall; and of an epidemic of cholera, which had already caused 114 deaths in Liverpool.

---

[32] The programme included favourite glees, a song specially written by Hayden and prettily sung by his son, comedy songs, the 'March of the Men of Harlech', and the less topographically apt 'Banks of the Blue Moselle'; these and other details from the *North Wales Chronicle*, 22 May 1849.

The Bridge, too, claimed its victims. On 15 July 1848 'Henry Jones, a labourer employed on the Britannia Bridge was . . . crushed to death by a descent of stone and rubbish. The unlucky deceased was a native of Llangefni, and a wife and seven children depended on his earning their daily bread'.[33] On 4 August the local newspaper reported the murder of John Rowlands, one of the watchmen on the site. On 17 August one tube being raised fell a few inches, throwing Clark off balance into the interior of the tower and killing a sailor. On 20 November another accident resulted in the death of another sailor and injuries to other workers.

Not for the last time a great technological project was subjected to criticism. In 1847 a Parliamentary Commission was set up to 'inquire into the Application of Iron to Railway Structures' and its Report was published in 1849. It

> urged the importance of leaving the genius of scientific man unfettered, for the development of a subject, as yet so novel and so rapidly progressing as the construction of railways, we are of opinion that any legislative enactments with respect to the forms and proportions of the iron structures employed therein, would be highly inexpedient.

But after the collapse of one girder bridge and the report of an Inspecting Officer of the Railway Board that he had just examined and found unsafe another girder bridge, engineers were afraid that 'the possible result might be the rejection of that magnificent monument of engineering, the Britannia Bridge'.

At this point Stephenson brought another engineer—a mathematical analytical expert—into his team. This was William Pole, who was not only a brilliant engineer but also an authority on whist, and a musician. A Birmingham man, he had once been organist of a Wesleyan chapel in the city. Pole was an early Bach enthusiast, playing that master's organ works as long ago as 1835. The Bach Society, founded at the time when the Britannia Bridge was being completed, claimed him as one of its early members. After moving to London he became organist of St Mark's, North Audley Street. In later years his achievements in the musical world were almost as remarkable as those of Grove, with whom he was ultimately associated in the RCM faculty.

In spite of all the alarms that had been raised the last stages of the work on the Britannia Bridge went well. The final alarm was on 5 February 1850 when the most violent storm since 1839 (when Telford's Bridge had been severely damaged) raged over the Straits. But the new bridge withstood the shock and a month later the first train, drawn by three flag-bedecked engines, the *Cambrian*, *St. David*, and *Pegasus*—on the first of which Stephenson rode in triumph—crossed to Anglesey.

---

[33] ibid., 21 July 1848.

The cost had been £674,000—three times the original estimate—but, as the workmen discovered in the shops on site, it was a time of inflation. Stephenson refused the knighthood offered to him, 'considering that, to be ranked with some of those who have the title, is no honour'.

CHAPTER THREE

Life in a Glass House

1850–1857

WITH the Britannia Bridge in commission Grove found himself at something of a loose end. He was restless, uncertain as to the direction he should take. He did not, it would seem, see his future as always that of an engineer, for whereas his brother Edmund progressed in the profession to become an Associate of the Institution of Civil Engineers in 1850,[1] George did not attain this rank. He had, however, made a favourable impression on the influential, and a distinguished trio comprised of the engineers Stephenson and Brunel and the architect Sir Charles Barry pushed him into his next assignment. They advised him to return to London and to put himself forward as a candidate for the post of Secretary of the Society of Arts which was to become vacant on the expected resignation of John Scott Russell. A Scotsman and also an engineer, the brilliant and somewhat unpredictable Russell before coming south had worked in the shipyards at Greenock, during the time Grove was in Glasgow. He had been appointed Secretary of the Society in 1845.

The Society of Arts was intended to embrace both the pure and the applied arts, and—through the insistence of Henry Cole, an official at the Record Office—had lately been reorganized. In 1847 the Society had held an Exhibition of Art Manufactures—intended to be held annually—from which grew the idea of a large general exhibition which should serve as a shop-window for British industry. By 1849 an executive committee had been formed to plan such a project, and on 3 January 1850 this was confirmed by a Royal Commission. Cole was given leave of absence from the Record Office to devote himself to organization of the scheme, which culminated in what was to become forever known as the 'Great Exhibition'.

Already known as the force behind the new postal system and the inventor of the Christmas card, Cole is one of the unsung geniuses of the Victorian era. Often he was a real power behind the real throne.

---

[1] 'Edmund Grove . . . in the early days of railway development . . . was engaged on the survey and construction of a number of lines, especially in the eastern counties. Later, he joined in founding the firm of Cochrane, Grove & Co., of Cleveland. . . . Associate, 3 December 1850, and subsequently on Roll of Associate Members'; *PICE* CLXXXVII, 1911, p. 387.

His principal colleagues on the exhibition committee were Robert Stephenson; Matthew Digby Wyatt, an architect, who was sent to Paris to study the layout of the 1849 Exhibition in that city; and Charles Wentworth Dilke, sometime Chairman of the Society of Arts and an expert in horticulture. The President of the projected exhibition was Prince Albert, to whom—despite the efforts of others in setting it up—went most of the credit.

A competition was held for the design of a suitable exhibition centre and the successful entry, submitted by Joseph Paxton, was accompanied by a tender for construction from Fox and Henderson[2] with an under-taking to complete the building within nine months.

During the preparatory period the Society of Arts, directed by Scott Russell, had conducted feasibility studies, tested the enthusiasm of British manufacturers as well as of potential exhibitors in other parts of the world, and persuaded the City of London to put up a guarantee of £50,000. But somewhere along the line Russell, who had successfully handled exhibitions of Modern British Paintings and of Ancient and Medieval Decorative Art, began to feel he was being left out of things. Believing that his contribution to the major scheme had been considerable, and conscious of his professional standing (he had become F.R.S. in 1847), he decided to return to engineering.[3] On 29 January 1850 he was at a meeting of the I.C.E., discussing the design of girder bridges in general, and of the Torkesey Bridge for the Manchester, Sheffield and Lincolnshire Railway in particular, a subject in which both the Grove brothers were interested.

A week later George Grove was appointed Joint Secretary of the Society of Arts on the understanding that if he proved himself an efficient administrator within a probationary month he would be left on his own. The month passed and the Committee responsible for his appointment were more than satisfied that they had found the right man for the job.[4]

Grove had fallen on his feet. He could not have received an appoint-ment better suited to his multifarious interests, even though the salary was relatively modest.[5] The offices of the Society were in the Adelphi,

[2] Sir Charles Fox (1810–74), a member of the Society of Arts, was formerly a con-struction engineer on the London–Birmingham railway.

[3] He was to become known to posterity as joint designer with Brunel of the ill-fated ship, the *Great Eastern*.

[4] Grove was the third engineer to act as Secretary of the Royal Society of Arts. Francis Wishaw, author of *The Railways of Great Britain and Ireland* (1840–1), preceded Russell, holding office from 1843 to 1845. Grove was 'a thoroughly capable official—in this respect superior to his immediate predecessors—and with a longer period of service he would doubtless have left his mark on the administration of the Society'; H. T. Wood, *A History of the Royal Society of Arts* (1913), pp. 363–4.

[5] 'Cheer up, old man, I began life on £150 a year and had that income till after I married (at 31 years old) so I know all your feelings'; letter to [R.H.] Legge of 26 Mar 1896, in private possession.

where he had rooms. Here also was the Exhibition headquarters, and the new Secretary found that he was quickly having to turn himself into a public-relations expert.

As George moved forward in the large world of affairs the household in Clapham looked on with pride. Thurlow Lodge was still well occupied. His father, now aged seventy-seven and retired, was blind. His mother, ten years younger, helped by two eighteen-year-old servants from the country, was fully employed in looking after Thomas jun., now a Master Fishmonger, Eliza (later on she insisted on being called Elizabeth), Kezia, Anna, Eleanor and Edmund.[6]

While the Exhibition was being prepared George was in the last stages of a decorous courtship, which took him often to Clapham. The object of his attentions was Harriet, sister of his old school friend, George Bradley: 'Old Bradley had a very large family—12, of whom my wife [the fifth daughter] was the youngest, but one—his wife died; and after 12 or 14 years he married again, a delightful woman a third of his age, who still lives and is a dear friend of mine—and then had 8 more children.'[7] Grove married Harriet Bradley on 23 December 1851.

Meanwhile, as in the old days when he was in Fludyer Street, Grove managed to leave the Society office from time to time to further his musical interests. One day he was introduced to the eccentricities of the virtuoso:

I knew [Pauer] first in 1850; figurez vous! He was living in a little top room at Broadwoods in Pulteney Street; and when I called he was practising a concerto of Hummel's for the Philharmonic, and he had worn the skin off the corner of his little finger by practising a *glissando*, and the blood flowed freely, and made a great impression on me, who had seen no artists and knew none of their ways.[8]

Hummel's A minor Concerto (Op. 88) is an effective display piece, with dazzling scales, arpeggios, strings of helter-skelter thirds and first inversions. (Any glissandi, however, were added by Pauer for good measure.) Grove was soon to get to know many other artists and many of their ways.

On May Day 1851 the Great Exhibition was opened by the Queen,

[6] The national census held on 30 March 1851 records as also staying in the house a Catherine Bennett, of Salisbury, a girl of nineteen and of independent means, who was presumably Mary Bithiah's stepdaughter.
[7] E.O., Monday night [14 Apr 1894]. Bradley's first wife, who had borne him thirteen (not twelve) children, died in 1831. Eight years later he married Emma Linton, daughter of a stockbroker living in Clapham, by whom he had a second large family of eight children.
[8] E.O., Saturday night 10.30 p.m. [19 Jan 1891]. Pauer played the concerto at the Philharmonic Society concert on 23 June 1851.

dressed in pink and gold brocade. The Duke of Cambridge saw it as a 'great "festival of peace", which, by drawing men together in the common pursuit of moral and material progress, was to mark the end of war and the beginning of a new golden age of universal amity'. At the opening ceremony Paxton's great glass-house—nicknamed 'the Crystal Palace' almost as soon as it was built—resounded with organ music, played by S. S. Wesley, E. J. Hopkins, George Cooper, Henry Smart and J. L. F. Danjou, on instruments built by Willis, Hill, Ducroquet of Paris, Schulze of Thuringia and others. So much organ music ensured that the British public drew the right conclusions. Soon after the opening Charles Overton preached a sermon on 'The Crystal Palace; or, the Half not told' both in Cottingham and St Mary's churches in Hull. 'Let it', he thundered, 'solemnly admonish us to prepare for THE GREAT EXHIBITION that will be made in the day of judgment'. He passed on in ecstasy:

When you come to the entrance . . . [and] see the lofty trees with all their green honors, stretching their gigantic boughs in full liberty beneath that mighty dome; there you see the sparkling fountains, and hear the distant music, and gaze upon the honor and glory of the nations, and the multitudes that are gathered together within those shining walls, you are reminded of *Christian's* entrance into the Celestial City.

The Exhibition was closed on the Lord's Day, and this the preacher took as a sign of 'England's regard for the God of the Sabbath'. On week-days there were shelves of books in various languages supplied by the British and Foreign Bible and the Religious Tract Societies for the benefit of all comers. Here was the 'open bible'—the guarantee, concluded Overton, of happiness and freedom.

Charles Kingsley was present at the opening of the Great Exhibition. No one felt more profoundly the distance between the noble aims said to be inherent in the enterprise and their realization, and on 5 May, in St Margaret's, Westminster, he preached a sermon concerning the apparent inability of nineteenth-century man to recognize the source of his achievements as divine. Kingsley's acknowledgement of a growing rejection of religious beliefs was one mark of a general change in thought, brought about by the Reform Bill, the repeal of the Corn Laws, the Oxford Movement, the 'hungry Forties', Chartism, the social criticism in the novels of Dickens and Mrs Gaskell, by the quickening of the processes of industrialization, and rapidly improving communications; all of which helped to bring into being as many fears as hopes, doubts as certainties, and a counterpoint of conflicting opinions. Kingsley, F. J. Furnivall, F. D. Maurice, J. M. Ludlow, John Hullah, Tom Hughes and Septimus Hansard—some ordained clergymen, some laymen—all affected by the inequalities and injustices evident around them, and by the conflicting claims of revolutionaries and reactionaries, formed a loose federation of idealists owing loyalty to the emerging principles of Christian Socialism.

A main instrument of change was to be education, in which King's College, London, was already playing a distinguished part; in *Politics for the People,* first issued in 1848, Kingsley, in the guise of 'Parson Lot', suggested (in an essay on the British Museum) that a new sense of brotherhood might be forged by making the nation's heritage freely accessible to the nation as a whole. The idea was later taken up by Henry Cole and William Morris, to the general benefit.

This wave of idealism caught Grove at an impressionable age. He met various members of the Christian Socialist circle in about 1849 and tentatively dipped his fingers into the warm waters of their ideology.[9] Meanwhile, as Secretary of the Society of Arts, he was carrying out the instruction of the Prince Consort to engage eminent persons to give popular lectures in the Crystal Palace. Such lectures, said the Prince, should 'be delivered by none but those most eminently qualified to treat of the several departments of the Exhibition'.[10] Richard Owen, Hunterian Professor of Anatomy, was therefore invited to hold forth on the 'Animal Raw Production of the Exhibition . . . on the novelties in it which were brought into notice by the exhibition, their probable influence on the commercial, scientific, or general welfare of this or other countries'.

The energetic Cole, now Chairman of the Society, knowing that his Secretary was like himself a glutton for work, kept him busy in all directions. So, while dealing with Professor Owen, and others 'most eminently qualified', Grove was also deciding how to set up enquiries into such subjects as the manufacture and supply of coal gas, and the supply of water to London, the manufacture of sugar in the British colonies, and the adulteration of food. And following Cole's commitment to free education, in 1852 the Society proposed to review the working of the Museums and Free Libraries Act, as part of a serious attempt to lay the foundations for a broadly based adult and polytechnical education based on the existing 'Mechanics' and other 'Institutions'. Such institutions should, for a start, offer 'improved lectures of a more practical cast' by the most able men. Among those to whom Grove wrote, inviting their cooperation, was Charles Babbage, F.R.S., the mathematician and statistician, inventor of an early type of computer. Babbage, while excusing himself from performing an active part in the scheme—and informing Grove that what the Society of Arts was thinking of he himself had already promulgated—promised to lend his general support.[11]

[9] F. J. Furnivall considered Grove to be 'a cheery, bright, dear little fellow, a happier-natured man than whom [he] never knew'. The Faustian divide in Grove, deep though it was, was not to become apparent (and even then only to a very few) until later in life.
[10] Letter to R. Owen, 31 Oct 1851; BL, Add. MS. 42578, f. 96.
[11] Babbage wrote to Grove on 10 June 1852: '. . . it is now many years since I cir-

But by now Grove was working out his notice, for in May 1852 he was appointed Secretary to the Crystal Palace Company, which had purchased that structure from Fox and Henderson for £79,000, with the intention of removing it from Hyde Park and re-erecting it at Sydenham. As a salaried official, now with a steady income of £600 a year, and a ten-year guarantee, Grove had enough to sustain himself, his wife and any children in at least reasonable comfort. That year the Groves left the rooms in the Adelphi in which they had lived since their marriage and moved into a house known as Church Meadow, near Sydenham Station; there, on 25 April 1853, their first child, Lucy Penrose,[12] was born.

Grove had given up certain engineering consultancies which had from time to time taken him out of London to inspect railway installations in other parts of the country. But he had no intention of underemploying his talents. He began to move into literature by undertaking a translation of François Guizot's *Études sur les beaux arts en général*—a work illustrated by George Scharf, an artist engaged to design the Greek, Roman and Pompeian Courts at the new Crystal Palace. In the autumn of 1852, writing to Alexander Macmillan to request a copy of F. D. Maurice's 'new book of sermons', if they were yet published, he remarked that he had been reading Kingsley's *Phaethon, or Loose Thoughts for Loose Thinkers* just issued by Macmillan and had enjoyed it except that he thought 'Mrs. Windrush a little overdrawn'.[13] As far as literature was concerned, Grove consistently took a middle course.

He was not so cautious in his musical tastes. For some time past his idealism and his respect for history had led him to follow up his early enthusiasm for J. S. Bach. On 31 March 1853 he wrote to Anthony Panizzi, Keeper of Printed Books in the British Museum, with a list of published works of that master, which he considered the Museum should acquire. 'I hope', he said, 'you will not consider me intrusive or impertinent in thus writing to you. I am a great deal amongst young musicians (among whom the study of Bach is making great progress) and I have

---

culated in MSS a paper for the Federal Union of Scientific Societies in one large building as the means of economising greatly the funds voluntarily raised for the purposes of Science. . . . My own pursuits entirely prevent my giving any assistance on the subject of lectures. I heartily wish the Society of Arts success in exertions so highly honorable to its character'; BL, Add. MS. 37195, ff. 87–8.

[12] She was named after Francis Penrose, a relative of Matthew Arnold (whose wife, incidentally, was called Lucy) and a close friend of Charles Kingsley at Cambridge. The original of Amyas Leigh in *Westward Ho!*, Penrose in 1852 was architect to St Paul's Cathedral. He was also one of the directors of the Crystal Palace Company.

[13] Letter to Alexander Macmillan, 18 Oct 1852; BL, Add. MS. 54793, f. 11. The Macmillan brothers, Alexander and Daniel, partners in a relatively new publishing house in Cambridge, were friendly with F. D. Maurice and sympathetic to his school of thought.

very often to hear with pain their complaints of the want of the works of this great Master in the only Library accessible to them.' On 1 April Grove acknowledged a letter from Panizzi (who, on Grove's advice, had added the third volume of Winterfeld's *Der evangelische Kirchengesang* to the Museum's accessions), and indicated his willingness to help further in respect of Bach's works and their availability. Not long after this he began to stake his claim to critical authority by drawing attention to the virtues of Bach in a communication to the *Spectator* (11 June 1853).

Some days previously, at a Harmonic Union concert, Vieuxtemps had played the Chaconne for solo violin. Grove, who had heard Molique play this work at an anniversary concert of the Bach Society in 1851, and again at an Ella Concert earlier in 1853, took exception to the opinion expressed in the *Spectator* that Bach was primarily an intellectual composer:

Now the fact is, that Bach's learning was a very subordinate thing; and that not it, but feeling, sentiment, a burning genius, and a prodigious flow and march of ideas, are his characteristics. Learning he has in common with his contemporaries; fugal and imitative construction was the form music took in those days; but in the other qualities I have mentioned he stands quite alone. Germans know this well; in a few years perhaps Englishmen will do so: they will then find in Bach's work a tender passionate sentiment, showing itself in chords and harmonies which we are used to believe the sole property of Beethoven; grace and finish equal to those of Schubert; and melodic forms and peculiar idiosyncrasies and forms of expression which even young ladies have by heart from Mendelssohn's 'Songs without Words', but which we little imagine to have been drawn by him from his great predecessor.

There Grove laid down what were to be the principal lines of his life's work as a musical scholar. His views on Bach as stated here—and in his note on the *St Matthew Passion* of a few years later, for the second public performance of the work in England[14]—were based on the scores from which he had made his own choice excerpts, and from the experience of hearing certain works in more or less adventurous programmes of chamber music. He had also, typically, tried to find out all he could from the source. In his letter of 31 March to Panizzi he remarked that he had been in correspondence with a 'Mr von Bach'[15]. In later life he considerably modified his attitude to Bach; but to Beethoven, Schubert and Mendelssohn—the lode-stars of his philosophy of music—he remained adamantinely faithful.

[14] See p. 299.
[15] Possibly G. Bach, of Elberfeld, an acquaintance of F. Hiller. The letters to Panizzi, written from 3 Adelaide Place, London Bridge, are among the Panizzi Papers (1853) in the archive of the Department of Printed Books, Reference Division, the British Library (ff. 145 and 150 respectively).

At this time Grove was becoming increasingly disturbed by the heavy
Evangelical artillery being trained on that great pleasure dome the
Crystal Palace. Throughout its life on both its sites the Crystal Palace
performed a singular service for music, and it is unlikely that any building
ever did more to accustom working people to the enjoyment of music.
Its structure and its acoustics enthralled the senses, and the magnification
of otherwise commonplace sounds into a *mélange* of consorting and
conflicting sonorities was overwhelming. (Grove himself always showed a
tendency to be overwhelmed by music, and even by the thought of
music.) As early as 3 April 1852,[16] the music of Costa, Lortzing, Mendelssohn, Meyerbeer, Rossini, Weber and HRH the Duke of Saxe-Coburg-
Gotha, played by Guards' Bands disposed over the tall central nave, the
galleries, aisles, and the arched transept of the Palace, enchanted curious
visitors. But the more enthusiastic the response of people to the building
the louder the cries of protest. The recently formed Evangelical Union
claimed to be concerned for working-class morality (the morality of others
was beyond repair), and some of its adherents suspected that some
persons—Directors of the Crystal Palace Company who were also
Directors of the Company that intended building two new railway
lines to the Sydenham site—were going to make a good deal of profit
out of the moral turpitude to be carried to South London by excursion
trains.

On 29 April 1852 Lord John Manners, First Commissioner of Works,
speaking for the Government during a debate on the future of the
Crystal Palace, proposed that for the particular benefit of the working
classes there should be one area reserved for Church of England services,
with 'appointed reading-rooms' for Dissenters set up in less conspicuous
places. Conscious of the flood of pamphlets then being issued opposing
Sunday opening of the Palace he opined that if this came to pass, 'Then
they [would have taken] the first step—and it might be described as a
stride—to the introduction into this country of the continental method of
observing the Sunday.' Already there was desecration enough: steam-
boats plied on the river and omnibuses in the streets, while the railways,
by introducing 'Cheap Excursion Trains', were persuading people to
'forsake the houses of God and their own homes'. Worst of all, 'thousands
[were] already enslaved for work on the Lord's day for the pleasure or
profit of others'.[17]

On 14 September 1852, as if in token of divine disapproval of the decay

[16] The day after the death of old Thomas Grove.
[17] This idea was developed by an anonymous contributor to the debate into a shrewd
thrust at the profiteers from Sabbath-breaking: 'If you have so generous, so philan-
thropic, so disinterested a desire for the comfort and well-being of the million—then
let it be shewn by some great, general combination to release the million one half-day
in the week, without diminution of the six days' pay'; Anon., *The Removal of the Crystal
Palace* (1852).

in British morality, mortality claimed the old Duke of Wellington, a friend of Joseph Paxton from whom Grove heard many stories about the Duke.[18] On the death of the old Duke an Elegy was hawked round the streets of London in which, mindful of the libretto of Handel's *Acis and Galatea*, the chorus commanded:

Mourn Britannia and that soldier's loss deplore,
For thy great warrior he is no more.

But Wellington's death did not silence the Evangelical campaign against Sunday opening. Grove consulted his Christian Socialist mentors. He talked to Kingsley, who consulted Maurice—and both were sure that Sunday opening would be a good thing, if only to help in reducing drunkenness.[19] At the beginning of 1853 the minister of the Brixton Independent Church, the Revd. Baldwin Brown, published a supporting pamphlet, and hoped that the agitation of the extreme Sabbatarians would not damage Christianity. In another pamphlet the Lady Fanny Seymour asked fashionable, open-minded questions, to which Miss Caroline Howard replied with a beguiling mastery of Evangelical propaganda:

L.F. Why then not give [Sunday opening] a trial?
C. Because we have no right to make experiments where spiritual interests are concerned, or for a vain attempt to save the few, run the risk of endangering the many . . .
L.F. Still, Caroline, when I think of the poor and toil-worn doomed to labour all the week in an unwholesome atmosphere, I cannot find it in my heart to prevent their taking on the only day they are at liberty to seek it, one of the choicest blessings which God has given them, the fresh air of heaven.
C. And who could be found cruel enough for denying them so pure an enjoyment? but I have not yet heard that in the month of May so great a national calamity is to befall us as to make the fresh air so scarce and precious that the poor man even can only get it by *paying* for it at Sydenham. . . .[20]

The effort to secure public morality—often a cover for the suppression of private guilt, or an outlet for personal obsessions—which conveniently hinged on Sabbath Day observance led early in the next year to another

[18] Letter in the *Spectator*, 3 Feb 1894.
[19] In *Why not open the Crystal Palace and Park on Sunday Afternoons* (1855), p. 7, the Revd John Griffith, Vicar of Aberdare, put in an impassioned plea for his own people: 'Let us have a Crystal Palace at Cardiff, at Swansea, at Newport, at Merthyr—aye, and at Aberdare. I will hail the project with thankfulness, as a new era in the existence of the Welsh artisan. We shall then have far less Sabbath-breaking, less cursing and swearing, less drinking and rioting, less gambling and fighting.'
[20] *The Crystal Palace in 1853: a Dialogue between Lady Fanny Seymour and Miss Caroline Howard* (1853).

familiar aspect of philistinism. 'Thirteen eminent persons' wrote to the Directors of the Palace complaining that the statues of nude males intended for permanent display, being accurate in detail, would in 'exhibition to promiscuous crowds of men and women prove very destructive to that natural modesty which is one of the outworks of virtue, and which a great French writer has called "one of the barriers which Nature herself has placed in the way of crime" '. Whether on Grove's advice or not, the Directors gave way to pressure and, finding fig-leaves in short supply, ordered emasculation by hammer and chisel.

The task of transporting and re-erecting the Crystal Palace was one of great complexity. Paxton, whose inspiration for a glass-house for a water lily had developed into the original plan, with half-a-million pounds now at his disposal reshaped and enlarged the original building, and invited Brunel to design two great towers to hold the water for the myriad fountains that were to play within. So efficient was Paxton in marshalling the navvies on the site into effective labour units, that his methods were taken as the model for the army work corps during the Crimean War.

In spite of the concern expressed by so many for the welfare of the working class, human life was cheap. The Britannia Bridge cost seven lives. At Sydenham more than that number perished on a single day. A broadsheet ballad bore this epitome of its contents:

Full Particulars of the Dreadful Accident with the loss of twelve lives, at the Crystal Palace, Sydenham.
On Monday last, the 15th day of August [1853], shortly after two o'clock in the afternoon, the scaffolding of the middle transept of the Crystal Palace fell with a loud noise, that was heard for miles around, and dreadful to relate, killed twelve men besides wounding many others, who were immediately conveyed by Railway to the London Hospitals.

The coffins of the victims (thirteen according to the newspapers) were assembled in the central nave of the Palace on the day of the funeral.[21] All work was suspended and at the cemetery in Sydenham there was a crowd of several thousand. In church the vicar exhorted the mourners to take heed of the 'awful warning' given to them. Messrs Fox and Henderson subsequently carried out their obligations and, according to their invariable practice when any of their workmen were killed at work, allowed the widows 10 or 12 shillings a week for the first year of widowhood, and promised that they would introduce any orphan children 'to habits of industry in their own service'.

[21] This was the day (27 Aug 1853) on which the *North Wales Chronicle* reported the Queen's visit to Holyhead to open the Royal Victoria Harbour, for the service of which the Britannia Bridge had been raised.

Since Wordsworth had died in 1850, by the time the matter of the opening of the re-erected Palace at Sydenham came up there was no doubt as to who should compose celebratory verses. The collected *Poems* of 1842, the *Ode on the Death of the Duke of Wellington,* and *In Memoriam*, were all accepted as abundant proof of the fact that Tennyson was the greatest living English poet. Someone had the further idea that the Ode which Tennyson would write for the Crystal Palace should be set to music by Berlioz.[22]

Many years later Grove remembered his expedition to Farringford, to seek the cooperation of the Poet Laureate:

It was early in May 1854 when I had to go down to Tennyson's in the Isle of Wight to ask if he would write an Ode for the opening of the Crystal Palace, to be set to music by Berlioz. I was left by the train at Brockenhurst in the heart of the New Forest to find my way to Lymington at 12½ at night. I sent my bag over by the mail cart, and walked myself. The spring was just bursting, and I looked through not only the things you describe [in a recent letter] (except that the deer were cows, who *munched* away vigorously) but many others. It was as if nature were all in action around me, and the air full of invisible things—such strange noises of bubbling and screaming and groaning;—frogs and other animals of the night making the strangest sounds; almost startling. There was no moon so that more was left to the imagination though I wanted the beauty of the moonlight. It was a memorable night, and the more exciting because of my errand. I had never seen A.T. before and was in some trouble how to put my wants before him. But, with all that, I thoroughly enjoyed it and have all the *feel* in my mind quite fresh.[23]

The Ode did not get off the ground—to which, literally, the poet directed Grove's gaze while he soliloquized on the differences between cowslip and oxlip. As it happened a combination of Tennyson and Berlioz would have ill suited the programme to which the Queen and the Prince Consort were subjected on 10 June 1854. At enormous expense (which seemed minimal, however, beside the cost of assembling 1,650,000 square feet of glass at almost £1 per square foot), 1700 vocalists and instrumentalists were mustered under the general control of Michael Costa, the Neapolitan conductor of the Philharmonic Society and of Covent Garden. The forces included members of the German and Italian opera companies in London and the beloved Clara Novello, whose 'thrilling, piercing long-sustained [high] B flat' in the national anthem

[22] This more surprising suggestion was the result of Berlioz's visit to London two years before. The then newly formed New Philharmonic Society—of which one of the founders was Thomas Brassey, a railway contractor with whom Grove had worked at Chester—had invited Berlioz to conduct a series of concerts, and on 12 May 1852 he directed a performance of Beethoven's Ninth Symphony. Grove was present, and the occasion was a landmark in his own musical development.

[23] E.O., Ragatz [*sic*], Wed. ev. Sept 6 [1893]. Lymington is about five miles from Brockenhurst.

aroused ecstasy in 30,000 breasts and brought her contracts from all over Europe.

Well before the appointed day the Prince Consort had sent for Costa, to inform him that the music for the opening of the 1851 Exhibition had been 'below criticism', and that he expected better this time. The programme he heard comprised, besides the national anthem (twice), the Hundredth Psalm (which was said to have been better performed at the 1853 Dublin Exhibition held to advertise the new rail–sea link via Holyhead); and the inevitable Hallelujah Chorus. In the latter, J. W. Davison grumbled in the *Musical World* (17 June),

the new brass band of foreigners, conducted by Herr Schallehn, a foreigner, was seldom in time and always out of tune with the choir; and the parts for all sorts of brass instruments, added to the score by some bold and uncompromising hand, helped rather to mystify than augment the effect of Handel's tremendous paean, which, had an English musician been appointed conductor, could have been left alone in its glory.

Heinrich Schallehn, a German bandmaster, a colleague of Thomas Sullivan on the staff of Kneller Hall, at this point becomes a key figure in English music. Among the amenities of the Crystal Palace a wind band was expected to have a high place. In addition to the music already mentioned Schallehn, rejoicing in the title of Musical Director of the Crystal Palace, performed the following items on the opening day:

I	1 Grand March—"Aux Flambeaux"	Meyerbeer
	2 Overture—"Stradella"	Flotow
	3 Aria—"Il pirata"	Bellini
	4 Fantaisie Militaire	Bonnot
	5 Waltzes—"The Royal Birthday"	Kohl [, Auguste]
II	1 Fantaisie on "La Norma"	Bellini
	2 Quadrille—"Carabinier"	Wacker
	3 Romance—"Le Baiser d'Adieux"	Blencoco
	4 Galop—"Death or Glory"	Schallehn
	5 Schottische—"The Queen"	Tolkien [, Alfred]

The fourth item of the second part, 'dedicated to the Allied Forces', showed Schallehn in a favourable light to those who held the brief that Anglo-French firmness in the face of Russian expansion into the Middle East justified a war in the Crimea which was ultimately to cost 25,000 English lives. Schallehn's sense of commitment, however, was in conflict with his talent for exploitation, out of which came disaster for him and opportunity for another.

On 1 May 1854 August Manns, also a German, had been engaged to play the E flat clarinet in, and to act as sub-conductor of, Schallehn's band. He was also expected to perform other chores, such as checking and copying parts, and making arrangements. In September there was a fête in aid of a Patriotic Fund. On instructions from his superiors, Manns compiled a set of quadrilles based on English, French and Turkish melodies, together with some original padding material, entitled 'The Alliance Quadrille'. Having done the work Manns expected that he would receive any fee offered by a publisher, and he had been so advised by Schallehn. However, when £50 became available from such a source, Schallehn kept £49 and allowed Manns £1. Not unnaturally the latter was less than pleased when Schallehn not only dismissed his claims but, on account of alleged impudence, his person. On 9 November 1854 Manns wrote a letter to *The Musical World* claiming wrongful dismissal. Davison, the editor, who was already disaffected by the privileges accorded to some highly paid foreign musicians, generously took up the case. As a result Schallehn was dismissed and Manns—who in the meantime had found other occupation—recalled to take his place.

On 21 July 1855, on behalf of his Directors, Grove formally offered Manns the job of conductor of the Crystal Palace band at a wage of £30 a month. At the beginning of October—with a commission to reduce the numbers of the band from 58 to 36 in the interests of economy—Manns took up a post which he was to hold for half a century. The combination of Manns and Grove was to prove formidable, and, perhaps, the true generator of modern British music.[24]

In the letter of appointment to Manns Grove commented on some of the works which the German had lately conducted in Amsterdam. Although only five years older than Manns, Grove begins to sound elderly:

The overture [Beethoven's 'Consecration of the House'], op. 124 has only been done once in London in my recollection. Weber's "Clarinet Concerto", *never*. Berlioz's "Invitation à la Valse", *never*. Nor do I remember hearing of Mozart having written a finale to Gluck's *Iphigenia*. Your playing three rare works does you the highest honour. . . .[25]

At first, Manns disposed his military band in the centre transept of the Palace, but a few days after his arrival he took temporary possession of the so-called Court of Musical Instruments—subsequently renamed the Bohemian Glass Court—and presented a concert with a string band comprising some of the 'double-handed' among his players with some importees. On 1 December 1855, with a full orchestra, Manns conducted the Allegretto and Presto movements of Beethoven's Seventh Symphony, from which point the Manns–Grove partnership began really to take effect.

[24] Their respective contributions were equal and indivisible, in spite of Manns's later temporary misgivings as to the allocation of credit. See pp. 127–8.
[25] H. Saxe Wyndham, *August Manns and the Saturday Concerts* (1909), p. 32.

On the following Saturdays the Fourth, Second and First Symphonies (in that order) were played, and on 12 January Mozart's G minor (No.40). On Saturday 26 January 1856, to mark the centenary of the birth of Mozart, music by that composer was performed in the 'Music Room— by the Queen's Apartments; North Wing', by the Company's band. Mozart's birthday was actually on 27 January, but (as noted in the *Musical World* of 2 February) 'the Crystal Palace was interdicted from opening its doors to the public on the Sabbath'. But one Saturday having already led to other Saturdays, the interdiction merely helped to stabilize the institution of the 'Saturday Concerts'.

The 'Music Room' (burned down in 1866) was a very temporary auditorium, which could hold 900 people at most. As 1500 turned up for the Mozart concert, 'many had to leave without hearing a note of music', as the *Musical World* of 2 February sorrowfully remarked. It was particularly sad, commented the same journal, since 'the directors of the Crystal Palace have put to shame all the musical societies in London, they alone (with the single exception of the Panopticon on the preceding Monday) having had the good taste to hold a "festival"—albeit on the mildest possible scale.'

What was more, care was taken to inform the audience, who were provided with extensive historical and analytical notes on the programme, written by—but not ascribed to—the indefatigable Grove.[26] The Mozart centenary programme was as follows:

Overture—*Idomeneo*
Duet—"Dove scorre" [of doubtful authenticity]
    Grace Alleyne and [Bessie] Palmer
Sonata in B flat, Pianoforte and Violin
    W. H. Adams and A. Manns
Song—"Batti, batti" [from *Don Giovanni*]
    Grace Alleyne; Violoncello obbligato, W. F. Reed
Pianoforte Sonata in F
    George Russell [pupil of Sterndale Bennett]
Song—"Io ti lascio [, cara, addio" K.Anh. 245]
    Bessie Palmer
Allegro, from the Concerto in D minor, for Pianoforte and orchestra [K.466]
    Piano: Master John Francis Barnett
Recitative [Scena] and Aria [Rondo]—["Non più, tutto ascoltai",] "Non temer [, amato bene" K.490]
    Grace Alleyne; Violin obbligato, A. Manns
Scena [Recitativo] and Aria—"Ah questo seno [deh vieni", "Or che il cielo a me ti rende" K.374] Bessie Palmer
Andante and Finale, from the Symphony in E flat [K.453?]

---

[26] Grove shared the writing of programme notes with Manns until 1868, when he took more or less complete control.

3

Grove's introduction to this programme may be taken also as an introduction to his philosophy, in that it enshrined a sense of duty; to inspire in the minds of the general, listening public 'a sort of personal affection' for the great composers. In the brief biography of Mozart (presumably by Grove) for the *Handbook to the Portrait Gallery of the Crystal Palace* (quoted in the concert programme) there is by way of conclusion an excess of generosity in appraisal:—[27] 'In all the relations of life Mozart was blameless: he had a generous soul, and we are pained to think so rare and so richly endowed a genius should at any period of his career have suffered anguish from poverty and distress.' The centenary concert programme recommended the Mozart biographies of Alexander Oulibishev and Edward Holmes, and drew attention to the Mozart criticism contained in A. W. Lenz's *Beethoven et ses trois styles*.

In so far as commentary on the music is concerned, at this stage Grove mainly presents anecdotal material taken from approved sources, supported by an occasional expression of his own enthusiasm and a dissatisfaction at the neglect which often attends fine works. Of the B flat sonata played by Adams and Manns at the Mozart centenary concert he observed:

This fine Sonata is rarely if ever played in public. In this it shares the fate of many other masterpieces of the Classic writers, which are suffered to lie on the shelf, while others often of less merit, but giving more opportunity to the player for display, are hacknied and worn threadbare.

The tradition which the centenary concert proved to inaugurate was to be distinguished by its provision of opportunity, both to executants and to composers. The eighteen-year-old soloist in the D minor Concerto movement, J. F. Barnett, was from a celebrated immigrant family of musicians. Holder of the Queen's Scholarship at the Royal Academy of Music, he had (so the programme informed his listeners) played Mendelssohn's D minor Concerto from memory at a New Philharmonic Society concert, conducted by Spohr, in the previous year.

On the Saturday following the Mozart concert Manns gave a varied programme, of which the highlights were Beethoven's *Namensfeier* Overture (op. 115), three movements from Mendelssohn's 'Scottish' Symphony, and Rossini's *William Tell* Overture. By 1 March, the institution of the Saturday afternoon concert of serious—in a fairly free sense—music appeared established. On that day—on which Sonnenberg, the clarinettist, played the solo part in a potpourri based on *Der Freischütz*, and the orchestra presented four movements of Mendelssohn's First Symphony in C minor—an attempt was made politely to discipline the audience towards accepting a new-style concert behaviour. The pro-

[27] Or so it would have seemed before Bernard Levin's pious proposal in the spring of 1977 that Mozart should (omitting the stage of beatification) be sanctified.

gramme contained this note: 'Visitors are requested to keep their seats during the Performance of the Music. An interval will be allowed between the Pieces, and between the Movements of the Symphony, which can be taken advantage of by those who wish to move.'

Later concerts in the series that year, now accommodated in an enclosure in the Centre Transept furnished for the purpose, included performances of Schumann's Fourth Symphony (16 February and 15 March) and Schubert's 'Great' C major symphony (5 April)—both hitherto unheard in England—and a selection from *Tannhäuser*, made by Manns from a full score which had by chance come his way in 1848 when he was a Prussian military bandsman stationed in Posen.

Military bands still provided the most familiar sounds and those of the famous Regiments of Guards were unfailingly popular. The last day of May was particularly festive: 'In order to afford an opportunity of visiting the Crystal Palace, at Sydenham, to the numerous Excursionists now in London, as well as to the Londoners having a holiday on that day, SATURDAY the 31st of MAY will be a SHILLING DAY.' At 12.30 and 4.00 the Band of the Company played under Manns; at 2.15 and 5.45 the Band of the Coldstream Guards, conducted by Charles Godfrey, founder of a famous dynasty of conductors. In 1831 Godfrey had been appointed a Musician in Ordinary to the King, and his concern for his duties was in large measure the reason for the efficiency and musicality of British military music in later years.

Grove too was ever dutiful. During March 1856 he had suffered the death of his mother, and now that both parents were gone the old home at Thurlow Lodge began to be broken up. But his devotion to his work was absolute. The directors of the Palace were, above all, concerned with profitability; concerts were but a minor part of a growing concern; and Grove recognized—as he was often to do in the future—that private grief should never be allowed to interfere with public responsibilities.

As Secretary of the Crystal Palace Grove was responsible for determining what took place there, albeit having to take due notice of what the directors proposed and also of public opinion. Although he made his name through his musical enterprise, he superintended exhibitions of all kinds, religious gatherings, public lectures, animal shows and further education. It will be seen that in many ways he was continuing the policy of the Royal Society of Arts and fulfilling the intentions of the Prince Consort.

For anyone with a cause to promote, the Crystal Palace was the best place in which to do so. In 1856 the preacher Spurgeon conducted a Day of National Humiliation there, in respect of the unsatisfactory performance of the British in the Crimean War, and attracted some 23,000 penitents. In the next year Spurgeon suggested himself as a permanency in the Palace, for Exeter Hall could not hold those who

flocked to his denunciations of sin. But Grove was not at all partial to the
idea that he should be given a platform at Sydenham. At the time of
Spurgeon's death he remembered how, 'I heard him once, ever so long
ago, and it offended my taste'.[28]

In June 1856 music at the Palace was wrapped round the Opening of
the Picture Gallery, a Bazaar for Queen Adelaide's Naval Fund, Displays
of the Grand Fountain, and a Flower Show. On Friday afternoons that
month there was a series of opera concerts. Those who had bought
season tickets for the Palace were gratified that there were so many
delights, which included the impeccable conduct of the Secretary. If
anyone, for instance, lost his ticket, he would always find Grove helpful.
The great Babbage suffered this calamity, but was assured by the Secretary that the doorkeepers would search diligently for the lost ticket, while
suggestions made by Babbage concerning possible administrative
improvements would be communicated to the directors.

In 1857 Grove promoted performances by Henry Leslie's two-year-
old choir, and by the Cologne Choral Union. But most significant,
because of its future influence, was the 'dry run' for a Handel centenary
festival. The architect of this festival was Robert Bowley, the Librarian
of the Sacred Harmonic Society, who in 1858 was to become General
Manager of the Crystal Palace, a position which he held until his death
twelve years later. One of his first acts was to arrange for the transference of the orchestral concerts to a concert area set up according to
his design. Not notable for his general knowledge of music, Bowley
was remembered as a 'character'.[29] Weighing, it was said, 'towards 30
stone', he was one who may be said literally to have sunk under 'the
burden of the flesh'. During Handel Festivals he sat at a distance from
the main section, but, singing the bass line in oratorio choruses, would
adjure the other, distant, basses: 'Now, you boys, remember I am with
you!'

Bowley's predecessor as General Manager was James Fergusson,
who joined the staff in 1856. Known to the general public as the initiator
of the so-called Assyrian Court at the Palace, by a smaller company of
scholars Fergusson was considered one of the finest archaeologists and
authorities on ancient architecture of his day. During the time he was
working in Calcutta, first for the family firm of Fairlie, Fergusson & Co.,
and then on his own account as indigo manufacturer, he studied the
architecture of India more thoroughly than anyone from Europe had

[28] E.O., Feb 17 [1892].

[29] With a wide ignorance of Latin, Bowley was, nevertheless, much given to mis-
quoting it. Grove once entered the General Manager's office in the kind of hilarious
mood to which he was frequently subject, to be quietened by Bowley's 'Seriatim, if you
please, Grove, seriatim!' As for the notebooks which he kept by him, Bowley described
them as his 'little vade-meca'.

done before.[30] He also studied and wrote with equal authority on the topography and architecture of the Holy Land.

The consideration of Middle Eastern historical geography had been stimulated on the one hand by a more objective biblical criticism, and on the other by strategic and military factors. Part of the cause of the Crimean War from 1854 to 1856 had been concern for the fate of Jerusalem and the surrounding country if controlled by an Islamic power. In 1855 Fergusson published a popular two-volume history of architecture, and the next year produced a technical paper on theories of defence in relation to the recent siege of Sevastopol. He was not only well qualified to administer the affairs of the Crystal Palace, and to contribute towards its development as a centre for popular education, but also to act as a member of a Royal Commission set up in 1857 to study the national defences.

Fergusson exerted a strong influence on Grove:

Fergus[s]on's "intense personality" was just the remarkable point in him. . . . He was always fighting for some truth or other which he fully perceived but which others were not sharp enough to perceive, and therefore thought him a *villain* for maintaining. I am bound to say that he treated them as if they were villains too! and so there was a lot of fighting. He was one of the *fullest* men I ever knew. The subjects of his works show it. Fortification—the sacred spots in Jerusalem. Architecture—to courses of India Tree and serpent worship.[31]

Already Grove was involved in some areas of research in which Fergusson was expert. With the support of the older man he was to prove, in his own way, and in due course, an almost equally valuable worker in the field of biblical studies.

[30] In due course he published an authoritative *History of Indian and Eastern Architecture* (1876), as well as (with James Burgess) *The Cave Temples of India* (1880).

[31] E.O. July 17/Monday night [1894]. Grove referred in particular to Fergusson's *Proposed New System of Fortification* (1849), *An Essay on the Ancient Topography of Jerusalem* (1847), *A History of Architecture in all Countries from the Earliest Times to the Present Day* (1865-7), and *Tree and Serpent Worship . . . in India* (1868).

CHAPTER FOUR

Mr Grove of Sydenham

1857-1867

ABOUT work Grove was obsessive. Among Victorians in this respect he was not exceptional, although his record of industry and productivity is not easy to match. At the basis of his obsession was a sense of insecurity. It was important that he should enjoy a sufficient income for him to be able to maintain the standards expected of a middle-class citizen with respectable city and suburban connections, and to sustain a family. But fame too was the spur. Those who had grown up under Pritchard's tutelage were not expected to fall by the wayside. Better educated than many of their contemporaries in public schools but often short on influence, they had to work rather harder to make their mark. Grove, from an academic point of view a late developer, lost no opportunity of seeking the means whereby he might in the end justify himself.

He rose early in the morning and, Trollope-wise, was at his desk hours before the household was astir. He worked long into the night. His companions saw him as bright, lively, curious and friendly. They rarely recognized—and, if they did, almost never mentioned—an *alter ego* anguished by a feeling of isolation. In more than one sense he led a double life. In his middle thirties he noticed that between himself and his brothers and sisters there was something of a rift. More sadly, his marriage seemed to be hardly more than a marriage of convenience.

As time went on he became secretly embittered as his wife failed to absorb his interests and enthusiasms, or to foster his egotism and his creativity. Harriet had been brought up in a family in which the male Bradleys were of exceptional academic talent. Whatever her own abilities, they had little outlet. Life was less than exciting for her, and it remained so. A dutiful wife, she looked after the household and acted as hostess to Grove's friends and acquaintances, especially on Saturday nights when guests were numerous. But she spent long hours on her own as her husband dedicated himself to his several professional interests. He for his part suffered the frustration of feeling largely unappreciated at home, while increasingly lionized and drawn into wider circles elsewhere.

On 27 January 1857 the Groves' first son, Walter Maurice, was born. His second name was a singular tribute to a man by whom Grove was much influenced, and whose principles had recently caused great offence to those who considered that religion and politics should be kept far apart. In 1853 F. D. Maurice had been dismissed from his post at King's College on account of theological unorthodoxy and Socialist convictions. His passion for achieving social reform by means of education led him in that year to organize a series of lectures for working-class audiences at the Hall of Association, off Oxford Street.[1] Emboldened by the success of this scheme, Maurice in the next year founded the Working Men's College in Red Lion Square, of which he became Principal. In 1854 and 1856 respectively, two important citadels of reaction began—largely through Maurice's campaigning—to crumble, as sanctions against Dissenters being admitted to the university were relaxed, first at Oxford and then at Cambridge. Grove, however, having gone along with Maurice in the first stage of his adult education enterprise, had reached a point in radicalism beyond which he would never go.

Having been brought up in Clapham, and having married into a clerical family, Grove was perpetually looking for an anchorage in religion. But the more he looked, the more his scepticism grew. At the same time the fascination of religious speculation touched his determination to search for truth in established facts, in which he was supported by a reverence for accuracy derived from his engineer's skills.

In the transitional period in which Grove began to find himself as a scholar, he was indebted not only to Maurice, but to another prominent churchman, A. P. Stanley, with whom he formed a friendship which was to be close and lasting. It grew out of an existing intimacy between George Bradley and Stanley who had been pupils of Arnold at Rugby; later Bradley had been a student at University College, Oxford, when Stanley was one of the fellows.

In the winter of 1852–3 Stanley, by then a Canon of Canterbury, set out on the first of his pilgrimages, to Egypt and Palestine. He was accompanied by Theodore Walrond, Matthew Arnold's close friend who proceeded from Rugby to a Fellowship at Balliol, and two other Oxford acquaintances, T. F. Fremantle, also of Balliol, and W. B. Findlay. With the public-school humour characteristic of the period (which rubbed off on Grove in due course), Stanley was known as 'the Sheykh', Walrond as 'the Pacha', Fremantle—from the shape of his cap—as 'the Fez', and Findlay, a sportsman of sorts, as 'the Father of Guns'. Out of this journey Stanley wrote a biblical travelogue, *Sinai and Palestine*, which was published in 1856. When the manuscript had accumulated he looked round for someone who might save him from some of the more tedious tasks of authorship, and, acting on Bradley's recommendation, enlisted the aid of Grove with whom, on 19 November 1853, a long correspondence commenced.

At home in Sydenham, when there were no guests, work was a kind of

[1] On 18 April 1853 Grove had shown his support for the scheme by reading a paper on 'Mathematical Principles Exemplified in Common Things'.

anodyne. Ever a willing horse, Grove at once made himself available
to Stanley. In the Advertisement to the book, Stanley wrote: 'For the
arrangement of the Appendix [a 'Vocabulary of Topographical Words',
with annotations], as well as for the general verification of references
and correction of the press, I am indebted to the careful revision of my
friend, Mr Grove of Sydenham.' In the introductory sentences to the
Appendix Stanley paid an unconscious tribute to his collaborator, writing
that 'the geographical passages of the Bible seem to shine with new light,
as these words acquire their proper force. . . .' And to Benjamin Jowett[2]
he observed, 'I never ought to write a book without a Grove . . . to correct
references and proofs.'[3]

In 1857 Stanley, now Professor of Ecclesiastical History at Oxford,
went to Russia to prepare for his *Lectures on the History of the Eastern
Church*, and wrote back to Grove details of dress, custom, and social
practices. Thus, on the achievement of Peter the Great:

> If you wish to bring out the dramatic effect of Russian history, it could not be
> better done than by the contrast between Moscow and Petersburg—the great
> Eastern nation striving to become Western, or, rather, the nation half-Eastern,
> half-Western, dragged against its will by one gigantic genius, literally dragged
> by the heels and kicked by the boots of the Giant Peter into contact with the
> European world.[4]

Having learned from Stanley the relevance of geography to history,
Grove in later life touched his study of Beethoven with a sympathy for
European Russia, considering the Rasumovsky Quartets 'another link in
the chain of connection between the republic composer and the great
Imperial court of Petersburg, which originated some of his noblest
works'.[5]

No sooner had Grove seen Stanley's *Sinai and Palestine* into the world
than, on his colleague James Fergusson's recommendation, he was
taken into the panel of experts assembled by William Smith—whose
Dictionary of Greek and Roman Antiquities (1842) was already a classic
of lexicography—to prepare a *Dictionary of the Bible*.[6] Grove was to

---

[2] At the time Jowett was suffering deprivation of his emoluments as an Oxford
professor on account of supposed heretical views (see below, p. 77).

[3] R. E. Prothero and G. Bradley, *Life and Correspondence of A. P. Stanley, D.D.*
(1893), vol. I, p. 476.

[4] ibid., p. 517.

[5] *Grove 1*, vol. I, p. 185.

[6] Apart from Fergusson the contributors to the first edition of *A Dictionary of the
Bible* included a number of people who had played, or who would play, a significant
part in the advancement of Grove's career, among them Henry Alford, Dean of Canter-
bury; Emanuel Deutsch, a Semitic scholar on the staff of the British Museum; F. W.
Farrar, a master at Harrow School and later Master of Marlborough College; Joseph
Hooker, Keeper of the Royal Botanic Gardens, Kew, later to be a friend of Alice
Roberts (later Elgar); A. H. Layard, a Departmental Head at the Crystal Palace and

labour on this project for seven years, at the end of which time it was clear that he had had a lion's share in its realization.

The methodical listing and systematic analysis of proper names, with particular regard for comparative etymology, undertaken for *Sinai and Palestine*, had left Grove with an abundance of material and a thorough knowledge of biblical sources, so that for the larger commission, the Bible *Dictionary*, he merely took up from where he had left off in Stanley's work. But he felt the need of first-hand experience of the biblical terrain, and in May 1858 let his house and, following in Stanley's footsteps, went with Harriet to Egypt and the Holy Land.

Grove was sometimes well served by a particular kind of modesty which sprang from a sense of educational disadvantage. In later life he revealed that at times he felt somewhat diffident in the presence of those who had been to universities. He was therefore always ready to pay attention to and to benefit from the knowledge of specialists. He met two such individuals in Haifa in 1858. Edward Thomas Rogers (1830–84), a keen student of Middle Eastern affairs, had lately been appointed Vice-Consul there, and Grove paid tribute to him for his kindness in making visits to various places and people possible. Since 1855 Rogers had been energetic in surveying the area and had conducted missions of inquiry in Hebron and Nábloos. His sister, Mary Eliza, was more remarkable than he, in that, at a time when it appeared grievously irregular, she travelled freely through Palestine, and established a close understanding with Jews and Arabs alike.[7]

Grove's first visit to the Holy Land also made him appreciative of Stanley's descriptive facility, of which, on 26 October 1858, he wrote to George Bradley: 'It is impossible for anything to be better or truer than the book [*Sinai and Palestine*], or to have caught more exactly the very air and atmosphere, as it were, of everything.'[8]

At the beginning of November Grove wrote to Smith that he felt

---

founder of the Assyrian Excavation Fund in 1853, and a politician; J. B. Lightfoot, the theologian; E. S. Poole and R. S. Poole, Arabic scholar and Orientalist respectively and sons of Sophia Poole, author of the celebrated *The English-woman in Egypt* (1844–6); Christopher Wordsworth, nephew of the late Poet Laureate and a Canon of Westminster; and William Aldis Wright, Librarian of Trinity College, Cambridge, and Examiner in Hebrew in London University, and one of Grove's closest friends. Charles Pritchard, now Secretary of the Royal Astronomical Society, was also a member of the panel of contributors.

[7] In 1862 Miss Rogers published a diverse and candid study entitled *Domestic Life in Palestine*. Dedicated to Holman Hunt 'in admiration of his work, and in remembrance of the pleasant visits which I paid to his studio on Mount Zion', this book is as exact in description as the paintings of Holman Hunt, but without his sententiousness and well irradiated with a robust humour. It is an ideal complement to the Palestine essays of Grove.

[8] Graves, p. 65.

compelled to resign some of the subjects he had accepted. On 8 April
1859 his second son, Julius Charles, was born; an event which reminded
Grove that money was hard to come by through contributions to biblical
literature. In one of his recurrent moods of depression he wrote suggesting once more the jettisoning of some of his commitments.

At this time the indefatigable Henry Cole was casting round for qualified persons to man the museum services he was persuading Lord
Palmerston's Government to institute. As Secretary of the Department
of Science and Art, Cole promulgated the sensible idea that there should
be scientific and art museums and galleries in all parts of the country,
and increased provision of such services in London—all of which was
bound up with his concept of a thorough and universal educational
service, extended to adults, suitable for an age of technological revolution.
He approached Grove with an offer of the post of Director of the Patent
Museum. Although at the beginning of 1860 this did not appeal to Grove,
he none the less looked around for a more lucrative appointment than
his salaried post at the Crystal Palace.[9]

Meanwhile, as was generally to be the case, he extricated himself from
the dark mood of the previous year and continued vigorously to apply
pen to paper. By March 1860 the first of the three volumes of the Bible
Dictionary was ready for the printer and John Murray, the publisher,
gave a celebratory dinner. Grove now put to Murray the idea of a general
'Dictionary of Persons'—an idea which was never carried out by Murray[10]
but which, in a more precise form, and not without Grove's involvement,
later emerged from another house as the Dictionary of National Biography.

In the summer of 1860 the Groves moved from Church Meadow into
a compact, though adequate, wooden house with a pleasant garden at
Sydenham, thought once to have been occupied by Charles James Fox.
That same summer Grove's restlessness was sublimated in a continental
holiday. Nominally, at least, it was a holiday, but as was always the
case with Grove there was an exacting and congested time-table. Harriet
went with him and the rigours of the expedition tested her stamina. She
'stood it most bravely', wrote Grove to Bradley at the end of the month's
pilgrimage, in which they saw Brussels, the principal Rhineland towns,
the tourist catchment areas of Austria and Switzerland, and Paris, with
particular attention to the Louvre.

The outstanding memory of their tour was of the Passion Play at
Oberammergau, an event not then so well known in England as it was
to become; and Grove wrote a descriptive essay which was published

[9] Grove even put in an unsuccessful application for the post of Secretary of the
Eastern Bengal Railway Company (incorporated 1857), whose line between Calcutta
and Dacca—to be opened in 1862—was at the time under construction.
[10] The project is not mentioned in George Paston (pseud.), At John Murray's—
Records of a Literary Circle 1843-1892 (1932).

in the form of a letter, in *The Times* of 5 September 1860.[11] In a significant section of these reflections, he interprets the character of Judas Iscariot, whom he saw as less a villain than a

narrow-minded, impulsive, vindictive man, really puzzled and annoyed at what he conceived to be the 'waste' of the 300 pence [John 12:5] on the precious ointment, and stung to the quick by the reproof so publicly administered to him by Christ, [who] never really believes that what does happen will really come to pass. . . .

This characterization, influenced by R. H. Horne's *Orion*, a popular epic poem published in 1843, and Richard Whately's liberal theology, comes near to that later adopted by Elgar and expressed in *The Apostles*.

Always unwilling to write at second hand, Grove decided on a second journey to Palestine in the summer of 1861. Among the reading he took with him were those excellent exemplars of descriptive topography, Mendelssohn's recently published Letters.[12] From this expedition came not only a number of *Dictionary* articles, but also the essay, 'Nábloos and the Samaritans', published in 1862 by Macmillan in Francis Galton's *Vacation Tourists and Notes of Travel*, as one of three 'vacation tours' undertaken in 1860 and 1861 by Galton, Grove and W. G. Clark, Fellow of Trinity College and Public Orator of the University.

In describing the whole day's ride under a burning sun from Jerusalem to Nábloos, and the fragrance of the valley of Nábloos, Grove indicates contrasts indigenous to a tradition whose problems are as intractable now as in his day. Gibbon pointed out that the Samaritans were 'a motley race, an ambiguous sect, rejected as Jews by the Pagans, by the Jews as schismatics, and by the Christians as idolators'. Grove, who had read Gibbon when in Glasgow and himself wrote in a near-Gibbonian style, extended these contrasts, pointing the differences between Samaritan and English culture, and between the appearances of Samaritans and native Christians, between the ways of distant antiquity and of the nineteenth century. And there are homely touches, indicating how often Grove's letters to familiar friends provided the foundation for loftier literary productions.

I brought away a primer from which little Samaritans are taught in their school at Nábloos, and it is covered with their sprawling forms of the venerable letters [of the ancient Hebrew alphabet], much more rude and complicated than the usual Samaritan type of the Polyglots.

[11] A. P. Stanley, to some extent using his friend's experience, contributed a larger piece on the same subject to the October issue of *Macmillan's Magazine* (which had begun publication in the previous year).

[12] *Reisebriefe von Felix Mendelssohn-Bartholdy aus den Jahren 1830 bis 1832* (Leipzig [Hermann Mendelssohn], 1861).

On 11 November Grove reached Nábloos, where he was received by Yakûb esh Shellabi who, alone of the Samaritans of Nábloos, had been able to travel abroad. He had visited London in 1856, whence, inspired by the English respect for education, he returned to encourage the Priest Amran to establish a school in Nábloos. Grove's meeting with esh Shellabi was facilitated by E. T. Rogers, who was now Consul in Damascus.

Grove attended the New Year ritual of Yom Kippur, which the Samaritans celebrated a month earlier than the Jews. Totally fascinated by the experience, Grove continually found that he needed to take bearings on his own cardinal culture points. A priest read 'some services in a loud, harsh, monotonous chant or plainsong, varied by occasional jerks or *barks*, and by stage gestures, as if because trying to bite violently something immediately in front of him'. The plainchant was similar to that of the Roman Church, 'but even more archaic in its turns'. At another service he

found that the speed of the recitative was increasing. At last it became a perfect race. Then they fell as before, only more decidedly, into a metrical pace

(musical notation)

but with a concord of *measure* only, not of *pitch*; now it was

(musical notation)

and now

(musical notation)

Grove was unable to pull away from the idea of the general superiority of European man. Music transgressing against the tonal and harmonic principles expounded in Western schools of music was to him less than perfect. The unorthodoxies of Samaritan music nevertheless stirred his imagination, and the excesses of the ritual antiphony between priest and congregation recalled 'the psalms for the day as performed at St George's-in-the-East during the riots, when a majority *said* and a minority sung them;[13] and even that wanted the force and energy which

[13] The reference was to an ecclesiastical *cause célèbre* which had inflamed many passions. In 1856 Bryan King, a ritualist, was appointed Rector of the London church of St George's-in-the-East, but the Vestry had the right of appointment of a lecturer. In 1859 one Hugh Allen was nominated to that post. This was done by means first of infiltration into, and then by take-over of, the Vestry by a group of 'no Popery' partisans, who more particularly represented those who objected to King's war on sweatshops and brothels. The Protestant cause, however, was respectable cover for sinister interests. On Sunday afternoons those who supported the Rector attended a service which came immediately after Allen's 'lecture'. Because the ritualists intoned it, the other side assembled early and said—or rather shouted—the Litany, so that to one observer it seemed as if there was 'a handful of singing-mice in a cage, surrounded by an army of

here lent such a dreadful life to the discord.' But Grove's sense of history was always alert to the validity of the prompting of tradition, and he finally concluded that the Samaritan manner of psalmody contained the probability of authenticity. If, he argued, the Samaritans had in less significant respects retained ancient practices, then they would surely have done so in such a central ideal of liturgy.

The enterprise in which Grove was engaged for so long for William Smith was to some extent an attempt to meet the demands of those who required that the assertions of religion should be tested by the criteria of scientific scholarship. But the *Dictionary* was clearly also related to the larger issue, of the relevance of such assertions to modern society. In 1859, the year of the St George's affair, J. S. Mill's *On Liberty* and Charles Darwin's *Origin of Species*—as well as FitzGerald's *Rubáiyát of Omar Khayyám*, George Eliot's *Adam Bede*, Meredith's *Ordeal of Richard Feverel*, Dickens's *Tale of Two Cities*—were published. In the following year *Essays and Reviews*, a challenge from within the Church to orthodox theological values, appeared. In the debate which followed an abortive attempt to prosecute two of its contributors, Henry Wilson and Rowland Williams, Grove was to declare himself for 'speculation and free enquiry'. He was appalled at the treatment of Jowett, whose 'Interpretation of Scripture' in *Essays and Reviews* was a landmark in the development of liberalism in theology, by the University of Oxford,[14] and also by the violence of the attacks on J. W. Colenso, a friend of Maurice and Bishop of Natal, for his study of the Pentateuch, a work, of which Grove had his own copy, which began to appear in 1862.

During the time he was working on the Smith project, Grove acquired a magnificent supporting library which he was sadly to dispose of some 30 years later.[15] The first edition of *A Dictionary of the Bible*, complete

---

starved cats'. After a year of such unseemliness, during which the police were often conscripted spectators, A. P. Stanley diplomatically intervened, proposing a sabbatical for King while the parish was for the time being entrusted to Septimus Hansard, who had already proved himself as a trouble-shooter in dealing with discontented Irish navvies in the East End, but who was no less concerned for social justice than King.

[14] See letters to Mimi von Glehn of 10 Feb and 9 Mar 1864; Graves, pp. 105, 106. A Subscription List was established for Jowett, to compensate him for his deprivation of emoluments and to register a protest against intolerance. On 14 Jan 1862 the testimonial was sent to Jowett with the information that £2000 had become available to him through the generosity of well-wishers, among whom were George Bradley, now Headmaster of Marlborough College, J. D. Hooker, Holman Hunt, Charles Lyall, Max Müller, F. T. Palgrave, Stanley and Tennyson, as well as Grove.

[15] Among works he owned which were particularly to influence his later career were D. F. Strauss's *Life of Jesus* (1846), W. M. Thomson's *The Land and the Book* (1859), J. L. Burckhardt's *Notes on the Bedouins and Wallabys* (1831), R. J. Schwarz's *Geography of Palestine* (1850), A. H. Layard's *Nineveh and Babylon* (1853), Renan's *Histoire des langues sémitiques* (1855), *Études d'histoire religieuse* (1857), *Livre de Job* (1859) and *Vie de Jésus* (1863), and W. Cureton's *Four Gospels in Syriac* (1858).

in three volumes at the end of 1863, was a handsome production. In the Preface William Smith paid tribute to his principal assistant:

There is, however, one Writer to whom he owes a more special acknowledgement. Mr George Grove, of Sydenham, besides contributing articles to which his initial is attached [Grove's contributions are signed 'G'], has rendered the Editor important assistance in writing the majority of the articles on the more obscure names in the First Volume, in the correction of the proofs, and in the revision of the whole book.[16]

Despite the calls made on him by *A Dictionary of the Bible* Grove was in the first instance a servant of the Directors of the Crystal Palace, and of the public, and he was nothing if not conscientious. Within a decade he had turned Paxton's glass-house, relocated in Sydenham, into a signal triumph for popular education and recreation. He had had his trials: 'I tell you what it is,' one Albert Smith was reported to have said to one of the Directors, 'this talk about elevating the people won't pay. You'll have to climb down, mark my words; it will end after all in climbing the greased statue of Rameses for a leg of mutton, as sure as you're alive.'[17] But Grove had found one way to convince the sceptical, by the old, well-tried medium of Handelian oratorio.

The experimental festival held in 1857 had been so encouraging that to wait until the centenary celebration planned for 1859 was placing too great a strain on the patience of the faithful. On 2 July 1858, therefore, a 'grand demonstration' was given by the Great Handel Festival Choir, including 'renowned singers from the Continent' (currently employed in the opera choruses in London), and—as far as the North was concerned —even more renowned choral singers from Bradford. In all, with choruses and orchestra and military bands, some 2500 performers sweated their way through a popular selection from the oratorios. Later that summer Maria Piccolomini—a sex symbol from the Royal Italian Opera then performing at Her Majesty's Theatre, whose figure compensated for the inadequacies of her singing technique—gave a farewell concert on the eve of her departure for the United States. Supported by the elegant but manic-depressive Giuglini and an orchestra conducted alternately by Arditi and August Manns, she had 10,000 fans in raptures.

At the beginning of 1859 the priority was to put the Palace into a state of readiness for Handel. New galleries and stalls were added, with a better view of the performing area, 216 feet in width; more stops were put into

---

[16] In the second edition (March 1893) of the *Dictionary* a prefatory note stated: 'The geographical articles by Sir George Grove, which have been justly considered one of the most valuable portions of the original edition, have been revised, at his request, by Sir Charles Wilson, and, in a few instances, by Major [C. R.] Conder.' For a discussion of Grove's contributions see chapter 14.

[17] *Sydenham, Forest Hill, and Penge Gazette*, 11 Jan 1895.

the Gray and Davidson organ; some 'gigantic steel kettle-drums, far exceeding in size any yet in use, and some deep-toned brass instruments' were built. Distinguished guests from every superior walk of life were invited to hear choral rehearsals in Exeter Hall. The consummation of all this devoted labour was the Festival over which Costa presided. On non-oratorio days during the Festival Manns was permitted to play secular music, surprisingly including some excerpts from Handel's Italian operas.

On 1 May 1862 a second Great International Exhibition took place in South Kensington. Initially the idea of the Prince Consort, it was held in the shadow of his untimely death in the previous December; and while ceremonial music for the opening had been ordered from Meyerbeer, Auber and Sterndale Bennett, it was imperative that the Hallelujah Chorus should touch the occasion with the sublime. It was then proposed that another Handel Festival should be held at the Crystal Palace. Stimulated by the prospect of large numbers of tourists in town, and stirred by the propriety of the music in that mournful year, the Directors wholeheartedly supported the arrangements. Their success was so complete that thereafter a triennial Handel Festival became a national institution. As a writer in the *Musical World* effused on the eve of the Festival of 1868:

Let honour, then, be paid to the man who was not merely a giant in his art, but who made his art the zealous handmaid of religion, the man who bequeathed to us *Messiah*, that most impressive and magnificent of sermons, which sets forth both precept and example in a language common to the world of civilisation— the musical apostle, in short, of revealed religion. Independent, however, of such grave considerations, the simple fact that the Handel Festivals which have already taken place comprised performances the like of which can find no precedent in the musical records of any country must suffice to create a general desire for their periodical continuance.

Meanwhile August Manns was establishing himself on the heights of British music. Inspired by a belief, to which Grove also subscribed, that nothing but the best was fit for those of whatever rank who wished to hear music, he made the Saturday concerts at the Palace a feature of London cultural life. He engaged the finest artists and ranged widely across contemporary music as well as the classics—which were not then considered, as they are now, as familiar. In 1859 the death of Spohr prompted a commemorative programme, while two weeks later Schubert's 'Great' C major Symphony was played. Manns commendably took in works of living British composers, by no means all with established reputations. The spring of 1862 was notable not only for the first appearance of Joachim, playing Beethoven's Violin Concerto, but also for the performance a week later of Arthur Sullivan's music for *The Tempest*.

And enhancing these events were the programme notes, some written by
Manns and some by Grove, and musical instruction to be had in the
School of Art, Science and Literature which was part of the Crystal
Palace amenities.

The permanent organist at the Palace was James Coward, an ex-
chorister of Westminster Abbey, a fine extemporizer, and a competent
composer, who was expected also to conduct musical-appreciation classes.
Among his extramural engagements was one at a school in Lambeth at
which a certain Joseph Erichson Parrott was a pupil. On 26 January
1863 the sixteen-year-old Parrott (whose spelling and punctuation were
at times somewhat disordered) wrote in his diary: '. . . got back to school
about 8.45 to hear a lecture on English music delivered by Mr Coward
one of our finest English composers which was illustrated by some first
class professionals it was well worth hearing and as good as a "Hampton
Court" concert. . . .'

On Saturday 11 July young Parrott, with a friend, went 'for a long walk
to the Crystal Palace and back before dinner—up Tulse Hill and High
Norwood to the Crystal Palace and back through Dulwich w[h]ere we
had some ginger beer and cake in a cottage by the wayside. . . .' South
London was still rural.

Ten days later Parrott was back at the Palace:

Didn't go to lessons this morning started for the Crystal palace about 10 along
with the boys got to Victoria Station about 10.30 and to the Palace about 11.15
when it began to rain and continued all day. The children's concert began at
3 o'clock before that we had dinner Mr Heller [teacher] treated us to sandwiches
and ale and pork pie at 4 o'clock a baloon ascended containing some gentlemen
and a lady. . . .

During the late weeks of summer Parrott and his fellows 'practised
the Crystal Palace music' for a great concert on the afternoon of Saturday
19 September. This was organized by G. W. Martin, organist of Christ
Church, Battersea, who conducted the choirs (and wrote or arranged
most of the music) on behalf of the Metropolitan Schools' Choral Society.
There were 5000 singers.

We went over Lambeth Bridge and got to Victoria Station in time to meet the
Boys etc. We arrived at the Palace at 10.30 and went up to the orchestra for the
rehearsal after which I met Alice [his sister] and Minnie [a friend?] and took
them up the Tower We then came down and walked about the Palace and then
had some dinner after which we met George and then Mr Bailey and Horace
etc etc. About 2.45 the boys went on the orchestra to sing while I staid behind
to collect a few stray boys I then went and took a seat near Mr B. and Alice etc
and did the audience instead of part of the performance after the concert we all
had Tea at Mr Heller's and Bailey's expense.[18]

[18] J. E. Parrott, at this time a pupil at a private school in the parish of Lambeth, in

For young Parrott the year 1863 was otherwise brightened by the entertainments which followed the marriage of the Prince of Wales in March. On the night of the wedding (when several lives were lost through the overenthusiastic behaviour of thronging crowds) the main buildings in London were 'lime-lit'. After the Prince and Princess had returned from the Holy Land (which had no effect on the Prince's moral conduct) there was a Panorama of the Holy Land to view in Her Majesty's Theatre.

For Grove too this was a period of special significance, in which the gap between the private person and the public figure widened. On 28 January 1862 his second daughter Millicent Stanley was born. Eighteen months later, on 15 June 1863, his elder daughter Lucy died of scarlet fever. This was a shattering blow, from which—since ever afterwards he was haunted by the idea of death—he may be said with some truth never to have recovered. For the rest of his life, which was regularly punctuated by the loss of those who meant most to him,[19] this outwardly gregarious man was fated to experience only a fugitive kind of love. But it was the death of marriage—already prefigured in their early years in Sydenham—that was the most tragic and affecting circumstance, for it left Grove in isolation at those times when he most needed comfort and support. The crisis brought about by Lucy's death came to mind once in later years when his attention had been drawn to Wordsworth's 'She dwelt among the untrodden ways';

That dear little poem has a force to me that it can have to very few because I have always applied it to the death of our darling Lucy our first child who died and altered the whole world to me. Religion, my family relations, my hopes in life—everything went into her grave and oh the difference to me! In one way it overthrew everything however firmly rooted—on the other hand it drove me into a new world of poetry, love, music, which has enormously extended my life and my sympathies.[20]

There were in 1863 some who knew the truth, but in their own interests they had to stay silent. There were some who must have guessed, but they too, according to the custom of the day, stayed silent. For the affection lacking at home Grove found substitutes, in work and in social

---

his last year acted as an assistant to the teachers. He played the organ, but his voice having broken he found singing an embarrassment. It is interesting to compare his school life, as candidly revealed, with that of Grove a generation earlier.

[19] His sister Mary Bithiah had died on Christmas Eve 1861, ten days after the Prince Consort, and less than two years after her husband James Bennett, who died on 16 March 1859, after an illness reported to have been of only an hour's duration, and was buried on the north side of the burial ground within the cathedral cloisters (where his widow was also to be interred). On the day of his funeral most of the shops in Salisbury closed as a mark of respect.

[20] E.O., Apr. 25 [1886].

engagements. He also sought new intimacies within the bourgeois respectabilities of Sydenham.

Grove's circle of acquaintances by now embraced such eminent persons as Bulwer Lytton, Browning, Wilkie Collins, Holman Hunt, Dickens and Gladstone—who praised his work for the Bible *Dictionary*. He knew rich and leisured families, in particular the Lehmanns and the von Glehns; and among the musical, Hullah, whom Grove supported in his application for the Gresham professorship; Felix Moscheles, son of Ignaz, whose close connection with the Mendelssohn family was one of the foundations of Grove's study of that master; Edward Dannreuther, pianist, lately arrived in London from Leipzig; Franklin Taylor, a pupil of Clara Schumann; and Henry Chorley, fluent music critic and littéra-teur, at whose house Grove first met Sullivan. The family of his sometime colleague, John Scott Russell, were neighbours, and it was at their house that C. V. Stanford, then a Dublin schoolboy, first encountered Grove. Another neighbour and friend was H. W. Phillips, an artist who regularly exhibited portraits at the Royal Academy Summer Exhibitions. In 1853 he had painted the children of Thomas Gambier Parry—including the five-year-old Hubert—and in 1861 he produced a portrait of Grove (which, however, was not an Academy exhibit).

Scott Russell, who in 1858 had taken over Napier's London shipyard for the construction of the *Great Eastern*, was by now one of the Directors of the Crystal Palace, and had much in common with Grove. He had three daughters, Luise, Rachel and Alice, known familiarly and respec-tively as 'Lady', 'Khenny' and 'Dickie'. Rachel was Sullivan's inamorata, until he was forbidden entry to the household by Scott Russell.[21] Grove admired all three girls, but with Luise he developed a special relationship, as he later disclosed:

Oh, they were so very nice—so clever, so handsome, so distinguées, so thoroughly different from every one else. Their home lay between Sydenham and Crystal Palace and I often used to go in there en passant. As Eaton (now Secretary of the Academy of Arts) once said to me—'I think Grove that your *daily transit of Venus* might be dangerous'. Some day I will tell you all about it when I can find the key of my desk and can send you some of [Luise's] letters you will get an inlook into her character which nothing else gives. . . .[22]

Luise's letters were distinguished by ' . . . great childish lines, and yet these little scraps of paper contained an extraordinary quantity of meaning. She had a way . . . of greeting or giving maxims in French—

---

[21] Scott Russell's anger with Sullivan would have been greater if he had known the full extent of Rachel's commitment, and greater still if he had realized that Sullivan had—while pursuing his amorous course with Rachel—also dallied with Luise's affections.
[22] E.O., Jan 27 [1892].

such as "tout comprendre est tout pardonner"—which set off her own scraps of wisdom.'[23]

Frederick Lehmann, the youngest of five sons of a German artist, had come to Britain as a young man to work in the iron and steel industry, in which, in due course, he made a fortune. For a time, at the beginning of his career, he worked in Leith. Here he met Robert Chambers, the Edinburgh writer and publisher, and more importantly, Chambers's eldest daughter Jane, whom he married in 1852. The Chambers girls were notable for their charm and their cultural capabilities. Their mother was outstandingly musical, and Jane especially inherited her mother's qualities in this respect. After she had moved south, to Sydenham, in 1859, she became a celebrated hostess, whose guests included Joachim, Clara Schumann, Henry Chorley and Pauline Viardot, as well as George Grove. Jane's parents also came south, so that Robert Chambers could the more conveniently work in the Reading Room of the British Museum. A younger sister of Jane, Amelia, having accompanied her parents to London, promptly fell in love with, and married, Frederick Lehmann's brother Rudolf, the artist.

Robert William von Glehn was an Estonian merchant who settled in England in 1835. Like Lehmann he married a Scottish wife and Agnes von Glehn made their home, Peak-Hill Lodge, a remarkable centre of artistic and intellectual energy. There were twelve children of this marriage, of whom a number, either directly or vicariously, made their mark in scholarship, literature and the arts. One son, Oswald, became a painter; another, William, married Sophie Löwe, a singer; a third, Ernest, was the husband of Marian Bradley, half-sister to Harriet Grove. The youngest of the girls, Louise, married Mandell Creighton, later Bishop of London. Olga, and Mary Emilie, who was a pupil of von Bülow, were very musical.

Mary Emilie von Glehn, called 'Mimi', was in a special category, the subject of significant recollections by Grove: 'At one time I violently rebelled by getting head over heels in love with another woman, a perfectly pure though *most passionate* attachment, which lasted for 20 years and only ended with her death.'[24] In another letter (written on the eve of Tennyson's funeral) Grove was even more explicit:

[23] E.O., Thurs 21 Jan [1892]. Luise Scott Russell died on 6 March 1878; Rachel The first real moment in my life came when I was 43 years old, when my Lucy

married an Indian civil servant and died in 1882; Alice married 'a Count [named Rausch] near Schaffhausen'.

[24] E.O., Thursday night [12 Feb 1891]. As a young man, Hubert Parry used to visit the von Glehns, whose house was 'the rendezvous of the coterie of which "G" was the central figure and Miss Mimi von Glehn, fragile, gifted and magnetic, the chief attraction'; C. L. Graves, *Hubert Parry* (1926), vol. I, p. 232. Parry also tells of Grove 'romping' at a party at the von Glehns, and how in so doing he split his trousers.

died, and I became madly in love with Mimi von Glehn. *There* was a passion! It lasted 20 years and more—till her death and with it came my first real insight into music, poetry, nature—everything.[25]

On 22 July 1864 a third son, Arthur, was born to the Groves. With Stanley—now Dean of Westminster—as one godfather, and Sullivan as another, his Christian name was doubly significant. For godmother Olga von Glehn was chosen. A few weeks after the christening Grove went off to Ragatz, in Switzerland, for a holiday with other members of the von Glehn family.

A third attachment of some emotional significance, which developed over this period, was with Arthur Sullivan, who 'for 4 or 5 years . . . almost lived here and was on the most intimate terms with us both (more so than anyone else)'.[26]

Between the first performance of the incidental music for *The Tempest* in 1862 and 10 March 1866, when Manns conducted his 'Irish' Symphony at the Palace, in no small measure at Grove's insistence, Sullivan became famous. At the end of 1866 his Cello Concerto, with Piatti as Soloist, was performed at the Palace, while *In Memoriam*, the overture commemorating the composer's father, Thomas Sullivan, was performed at the Norwich Festival.

After Lucy's death Grove had acknowledged Sullivan's message of sympathy:

Many thanks for your note. . . . Sometimes I think that I am as unhappy as ever and have terrible fits of grief. Sometimes I think that I am getting more contented and that at least I shall be able to think about her as happy and brilliant and waiting for us to join her. Anyhow it is certain that it is good for me to be at work—that is positive—whatever else is uncertain and variable. I am very much obliged to you for your kind expressions of affection. These things don't alleviate one's troubles exactly—but they are a certain support and comfort.

To this he added a postscript: 'I could not have imagined before I knew it from experience, how solitary one is under such a trouble as this. There is no companionship in these sorrows.'[27] These bleak words are reflected in a letter written three years later, after the death of Sullivan's father:

My dearest Arthur:

It's little I can say to comfort you. Only I have been thinking of you all through the day when I had a moment and I can't help telling you so—though I am sure you knew it before? It was a great thing for him to have lived to see your triumph—If he had died last year or even in February of *this* year, before our Symphony was done it would have been quite a different thing to him and he

[25] E.O., Oct 11 Thursday [1892].
[26] E.O., Sunday Feb 12 [1893].
[27] Letter of 23 July 1863, written from Crystal Palace; PML.

could not have felt such a satisfaction in the thought of your success as he did. *That* is surely a great thing to think of both for gratification in the present and encouragement for the future.

God help you my dear fellow; and thank you over and over for all your kindness to me and for your love—which is like a well of light every time I come near you.

Ever your's most affectly

G. GROVE[28]

The practice of keeping a stiff upper lip in public was much cultivated by Grove, but at a cost to his equanimity. In the time of Sullivan's grief Grove asked: 'Why don't I see you? I do long so for you—there is no man I care to be with so much—and it's really cruel that I never can fulfil my wish—you know how busy I am—I am quite killed with work—so do come and smile on me now and then my dear—'[29] At the end of this letter Grove asked whether Mrs Sullivan, for whom he had great affection, 'would value a few apples' from the garden.

Harriet Grove seldom emerges from the background. But there is a rare letter from her to Sullivan at this time, which makes poignant reading. In years to come she retracted her early affection for Sullivan, while her inability to lighten troubles was one factor contributing to a deterioration in her relationship with George. But to the young Sullivan after his father's death, she wrote: 'I am thinking of you and your Mother incessantly. How much I wish I could do anything for you to comfort you—But there is nothing one can do, to make such a trouble any lighter.'[30]

A few weeks later, on 24 October, Harriet's brother Jack was drowned at Oxford. It is not altogether surprising that at that time Grove found himself ruminating on the desolation of Tennyson's 'Tears, idle tears', and the stoical melancholy of *In Memoriam*.

It was very much a Tennyson year. In January Grove had been to Freshwater, when Tennyson also entertained George Bradley—to whose care at Marlborough College Hallam Tennyson had been entrusted—W. G. Clark, John Fowler, the designer of the Metropolitan Railway and the Forth Bridge, and Richard Owen. In February an article by Grove 'On a Song in "The Princess" ' was published in the *Shilling Magazine*,[31] and in the November *Macmillan's Magazine* (just before the

[28] 28 Sept 1866; PML.

[29] Tuesday Sept 1866; PML.

[30] Undated letter; PML.

[31] Three volumes (and one number for May 1866) only were issued of the *Shilling Magazine*, edited by Samuel Lucas and published by Tinsley Brothers, and Grove's piece appeared in the third and final volume. In the previous volume, in August 1865, Mimi von Glehn published the first of her excellent translations of Schumann's criticisms, under the heading 'Robert Schumann on his Contemporaries'. In vol. III two further selections of her translations of Schumann were published.

appearance of which Grove went to Freshwater once more, this time with Sullivan) an essay on 'Tears, idle tears'.

This was the period in which, Grove said, he first had insight into poetry. In confirmation of this there are some verses scribbled into a commonplace book (RCM 2134) dated 'Feb. 22 1865'. After excerpts from Mendelssohn's 'Trumpet' Overture in C major[32] and Mozart's Haffner Symphony—for which works programme notes were needed for a concert on 18 February 1865—is a poem of five stanzas, characterized by a curious turn of religious phrase indicative of a mood veering towards agnosticism. The poem ends with Tennysonian echoes:

> I cannot bear the coming ill
> I can but fling my prayers above
> To that inexorable love
> Which hears and works Its perfect will.
>
> To It I trust thee. Let me stand
> Beside thee through the painful years
> And give some comfort with my tears
> Though but the pressure of a hand.

Shortly before its first performance, Grove copied excerpts from Sullivan's 'Symphony No. 1' [*sic*] preparatory to writing his analytical note, after which comes a stanza picking up from *In Memoriam* VII:

> *In the train*
> Dark house, dark house, up there on the slope
> Why do you stand so dark and drear?
> You ought to be bright with the face of my dear
> To lighten and shine with the light of my hope.

There follows, in Greek, a section (lines 99–107) of the third of the extant idylls of Moschus, which again illustrates Grove's questing nature, and the lasting influence of his early classical training.

Grove's essay in the *Shilling Magazine* on the song at the beginning of Canto VII of *The Princess* is more remarkable for the light it throws on his feelings at that time of his life than for its value in the field of literary criticism. In respect of Tennyson's climactic third stanza Grove writes with orgiastic intensity:

And this time again what a different meaning do the familiar words contain. 'Ask me no more! Not because I will not grant, but because I can no longer refuse,'—because she sees how true is the instinct, how irresistible the fury, of real passion; because she is forced to admit how right as well as how powerful her lover has been in his obstinate perseverance; because she finds herself too feeble, and is compelled to give herself up to an influence which is too strong for

[32] Grove discusses the history of this overture in a letter to *The Times*, 21 Feb 1865.

her weak will to combat. And observe how readily and gracefully the concession is made, as all concessions should be, when the inevitable moment has arrived. 'No more, *dear love*, for *at a touch* I yield.' How wonderfully sweet is the 'dear love', following on the 'too fond', and the 'friend', of the former verses! Even to this it has come—'No more, dear love, for at a touch I yield'. 'A touch,'—yes! not yet an embrace, but a touch—the touch of hand on hand, which at such a moment does more than match to fire a magazine. 'No more',—yes, 'no more' *now*—no more importunity, but also no more resistance—*now*, silence and fondness, an unutterable union of hands to hands, and lips to lips, and heart to heart, and being to being.

The vocabulary of intimacy on which Grove draws here was to serve him not infrequently in the years to come.

This essay also gives additional support to the conclusion that for Grove music was a psychological necessity. Tennyson's economy of means is aptly compared with Mozart's; but in the end it is Grove's true *deus ex musica* who is seen to contain and to express his thoughts and feelings:

In considering, to conclude, the final impression which [the poem] leaves on one's whole being—ear, heart, intellect, imagination, memory—I find myself continually tempted to compare it with some of the masterpieces of the musical art, some of the slow movements of Beethoven's symphonies for example, which present the same astonishing combination of beauty of subject and beauty of general form, with perfect delicacy of detail, the same consummate art, with the same exquisite concealment of it—and which, like it, form a whole that satisfies both the intellect and the imagination, and, once known, haunts the memory for ever.

Within the years enclosed by his own and Sullivan's grief Grove was pushed in different directions. He had some of the discontent of an artist, but in so far as he was the Secretary of the Palace he had to steer a discreet course. On New Year's Day 1865, the *Musical Times* fired a shot across his bows by noting an apparent preference for 'the talent of all the German artists who find a ready welcome', and expressing 'a hope that the audience may occasionally be reminded that we have resident English performers'. At the end of the next year Grove's pessimism was not reduced by the fire that threatened to destroy the Palace, before being mastered by the London Fire Brigade under the command of the redoubtable Captain Shaw, who was to be immortalized in *Iolanthe*.

It appears that Grove was asked at this time to help with a new edition of the Bible, but the offer came, perhaps, too close on the heels of the Bible *Dictionary*, and he did not take it up.[33] Neither did he accept an

---

[33] Graves states (p. 101) that Dalziel Brothers invited Grove to help with a new edition of the Bible, but it seems likely Graves is confusing this with an offer from John

appointment at the South Kensington Museum—which in 1865 received a gift of musical instruments and music from Ella's Musical Union Institute—where Cole would have liked him as a Keeper. There was a suggestion that he should apply for the post of Librarian to the House of Commons, after the death of Thomas Vardon in April 1867, but this came to nothing, as Speaker Denison promoted the Assistant Librarian, George Howard, to the post.

But now, it seemed, Grove's career was too firmly shaped. On the one side those whose interests were in biblical research saw in him the ideal middle-man, one who was theologically broad to the point of neutrality, and as scientifically objective as it was possible to be. On the other, he was a beneficent agent of musical recreation and instruction at a crucial point in the history of education. The two areas of influence were linked by his special skills, as a catalyst so far as other writers were concerned, and as an essayist himself well qualified for eminence in the middle ranges of letters.

Like Stanley Grove had the art 'to popularise mouldy records, and to clothe with flesh and blood the dry bones of antiquity'.[34] In 1864 a fourth edition of *Sinai and Palestine* carried an 'Advertisement' referring readers anxious to supplement the book's contents to the 'numerous articles on Sacred Topography in the new "Dictionary of the Bible" signed by the well-known name of George Grove'. A month later, Smith, whose zest for providing popular but exact works of reference to meet an apparently endless demand was both inexhaustible and a strong support to the prosperity of the firm of John Murray, enticed Grove into accepting a further supervisory commitment. This was to *An Atlas of Ancient Geography, Biblical and Classical*, or *Dr William Smith's Ancient Atlas*, an important work of scholarship, finely produced and as accurate as the researches of Charles Miller and Henry Yale—chief authorities on the topography of the classical world and India respectively—and the critical attention of Grove could make it, which finally appeared in 1874.

Preparation of the *Atlas* overlapped with a practical exercise conducted under military auspices. As often in British imperial history, missionary and military ambitions combined, nowhere more so than in the Middle East. No region aroused so much feeling and sentimental interest as the 'Holy Land', where the purchase of land in 1855 by Sir Moses Montefiore for the purpose of providing a Jewish national home had created both

---

Murray, who projected 'an illustrated edition of the Bible', of which Stanley was to be editor and Grove assistant editor. Murray hesitated over whether such an edition would be accepted by the various sects, and in the end published instead 'the famous "Speaker's Commentary", but without the participation of either Stanley or Grove'; George Paston (pseud.), op. cit., p. 154.

[34] Review of 'On Historical Memorials of Westminster Abbey', *Chambers's Journal*, 21 March 1868, pp. 185-9.

interest and concern. Nine years later Captain C. W. Wilson of the Royal Engineers, a well-known military surveyor, went with a small group of sappers to make a survey of Jerusalem, ostensibly to organize a water supply for the city. Wilson's work, inspired partly by military curiosity and partly by acquaintance with a rapidly growing corpus of archaeological literature, further stimulated Grove, whose interest in the subject had been aroused by close examination of Ermete Pierotti's *Jerusalem Explored*, about which he had written to *The Times*. On 3 January 1865 he wrote again to the paper, this time in support of Sir Henry James, Director General of the Ordnance Survey, to whom Wilson was nominally responsible.

Characteristically Grove now brought into play his organizational talent. There was still in existence an Assyrian Excavation Fund, commenced by Henry Layard in 1853, and Grove saw the money there gathered, but for the time being lying useless, as the basis of a new Fund. If progress was to be made a Committee would be required. He wrote a series of letters to *The Times* to float the idea, and then prudently asked Stanley to use his influence to procure help from above. Among Stanley's papers is a copy of a testimonial written on Grove's behalf, probably to the Archbishop of York, on 23 March 1865:

My dear Lord:

I venture to introduce to your notice Mr Grove, who is very anxious to obtain your name to a Committee which he is desirous of forming for the purpose of prosecuting discoveries in the Holy Land. He is Secretary of the Crystal Palace, and is a person in whom complete reliance can be placed—He has long concerned himself in matters of Biblical Antiquities and Geography and I do not know anyone who is better qualified to promote the object that he has undertaken.

Yours . . .[35]

As many people as possible were invited to a preliminary meeting, over which the Archbishop was to preside. On 11 May, the day before the meeting, Grove wrote to Layard: 'I am very grateful to you for getting Lord [John] Russell to join—I fear there is no chance of your coming over to the Jerusalem Chamber at 5 tomorrow? It is of great importance to get the affair well started. Do come if you can.' (The letter continued with a reference to the forthcoming musical event for which Grove had responsibility: 'As to the Indian Princes and the Handel Festival, no difficulty whatever. I will see the proper people and they shall write to Colonel [Percy Egerton] Herbert as you request.')

After the meeting in the Jerusalem Chamber a Committee was appointed. But that all was not quite plain sailing is evident from a somewhat tetchy letter from Kingsley. On 25 May Grove wrote to him saying that

[35] BL, Add. MS. 35226, f. 80.

he did not understand why Kingsley objected to some of the members of the Committee, who, Kingsley seemed to suppose, might disapprove of the discussion of certain subjects—such as the origins of geological formations in particular volcanic areas—on the grounds that theological tenets might be assailed thereby. Grove assured Kingsley that he would see to it that scientific principles would prevail, and that someone of the academic stature of Andrew Ramsay, Professor of Geology at University College, London, would be sent out to Palestine as a nominee of the Geological Society. He added that he would be glad if Kingsley would send him a couple of guineas to ensure his place on the committee. In this connection Grove remarked, '(to you I don't mind saying it) I don't want too many parsons.'

The Palestine Exploration Fund was officially launched at a meeting on 22 June 1865 with the Archbishop of York in the chair. 'We are', observed His Grace, conscious no doubt of what Kingsley had said to Grove, 'about to apply the rules of science, which are so well understood by us in other branches, to an investigation into the facts concerning the Holy Land.' Grove was officially designated Honorary Secretary, the duties of which office he had, of course, already been conscientiously performing, and without which the enterprise would never have been started. He retained this position, but in 1868 Walter Besant was appointed paid Secretary, so that Grove's duties were lessened. But his interest was enduring, as is evidenced by his many later letters on the subject to the newspapers.

The whole adventure caught the imagination, so that on 29 July a useful article appeared in *Chambers's Journals*, saying:

Naturalists, geologists, archaeologists, topographers, and others are all agreed that our information on many essential particulars of the Holy Land is deplorably scanty, and, indeed, a reproach to our age. . . . Subscriptions . . . are dropping in, and competent explorers are ready to start; hence, for some years to come, we may expect a series of books, which will tell us all we wish to know about the geography, geology, natural history, and antiquities of Palestine.

Shortly after this had appeared—on 3 August—Stanley wrote to Grove, 'Gilbert Scott (the Architect) expressed so much interest in the P.E.F. that I told him I was sure you w$^{d.}$ be glad that he might be on the committee.'

On 11 August Grove informed Layard that a resolution had been passed with general instructions to Captain Wilson to concentrate on certain sites near Damascus, at the north-west corner of the Lake of Galilee, and in Jerusalem.[36] The politics of the situation were apparent to Grove. Layard, now Member of Parliament for Southwark and an Under-Secretary at the Foreign Office, was his close adviser; and in

---

[36] Letters from Grove to Layard are contained in BL, Add. MSS. 39117-8.

his letter of 11 August Grove included Wilson's advice that special favour should be shown to the Pasha of Jerusalem, particularly since a precedent had recently been set in the award to the Bey of Tunis of 'a G.C.B. or something of the kind'. It was, indeed, a vital investment, for unless in the Pasha's good books it would be impossible to carry on with the work. Already funds were low. Work on the excavation of a well near Jerusalem, which had gone down some 70 feet, had had to be stopped, as an initial grant had been exhausted. At the beginning of September 1865 Grove went to Birmingham to speak to the Geographical Section of the British Association about the necessity for a 'systematic, leisurely, and thorough investigation of the Holy Land'. As a result of his address the British Association made a grant of £100 to the Fund. At the end of the year Grove was again passing on requests from Wilson, now at Beirut, for assistance of one sort or another in respect of local political conditions to be rendered by the British Embassy in Constantinople.[37]

While Wilson, assisted by another officer of the Royal Engineers and a corporal who acted as photographer, zealously investigated the territory assigned to him, Grove kept the British public more than fully informed with a flood of letters to the press. Between December 1865 and May 1866 no fewer than 49 separate places, the positions of which were previously unknown, had been fixed and detailed sketches for maps (to be published under Grove's supervision by John Murray) prepared. In August 1866 Grove went again to the British Association meeting— this year held in Nottingham—to give an up-to-date account of the exploration.[38] At the end of his report he emphasized 'the importance of these researches as corroborating the statements of the Bible, which purported to be mainly a record of facts, and of facts about certain definite localities'.

As well as his *Atlas* Smith was now projecting a *Dictionary of Christian Antiquities*, and on 14 May 1867 Grove, announcing himself as one of the editors, and responsible for entries under 'Sacred Places, Art and Furniture, AD 50–850', asked if Layard would be willing to contribute

[37] It is typical of Grove's thoroughness that on 30 January 1866 he wrote to Layard, requesting the use of a map of the Turco-Persian frontier which had, he knew, been drawn but not yet engraved. After some correspondence and parliamentary questioning, it was stated that the map could not be used until after it had been communicated to the Turkish and Persian governments 'for the settlement of whose boundaries it was prepared'.

[38] In this report Grove mentioned his old friend Rogers, Consul in Damascus but shortly to move to Cairo, who was preparing for publication material on 'the modern Syrians'. Rogers was one of several properly qualified persons whose researches, while outside the main purpose of the original scheme, were being encouraged by the Exploration Fund—an indication of Grove's disinterested support for all kinds of scholarship.

articles. A month later, on 28 June, on the point of leaving for the half-yearly meeting of the Crystal Palace which he expected to be rather stormy, he wrote that no one knew better than he that the Board was in need of 'new faces' and he hoped that one of these might be Layard's. He wanted to keep 'the dear old glass house that we all love so much from sinking into a mere tea-garden'.

The Crystal Palace, as it had been conceived and as it had developed, was a good point of departure for most things. Arthur Anderson, chairman of the Peninsular and Oriental Company, about ten years previously had helped to provide 'specimens of Egyptian utensils and other articles'; Grove now used this connection as an introduction to a Middle Eastern potentate, Hekekyan Bey, who he thought might be able to provide information concerning surveys made of the Sinai Peninsula at the time of the building of a palace for the Egyptian Pashas at Jebel Asman. Grove was not one for leaving stones unturned.

During this period his friendship with Alexander Macmillan (whose authors included, among Grove's friends, not only Maurice but Arnold, Hughes, Kingsley and Ludlow) was rapidly developing. As was the case with other publishers, Macmillan was delighted to have to hand an exact man of literary talent whose reluctance to overstate his own originality and readiness to help others made him an ideal editor. Grove graduated on to the payroll of the firm as an assistant to David Masson, editor of *Macmillan's Magazine* since its inception. Inevitably a good many of the chores came his way.[39] Above all he tried to encourage simplicity and clarity. In respect of one passage from an unnamed author he wrote to Macmillan one Thursday night in 1866:

. . . such sentences as 'the morning dawned rather untoward for this anxiously expected ceremonial' and 'was engaged in the decisive battle of Trafalgar capturing on that occasion a Spanish 3 decker' which have no literary merit and are unnecessarily long might be altered to 'the morning was bad' and 'took a Spanish 3 decker at Trafalgar' which conveys all the meaning.[40]

On 27 February 1867 Grove wrote to Macmillan about an article for the Magazine by R. H. Shepherd, on Browning's *Pauline*, a poem which had not been reissued since its publication in 1833. Grove's consciousness of himself was to some extent matched by Browning's account of Pauline's lover, in whom a 'restlessness of passion meets in me/A craving after

[39] In the summer of 1866 he was writing to Mrs Margaret Oliphant in regard to Macmillan's new series of children's books, 'The Sunday Library for Household Reading'; and concerning the magazine to, among others, T. H. Huxley about a paper on 'A Lump of Chalk and all that hangs on it', and to Stanley apropos 'the Canadian Church as a type of the Irish and English Church of the future'.

[40] BL, Add. MS. 54793, f. 4.

knowledge'. In the same letter Grove referred to the death in January of Alexander Macmillan's sister-in-law, Daniel's widow:

... I only heard of your new loss a few days ago and was deeply grieved to hear it. The more I come into contact with Death the more hopeless it seems to be—to the individual I mean not to the race.[41]

However, I have not much time to think of such things for I never was so hard worked. My colleague has knocked up and all his work comes on my shoulders—Thank God I am very well but there is a limit to all things and I must get a holiday soon or I shall collapse.[42]

He did not get a holiday soon; and he did not collapse.

[41] Even as Grove wrote, the race's chances of survival were being improved, in London, by the efforts of Sir Joseph Bazalgette, who created the modern sewage system of the metropolis. In cholera epidemics in 1848–9 and 1853–4 more than 38,000 people died in London. On 11 May 1867 Grove's brother Tom emulated George in writing a letter to *The Times*.

As a proof of the improved condition of the Thames I beg to inform you that a fine well-conditioned sturgeon, upwards of 60 lb weight, was caught this morning at Westminster Bridge, and is now alive in a tank in my shop.
                                 Your obedient servant,
33 Charing-cross   Thomas B. Grove

This letter was published on 13 May. Three days elapsed and Tom wrote again to inform the readers of *The Times* that because it had been injured while being caught the sturgeon had been put under the care of Francis Buckland—naturalist, qualified doctor, and son of Stanley's predecessor as Dean of Westminster. Buckland, appointed Inspector of Salmon Fisheries in 1867, visited the fish daily until on 16 May he pronounced it well enough to be transferred to the Zoological Society in Regent's Park.

[42] BL, Add. MS. 54793, f. 8.

CHAPTER FIVE

In Search of the Ideal

1867–1876

ONE of the main occupational hazards of the greater Victorians was the incidence and infectious nature of a brooding melancholy which was the frequent companion to optimism in the thoughts of the well-circum-stanced. The discontents of daily life, which tended to include a sense of frustration at the non-fulfilment of the highest aims, were an incentive to philosophic speculation, if only because they required some explanation.

In that age music was a perfect catalyst, and Grove was neither the first nor the last to listen to and to study music believing it to have a therapeutic value. In 1867 he was in middle life, a well-respected citizen of Sydenham, a public servant, but with a commendable side interest (so it appeared to his neighbours) in literature. His private interest in music was deep and also well known. But this was the interest of an amateur—and he never claimed to be other than an amateur even when in later life he was at the head of musical affairs.

In the 1860s there was a growing interest in England in the music of Robert Schumann. Marie Wieck, Clara's stepsister, first played the Pianoforte Concerto at the Crystal Palace, on 5 March 1864. In the next year Clara Schumann met Grove, who was already among her late husband's keenest supporters, in Paris. There was at that time a reluctance on the part of English critics generally to accept Schumann's modernity, but Grove was not one of them. On 8 August 1866 he wrote an informed appreciation of Schumann's songs in a letter to a daughter of Sir James Paget, a royal surgeon. In his essay on Tennyson in *Macmillan's Magazine* in November, he referred to the atmosphere of gloom in Schumann's *Manfred* Overture, from which he cast an appraising eye over Schubert's work, 'at the base of which, almost without exception', he stated, 'there lies a profound melancholy.' This statement, qualified by proper references, is expanded in his great essay on Schubert in the *Dictionary*, and with hindsight it may be said that the idea for a dictionary of music really began germination at this point in Grove's life.

In a commonplace book begun in 1865 (RCM 2134), the first excerpts were from Mendelssohn, Mozart, Beethoven, Schumann and Sullivan.[1]

---

[1] Mendelssohn, Overture in C 'for Philharmonic Society', and Haffner Symphony in D (K.385), performed at Crystal Palace, 18 Feb 1865; Beethoven, Pastoral and Ninth Symphonies, Crystal Palace, 11 Mar, and 22 and 29 Apr 1865 respectively; Schumann,

But there were two pages devoted to quotations from various marches by Schubert, arranged by Liszt, Halberstadt and Manns.[2] In 1865 Kreissle von Hellborn's biography of Schubert appeared in its second and greatly enlarged edition, and this led Grove to sharpen an already alert interest in Schubert's works. On 21 April the 'Great' C major was again played at the Crystal Palace.[3] On 3 November the Overture to *Alfonso und Estrella*, a week later the Entr'actes in B minor and D major from *Rosamunde*—the parts of which had been sent from Vienna—and on 1 December the Overture in the Italian Style were given first performances at the Palace. On 16 March 1867 the 'Ballo' (no. 2) and 'Ballet Air' (no. 9) from *Rosamunde* were played, and three weeks later Manns introduced the 'Unfinished' Symphony. Manns's orchestration of the Marche Militaire in D (op. 51), noted in Grove's commonplace book, was played on 2 December 1867.

Grove by now was thoroughly absorbed in Schubert. He was also absorbed in Sullivan, with whom he spent some cheerful days in Paris in July 1867 during the Universal Exhibition. According to Grove's notes a favourite rendezvous was the Café Voisin. By September Grove felt again the need for a holiday—albeit a busman's—and Sullivan agreeing that the call of Schubert was irresistible, there followed an excursion to Vienna, to seek out the rest of the *Rosamunde* music and any other works of the master still in existence. The journey was made possible 'through the kindness of the Directors of the Crystal Palace, always ready to adopt any suggestions for increasing the interest and worth of the Saturday Concerts'.[4]

Just before starting his journey Grove went down to Marlborough to stay with his wife's sister and her husband. On his return to London he wrote to Stanley concerning his immediate plans, but also revealing in a striking passage his own inner turbulence: 'I had a very pleasant day at Marlborough yesterday. It is a happy house. I wish my pleasure there were not so mixed with envy at a happiness and a calm and a steady progress which I can never reach—not only reach but have no part in except as sharing that of others.'[5]

The story of a journey which was to become famous is told by Sullivan:

George Grove and Arthur S. Sullivan left London on Thursday night 26 Sept:

Sonata for Violin and Pianoforte in D minor (op. 121); Sullivan, Symphony No. 1 [*sic*], Crystal Palace, 10 Mar 1866.

[2] In May Louise von Glehn copied into the book 'Das Ringlein' (*Piefscień*, no. 14 of Chopin's op. 74) from G. F. Reiss's German edition of *17 Polnische Lieder* (Litolff, Braunschweig).

[3] Previous performances were on 5 Apr 1856 and 11 July 1857.

[4] Grove's note on Schubert's Symphony in C major in the Crystal Palace programme of 14 Dec 1867.

[5] Letter dated only 'Monday'; BL, Add. MS. 55226, f. 342.

1867, in company with Frederic Sullivan and arrived in Paris on Friday morning 27 Sept[6]—left Paris on Monday night 30 Sept and arrived in Baden Baden—Zahringer Hof Tuesday morning 1 Oct: visited Mad. Schumann and Made Viardot Garcia. Left Baden on Wednesday morning 2nd Oct in a fly and drove to Rastatt, took the tram to Munich via Carlsruhe, Stuttgart, Ulm, Augsburg and arrived in Munich the same night, stayed in Munich (Hotel Linzfelder) all Thursday and left early Friday morning 4th Oct arriving at Salzburgh 12 o'clock the same day. Stayed at Salzburg (Hotel de l'Europe—very good, but dear and waitresses uncivil) all day and left at 2 a.m. for Vienna. arrived in Vienna Saturday morng Oct: 5 put up at Hotel Kaiserin Elizabeth—excellent Hotel (haven't seen the bill yet).[7]

Fortunately Grove was reasonably fluent in German, which he had, he said, taught himself from studying hymns in that language.

Concerning the trip there remains a letter from Grove to Sullivan's mother written from Baden just before going to Lichtenthal—the village near Baden where Clara Schumann had a cottage:

Tuesday [1 October 1867]

Dear Mrs. Sullivan

I knew that this incorrigible infant of yours (why *did* I bring him with me?) has not told you a tenth part of the sweet things I am always saying about you so I must just give you a line myself though I have nothing but a hair pen to write with. In short I am always wishing for you—saying 'Look! Arthur, how your mother would enjoy that' or 'Don't you think Mrs Sullivan would take this view!' etc etc etc This is not mere nonsense (the nonsense of a boy of 7 and 40) but the sober truth.

We have had the pleasantest time hitherto—and agree like soap and water or bread and honey or any other agreeing things. This is a charming place—like the best of S. Leonards or Brighton only 1000 times better but it is nearly empty—all the theatres etc shut up and so Arthur and I will have to put off our little speculation in Rouge and noir till our next visit. We are just going off to see Madame Schumann—of whom, let me tell you, Arthur is in a terrible fright.

I can't make this hair pen go on any longer so I must leave off but I am not withstanding my dear Mrs Sullivan your ever sincerely

G. Grove

We are very economical. I don't mention this out of pride—but to give you pleasure.[8]

---

[6] Cf. Graves, p. 142: 'He accordingly started on September 24th, was joined by Sullivan on the 27th. . . .' In his letter to Stanley (see n. 5 above) Grove stated his intention to start on 23 September. He also said that there was a possibility of including Pesth (Budapest) in the itinerary. Stanley advised the travellers when in Salzburg to see the church at Maria Plain (for which Mozart composed the 'Coronation' Mass) '¼ hour before sunset', and in Prague the Jesuit Cemetery.

[7] 'Vienna-Leipzig' Diary; PML.

[8] PML.

As usual Grove took a good deal of reading material with him, and he was specially taken up with the recently published second edition of Otto Jahn's *W. A. Mozart*, in his copy of which he wrote at Baden, also on 1 October, 'A precious long yarn.'

On their second day in Vienna, it being Sunday, Grove and Sullivan visited Schubert's and Beethoven's graves—from each of which they picked some ivy leaves—in the village of Währing. Characteristically Grove made a note of those buried in the three graves between those of the musicians. They were Freiherr von Wecherd, and Graf Johann and Gräfin O'Donnell—with whom were interred memories of the 'Wild Geese' of Ireland. Almost opposite to these, and a little lower down the hillside into which they had been dug, were the graves of Ignaz von Seyfried, a pupil of Mozart and composer of a *Libera me* performed at Beethoven's funeral, and Franz Clement for whom Beethoven had written the Violin Concerto.

The travellers next made the acquaintance of Karl Anton Spina, who had succeeded to Diabelli's publishing business in the Graben in 1852 and who had been cooperative in the previous year in sending orchestral parts of Schubert's works to Grove for Manns's use. In the *Dictionary* Grove (considering his debt to certain publishers) a little ungenerously wrote that Spina was one whose 'enthusiasm for Schubert was not that of a mere publisher, as the writer from personal experience of his kindness can testify'. Sullivan noted how Spina made available for Grove and him:

Seligkeit, 2 Sonette (Schlegeal) Am Flusse (Gothe) [*sic*]; Trio in B flat, Overture in D, Hirtenmelodien, Entr'acte no 3ª Overture 3rᵈ Act, Marsch and Chor. Fierrabras, Klopstock's Stabat Mater, Catalog; some letters by Beethoven, a Quintett—100 Ducats, 4 Hand Sonate. Quintets with flute. Letter from Beethoven 1824.

In Spina's shop, continued Sullivan,

there was an old clerk v. Doppler who had known Beethoven and Schubert well [and he] told us many little things about them. Beethoven wore a *green* Polish coat with Frogs on it—and when in the shop generally leant against a wooden pillar by the counter whilst Czerny and Seyfried Stadler sat on a leathern sofa— They wrote down their conversations on a slate as B. was stone deaf. Doppler corroborated the story told by Jahn in his 'Aufsätze' of Beethoven's composing under a tree at Heiligenstadt. He it was who was told by the peasants. v Doppler said that the portrait by Kriehuber is the most like of all the portraits of Beethoven. Pointing to the 'Missa Solennelle in D' which is in B's hand in the engraving he said 'Ah, he sketched some of that in a storm—for he was lying under a tree writing—when it began to rain. He was however so engrossed in his work that he took no notice of the rain, and it was not until his paper was wet and his pen had gone through it that he left off.'

4

He told us that Beethoven was very absent and that, for instance, he would often order his beer, pay for it, and never drink it.
I said 'Did you know Schubert?' 'Know him!' said he,—'Why I was at his christening! and was a pupil of his father's.'[9]

Grove and Sullivan made themselves known to Schubert's nephew Eduard Schneider, son of his sister Therese, from whom they had MSS. of the 'Sinfonie in C major, Sinfonie in C minor (sogenannte "Tragisch"), Overture in D, "Die Freunde von Salamanca" ', and they went into the library of the Gesellschaft der Musikfreunde where Carl Ferdinand Pohl had lately been appointed Librarian. Pohl, who had lived in London from 1863 until 1866 in order to undertake research in the British Museum, was charming and helpful. He remained a friend of Grove and was among the more important contributors to the Dictionary.[10]
On 8 October Sullivan went through the autograph of the 'Grand Symphony in C', copying into Grove's commonplace book (RCM 2131) the salient themes, and adding his annotations.[11] Thus:

there are hardly any alterations certainly none of importance and towards the end the pen seems to rush without stopping for a moment—like the glorious music itself. The first 3 movements are crowded with alterations so much that the work looks as if it were made up of afterthoughts. The handwriting is neat and perfectly distinct.[12]

Immediately after the excerpts from this symphony come the first and only nine bars of the Scherzo for the B minor Symphony. 'This,' says

[9] Cf. Grove 1, vol. III, p. 324, n. 3: Grove, 'I cannot refrain from mentioning this gentleman [Doppler] who in 1867 was shopman at Spina's (formerly Diabelli's). I shall never forget the droll shock I received when on asking him if he knew Schubert, he replied, "Know him? I was at his christening!" ' To whom Doppler actually said this will never be known. The portrait referred to is a drawing of Beethoven (1826) by A. Dietrich which was lithographed by J. Kriehuber; it was reproduced in T. von Frimmel, Ludwig van Beethoven (Berlin, 1901).

[10] In his own copy of Kreissle von Hellborn's Schubert (1865) Grove kept a note from Pohl:

P.S. Sunday 23rd Feb [1868]: As the copyist did not come also this morning, I became anxious and went to Hernals where he lives. He gave me the Nr. 1 (Entr'acte) which was finished. (If I had known that there are only a few leaves I would have copied it myself.) The ouverture also will be ready by 4 or 5 o'clock and I send it also directly by the letter post. All the rest I told the man to bring to Spina that the whole shall be send [sic] to you—the [Jean] Becker Quartett is much liked here. Very disagreeable for Hellmesberger. God bless you!

Yours
POHL

[11] RCM 2131, ff. 10–12; simple annotations, without musical examples, are in Sullivan's 'Vienna-Leipzig' Diary, PML.
[12] This passage was transferred to, and developed in, Grove's analytical notes for the Crystal Palace concert on 14 Dec 1867.

the note, 'was shown to us by [Johann] Herbeck [Court Kapellmeister).'[13]

It was a busy week, but as it passed Grove became increasingly agitated. He had gone to Vienna principally to collect the remaining *Rosamunde* music, and in spite of what Spina and Schneider had been able to turn up, it looked as though he would go away unsatisfied in this respect. A valedictory call by him and his companion on the afternoon of 10 October, however, led to Schneider suddenly remembering some more music in the cupboard where the Fourth and Sixth Symphonies had lain, and which had been examined already by Grove and Sullivan. It was, indeed, what Grove had gone to seek; a complete set of part-books of the *Rosamunde* music.[14] Helped by Sullivan and the obliging Pohl, Grove—working into the small hours of Friday—copied the music he lacked and also had an index made of the complete set of *Rosamunde* pieces. When this task was completed Grove and Sullivan, without Pohl, went into the silent Vienna streets and released their exuberance by means of Grove's favourite pastime of leap-frog.

In the Appendix which he contributed to the English translation of Kreissle von Hellborn's *Life of Schubert* Grove expressed his enthusiasm in terms of another of his disciplines. The discovery of Schubert's forgotten music was like the monkish find of treasured manuscripts at Souriami, as described by Robert Curzon in his famous *Visit to the Monasteries of the Levant* (1849), or William Cureton's 'truly romantic discovery of the missing leaves of the Syriac Eusebius', described in *Four Gospels in Syriac* (1858), a volume in Grove's biblical library.

Sullivan had separately investigated other works, from which excerpts were taken and on which notes were made. These were the D major (no. 1, 1813), B flat major (no. 2, 1814–15), D major (no. 3, 1815), C minor (no. 4, 1816) and B flat major (no. 5, 1816) Symphonies. For the first three Sullivan had the autograph scores to work from, and for the fourth a copy ascribed to Ferdinand Schubert. The Fifth Symphony was, he noted, 'in the possession of Herr Herbeck. I saw the parts only. "Symphonie in b♭ von Franz Schubert aus dem original Partitur die Orchester Stimme copirt von Ferd. Schubert" '.

Sullivan left Vienna on Saturday afternoon for Prague, where he arrived late at night. Next day he went sightseeing, not omitting to visit the

---

[13] 'As these bars have not been printed, I cannot resist quoting them from the note-book of Mr Arthur Sullivan, with whom I saw the MS when in Vienna'; analytical note, 14 Dec 1867.

[14] See *Grove 1*, vol. III, p. 339: '. . . the parts were tied up and forgotten till the year 1867, when they were discovered by two English travellers in Vienna.'

72348

Judenviertel, the Jewish quarter of the city, where were the old synagogue and burial ground. Like Mendelssohn, Sullivan occasionally paid respect to his Jewish antecedents. While Sullivan travelled on to Leipzig, Grove stayed in Vienna, hearing one of Gluck's *Iphigénie* operas and Schumann's Mass at the Court Chapel. He went to the Picture Gallery, and once more to the graves of Währing, and—for the first time—he met Brahms. From Vienna Grove travelled to Leipzig by way of Prague and Dresden, spending some hours in the Library in the one city and in the Picture Gallery in the Zwinger in the other.

In Leipzig on Thursday, 17 October, with the composer he heard the Gewandhaus Orchestra play Sullivan's *In Memoriam* overture and was pleased at the warmth of its reception. After the concert Sullivan, Anton Rubinstein—who had played his own D minor Pianoforte Concerto, Barthold Senff, a music publisher, Ferdinand David and Grove went together to dine. They drank what Sullivan described as an 'excellent Bohle'; and so good was it that he wrote the recipe in his notebook:

> Three bottles of Moselwein
> One bottle of Champagne
> $\frac{1}{2}$ „   „   Rothwein
> $\frac{1}{4}$ pound of Sugar
> six to ten peaches cut in quarters. Ice ad lib.

After two days' respite Grove and Sullivan went to Dresden, and were disappointed that Sullivan's old teacher Julius Rietz—now conductor of the Royal Opera and Director of Music in the Catholic Court Church —was not at home. They heard Wagner's *Rienzi*—'a great disappointment,' wrote Sullivan, 'a mixture of Weber, Verdi and a touch of Meyerbeer. The whole very vulgar; commonplace and uninteresting.' Dresden was then much favoured by the English, who were either rich and idle, or poor and artistic. Here, by chance, Sullivan ran into an acquaintance, the Revd Thomas Fuller, incumbent of St Peter's Church, Eaton Square, since the establishment of that church in 1827. Being a clergyman, Fuller was at least moderately poor, and as a Fellow of the Royal Society of Literature he could be thought of as reasonably artistic.

On 22 October Grove took the train to Berlin, arriving at the Anhalt Station late at night. During his brief stay in the city he paid homage at Mendelssohn's grave and went to one of Joachim's concerts,[15] before setting out for England on 26 October. He reached Sydenham the next evening.

[15] The impression that those were heroic days and nights is heightened by the details of the concerts which Joachim directed, and in which he appeared as composer and soloist as well as conductor. When Grove was in Berlin there were offered at the Joachim concerts concertos by Bach, Beethoven (with Joachim's cadenzas), Mendelssohn and Joachim (the Hungarian concerto and that in G major), as well as vocal items, the latter including Schubert's *Allmacht* orchestrated by Bernhard Hopfer.

On 1 November Sullivan wrote a brief account of the Vienna part of the expedition to J. W. Davison, observing that 'no pleasure was equal to the delight of travelling with G.G., whose looks, manners and conversation won all hearts there, even as they have won yours and mine'.[16]

Grove's mind was unceasingly active, and he moved from one idea to another but never without ensuring that his main lines of communication were intact. Thus the musicologist and concert promoter, lately returned from Vienna, on 20 December 1867 put to Alexander Macmillan the desirability of an English edition of Jahn's *Mozart*:

I have for some time past been in treaty with Mr Otto Jahn of Bonn, the first living musical writer and biographer, for a translation of his Life of Mozart, a work which has already gone through one large Edition and has just been republished in a rather smaller form. . . . I have got a translator—a lady who lives in Sydenham [M. E. von Glehn?] and with whom I am in frequent communication. She is the daughter of a German father and talks and writes German like a native—and has already had a good deal of practice in translating musical literature, which she is very well qualified for—being a very accomplished musician—I purpose to make the necessary compression in the work and to revise the translation.[17]

Grove pointed out that by omitting certain 'dissertations' put in by Jahn, which in Grove's view impeded the narrative, the biography could be contained in two volumes rather than three. Having, as he said, taken the book with him on his recent journey, he had done some editorial work on it. The translator he considered should receive £100, the original author £25 (to allow which 'would be a graceful and proper thing'), and as editor he would like a share in the profits. 'The Book is a *thoroughly* good book and would be a standard work for years to come. I don't think it would have a brilliant sale, but it ought to command a good one.'[18]

By this time the new concert season at the Palace was well under way. On 2 November there was a performance of Handel's *Acis and Galatea*. Manns wrote the programme note on this work, as he did a week later for the *Prometheus* overture of Woldemar Bargiel. The stepbrother of Clara Schumann, and himself a Schumann-inspired composer, Bargiel had been introduced to the Crystal Palace audience in 1863, with his *Medea* overture. *Prometheus* took the place of Sullivan's *Marmion* overture, which was put off until 7 December as the orchestral parts were not yet ready. At the next Saturday concert Schubert's 'Great C

[16] PML.

[17] BL, Add. MS. 54793, f. 15. Mimi von Glehn had proved herself as a competent translator in the *Shilling Magazine* (see p. 85).

[18] The English edition of Jahn came out in 1882 from Novello, not Macmillan, in a translation by Pauline Townsend. See below, p. 129.

major' was again performed and Grove's analytical note, containing a brief account of the Schubert adventures in Vienna, was for the first time signed 'G'.

On Saturday afternoons during that winter, as the special trains backed into the departure platforms at Victoria, all the talk among the Palace-bound travellers was of Schubert, 'who then was, for the first time, shining in all the glory of his heaven-descended art'[19]. The critics and their friends assembled early at the Palace, fortifying themselves in one of the bars opposite the 'Music Room'; prominent among them were Davison; Chorley; Grüneison of the *Morning Post*; Campbell Clarke, Bennett's predecessor on the *Daily Telegraph*; Henry Lincoln of the *Daily News* and an early champion of the works of Bach; Desmond Ryan of the *Standard*; Tom Mudie, brother of the librarian and composer in the household of Lord William John Monson; Alexander Durlacher, a committee member of the Sacred Harmonic Society from 1848 and a generous donor; and even John Goss, the revered veteran organist of St Paul's Cathedral, who was then living in Brixton.

If those were great days for Schubert they were no less so for Schumann, in the promotion of whose works Grove was almost equally fervent. Clara had become a familiar figure in England and her appearances aroused all Grove's sense of chivalry. Schumann's music to him was the necessary complement to that of Schubert, for within his own personality there was a complex of emotional traits similar to those to be understood from the works of the two composers.

'The issue of an autumnal document, signed 'G. GROVE Secretary', has come to be looked for with interest and curiosity,' wrote one of the papers in 1868.

No higher tribute to the excellence of the Saturday Concerts and the enterprising zeal of its managers could be paid. The public know—as they ought after thirteen years' experience—that so long as improvements are possible improvements will be made, and that so long as there are treasures unheard no pains will be spared to secure them an audience.[20]

The programme for the season as then announced included 'Symphony in C, No. 6 M.S.—Schubert (From the Vienna treasures; never before performed entire)', as well as excerpts from the same composer's *Die Verschworenen* and *Miriams Siegesgesang*, Schumann's Third Symphony and the overture to *Hermann und Dorothea*: Handel's Ode for St Cecilia's Day; Max Bruch's Violin Concerto in G minor (no. 1); and works by Mendelssohn, Sterndale Bennett, Beethoven, Wagner, Rubinstein and Sullivan.

At that time the last-named was in the highest favour and his 'Irish'

[19] J. Bennett, *Forty Years of Music 1865-1905* (1908), p. 337.
[20] *Sunday Times*, 27 Sept 1868.

Symphony had been performed for a second time on 11 April 1868. By the autumn of that year its successor had been commissioned, and among the forthcoming works listed at the end of the programme of 3 October the following statement, establishing its tonality, seemed to indicate that a major work was taking shape:

A new Symphony in D, composed expressly for these Concerts by Mr Arthur Sullivan . . . Of Mr Arthur Sullivan's new Symphony we can say nothing save that it will be welcomed with heartiness, and heard with an interest inspired by the remembrance of works which have made this composer the object of many and high hopes.

That is one of the most important non-works in British music—the one which might have turned Sullivan into the symphonic composer expected by the nation. That he did not fulfil these hopes was no fault of Grove.

The banners of Schubert and Schumann were waved frequently in 1868. On 29 February the Palace audience, having read how the C minor Symphony of the former had lain in 'dusty retirement', were invited to see the 'cartes de visites of Schubert's Tomb and of the Bust [which] may be obtained from Negretti and Zambra, in the Nave; Price 6d each'. On 14 November the *Song of Miriam* was performed for the first time, and a week later the C major Symphony (no. 6). During that year Paul Mendelssohn, brother of Felix, presented to Grove the MSS. of Schubert's unfinished E minor–major Symphony, which was put into shape for performance a few years later by J. F. Barnett.

On 28 March the performance of the complete *Rosamunde* music necessitated a long programme note, which relates how the author had scoured Vienna not only for the music but (unavailingly) also for a copy of the libretto of Helmina von Chezy's play.

As for Schumann, Clara played the Pianoforte Concerto on 8 February. On 7 March she was present for a performance of her husband's Second Symphony, was the soloist in Mendelssohn's D minor Concerto, and played some pieces by Chopin. Next month her interpretation of Beethoven's Sonata in D minor (op. 31, no. 2) caused an anonymous contributor to the *Pall Mall Gazette* (11 April) to write that it could not be heard 'without stirring the listener's sympathies to their depths'. This sounds very much like Grove, for whom this player and this work remained the *ne plus ultra* of the 'sublime'. At the beginning of the new concert season, on 24 October, Schumann's Third Symphony was for the first time given a complete performance at the Crystal Palace, and in the *Pall Mall Gazette* of 30 November that this composer's reputation had appreciated was ascribed to the faith of the organizers of the concerts 'at which Schumann has been exhibited through evil as well as good report with a consistency that deserves success'.

An innovation that year was the introduction of the organ into the

Saturday concerts. Through Grove's insistence John Stainer, University organist at Oxford, appeared on 7 November, when he played a 'Pedal Fugue in G minor' by J. S. Bach and Mendelssohn's Fourth Organ Sonata.

The persistence of Manns and Grove in respect of the Saturday concerts was little short of heroic; but the heroic properties of the enterprise have gone largely unrecorded. The concert hall, in spite of its magnificent setting, was but a make-shift auditorium. Access to the Crystal Palace by train, despite protests, was always less than satisfactory. The orchestra—the permanent 'Band'—was augmented for the Saturday concerts, but even so was smaller than Hallé's orchestra in Manchester—where the secure backing of the German community in the city, the excellence of the Free Trade Hall, and a native enthusiasm for good music evident in hundreds of local choirs, provided a more encouraging environment. Manns, however, was dogged—sometimes he paid for rehearsals out of his own pocket—and Grove was persuasive. The concerts grandly rode over rumours of collapse, and determined attempts by some unsympathetic shareholders to induce collapse, for half a century.

Grove sat through the concerts in the gallery at the back of the hall, and there he entertained his friends, not infrequently allowing the sounds of hospitality and conversation to overflow into the ears of the audience. Once Hans von Bülow was among the elect and on hearing what Manns was doing to the *Coriolan* Overture threw the score he was following to the ground and shouted, 'What can you expect from a bandmaster?'[21]

Joseph Bennett saw a good deal of Grove at this time and noted a degree of sensitivity in him that sometimes led him to misunderstand the intentions, or the integrity, of others, and to 'exaggerate what he regarded as offensive in their remarks'. Bennett perceptively noticed that Grove 'loved Schubert with almost feminine devotion'.[22] Throughout 1868 Bennett was aware that he was not in Grove's favour when he made less than enthusiastic comment on Schumann. This was an issue in respect of which the young writer could not win. On 30 November an appreciation of Schumann by Bennett appeared in the *Pall Mall Gazette*. Grove was overjoyed, remarking that the article marked 'an epoch in English musical criticism'. Davison, of *The Times*, on the other hand, was appalled. A defection from the anti-Schumann faction to him was a serious matter.

If Grove took some things too seriously, his boisterousness provided frequent contrast. The domestic scene was enlivened by noisy parties of 'Muttonians', the designation of the members of a dining club invented by Davison, and noticed weekly in diversionary manner in the

[21] E. Speyer, *My Life and Friends* (1937), p. 35.
[22] J. Bennett, op. cit., pp. 112–13.

Musical World, of which he was editor. When invited to dinner at the Groves' Bennett was sometimes told that the guests would be 'Dishly Peters, Dr Shoo, and Dr Silent'—all concealing Davison, 'Thaddeus Egg'—Bennett, 'Shaver Silver'—H. Sutherland Edwards, 'Drinkwater Hard'—Clemow, a contributor to the *Musical World*. Sullivan was known in this embarrassingly hilarious company as the 'Prodigal Son', and Grove himself as 'Flamborough Head'.

These years were truly *années de pélerinage*. No eighteenth-century lordling could have been more intent on absorbing the European cultural heritage than Grove. A man who was simultaneously editor of an important literary journal, a musicologist with primary interests in foreign soil, a principal in the Palestine Exploration Fund, an authority on geography, and responsible for thinking of ideas for exhibitions in the Crystal Palace, could justify almost any expedition.

In the spring of 1868 Grove had devoted almost seven weeks to a tour of Italy, which took him twice to Florence, to Naples, Rome, and Turin, as well as other places on the conscientious sightseer's list. He climbed Vesuvius three times, on 30 March, 1 and 3 April, and noted every detail of each ascent. After the first he wrote how

. . . we then continued the ascent to a small funnel-shaped hole not more than 40 feet [across] and some 25 feet deep. It was full of vapours of sulphur, so strong, that it was all we could do by stuffing pocket-handkerchiefs into nose and mouth, and holding breath, to stand it. It was only now and then, when the wind blew stronger than usual, that we could manage it. It was a horrible little pit—brown and dry and sandy—it looked merciless and hellish—dead. The guide rolled down some stones to the bottom, and in a few moments eight or ten bubbles appeared and blew up (like a crater) a horrid sulphurous vapour.

Unwilling to miss any opportunity of informing his fellow-countrymen of the wonders of the world, Grove described the eruption of the volcano in a graphic letter in the *Pall Mall Gazette*. In November of that year specimens of volcanic ash and volcanic minerals and photographs of Pompeii were exhibited in the Pompeian Court of the Crystal Palace and the latest activities of Vesuvius described in a concert programme, in a vivid letter reprinted from *The Times*.

In Rome Grove stayed in rooms once occupied by Mendelssohn, and one night, as he wrote to Alexander Macmillan, he sat next to Elizabeth Garrett (Anderson, after her marriage in 1871), the celebrated doctor. 'She is', commented Grove, 'quite as killing as any of her own drugs, a charming, natural, sweet, nice, person. Nature's lady. She stuck her lancet through my too penetrable waistcoat into my too susceptible heart in a minute. I bled *freely*.'[23]

[23] Letter of 8 Apr 1868; BL, Add. MS. 54793, f. 46.

Grove met Liszt in Rome, and heard him play works by Bach, Raff and von Bülow. Before he left England Stanley had given him letters of introduction to officials of the Papal Court, and so he was able to meet the Pope. In Florence he saw the festivities in honour of the entry into the city of Prince Umberto, eldest son of Victor Emmanuel I.

Grove returned home that spring to find that his application for the post of Secretary to Lloyd's—in support of which Tom Hughes, now Chairman of the Crystal Palace Board of Directors, had written a testimonial—was unsuccessful. The submission of such applications came from a feeling that he was not yet secure in the style of living to which he assumed he was entitled. In the circles in which he moved a certain liberality was expected (Grove's Saturday night dinners were quite an institution), as well as a degree of self-indulgence. Out of luck, in respect of Lloyd's, it was back to the Palace, with its 'Shakespeare House' (including a facsimile of the birth room of Stratford), new Reading and Chess Room, Theatre of Mechanical Arts, and School of Art, Science, Literature, and Music, to administer as well as the concerts.

Dining out occupied a good deal of time, particularly as dining clubs of one sort or another proliferated. In 1869 a Metaphysical Society was founded by Charles Pritchard (whose relationship with Grove was a constant), James Knowles, architect and littérateur, and Tennyson, and this required attendance once a month, ostensibly to discuss the evidences of Christianity. This company was an inter- (and, indeed, extra-) faith group, containing bishops, deans and other dignitaries of the Established Church and notable members of the Catholic community, as well as dissenters and sceptics, scholars and writers,[24] a number of whom had crossed or would cross Grove's path at some point or other.

It was all very challenging, and keeping up with such society required frequent attention to the abstract or the exotic. In the autumn of 1869 Grove went off to Naples with the firm intention of conducting an examination into the supposed miracle of the liquefaction of the blood of St Januarius on 19 September.[25] Accompanied by the young, noble and

[24] Among them were Cardinal Manning, John Dalgairns, and the contentious W. G. Ward—a hard-liner on dogma; the Unitarian James Martineau, Frederic Harrison, a Positivist who was authoritative on trades unions and jurisprudence, Thomas Huxley, and John Tyndall, natural philosopher and one-time railway engineer; Henry Sidgwick, who resigned his Cambridge Fellowship as a protest against religious tests, Mark Pattison, W. B. Carpenter, an expert in forensic medicine, and James Hinton, surgeon and philosopher; and Bagehot, Froude, R. H. Hutton, Roden Noel and Seeley. W. E. Gladstone, an occasional member of the Crystal Palace audience, was also a member.

[25] Failure of the blood to liquefy was taken as a mark of divine disapproval and threatened ill fortune for the Neapolitans. In 1976 initial reluctance of the relic to perform its miraculous function was attributed by some to the influence of a Communist administration of the city.

Reverend Augustus Legge, Vicar of St Bartholomew's Church, Sydenham, and his wife Fanny, and F. A. Eaton, editor of some of Murray's Handbooks and one-time Secretary of the Royal Academy, Grove conducted his researches with his customary diligence. He communicated them to *The Times* on 28 September, and on 23 October, amplified his account on what had transpired in Naples for the *Spectator*—which properly described what had appeared in *The Times* as 'a very amusing account'. If the miracle failed to come up to expectation, Grove showed himself as in some ways susceptible to the ambience of continental Catholicism. He loved the 'splendid decorative lighted candles—the long thin ones', which he had seen in the Franciscan church in Vienna, the chapel of the convent of French Nuns in Rome, and in churches in Loreto and in Naples.

Against these events and activities another pattern was being traced through the agency of Henry Cole, still bringing his considerable influence to bear on the enhancement of the nation's culture. For the variety of his interests his only rival, perhaps, was Grove himself, and their respective interests converged in musical education. Cole, who had in 1869 proposed the holding of 'a conference of working-class representatives . . . to continue the question of primary education'[26] under the auspices of the Society of Arts, was responsible for much of the groundwork for the Education Act of 1870. At the same time he sought the cooperation of the Church of England to extend an appreciation of music. A friend of W. J. Irons, hymn writer, theologian, supporter of the principle of compulsory universal education and Vicar of Holy Trinity Church, Brompton, he made a hitherto little noticed intervention which was not without its wider significance. He persuaded Irons to hold a week-day musical service in his church, in which the organ was to be supported 'as at St Paul's Cathedral, with drums, trombones and trumpets,' under the direction of Mr Arthur Sullivan. Cole laid it down that Irons should preach on these occasions but for not more than ten minutes—a condition which the Vicar tolerated with equanimity. 'Workmen with their wives and families were especially invited to come, and to take part in the services.' The costs were underwritten by Cole's friends and the offertories of pennies and halfpennies given by the 'working and poorer classes from the neighbourhood'.[27]

On 29 March 1871 another scheme of Cole's came to fruition with the opening by Queen Victoria of the Albert Hall, the musical arrangements for which were in the hands of Costa, who had also acted as adviser in respect of the acoustics of the building. Not the least of the features of the hall was the great organ built by Henry Willis, in which the

[26] *Fifty Years of Public Work of Sir Henry Cole, K.G.B.* (1884), vol. I, p. 398f.
[27] Ibid., pp. 383–4. Cf. Grove's letter on 'Sunday Music', *The Times*, 22 Mar 1886.

disposition of the pipe-work was after an arrangement Cole had noticed in some Spanish organs during a recent holiday. Cole's ambition to make South Kensington a cultural metropolis of unrivalled opportunity for the broad mass of the British people led him to pick up an ongoing idea for a national school of music first projected by Her Majesty's Commissioners of the 1851 Exhibition.

In 1854 the Director of the Royal Academy of Music had petitioned to be allowed part of the Exhibition site for a new building. The Commissioners considered the proposal for ten years, by which time it had gone cold. In 1866 the Royal Academy of Music made fresh overtures to the Government which resulted in agreement that the Academy should be reconstituted, that it should be housed—temporarily at least—in South Kensington, and that Costa should be appointed Director. Costa accepted the appointment at £1200 a year. But after discussion between the staff of the Academy and the Department of Science and Art, the negotiations were suspended. By the time the Albert Hall was opened it was apparent that productive collaboration with the Royal Academy was not possible. With the aim of raising money for a new national school of music six concerts were therefore given in the Albert Hall, but with a loss of £100. Cole now fell back on the principle of sponsorship, hoping that he could encourage some who wished immortality for themselves to promise funds for a 'Scheme of Musical Scholarship'.

This ploy worked. An encouraging body of support was forthcoming from among the aristocracy, members of Parliament, leaders in the world of commerce, and the Church.[28] In 1872 the Duke of Edinburgh joined the Music Committee of the Society of Arts, and eventually the offer of C. J. Freake (later Sir Charles Freake), a Kensington builder and contractor, to provide £20,000 for the building of a school of music enabled the Commissioners to release the necessary land. On 18 December 1873 the Duke of Edinburgh laid the foundation stone of the National Training School for Music[29]—at which point Cole characteristically turned his attention to the possibility of establishing a sister foundation, a National Training School for Cookery. In 1874 a Prospectus of Management was produced for the School of Music; on 15 June 1875 the Prince of Wales held a meeting 'to promote the establishment of Free Scholarships for the Metropolis, in the New National Training School for Music'; and on 17 May 1876 the new foundation opened its doors to take in the first 50 students, each sustained by a scholarship.[30]

---

[28] The only collective body on the initial list of sponsors—the Fishmongers' Company —was the one associated with the Grove family. An interesting individual sponsor was T. Gambier Parry, father of Hubert and president of the Gloucester Choral Society.

[29] The building is now the Royal College of Organists.

[30] Arthur Sullivan—once a professor in the Crystal Palace School of Music—was Principal and his assistant staff included J. F. Barnett, J. F. Bridge, J. T. Carrodus,

The war years of 1870 and 1871 had affected Grove in many ways. As far as music was concerned, however, the events in Europe were taken to underline the might not only of Prussian arms but also of German music. In 1870 Grove acquired *Beethoven, A Memoir*, by Elliott Graeme. It was, he noted on the flyleaf, 'a book ludicrously full of mistakes of all kinds'—some of which he corrected in the margins. The significant part of the book, however, was an essay, 'Quasi Fantasia', by Ferdinand Hiller. Of this the meaning was unmistakable:

There are, perhaps, no two German names which can rejoice in a popularity—widely diffused in the most dissimilar nations—equal to that of Mozart and Beethoven. And Haydn, and Weber, and Schubert, and Mendelssohn! What a propaganda they have made for the Fatherland! That they speak a *universal* language does not prevent their uttering in it the best which we possess as Germans.

The Beethoven centenary year of 1870 was celebrated at the Crystal Palace in a big way, and although the preparations were disrupted by the death of Bowley,[31] by 1 October everything was in order for the beginning of a festival of twelve concerts. Manns, who had enjoyed a benefit concert in the preceding year, organized programmes together with Grove which included all the symphonies, the violin and piano concertos, the Mass in C, and a number of other works. In the Centre Transept there was an accompanying exhibition, of photographs, 'relics' (including two autograph letters), and two pages to show improvements in recent issues of printed orchestral parts and to remind the public 'how *impossible* accurate performances must have been when the only copies accessible were so bad'. A desire to preserve a balance between the living and the dead led to the interpolation in the Beethoven programmes of new symphonies by Hiller and Gounod, and Sullivan's *di Ballo* Overture.

During the Beethoven Festival the Directors of the Palace approved a display which would not seem out of place in the television age. In the so-called War Department of the Palace, crowds were attracted by the War Map and the Original War Sketches laid out—as were the Beethoven relics—in the Centre Transept. On 9 November C. T. Brock organized a display of fireworks (killing two birds with one effort) showing 'The presentation of a Battle, by Batteries of Guns, Maroons, Bombs, and Explosions'. To add to the excitement there was 'A Fleet of Magnesia Balloons (as used in Paris to display the besiegers' Lines) for the conveyance of Visitor's message cards'. The performance of Sullivan's *Cox and Box* at four o'clock that day seems, perhaps, incongruous.

Ernst Pauer, Ebenezer Prout, John Stainer, Franklin Taylor, Albert Visetti, and 'lady professors' in Signora Mazzucato and Edith Jerningham.

[31] Bowley died on 25 Aug; see *Grove 1*, vol. I, pp. 266–7.

Grove's election on 27 February 1871 to membership of the Athenaeum, for which Arthur Stanley and William Smith were sponsors, pleased many people, including Browning and Frederick Lehmann. His election was largely because of his biblical researches and the energy expended in request of the Palestine Exploration Fund. This was a continuing obligation and only a few months previously Grove had been delegated to ask Stanley to write a Preface to a volume of papers on Palestine by those most closely associated with the work.[32] Stanley for his part performed a useful service for music. As a boy he had become friendly with Jenny Lind, when she sang in Norwich where his father was Bishop. From her he learned to reverence Bach, so that in the spring of 1871 he arranged for a performance of the *St Matthew Passion* to take place in Westminster Abbey, as part of his policy to widen the scope of the influence of the place.

Throughout the early months of 1871 the thoughts of all European-minded people were directed to France, where, after the capitulation, civil strife was acute. Demonstrations, wanton destruction and sabotage, the rising and suppression of the Commune, a virtual reign of terror in Paris, appalled and distressed those who were either sensitive or visionary, even those who had rejoiced at the Prussian victory. In the January issue of *Macmillan's* Grove had published an article by Scott Russell on the state of France during the war. In the following May, together with William von Glehn, he went to Paris, where he met Sullivan and William Simpson, a war artist and newspaper correspondent. Grove was shocked by what he saw. Back in England he heard Julius Stockhausen sing lieder by Schubert, on 5 July, and two days later Brahms's *Requiem* for the first time. Both experiences made a deep impression.

At this time William von Glehn's sister Louise was thinking of going to live in Oxford for a year, believing that she might learn something. J. R. Green, however, thought she would do better by staying in Syden-ham, since Grove and other sages of the neighbourhood were better able to give her a broader view of life than anyone she was likely to meet in Oxford—except Max Müller, whom, Freeman suggested, she would not be likely to meet anyway.[33] Louise, however, knew her own mind. She went to Oxford, distinguished herself as an aesthete by sporting a yellow scarf and by attending Ruskin's lectures. At one of these she met Mandell Creighton, a young tutor, to whom she became engaged three weeks after their first meeting. The Mandell Creightons became firm friends of Grove, who admired their talents and envied them their happiness.

In this summer of 1871 Grove suffered acutely from depression. For the first part of his summer holiday, he went to Bonn for the Beet-

32 Letter of 25 May 1870; BL, Add. MS. 35227, f. 112.
33 Graves, p. 192.

hoven Festival, conducted by Hiller, and from the Rhineland he made
for Switzerland. At Lucerne on 31 August he copied out some passages
from Haydn's last String Quartet, in B flat (op. 103). A passage in one of
his notebooks, quoted by Graves, gives an insight into his state of
dejection. Looking out at the breath-taking mountain scenery from
the Brünig Pass, he commented: 'I am not sure but when one is in
these panic states one sees a great deal of beauty and gets a great deal
of feeling out of scenes and things that would pass unnoticed in rude
health.'[34]

He went on to Mürren in the Bernese Oberland, musing on Wordsworth and on Newman, the words of whose 'Lead kindly light' he wrote
into his commonplace book (RCM 2135). Years afterwards he recalled:

I have known that hymn for years and always recur [sic] to it when out of heart
or weary. It is intimately connected with one or two spots in Switzerland where
I have poured out my heart in that way which endears a place or a time more to
one than anything else does. It is so good, I think, to have a store of poetry in
one's recollection for such times.[35]

The commonplace book into which Grove's words were written was
an important companion for the next few years, and indicates a growing
concern with musical analysis, and in particular with the structural
procedures of Beethoven. From a full store of observations on carefully
chosen excerpts may be cited Grove's annotation of 'vacillation'
between major and minor tonality in the Pianoforte Sonata in B flat
(first movement), op. 22, canon and double counterpoint in the Second
Symphony, 'the mode of arriving at the 2nd subject' in movements of
the first three symphonies, repetition of motif in different movements of
the Second Symphony, and similarities of phrase structure in various
symphonies and overtures. Many of these notes were to find their way
ultimately into *Beethoven and his Nine Symphonies* (1896), either directly
or by way of programme notes.[36]

After his return from Switzerland in 1871, Grove again considered the
wisdom of ridding himself of the Crystal Palace appointment. He could,
he reckoned, survive financially if he did so and he would be able to do
more of the things he really wanted to do.[37] In the summer of 1872

[34] Ibid., p. 194.
[35] E.O., Sat. Aug 16 [1890].
[36] Grove moved nearer to a scientific scrutiny of the material of music as others were
proceeding in a different direction—as shown, for example, by Karl Mendelssohn's
Goethe und Mendelssohn (1872), which Mimi von Glehn was to translate and Grove to
edit. Herein, though none remarked it at the time and few (if any) since, was a purposeful
combination of music and politics.
[37] One of these was to write a geography primer. That a good one was needed was
clear; for few saw as did Grove—having learned this from Pritchard and Stanley—
that geography was an indispensable foundation for all humanistic studies. It was

Grove holidayed in Scotland, and in the following year he was once more in Germany.

He was at Bonn for the Schumann Festival, for which Joachim was responsible. Brahms was there and so too was Charles Villiers Stanford—with a sizeable Irish contingent. Clara Schumann's playing, the singing of Frau Joachim and of Stockhausen were inspiring. Grove was carried away by the *Faust* music, passages from which also went into his book. From Bonn he slowly went to Thuringia and into the countryside of the Bachs. 'I have', he wrote to Macmillan, 'come on here (slightly remote but well worth being at) on a visit to a friend of mine who is a grandee in these parts.'[38] Among the woodlands of the duchy of Saxe-Meiningen was the little watering place of Liebenstein, where the 'grandee', the Duke, had his summer palace, the Schloss Altenstein. The Baroness Heldburg, morganatic wife of the Duke, was a friend of the von Glehns through whom Grove had his first introduction to the family.

Meanwhile he had taken a firm decision in the matter of the Crystal Palace; after returning to England, his resignation as Secretary became effective. Though he remained significantly connected with the Palace, having been elected a Director in this year, he now began to turn himself towards what was to be his principal monument. A prospectus for a *Dictionary of Music and Musicians*, in two volumes, was issued in January 1874.

He had by now a great deal of musical experience behind him. He was acquainted with the leading musical figures of the day. He was a careful student, methodical in research and careful in analysis, a competent and shrewd editor, and a passable writer. And he had essays, written over many years, which could be turned into lexicographic entries at the drop of a pen.

As a writer, in an absolute sense, Grove is not to be reckoned among the greatest. He was neither profound nor particularly stylish, and his defects in respect of style were continually in his mind. His predecessors and some of his contemporaries in the field of musical criticism and journalism for the most part pursued literary elegance, often at the expense of veracity. The engineer in Grove always urged him to consider the exact measurements of a situation. He was dogged in the pursuit of facts. A prototypical late developer, he had neither intuition nor brilliance on which to depend; only the mass of material quarried from many repositories of learning, and tenacity of purpose. He wrote down all that he observed. But he had a genius for often seeing what others did not see, as well as a conviction that nothing was too insignificant to be

characteristic of him that in his *Dictionary* article on Schubert, an early footnote refers to his scrutiny of a large map of Vienna, of the right date, in the British Museum.
[38] Letter dated 'Saturday Aug 23 [1873]'; BL, Add. MS. 54793, f. 68.

written about. In his finest work—in the field of music, notably the biographies of Schubert, Mendelssohn and Beethoven—there are frequent touches of the commonplace which give a setting to what is generally taken to be genius. In a sense, it is from his commonplace qualities that Grove's own kind of genius, which finally rendered him the most influential figure in English musical literature, sprang.

CHAPTER SIX

The Editor's Chair

1867–1875

THE first issues of *Macmillan's Magazine* appeared on 1 November 1859, two months before Thackeray launched *The Cornhill*, with which for many years it maintained a rivalry. That *Macmillan's Magazine* was so called was due to David Masson, a friend of Alexander Macmillan. Masson was of the opinion that this title was to be preferred to the more pretentious *The Round Table*, Macmillan's first idea.

An Aberdonian and a friend of the Carlyles, Masson had edited educational works for William and Robert Chambers in Edinburgh before coming south to establish himself in London in literary and artistic circles. He belonged to a select group named 'our Club', where he met, among others, Thackeray, Douglas Jerrold, Charles Knight and Mark Lemon; D. G. Rossetti, Thomas Woolner and Holman Hunt were frequent guests at the house of his wife's art-loving parents. In 1853, in succession to A. H. Clough, Masson became Professor of English Literature at University College. The early harvests of his professorship produced popular critical works, *Essays . . . on English Poets* (1856) and *British Novelists and Their Styles* (1859); also in 1859, the year in which Macmillan invited him to undertake the editing of *Macmillan's Magazine*, appeared the first volume of the massive work on Milton by which he was to be chiefly remembered.

In preparation for the first issue of the magazine Masson and Macmillan went down to Farringford to receive Tennyson's blessing, made the more valuable by his offer of a new poem, 'Sea Dreams', for inclusion in it. On the way back, their way lying through Hampshire, they called on Charles Kingsley at Eversley.[1]

The character of *Macmillan's Magazine* was set by its first editor, a man of wide interests, by the philosophic enterprise of the publisher and by a strong radical influence. Hughes, Huxley, Ludlow, Maurice and Herbert Spencer, as well as F. T. Palgrave and D. M. Mulock (Mrs

---

[1] As it turned out, this was a fateful encounter, in that Kingsley's involvement with the magazine led in January 1864 to the famous review of Froude's *History of England* (vols. VII and VIII), in which he exposed in injudicious terms his mistrust of Catholic obscurantism. This spurred Newman to protest in response to which Kingsley published 'What, then, does Dr Newman mean?'. Newman's riposte to this was his *Apologia*.

Craik), were contributors to the first number, which also contained an article on British musical taste (signed 'M'=Masson?). Grove having been in the environs of the enterprise from the start, when Masson wished to devote himself to matters other than editing the magazine, was the natural successor. By the summer of 1867 it is clear that Grove was playing a major role in its policy and preparation. On 26 August, on the eve of his journey with Sullivan, he informed Macmillan that he would be going to Vienna probably on 1 October, and that he would be talking to Macmillan's partner, George Lillie Craik, about this.[2]

On 23 December Grove wrote to Macmillan that he had received from Mrs Tennyson '2 verses very pretty and strong—a sort of pendant to The Will ('O well for him')[3] being 'Wages', which was published in the February 1868 number of the magazine. In the same letter Grove asks that copies of the magazine should be sent to Hermann, son of Wilhelm Grimm; there is another reference to the Grimms in an undated letter of that time which shows how Grove's literary activities and his continuing Crystal Palace responsibilities in respect of programme notes were infringing on his domestic life:

... I got home to dinner at 8½ and have now 23 letters to write! And 4 pages (close print) description of the Symphony on Saturday—and a bag full of magazine things Hurra!
P.S. The enclosed unpublished letter from Walter Scott to one of the Grimms at Cassel has just been sent me by Hermann Grimm of Berlin who shewed it me when I was there. Would it do to reprint it in the Magazine or shall I send it to that beast Dixon [editor of the *Athenaeum*]? I think it would make a very nice little article for us. . . .[4]

Grove was perhaps most secure and happy within the domain of letters. Intellectually he was adaptable, as instanced by his transition from engineering to biblical research, and from both of those to music. Because of the width of his reading, and the limits he set on his own capabilities as a writer, he was well placed to be a good editor. He had an instinct for what was intrinsically interesting. He was exact without being censorious. He was encouraging and sympathetic without relinquishing refinement in discrimination. But his best recommendation to

---

[2] BL, Add. MS. 54793, f. 12. As postscript to this letter he referred to an ambitious project of his own, which he was never able fully to realize. 'David', he wrote, 'proceeds —but only slowly. We have had nieces with us who are a drawback to literature, however pleasant in themselves (and these *are* pleasant).' The nieces cannot be identified; a *Life of David*, a by-product of Grove's biblical researches, was thought about, in part sketched, but at this juncture laid aside.
[3] Ibid., f. 17.
[4] Ibid., f. 173. The brothers Grimm, of Kassel, were celebrated scholars, but best known for their *Kinder- und Hausmärchen*, or fairy-tales; the Scott letter in question was published in *Macmillan's* for February 1868.

a publisher was his complete dependability: if he promised copy for a particular day, it arrived on that day. When he took over *Macmillan's* from Masson at the beginning of 1868—at a beginning salary of £250 a year[5]—he went about his task with his usual formidable energy and conscientiousness. He also increasingly took on the role of a general literary adviser to Macmillan; and within the firm he was often able to counterpoint the brusqueness and occasional downright discourtesy of George Craik.[6]

The first volume of *Macmillan's* on which Grove's imprint is clear is that containing the middle issues of 1868. The year had opened with him constricted by lumbago—'the worst bout I have had for years', he wrote to Macmillan—and unable to go to Farringford to discuss with Tennyson the newly composed *Lucretius*. This work presented editor and publisher with a crisis to resolve. To have another opportunity to be the first to publish a major poem by the man generally esteemed to be the greatest living poet was not one lightly to lose, and Grove considered the event sufficiently important to warrant its advertisement in the *Athenaeum* and the *Pall Mall*. But Tennyson's treatment of the theme of the self-destruction of the Epicurean philosopher (on whom an unsigned scholarly article had appeared in *Macmillan's Magazine* in May 1865) under the influence of

> the Gods, who haunt
> The lucid interspace of world and world

was both passionate and pessimistic, providing additional evidence of a growing impatience with accepted interpretations. In essence, *Lucretius* is near to the spirit of Hardy (whose *The Poor Man and the Lady* and *Desperate Remedies*, of 1868 and 1871 respectively, were both rejected by Macmillan), but it was the directness of Tennyson's descriptive vocabulary that caused the head-scratching. Tennyson himself was on the point of withdrawing the poem from Macmillan, and only Grove's diplomacy prevented this.

'The subject is not pleasant', wrote Grove to George Bradley, a good friend of Tennyson, 'but it is a grand poem; one of the grandest of all his works.' However, it contained this passage:

[5] Arranged with George Craik, as stated in Grove's letter of 6 Mar 1868 to Macmillan; BL, Add. MS. 54793, f. 31.

[6] W. H. Stone, a physician at St Thomas's Hospital and an expert on wind instruments whose contributions to *Grove 1* were much valued by the editor, once called at Macmillan, by appointment, to see Grove. About to enter the premises by the side door, he was accosted by Craik and peremptorily ordered to the shop door. Stone was not pleased, but in his letter of protest to the firm he insisted that the 'utmost kindness and consideration' was always accorded him by Grove; S. Nowell-Smith, ed., *Letters to Macmillan* (1967), pp. 148-9.

And here an Oread—how the sun delights
To glance and shift about her slippery sides,
And rosy knees and supple roundedness,
And budded bosom-peaks—who this way runs
Before the rest—A satyr, a satyr, see,
Follows . . .

Not even the most liberal-minded of British editors and publishers
could let those lines pass, which represented 'that abandonment to
physical beauty which swayed the Pre-Raphaelite school . . .'[7] To do him
credit, Grove had his doubts about accepting Tennyson's reduction to

And here an Oread—and this way she runs—

and sought Masson's advice. Masson adjudicated from Edinburgh in
favour of the shortened version, concluding his letter: 'The poem is a
most powerful one—a strong rendering of a high and difficult idea
throughout, and with passages of large force. But I dare say it will not
pass without yelping on various sides.'[8] In respect of American publication of the poem by Ticknor and Fields, of Boston, Tennyson instructed
Grove to send them the 'full passage . . . they are not so squeamish as we
are'.

In his first editorial year Grove, secured by his wide range of intellectual
acquaintances, was engaged with Maurice, who wrote an essay on Baron
von Bunsen, for long the Prussian Ambassador in London, whose
memoirs had just appeared; with Scott Russell, who contributed articles
on 'Technical Education—a National Want', and 'Faraday';[9] and with
Harriet's brother, seventeen-year-old Andrew Bradley, 'a dear fellow'[10]
whose poem 'A Sea Shell' raised, in the author's mind at least, the hope
that he might become a poet. Mindful of his continuing concern for
exploration and for a due respect being paid to geography, Grove was
pleased to have a substantial article, published in serial form, from
Clements Markham, Secretary of the Royal Geographical Society,
superintendent of geographical work in the India Office, and official
geographer for Sir Robert Napier's punitive Abyssinian campaign.
Present at the capture of Magdala and discoverer of the slain body of

[7] A. Waugh, *Alfred, Lord Tennyson* (1902 ed.), p. 164.

[8] Nowell-Smith, op. cit., p. 114. The June 1868 number of *Macmillan's* contained an
appreciation of *Lucretius* by R. C. Jebb, then a young Fellow of Trinity College,
Cambridge.

[9] 'Thursday night' (Sept 1868) to Macmillan: 'I have asked [J.] Tyndall to do a life
of Faraday; and Huxley to send me some notes from Dundee. If he won't then I'll ask
[Archibald] Geikie for a résumé of his lecture'; BL, Add. MS. 54793, f. 21.

[10] E.O. Monday night [April 1894]. In 1871 Andrew [Cecil] Bradley's hopes of
becoming a poet were dashed by Macmillan's rejection of a volume of his verses. He
did, however, become a distinguished Shakespearean scholar and critic.

the Emperor Theodore, Markham was able to write authoritatively on
'The Abyssinian Expedition'.[11] Macmillan and Grove shared a belief in
the efficacy of education and the August issue contained 'Primary Education, Suggestions on, and a Short Notice of the Method of Teaching
Reading and Writing in Germany', signed by 'A.J.C.' [A. J. Carver,
Headmaster of Dulwich College?]. Still on the side of social responsibility, an article by F.W.F[arrar] on 'The Wounded Soldier in Modern
Warfare' took up where Florence Nightingale had left off, at the
same time pleading for a saner method of solving problems between
nations.

J. R. Seeley, who was shortly to succeed Kingsley as Professor of
Modern History at Cambridge, and whose humanistic life of Christ,
Ecce Homo, had caused a tumult of controversy in 1865, was an early
contributor under Grove's regimen; his essay on 'Milton's Poetry' was
published in vol. XIX. In the same volume was Matthew Arnold's
'On the Modern Element in Literature'; Grove 'knew Arnold pretty well'
and was charmed by his 'warmth of affection to his mother, sister, and
child'.[12] Among other contributors Grove welcomed Thomas Huxley,
whose concern for wider educational opportunity stimulated him in
1868 to offer for publication one of his lectures 'for Working Men';
Charlotte M. Yonge, adviser to Macmillan on devotional and children's
books;[13] and Harriet Beecher Stowe. Macmillan could not be criticized
for failure to consider female talent; Craik's wife, Diana Marian Mulock,
author of *John Halifax, Gentleman*, was a profitable part of the firm, and
in addition to those already named, George Eliot, Annie Keary, Frances
Martin and Mimi von Glehn (as translator) became valuable collaborators.
Among early musical contributors were Joseph Bennett and John Hullah,
whose essays are noticed in chapter 7.

Macmillan's Magazine was designed for family reading, and for profit.
In a letter (not otherwise dated) of 1868 Grove informed Macmillan
of a 'pleasant set-off to The Spectator's bile' from Thackeray's sister. He
reacted in reassuring terms to a gloomy prognosis concerning the business
side: 'Cheer up, old man', he wrote, 'we shall beat the Spectator, and all
the other 'ators and get up to 20,000 a month yet, and that by fair means.'[14]
Part of the policy was protection of female interests, and also of the ideal
of virtue. Charlotte May Yonge was one who was capable of adding a

[11] *Macmillan's* XVII, March 1868, p. 435. In August of that year Grove was present
at the British Association meeting at Norwich where Markham read a paper 'On the
Physical Geography of the Portion of Abyssinia Traversed by the English Expeditionary
Force'; see *Athenaeum*, 29 Aug 1868, p. 279.
[12] E.O., Monday evg. Dec 8 [1895].
[13] Miss Yonge had two serials running in *Macmillan's* at the same time, though neither
was directly attributed. *Realmah*, 'by the author of *Friends in Council*', and a *Chaplet
of Pearls*, 'by the author of *The Heir of Redclyffe*', were both by her.
[14] BL, Add. MS. 54793, f. 51.

not uninfluential voice to the chorus of those who were beginning to ask for female emancipation—albeit in moderation. In an essay on 'Children's Literature of the Last Century' in vol. XX of *Macmillan's* she produced an epigram which is still pertinent: 'Our own private theory is that we ought to *teach* girls less, while we should encourage them to *learn* more.' As editor of the Sunday Library, Miss Yonge urged the need for understanding how—in respect of the geography and history of the lands of the Bible—children's interests could best be aroused; certainly not, she protested, by cutting up chunks of travellers' tales and stringing them together. Annie Keary, a sensitive and perceptive writer, she thought to be an ideal contributor to her series, and so did Grove. Miss Yonge, whose *Monthly Packet* was primarily an exposition of High Church doctrine, needed to be balanced by Frances Martin, a radical Christian of the Maurice school and founder of the College of Working Women, who also became editor of the Sunday Library.

The years in which Grove was principally occupied with *Macmillan's Magazine* were of great political significance. On 7 December 1869 after a week's 'writhing' with a 'violent colic' he wrote his intentions for the coming issues, which would include contributions on Admiralty reform, and the Irish Land Question (in which Grove in later years was quite fortuitously to become entangled); but regarding another issue he surmised, 'the Public will have quite enough of the Suez Canal long before February.' Some time later he questioned the propriety of the article on the Admiralty as it stood. 'I have', he wrote, 'been re-reading [it] and the only thing I can take exception to is the paragraph about the resistance of the officials which perhaps is too personal in tone.'[15]

On 19 July 1870 the French government declared war on Prussia and two days later Grove wrote to Macmillan about the possibility of an article for *Macmillan's*—political rather than cultural—either from H. M. Hozier or Colonel Charles Chesney:

I hesitate about asking Hozier because the line I would like to take would be one which I think he would not take. I want to draw the lesson from war of what a wicked and costly proceeding it is and how much the drama of it would be lessened if the men of the world understood how much misery it brings and how much of their money it spends.

Now Hozier, who is a more sharp clever (very clever) soldier will not take that line while I think Chesney will take it or some similar line—certainly he will if he wrote the article in the Pall Mall of Monday.

I hope you will agree with me—our [the magazine's] character is very good and I think we may take a high line before Christian men with advantage both to our consciences and our Magazine.[16]

[15] Ibid., f. 54.
[16] Ibid., f. 60. Charles Cornwallis Chesney, whose 'Waterloo Lectures:

Grove had been in Paris in the aftermath of the 1848 revolution. In August 1870, fearful of the consequences of the new outbreak of hostilities, he visited the city briefly, in the company of C. A. Fyffe. A Balliol man who was Paris correspondent of the *Daily News*, Fyffe had been taken by Grove, with Sullivan, to dine with Alexander Macmillan six months previously.

The Franco-Prussian War was a severe test for Grove, who deplored war on principle, but he was aware that the unity of Germany was a consummation to be wished for by many for whom he had a high regard, as the realization of a national cultural development. In respect of music Grove had one view, in regard to politics another. He published in *Macmillan's* an article by Seeley of which the theme was the need for a 'United States of Europe'. Prophetically Seeley proclaimed: 'I infer that we shall never abolish war in Europe unless we can make up our minds to take up a completely new citizenship. We must cease to be mere Englishmen, Frenchmen, Germans, and must begin to take as much pride in calling ourselves Europeans.'[17] No one, of course, could complain that Grove was other than a good European; indeed, it was said about the Crystal Palace programmes that they favoured foreign performers, and it was to be said later—when Grove was endowed with special responsibility in this respect at the Royal College of Music—that he had too little concern for British composers.

The age was one in which historians enjoyed special prestige. As well as Seeley, whose understanding of contemporary values was expressed serially in 'The English Revolution of the Nineteenth Century' (vol. XXII), Grove also accommodated E. A. Freeman, J. R. Green, W. E. H. Lecky and Mandell Creighton whose *Macmillan's* articles on Pope Pius II were a worthy prelude to his greater works. History as a foundation for politics was becoming increasingly dialectical, and historians more and more inclined to mutual dislike. J. A. Froude, at the time editor of *Fraser's Magazine*, published the last volume of his *History of England* in 1870. Freeman castigated Froude's inaccuracies in 'The Use of Historical Documents'—ostensibly an article on William Stubbs as historian—which was published in the *Fortnightly Review* (September 1871) after having been rejected by Grove. Not wishing to offend either Froude or Freeman, Grove at this point forgot his talent for diplomacy:

---

a Study of the Campaign of 1815' were popular in 1868 (see *Athenaeum*, 5 Dec), was the author of *The Military Resources of Prussia and France* (1870). The Government sent him to France to report on the Franco-Prussian War. Henry Montague Hozier was the author of *The Franco-Prussian War*, 2 vols. (1870-2).

[17] *Macmillan's* XXIII, March 1871, p. 436; based on a lecture delivered to the Peace Society.

August 17, 1871

My dear Freeman:

Thank you for yours of the 9th which should have been answered before, but for the business of the C[rystal] P[alace].

I am sorry to differ so radically about personalities—to me the paper seems more or less permeated with them—you assume throughout that because, in your opinion, Froude is inaccurate, therefore he is so of design and malice, and is an imposter. A kind of Procrustean rule that is intolerable—at any rate cannot be allowed in Macmillans magazine as long as I am Editor.

I am sure you will pardon my saying that I think this line of conduct always more or less likely to defeat itself. In this particular instance I know that my sympathies for Froude and Stanley have been very much quickened and increased by the strong personal animosity displayed in the articles. I am sure that the same thing has happened to hundreds of others. It is intolerable that scholars and gentlemen are to be browbeaten and abused because they hold their own opinion on certain points.

With regard to this article I should very much regret not having it because half of it seems to me so very good, and because I respect Stubbs and wish the world to know how good and great he is, but the portions of which I complain must come out.

I am just off to the Continent,

Yours . . .
G. Grove.[18]

Freeman was very angry, and—one of the few people ever to utter a word of criticism of Grove—he expressed his feelings to Macmillan in this ferocious manner:

Grove evidently does not know that there is such a thing as truth. He thinks that every protest in its name is a sign of 'personal animosity', as if Froude or Stanley were of any consequence to me personally. He thinks that careless and culpable blundering is matter of 'opinion'. As for what 'permeated' may mean—that I leave to the editor of the *Daily Telegraph*. The man is simply insolent. I am ready to hear anything from you, but no more dealings with him.[19]

Froude's sins of omission and commission did not, however, escape rebuke in *Macmillan's*, for the arguments continued in the first volume of *The English in Ireland in the Eighteenth Century* were harshly refuted by Lecky in 'Mr Froude's English in Ireland'.[20] Because of the Disestablishment of the Church of Ireland and the Land Act of 1870 Ireland was once more at the centre of political consideration. Lecky, a young alumnus of Trinity College, Dublin, had risen meteorically in the literary world, through his *History of Rationalism* (1865) and *History of European Morals* (1870).[21] A contemporary of Lecky at Trinity College, also soon

[18] BL, Add. MS. 54793, f. 62.
[19] Nowell-Smith, op. cit., p. 125.
[20] *Macmillan's* XXVII, January 1873, p. 246.
[21] See R. H. Hutton, 'A Questionable Parentage for Morals', *Macmillan's* XX, July 1869, p. 266.

to become a contributor on various subjects to *Macmillan's*, was J. P. Mahaffy, the most talkative and versatile Irish scholar of his time.

Two pieces, classics of their kind, which Grove sponsored were J. R. Green's lengthy disquisition on 'The Development of the Common Law' and James Fergusson's essay on Street's new Law Courts.[22] The former was significant because it aimed to make intelligible for the plain man what otherwise appeared as a mass of obfuscation; the latter because it called for a new approach to architecture. Street, Fergusson deplored, in 'choosing to devote his undoubted talents to reproduce the art and fashion of the 13th century is resolutely shutting his eyes to the fact that we are living in the 19th.'

Sociological issues were entrusted to the old firm, as it were. The voice of Thomas Arnold was echoed by many contributors, in particular by Tom Hughes and Matthew Arnold. The latter, whose *Thyrsis* was published for the first time in the magazine in 1866, sometimes appeared in his capacity as Inspector of Schools to show how idealism nurtured in the confines of Rugby was chastened by experiences in the wide world, and by the reality of attempting to evolve a universal system. There is a fine passage which bears on our own age in an address given by Arnold in 1873 to the Association of Public Elementary Teachers and later published in the magazine: 'We must be patient, however; things cannot move as fast as our wishes would have them move. Our schools will not in our lifetime be what we could wish to see them. We shall not live to do more than a very small part of what has to be done for them.'[23]

Grove kept up with his biblical-geographical studies, and on the practical side there was a continuing interest in the Palestine Exploration Fund. From time to time he solicited Layard's aid in bringing Foreign Office pressure to bear on other governments. On 12 October 1871 he sent a note to Layard, expressing the hope that Lord Granville might be able to persuade the French to allow Clermont Ganneau, formerly a dragoman in the French Consulate in Jerusalem, a sabbatical year in order to help with the excavations. Two years later Grove sought Layard's permission for the reproduction of one of his illustrations from *Discoveries in the Ruins of Nineveh and Babylon* (1853) in Samuel Sidney's *The Book of the Horse* (1873–5).[24] All this time Smith's *Ancient Atlas* had been going forward, to appear in 1874, where it was told how the impulses

[22] For Green, see *Macmillan's* XXIV, August 1871, p. 287; for Fergusson, ibid. XXV, January 1872, p. 250.

[23] *Macmillan's* XXIX, 1873–4, p. 361; the lecture was given at the Westminster Training College on 6 Dec 1873.

[24] Sidney was the nom de plume of Samuel Solomon (1813–83), a versatile writer with interests ranging from railway engineering to emigration. In 1851 he was an Assistant Commissioner for the Great Exhibition and later sometime Assistant Secretary to the Crystal Palace Company.

from Robinson's researches of the 1830s and Stanley's enthusiasm had led to the ordnance survey of Jerusalem and then to the Palestine and Sinai Exploration Societies. At this time, as Grove mentioned in his letters to *The Times*, the military team working in Palestine was led by C. R. Conder, who became a respected scholar in this area of archaeological research. In the summer of 1874 his assistant was Herbert Horatio Kitchener—in due course to become a Field Marshal, whose influence on history derived not a little from the knowledge gained as a young lieutenant under Conder's supervision.[25]

Also among Grove's acquaintances at this time was the Leipzig publisher Tauchnitz, whom he had met during his 1867 tour in Germany. In 1869 the thousandth volume in Tauchnitz's Collection of British Authors had appeared in the form of an annotated edition of the New Testament by Professor Tischendorf, of which Grove wrote a substantial review in *Macmillan's*. Covering a great deal of scholarly ground with an enviable suggestion of familiarity, he discussed Tischendorf's use of Vatican, Alexandrine and Sinaitic codices with particular authority.

Examination of this edition may to some extent have influenced Grove's transition from faith to scepticism. He noted that some of the best-known quotations from the New Testament were the result of fortuitous misapprehension, and correction by persons far removed in time from the apostolic age. Then there were the additions—'those', wrote Grove, 'which contain some of the most characteristic and "Christian" sentiments in the whole of the New Testament'. Since he had perpetually to wrestle on his own account with one aspect of sin (as it was then understood), it is not surprising—although it may have appeared so at the time—that Grove chose to illuminate the case in this manner:

There are few who, if asked to name the incident which most clearly embodied the justice, mercy, and tenderness of Christ and supplied us with the most precious traits of his personal manners, would not quote the story of the woman taken in adultery. And yet there can be little doubt that this story did not exist in the original Gospel, in fact, did not make its appearance in any edition before the middle of the 5th century.

While claiming for himself in this field no more of authority than was allowable to an informed layman (here he tends at times to confuse himself), Grove's sense of stern discipline brought him to a conclusion which has relevance to the scholarly appreciation of source material in general, and to methods profitably applied to musical research. He suggested that the reader should mark passages in the New Testament

[25] How hazardous archaeological research then was is illustrated by the fact that in 1875 both Conder and Kitchener, as well as others in their party, narrowly escaped death after being ambushed in the hills north-west of the Sea of Galilee. Later in that year Grove had a first-hand account of the affair from Kitchener.

which were not to be found in the three named codices—or at least in two of them:

And if at first the phrases seem balder and the sentences less fluent and abrupter than before, he will find these deficiencies made up for by greater life and greater reality, and will have the satisfaction of knowing that he has come much closer to the original of a document which all must desire to possess as nearly as possible in its original form, and has caught a trifle less faintly the echoes of that divine voice, for the tones of which men were never more eagerly listening than they are now.[26]

The end of the passage is a reminder that Grove was closely associated with two Deans of Westminster, Stanley and Bradley, for both of whom he had the greatest respect.

On 12 May 1873 Emanuel Deutsch, a friend for whom Grove felt a particularly strong affection, died of cancer at Alexandria. Born in Silesia, educated by an uncle who was a rabbi, Deutsch had a brilliant career in the University of Berlin and early distinguished himself in Hebrew, classical, theological and German scholarship. He was not only a fine scholar but a fine writer, capable of infusing his poetry and fiction with a charming romantic fancy, and his more serious works with a gravity unallied to dullness. Very much a Grove man, Deutsch contributed to the Bible *Dictionary*. But his outstanding work of scholarship was a paper on the Talmud published in the *Quarterly Review* of October 1867.[27] Soon after his death the *Edinburgh Review*, true to its tradition of severity, offended Grove's sense of propriety and also of justice by setting beside Deutsch's acknowledged brilliance an alleged 'superficiality' in exposition.

On 21 July, while at Wildbad during his summer holiday, Grove wrote a noble rebuke to the *Edinburgh Review* which was published in the August issue of his own magazine. He felt particularly strongly about this matter, for Deutsch, living nearby in Sydenham, as he worked on his *Quarterly Review* essay had discussed it in detail with Grove. Superficiality, said Grove, signified the omission of such infelicities as 'repulsive Hebrew terms in inadequate English dress' and a '*catalogue raisonné*. . . . well stuffed with names and references'. In rehearsing Deutsch's qualities Grove stated his own ideals and in his comment are principles which inspired the *Dictionary of Music*:

Let a man write a book or an article for which the ordinary world is grateful; which shall make some obscure unknown subject plain to the general reader,

---

[26] *Macmillan's* XX, May–October 1869, pp. 428–32.

[27] 'The author of the glorious article on the Talmud', George Eliot noted, 'is "that bright little man" Mr Deutsch—a very dear, delightful creature'; letter to Mme Bodichon, 9 Dec 1867, quoted in *George Eliot's Life . . . in her Letters and Journals*, ed. J. W. Cross (1885), p. 418. It was from Deutsch that George Eliot learned Hebrew.

shall set all its difficulties in broad daylight and bring out its connexions in many
an unexpected point with things already familiar to us; let him, in a word, show
that learning is with him not an end but a means to an end—and one is at once
assailed by the owls of literature, who because they cannot themselves fly in the
sunlight would fain prevent others from doing so.

The accusations levelled at Deutsch were also, commented Grove,
heard in respect of Stanley. Like Stanley (though not to the same extent)
Deutsch committed the cardinal sin of achieving popularity, the copies
of the *Quarterly* carrying the article left out in the *Athenaeum* for the use
of members being said—somewhat unflatteringly—'to have been black
with finger-marks'.

Deutsch had spent his last days in Egypt, vainly seeking recovery.
Discovered by friends still labouring amid his books and his notes, he
was not to finish the 'great work' on which he had set his sights. Grove
orchestrated the coda of his tribute richly:

> He has left no successor. Great Hebrew scholars there will always be; but the
> rabbinical department of the language has attractions for few, and many a
> generation must pass without seeing again that special union of scholarship and
> poetic insight, combined with an unusually wide range of general knowledge,
> and with a devotion to the literature and the memories of this nation almost like
> the fervent love of a son to his mother, which made Mr Deutsch's short career
> so remarkable.[28]

Grove's championship of Deutsch is one of the outstandingly generous
acts of his life; it came not only from a deep well of affection but also
from a perceptive conviction that the ideals held by Deutsch were of
significance to the world.[29]

During his first phase of editorship Grove was affected by the deaths
of two other friends who had considerably influenced his development:
Maurice and Kingsley. Kingsley, then being a Canon of Chester, wrote

[28] *Macmillan's* XXVIII, August 1873, p. 382.

[29] Deutsch was one of the first—if not the first—among Jews in Britain to promote
the ideal of a national home in Palestine. When George Eliot published *Daniel Deronda*
Grove (who had taken her *Jubal* for *Macmillan's* in 1870) wrote to her that it made him
think 'of our dear Deutsch'. He had in mind particularly the portrayal of Mordecai in
chapters 42 and 43 (Book VI). That *Daniel Deronda* met with disapproval, even hostility,
from others besides George Saintsbury in his *A History of Nineteenth Century Literature*
was not unexpected. George Eliot remarked in a letter to Harriet Beecher Stowe how,
'Not only towards the Jews, but towards all Oriental peoples with whom we English
come into contact, a spirit of arrogance and contemptuous dictatorialness is observed
which has become a national disgrace to us.' In *Macmillan's*, in May 1877, appeared
' "Mordecai: A protest against the Critics", by a Jew (Joseph Jacobs)', in which the
honour of Deutsch and of George Eliot too was eloquently upheld: 'But surely the
critics had no occasion to doubt the possibility of a Jew like Mordecai at a time when we
still mourn the loss of one who laid down his life for the regeneration of our views of
Israel, just as Mordecai sacrificed his for the elevation of our hopes of Israel's future.'

the obituary of Maurice for the May 1872 issue of *Macmillan's*. Here
with a concern for common humanity is depicted the idealist, the scholar
and the rebel.

If any man is in search of a mere philosophy let him beware of Mr Maurice's
books, lest, while searching merely for 'thoughts that breathe', he should
stumble upon 'words that burn', and were meant to burn. His books, like himself, are full of that θυμός [soul], that capacity of indignation, which Plato says
is the root of all virtues.[30]

It was the 'Divine discontent' of Maurice, that source of self-criticism
rooted in idealism, but shaped by daily experience, that also distinguished
Kingsley. He died at the beginning of 1875, and the notice contributed to
Macmillan's by A[rthur] H[elps] contained this apostrophe to his kind
of *saeva indignatio*: 'He was, if one may use the word, tempestuous in
his indignation when any conduct that was *per se*, mean, or cowardly
(he could not endure a coward) was brought before him. On the other
hand he was tolerant as regards the ordinary frailties of mankind.'[31]

At this point a new writer made his appearance in *Macmillan's*. In
May 1875 six poems, somewhat after Meredith in applying a humanistic
philosophy to lyrical themes, were published under the title *A Sequence
of Analogies*. Their author, 'C.H.H.P.', was a young man who was a
pupil of Dannreuther[32] and a frequenter of the Crystal Palace concerts.
Recognizing fresh talent, Grove gave Hubert Parry, who was thus
modestly introduced to the world as a poet, an opportunity not only to see
his verses in print, but also to get to grips with the serious matter of
musical scholarship. By the autumn of 1875 Parry was busily occupied
in helping Grove in the first stages of the most ambitious undertaking
of his life.

[30] *Macmillan's* XXVI, May 1872, p. 84.
[31] Ibid. XXXI, February 1875, p. 376. Sir Arthur Helps (1813–75), a distinguished
civil servant, was a friend of Hullah, Kingsley and Grove, and had previously contributed
to *Macmillan's Magazine*. He died less than two months after Kingsley.
[32] 'From 1874 to 1880 [Parry] studied with Edward Dannreuther, wisest and most
sympathetic of teachers, who realised at once that his pupil was a man of genius and
gave him a free hand'; W. H. Hadow, 'Sir Hubert Parry', in *Collected Essays* (1928),
p. 153.

CHAPTER SEVEN

Towards *Grove I*

1874-1878

IN retrospect it may be said that Grove's whole life was directed towards the production of *A Dictionary of Music and Musicians*. In an age of lexicography music was the one area in which the needs of the times had not adequately been met. Of musical scholars and critics there was by 1874 no dearth, but what was required to make the most effective use of them was the genius for organization which Grove had shown himself in so many ways to possess. During his first editorial years with Macmillan he had never been far away from musical affairs, and the accumulation of ideas that came to him from his own musical experience, from his thousands of words of commentary on Manns's programmes, and from his relentless pursuit of information concerning his heroes enabled him to persuade Macmillan, at the beginning of January 1874, to announce the intention to furnish the musical reader with a compendium of two volumes, each of about 600 pages,

from which an intelligent enquirer can learn, in small compass, and in language which he can understand, what is meant by a Symphony or Sonata, a Fugue, a Stretto, a Coda, or any other of the technical terms which necessarily occur in every description or analysis of a concert or a piece of music; or from which he can gain a readable and succinct account of the history of the various branches of the art, or of the use and progress of the pianoforte, and other instruments, or the main facts and characteristics of the lives of eminent musicians.[1]

Just at this time, however, when Grove wished to be able to concentrate on the new undertaking which was uppermost in his mind, there was a hint of a rift in the Manns–Grove partnership. Grove's anxiety that

---

[1] Preface to *Grove I*, dated 1 Apr 1879. There were eventually four volumes, 3125 pages in all, and an Index of 188 pages. The Prospectus issued by Macmillan in 1874 underlined the need for such a compendium:

The want of English works on the history, theory, or practice of Music, or the biographies of musicians accessible to the non-professional reader, has long been a subject of remark. The 'Biographical Dictionary of Musicians', the latest English book of the kind, was published in 1827, and even for that date is very incomplete. Dr Callcott's 'Grammar of Music', though issued in 1817, is the latest attempt to give a general account of the form and terms of the art in a popular style. But to Dr Callcott modern instrumental music was (naturally) a *terra incognita*—the name of Beethoven occurs only once in the entire volume.

his old friend should not feel relegated to a subsidiary role in the Crystal
Palace concerts is expressed in a letter to Joseph Bennett:

Private   January 30th 1874
Dear Bennett:
I want to ask a kindness from you—Manns is in a terrible state of grief owing to
various remarks in the Papers recently which seem to give *me more* credit than
is due—or rather to give *him less*—in reference to the Saturday Concerts.

He urges that I am spoken of as if the choice of the programmes, and the
excellence of the execution, and the entire success of the concerts, were due to
me—I can't see the inference, but he does, and is terribly hurt and distressed.
He is over-sensitive,—but on the other hand he is so able and devoted, and has
done so much more for music than any conductor that I have ever had to do
with in England that I should be very glad if he could be relieved in some way.
He urges me to write to the Papers, but this I am determined not to do. But it
occurs to me that you could easily say something in your next notice which would
heal the wound, and I am sure you will be glad to do so both for my sake and his
—I am writing to [Desmond] Ryan [junior] and J.W.D[avison] in the same
spirit.

Ever yours
G. Grove[2]

When the mollification of Manns had been accomplished Grove went
into the matter of a new contract with Macmillan, and on 26 February
a comprehensive agreement was drawn up with the firm, which assured
Grove annually of (1) £300, as editor of *Macmillan's Magazine*, (2) £600,
for 'managing the literary side of their business', and (3) a guarantee of
£400 per annum in the event of profits from the sale of books or series
of which he was editor or compiler not amounting to that sum in any
one year. The agreement[3] was for seven years. Immediately he began to
draft subject-headings for the *Dictionary* and to give thought to the matter
of contributors. Craik was the arbiter on the business side, while George
Macmillan, Alexander's son, now on the point of leaving Eton, being
musical was also to be associated with the administrative side of the
project.

For many years Grove had been hoarding both ideas and material (he
was not among those who thought the insubstantiality of the former to
be sufficient in itself) as for an encyclopedic work. Editorially he had
proved himself to be much more than merely competent with his handling
of the *Bible Dictionary* and the wider areas of *Macmillan's Magazine*.
In one of the earliest numbers of the latter under his editorship he had
taken 'a capital article on "The Messiah"—that is Handel's oratorio

---

[2] The original of the letter is in the PML. Bennett published it in *Forty Years of
Music 1865–1905* (op. cit., p. 117), but misread the unclear writing to give it a date of
1876 in error.
[3] BL, Add. MS. 54793, f. 74.

thereof à propos of a very curious facsimile of the original MS which has just been published, that I think will be very interesting'.[4] This article was by Joseph Bennett, who was also hoping at that time that Grove would commission from him an article on 'Cathedral Choirs'; but this was not a subject which rated high in Grove's scale of values, and the article never appeared. Bennett, having retired from the practice of music to pursue its criticism, was grateful for Grove's interest at this time and was to become a friend. Next year John Hullah, pioneer in both popular education and musicology, sent in a piece on 'Popular Songs of the Last Century', which to Grove's chagrin had to be shortened to accommodate an essay which interested him much less, by a Scottish divine, Hugh Macmillan (no relation to the firm). The admirable and lovable Hullah, well known to the Sydenham intellectuals, was an old acquaintance of Grove. Both Hullah and Bennett were among the contributors to the *Dictionary*.

But larger items came under consideration. On 20 February 1868 Grove had written to Macmillan: '. . . I have just received from Vienna, from a German friend of mine well known in musico-literary circles— a little book of his (small 8vo 180 pages) on "Mozart in London" giving an account of his visit in 1764 as well as a very curious and minute picture of musical London at that date.'[5] Of even more interest was Jahn's great study of Mozart, of which Henry Nettleship, a musical Germanophile and a master at Harrow, had now promised a translation. Grove was disinclined to place much reliance on intentions which were unsubstantiated. He wrote to Macmillan as follows:

Nettleship's Mozart. I have not seen any of this—indeed N has always spoken as if a line were not written—and I think it would be adviseable [*sic*] for you to ask to see a Chapter or two before making your final decision. The book, if well done, would be a good one and command a long steady sale—not large but permanent—because Jahn's book contains *everything* about the man and the subject and only requires judicious compression and rewriting in good lively English. . . .[6]

Even more absorbing at this time was the subject of Mendelssohn. As a result of a lecture given in Freiburg (im Breisgau) by his elder son Karl, Professor of History in the University there, in celebration of the establishment of the German Empire, *Goethe und Mendelssohn*—an

[4] Ibid., f. 48. Bennett's article was published in *Macmillan's* XVIII, August 1868, pp. 328f.

[5] i.e. C. F. Pohl, *Mozart und Haydn in London* (Vienna, 1867).

[6] Grove's letter bore no date. Jahn's *W. A. Mozart* was published in Leipzig by Breitkopf & Härtel in 1856-9 (4 vols.) and 1862 (2 vols.) When the book did at last appear in English (in 3 vols., with a Preface by Grove), the translation was not the work of Nettleship. See above, p. 101.

expansion of the lecture—was given to Mimi von Glehn to translate. Regarding the copyright of the book, Grove advised Craik that a payment in the region of £7–£10 should be made to Mendelssohn, in token of the firm's wish 'to do justice to his father's memory' and their gratitude for the help given by him and his sister, Marie Benecke, in regard to the translation. The next year, Ferdinand Hiller's *Letters and Recollections of Mendelssohn* (also in Mimi von Glehn's translation) began to be serialized in *Macmillan's Magazine*, afterwards coming from Macmillan in book form. In his Preface Grove lamented the recent death of Paul Mendelssohn, the composer's brother.

Grove worshipped Mendelssohn only just this side of idolatry and he rarely lost an opportunity of promoting his cause. He was fascinated by the variety of Mendelssohn's accomplishments and by his social graces, and he was friendly with many members of the Mendelssohn family. In 1871 he had published letters taken from a recently issued collection[7] and put two communications from Mendelssohn to Julius Maier of Freiburg into a Crystal Palace programme. The second of these letters, from Interlaken, at the end of July 1847, has a plangent character, being from one near death yet, in another sense, full of life.

Another kind of sadness attaches to a letter of 21 October 1873 which Grove received from George Macfarren. Despatched from the Royal Hotel, Bristol, this was in the hand of an amanuensis, Macfarren by now being virtually totally blind. Grove had sent one of his essays for Macfarren's observations; as always he was anxious to be precise in what he wrote. The reply began:

My dear Grove:

Your singlicate came never to hand but the duplicate arrived safely and the hearing of the article on the A minor ['Scotch' Symphony] made the journey hither truly interesting. I have always told you how capital was the infection of your enthusiasm and I never felt it to better advantage. I have personal knowledge of some incidents in the Symphony's history which in order to define some lines which are wavy in your account I will repeat. . . .

Whereupon Macfarren proceeded to set down, through his amanuensis, his very precise and full recollections of the Symphony's first performance in England, under the composer's baton, at a Philharmonic concert on 13 June 1842.[8]

---

[7] *Acht Briefe und eine Facsimile von Felix Mendelssohn-Bartholdy. Zum besten der deutschen Invaliden-Stiftung* (Leipzig/Grünow, 1871).

[8] 'M.', wrote Macfarren, 'was most pertinacious in adhering to his own prescription against stops between the movements and thus went ever so far into the Adagio (I would say 40 or 50 bars to any one of less accuracy than you in bar counting), whereof never a note was heard by reason of the applause to the Scherzo. But at length in spite of himself he broke off and repeated the Scherzo but then went on to the end with no stop. Save

Communications of this kind, linking past with present, were invaluable in enabling Grove to imbue his writing with a special quality of veracity. Nowhere is this more evident than in what he communicates concerning Mendelssohn, whom he admired so greatly. On 9 June 1874, therefore, he was pleased to take his place on the committee of the Mendelssohn Scholarship Foundation, the other members of which were Benedict, Goldschmidt, Hullah, Leslie, Julian Marshall, Kellow J. Pye, Stainer and Sullivan.

On 10 July 1874 Grove wrote to John Ella:

Dear Ella:
Thank you for your congratulations and all the good wishes. My book is a Dictionary of Music, including biographies. . . . Don't you think Alex[andra] Palace will beat C.P., but serve neighbourhood.
I have got your Sketches and will look at the chit-chat you mention. I agree with you that musical criticism is at a very low ebb here, but so it is surely everywhere. I get most of the German and French papers and except Hanslick or an occasional letter by Hiller it is all bad—and so it has always been. . . .
The *trees* of my *grove* are hardly saplings now—one 18—just leaving school and the others 16, 13, 11 . . .[9]

The *Dictionary* was to be a principal concern for the next nine years, but Grove's lesser obligations were more than those which would occupy a normal man. He was not a normal man, however, and the intensity to which he drove himself increasingly brought him to the edge of nervous disaster. The pressure under which he laboured was such that he had occasionally to let someone know the truth. He was generally supported by extreme pride combined with punctilious observance of contractual obligations, but was sometimes placed in a difficult position because of an inability to refuse a commission, or a request from a friend. In 1875 Joseph Bennett commenced a weekly journal, *Concordia*, which was to combine discussion of all the arts, for Novello. As had been the case with the *Shilling Magazine* a decade before, the timing was unfortunate, and like the *Shilling Magazine* the *Concordia* died after little more than a

---

for this interuption [*sic*] there was no applause at ends of movements till the conclusion. M. showed me the autograph—it was an 8vo book bound in blue silk, I think watered, and lettered in silver on the side "Cecile". His wife he said had asked him to write something for *her* so he had had this vol. bound and fronted with her name wherein to put it on paper . . .'; BL, 7898.o.12 (vol. 2), written in pencil.

[9] BL, Add. MS. 42233, f. 2. The Alexandra Palace, intended as a North London counterpart to the Crystal Palace, was opened in 1873. Ella's *Musical Sketches at Home and Abroad*, largely based on his programme notes, had been published in 1869.

Walter Maurice Grove had been a pupil at Marlborough College since January 1873. Grove went to the school Speech Day shortly after writing to Ella, but Walter did not leave school for another year.

year. One of Bennett's difficulties was that the people he would have liked to be contributors were already well occupied. It would appear to be in respect of this that Grove, who had had a Prospectus and had been made aware of the scheme by Henry Littleton, the owner of Novello, wrote to him:

I would do anything to help you, my dear old fellow but I really ought not to have my name put down. I have 3 books to write for my Firm and until I have done them must hold my hand from outside work. I am obliged carefully to keep the real nature of even my Saturday Programme work from my Chief [Craik] or he would kick and that reasonably enough at the strain it is on my power. I should not like working with Haweis I confess. I have a thoro' contempt for him as far as manliness and morality are concerned but that would not influence me if I had the time and strength to do it. All this of course is *strictly private*.[10]

Determined to be master of his subject—which by now was essentially musicology—Grove had concluded that he must be a master of all subjects. There is to be appreciated in his maturing musicological work a synthesis of his skills in engineering, his perception of the fundamentals of culture in terms of geography, his insistence on conceptual clarity, his musical intuition and his humanist idealism. Some of these qualities were to be recognized in 1875. Considering it a disgrace that Grove had received no recognition of his contribution to scholarship, A. S. Farrar, Professor of Divinity and Ecclesiastical History in the University of Durham, had urged in an impassioned letter in the *Durham County Advertiser* of 8 December 1874 that the University should confer an honorary degree on the 'illustrious geographer'. On 29 June 1875 this wish was fulfilled when Grove was made a Doctor of Civil Law. Never tired of seeing the masterpieces of English medieval architecture, Grove was delighted to have the opportunity to look at Durham Cathedral, with E. A. Freeman as his guide. At the back of his mind, however, there was the feeling that it should have been not Durham but Oxford—where he had many friends—which offered him its accolade.

But of what significance was it? In a state of uncertainty he wrote, on 12 August, to his sister-in-law Marian Bull:

Tomorrow I am 55 years old and what am I? As much a slave as I was at 35, as little near the attainment of any settled position of mind and spirit as I ever was. I am active and energetic and ready to do my best, but the day for *that* is gone. I ought now to be reaping the fruits, and feeling like Stanley or Jowett or other men of my own age that I am enjoying the harvest of my earlier years. . . . I ought not at my time of life to be a mere shuttlecock at the sport of all the people who

[10] The letter (PML) carries no date other than 'March 9'. The Revd Hugh Reginald Haweis (1838–1901) was a popular lecturer and writer on musical subjects. In the same letter Grove recommended that Bennett seek aid from Ebenezer Prout whom he described as 'an excellent fellow, willing and able and . . . quite biddable'.

employ me or have the least claim on me. I ought somehow to have more weight and leisure—but I can't get it. And yet I feel in myself plenty of capacity.[11]

Grove's capacities continued as always to be at the service of *Macmillan's*. At the end of 1875 he pulled up his young brother-in-law A. C. Bradley, now a Fellow of Balliol, for some remarks, in a review for the magazine of Browning's *The Inn Album*, which he thought disrespectful.[12] He himself had already committed himself, having written a letter to Browning expressing his admiration for what was a striking essay in poetic realism. He received a grateful letter in return, in which it was stated that the basis of the tragedy was factually true—a circumstance attractive to Grove, the seeker after truth, but one which he found difficult to accommodate on other occasions.

At this time Grove was endeavouring to bring W. E. Gladstone—a long-time admirer of the music at the Crystal Palace—into *Macmillan's*, by inviting him to review H. C. Maxwell Lyte's *A History of Eton College, 1440-1875*, recently published by the firm. He was also interested in Alexander Macmillan's intention to publish a Chinese primer, by Richard Douglas, sometime of the Chinese consular service and an assistant in the British Museum.

Meanwhile he was pulled back from the Far to the Middle East, in which he had lasting involvement, by reports of the romantic archaeological activities of Heinrich and Sophie Schliemann, at that time commencing excavations beneath the Lion Gate in Mycenae. At the end of 1875 a translation of *Troia und seine Ruinen* appeared in London. A year later—such was the authority of Britain at the time—Schliemann was invoking the aid of Gladstone (although out of office at the time) in an effort to obtain permission from the Greek government to work at Mycenae, the home of Agamemnon. That Hissarlik was the site of Homer's Troy, as Schliemann contended, was subjected to a critical, but not unsympathetic, examination by W. H. Mason in *Macmillan's*

---

[11] Graves, p. 214. Contentment allied to prosperity in the Grove family lay with George's brothers. Thomas, a Master Fishmonger, lived in squirearchic affluence in Penn, he was a pillar of local society, a strong supporter of the church, and—at least in George's view—thoroughly unimaginative and rather boring. Edmund was a partner in the engineering firm of Cochrane, Grove & Co., of Cleveland, in Yorkshire, and music was his hobby. His house, Glenside, at Saltburn, was a frequent place of relaxation for George until Edmund's retirement, when he moved south to Sussex, where he was, of course, more accessible.

[12] Bradley's article, lightly revised, appeared in February 1876. It does not attempt to disguise a sense of concern on account of the body-blow which Browning appeared to have delivered to the integrity of poetic expression, by his use in many passages of local and 'temporal colouring which hardly befits any form of serious poetry except satire'. Grove's opinion of this poem—the 'great triumph of Browning's later career', according to Hugh Walker in 1910—has been thoroughly vindicated. It is, according to J. S. Atherton, in a more recent critique (*Times Literary Supplement*, 16 Apr 1976, p. 464), 'one of the greatest neglected peaks of English literature'.

in August 1876, after which the new science of Homerology—as Gladstone named it—opened up new areas for speculation and observation, as the spade gave way to the pen.

For two years the Schliemanns worked hopefully and devotedly, and their discoveries of tombs—veritable treasure-troves—and their priceless contents were a watershed in archaeological scholarship. The success of the Schliemanns aroused envy, and captious critics were abundant. In England, however, the Royal Archaeological Institute, through its president, expressed its pleasure at such scientific enterprise and, enrolling the Schliemanns as honorary members, asked Heinrich Schliemann 'to remember how entirely [your labours] are appreciated by your friends in England'.

Grove, still with residual archaeological responsibilities, watched the reports of the Schliemanns' progress with deep interest. On 18 January 1877 he wrote to Gladstone, a Greek scholar who had kept up his classical interest since his Oxford days and had recently published his *Homeric Synchronism*:

Everyone is burning to know what you think of Schliemann's new discoveries. . . . What a wonderful find it is—I always look forward to the findings of the Tombs of the Kings in Jerusalem as the climax of my Palestine labours but even supposing we had found them and that the treasures had not been taken by Herod or some later 'explorers' they would be nothing to compare with them.

I suppose you will go and see them. I hear that [James] Fergusson and others are to be off very shortly. The question of the date [which] has arisen—whether pre-Homeric or Hunnish—is absurdly premature at present.[13]

Grove once more was fishing for an article for *Macmillan's*.[14] He also informed Gladstone that he had been working at a 'little geography book', of which he proposed to send him a copy. On 20 August, however, he was able to express his pleasure in accepting Gladstone's offer of a piece on 'The Dominions of Odysseus'.[15] When this arrived he noted one remark of the author with particular pleasure, about 'Homer's knowledge of places not being merely that which he would get from a map', which Grove compared to what Kinglake had written in the Preface to *Eōthen*, one of his favourite books.

At the time he was himself busy with maps, for his 'little geography

[13] BL, Add. MS. 44453, f. 48.
[14] In May Grove had read in *The Times* that Gladstone proposed writing about Sir James Brooke and the Dyaks of Sarawak, and if this was the case he asked that it might be published in *Macmillan's*. That article went into the *Contemporary Review*, but Gladstone's name was brought into the magazine in a review of Gertrude Jacobs's two-volume *The Rájà of Saráwak, an Account of Sir James Brooke* (*Macmillan's* XXXVI, May 1877, p. 145).
[15] *Macmillan's* XXXVI, May-October 1877, p. 417.

book' was among the pedagogic works that poured out in profusion after the passing of the 1870 Education Act. It was one of a series edited by J. R. Green for Macmillan. When he considered the matter of his own style seriously Grove fell back on the inflections of the King James Bible. The opening of his school book carries a solemnity of style less common in such works since his day:

Geography is from two Greek words, γῆ, ge, the earth, and γραφὴ, graphè, description;—and that is what it is, a description of the earth; not of what is below the surface, for that is geology, but of all that is to be seen on the face of it—the land, the sea, the mountains, the valleys, and rivers, and lakes, and all the rest that meets the eye.

But Grove was a writer of illuminating asides. There is a charm in the way in which he discusses the transference of meridians and parallels from a sphere to the flat. It is, he observes, 'called projection—a pretty word'. A contemporary school book editor would allow neither the whimsy of that nor the mixture of practicality, puckishness, and poetry concluding the discussion of the North Cape, where the reader is informed that 'by joining one of Cook's tours you may go there next summer and see for yourself the "midsummer, midnight, Norway sunset in sunrise" as the poet says'.

That Grove had a capacity for teaching is self-evident. That is what the *Dictionary* is about. The geography primer, in its more modest way, shows why he was a good teacher, for he was always ready to draw the homely point that can clarify an argument and illuminate an explanation. Concerning the necessity for a common standard of time (Greenwich Mean Time was adopted only in 1884), he fell back on an illustration drawn from his railway experience. After the coming of the railways it was 'very inconvenient to have one time in London and another at Exeter or Birmingham'. London time was therefore adopted in England, so that a train requiring four hours to reach Bristol from London and leaving at nine o'clock would arrive at its destination at one o'clock and not (as it would do without a time adjustment) at 12.50.

While Grove was immersed in literary tasks the musicological stream was becoming broader, and running in deeper channels. Although concerned to gather material for the *Dictionary* from the best authorities he was increasingly aware of his own special commitments—to Beethoven, Mendelssohn and Schubert. In 1875 the Lower Rhine Festival had taken place at Düsseldorf, from 16 to 18 May, and Grove was present and delighted with the programme. On the first day Joachim conducted the *Missa Solemnis*, on the second Handel's little-known *Hercules*, and on the third Schumann's First Symphony. Also on the programme for 18 May was Mendelssohn's 'Calm Sea and Prosperous Voyage', conducted by

Julius Tausch, who was taken on board by Grove to provide the *Dictionary* entries on the Festival.

At this time the main force of Grove's musical energy was concentrated on Beethoven, and he was working at his *Dictionary* article even while he was attending the Festival. His commonplace book (RCM 2135) is replete with references, excerpts and commentary built up over the previous years.[16] As has already been shown, in RCM 2135 a growing concern with musical analysis is evident; but Grove wished not so much to analyse the works in themselves as to see them as elements in Beethoven's processes of thought brought into meaningful unity. A perfectionist in respect of detail, he welcomed the help of those who had special knowledge, and among his allies one of the best informed regarding Beethoven was Edward Dannreuther.

An article by Dannreuther in *Macmillan's* in March 1876 laid a German philosophical scent which Grove in the years to come was much inclined to follow. On the day on which his article was published, 5 March, Dannreuther wrote from 12 Orme Square in this amusing manner:

My dear G:

A propos of Beethoven's cat and kittens:

(1)

(*Moscheles* informed me that the tune (bar 17 et segue) in the same movement was a popular one in his time, beginning

[16] The last item relating to the 'Eroica' was dated 'Chamonix, Aug 10 1874', but he was working on the other symphonies as well. ('Mr George Grove ("G.G.") was lately at Chamonix', noted the *Musical Times* for 29 Aug 1874, 'ascending in imagination to the heights of Mont Blanc, as he ascends in imagination to the heights of the symphony "No. 9"—Mont Blanc of Beethoven.') More than twenty years later Grove remembered that visit: 'My recollection of Chamonix are charming and range from a huge ants' nest in one of the woods at the back to the *celestial* light on the glaciers of Bossons and Taconnes which I told you of'; E.O., Tues. Aug 6 [1895].

Ich bin lie-der-lich, Du bist lie-der-lich, etc.

Would you ask Nottebohm[17] whether he has gathered the rest of the words (which Moscheles could not remember) and whether he has found the original tune?

(2) line 4 about the kittens is garbled—it should stand:

Das is schön, das *main* i'.

i.e. das ist schön, *das mein ich* (compare the popular colloquialism 'das will ich meinen')

(3) I am certain that the modernised version of the 2nd song is also incorrect—both in the 2nd and last line. But it would be rash to say how or why as long as the first line is missing—Some fellow at Vienna should hunt up all songs and texts used by Beethoven—I have got nearly all the tunes he transfigures in his 3rd period and mean to write this monograph—the subject is most interesting and I can throw a sharp light on it.

(4) Both songs and the letter are printed in Nohl's Briefe—vol 2 p 1 and he refers to Niederrh. Musikz.

(5) letter to Ries, Nohl, vol 2 p 217

E. Dannreuther[18]

It was at this point that Grove's acquaintance with Edward Speyer began to deepen into friendship. Son of a Frankfurt businessman and himself a person of substance, Speyer having settled in England took British nationality in 1869. The Speyer family had been brought up in a musical atmosphere and Edward's knowledge and competence were considerable. The reference in Dannreuther's item (4) is to letters of Beethoven,[19] presented to Speyer's father by their recipients—N. Simrock and F. Ries—which Grove had published in a Crystal Palace programme understanding this to be their first publication. On 8 March he wrote to Speyer about the letters and was told in reply that Nohl when once visiting the Speyers in Frankfurt had surreptitiously copied them.

There were other matters relating to Beethoven which Grove referred to Speyer at that time. On 10 March 1876 he was thinking about the Austrian Finance Act of 1811 by which the currency was devalued by some 20 per cent, and what effect this had on Beethoven's pension. 'I am',

---

[17] M. G. Nottebohm (1817–82), friend of Mendelssohn and Schumann, a pioneer in musicology and among the first to study Beethoven's sketchbooks.

[18] RCM 2267. Dannreuther's article in *Macmillan's* (XXXIV, March 1876, p. 193) has interesting references to Beethoven's affinity with folk-song.

[19] See L. Nohl, *Neue Briefe Beethovens* (Stuttgart, 1867), pp. 190, 251; the letters in question were stated by Nohl to be in the possession of Herr Wilhelm Speyer, Frankfurt.

he wrote, 'doing the Life of B. for my Dictionary and want to know exactly what happened.' He threw in the fact that the Saturday concerts (still much his concern despite his no longer being Secretary of the Crystal Palace) were 'all safe for 1876–77 at least', and that Brahms was expected to come over in February or March. It was on 15 June that Grove acknowledged Speyer's information on the currency problems: but he had further questions:

What was the effective value of money in Vienna in 1816–20 compared with 1876? If Beethoven had £136 a year what was it equivalent to nowadays?

When he was a child at Bonn his father's salary was 300 florins per annum. Nominally that would be £30, but what would it be equal to now?[20]

As background to this pattern of exploration—archaeology and musicology being separate facets of the same underlying intention, to gain and to share knowledge—Grove enjoyed new musical experiences. Joachim came to the Crystal Palace on 4 March 1876. As he had done many times before he played the Beethoven Violin Concerto. But he also presented his orchestration of Schubert's Grand Duo in C Major for piano (op. 140, D813). The attempt thus to express Schubert, after a hint from an unduly dogmatic Schumann on the composer's presumed intention, was not very successful; but Grove, affected by Schubert-mania and his affection for Joachim, believed the work of refurbishment well justified.

At this point Joachim and Brahms, bound together in the enthusiasm of the Germanophiles in British musical life, were viewed as the bringers of a new message. In the mainstream of musical thought Grove tried to prevent his concern with the past from interfering with a duty to the present. He was no committed Wagnerian, but just as he had been one of the first fully to appreciate Schumann, so, for example, he was among those who formed the vanguard in appreciation of Brahms. The Serenade in D (op. 11) had been played at a Crystal Palace concert as far back as 25 April 1863; on 26 September of that year the *Ave Maria* for women's voices (op. 12) was performed, and there had been other performances of his music in the 1870s.[21]

[20] The letters to Speyer quoted are in BL, Add. MS. 42233, ff. 4, 6, 8. The effect of the Austrian *Finanz Patent* of 20 Feb 1811 is dealt with in detail in the Beethoven article (*Grove 1*, vol. I, p. 189).

[21] On 9 Mar 1872 the Piano Concerto in D minor was given its first performance in England, with a Miss Baglehole, a pupil of W. H. Holmes at the Royal Academy of Music, as soloist. Sophie Löwe, Catherine Penna and Stockhausen also took part in a Brahms-orientated concert. In the following season Joachim, accompanied by Franklin Taylor, played the Hungarian Dances, and in March 1873 the *Schicksalslied* was heard. In February 1875, the same month in which he attended Sterndale Bennett's funeral in Westminster Abbey, Grove had a translation prepared, for a Crystal Palace concert programme, of a notice by Hanslick of the second version of the *Deutsches Requiem*.

As he had indicated in his letter of 10 March 1876 to Speyer, Grove had expected that Brahms would come to London for a Crystal Palace concert in the following season. It was also expected that he would receive an honorary degree at Cambridge where his case had been presented by the ardent twenty-four-year-old C. V. Stanford. But Brahms's dislike of the English overpowering any ambition to receive a high honour, he decided not to come, thus rendering himself ineligible for a degree which had to be conferred in person. This was a disappointment to the Brahmsians in the University, where the *Requiem* was performed in 1876 (its second English performance), and the *Neue Liebeslieder*, the Alto Rhapsody and the First Symphony in the following year.

The last work, receiving its first performance in England, was conducted by Joachim, who was himself receiving an honorary degree, in the Guildhall on 8 March 1877. Joachim played the Beethoven Concerto and also conducted his own Elegiac Overture in memory of Heinrich von Kleist (op. 13). The performance of Brahms's First Symphony was a musical event of national significance—blessed by the fact that the composer, by some extrasensory perceptiveness, appeared to have included the familiar chimes of Great St Mary's Church in the last movement. Robert Browning, Frederic Leighton (keenly musical and, because of his education in Germany, an admirer of German culture in general),[22] Felix Moscheles, Manuel Garcia, Manns and Grove—who was to become a Vice-Patron of the University Musical Society—were among the audience.[23]

The real hero of the hour, perhaps, was young Stanford who had engineered the function. After the concert Joachim wrote to Brahms: 'Since Cambridge the future of your work in England is assured.' The symphony was played twice more that month at the Crystal Palace, and was hailed with spacious praise by Grove. The next year Stanford married a daughter of one of Grove's friends, Jennie Wetton. She was a lively girl and a singing student, whose apparent promise persuaded Grove to refer her to Sullivan, who advised her to study in Leipzig.

The excitement over Brahms overlapped that aroused by Wagner's visit to London. On 30 April he and Cosima arrived in England and went to stay with Dannreuther in Orme Square. He was welcomed respectfully by the champions of modern music and graciously by the Queen, who received him at Windsor, about which he expressed his appreciation to

[22] 'I have pleasant recollections of Sir Frederick [*sic*] (afterwards Lord) Leighton. He had been at school with my father in Frankfort. . . . He spoke excellent German (and other languages) and was a great society man'; C. Fuchs, *Musical and other Recollections* . . . (Manchester, 1937), p. 52.

[23] The Cambridge programme opened with Sterndale Bennett's 'Wood Nymphs' Overture, and otherwise contained the *Schicksalslied*, and unaccompanied (and unspecified) Bach played by Joachim. On 18 Mar Joachim played his own Hungarian Concerto at the Crystal Palace.

Cusins, Master of the Queen's Music. Dannreuther brought to his house
to meet his guest some of his associates who had close connections with
Germany, including Browning, George Eliot, G. H. Lewes,[24] George
Meredith and Grove. Grove (prospecting for a Wagner appearance at
the Palace) having met the Wagners at Dannreuther's was pleased one
day to make up, with William Pole and William Siemens, a remarkable
engineering trio to entertain Wagner to lunch at the Athenaeum.[25]

There were eight Wagner concerts at the Albert Hall that month, the
last two being hastily put on in a vain attempt to make up for the losses
incurred in the first six. For Grove, however, a little Wagner went a
long way, and he appeared to put himself firmly on the side of those who
thought the German composer little more than an interloper in the high-
principled world of serious music. Brahms—whose name Grove mentioned, catastrophically, to Wagner—was his ideal of a modern composer.
The article on Brahms for the *Dictionary* was written by A. Macewski:
an uncompromising declaration of belief in Brahms's exposition of the
sublime, it summed up what Grove himself thought.

That summer of 1877 Grove was obliged to report to his employers on
progress on the *Dictionary*, and the timetable for the next three years:

July 29 1877

My dear Craik:

I found your note on Saturday night. Since our conversation a month ago I
have given constant attention to the dictionary. I believe it will be possible to
complete it in 2 vols., say in 1500 pages in all—and at the following dates:

A–D	Aug 31,	1877
E–G	Dec 31	,,
H–J	June 30	78
K–M	Oct 31	,,
N–P	June 30	79
Q–S	Dec 31	,,
T–V	June 30	80
W–Z	Dec 31	,,

[24] 'Your husband', said George Eliot to Cosima Wagner on this occasion, 'does not
like Jews; my husband is a Jew.'

[25] William Pole (1814–1900), born in Birmingham and trained as a civil engineer, had
worked on the Britannia Bridge; he advised on railway construction in many parts of
the world. Pole was an accomplished musician (Mus. D. Oxford, 1867) and had contributed articles on music to *Macmillan's* (IV, VII). A report by him in 1875 on the Crystal
Palace orchestral concerts had persuaded the financially cautious Directors to keep them
going. William Siemens (1823–93), born near Hanover, naturalized British citizen, was
one of the great inventors of the nineteenth century. Among his inventions the most
important was the Siemens furnace. He made significant contributions to the development of electrical power.

Also I believe that the corrections can be materially reduced below those of the portions submitted—probably by quite a half.

To do this, however, will require my whole time beyond the Magazine and the 3 days at the office as at present. To drive a team of contributors half of whom are amateurs, and half can get 3 times the pay we can give them elsewhere, takes a frightful amount of goading and coaxing and correspondence: and the editing and correcting and checking and completing—as I feel bound to do it— is a matter of great labour and *incessant* thought and occupation. But at this I do not grumble for a moment—and am quite prepared to give it my whole energy and devote any faculty to it—and now that I find from your letter you do not expect the geography book[26] at the same time I am now so relieved from the responsibility that that has been burdening me, that I can go to work with renewed vigor.

I think it will be quite possible to do what I have stated above provided of course no illness or other cause out of my control interferes—I am bent on doing it and see no reason to the contrary.
Yours ever sincerely

G. Grove

I have to go to the Dentists on Monday morning and may be late in making my appearance.[27]

This was a critical point in the fortunes of the *Dictionary*, for despite his willingness to observe the timetable Grove had felt that contractual obligations to write a class-book geography, in addition to the primer, and regularly to attend the office in Bedford Street had been making realization of his intentions problematic. But Macmillan wrote their approval of his postponement of the geography book and their agreement that he should only come to the office when it was vital for magazine or *Dictionary*. If Grove were not to finish the latter on time—extremely unlikely, it was conceded—then he must do so at the earliest possible moment and without further payment. In relief Grove wrote to Craik again.

August 3, 1877

My dear Craik:

Thank you very much for your letter. I am very sorry to [give] you the trouble of writing and reading business letters while you are away.

I was in a terrible dilemma between Dictionary and Geography. In the one hand my duty to my family and to the Firm urged me to the geography; on the other hand I felt myself so far committed that I could not give up the Dictionary. I must now work like a steam engine and try to finish it within the dates named.

As to the geography of course it is for you to do as you like. There must be many men who can do it though I hope you won't attribute it to vanity if I say

---

[26] One of the three books (a Class Book) mentioned in his letter of 1875 to Bennett (see above p. 132). IV was never completed.

[27] BL, Add. MS. 54793, f. 83.

I don't think anyone could do it quite as well as I because I have such a very strong feeling of my own shortcomings and ignorance. I know what I do not know, and that must be, as a rule, what most ordinary people do not know; and then I set myself to work to find it out and to tell it to others just as it has struck me—not much to be proud of certainly.—If you decide on anyone else I need not say I shall be happy to give all the aid in my power. . . . Stanley wants me to take a week at the end of August and go to the Rigi with him. But I don't feel its coming off.

> Ever yours affectionately.
>
> G. Grove[28]

Craik duly went on holiday to Arran with Alexander Macmillan and in September, unable to join Stanley in Switzerland, Grove disappeared to his brother's at Saltburn. During his stay there—as if to mark his removal, however temporary, from the metropolis—he met a Mr Ayrton, who remembered in his youth having seen hay cut in St James's Park, London, and carried away in carts drawn by oxen. It was known as 'King George's hay'.[29]

But it was not all vacation for Grove at Saltburn, for letters between him and Macmillan passed almost daily.[30] There were matters relating to Gustav Hirschfeld and his article on 'The discoveries at Olympus'; Nettleship on Bunyan; Mahaffy on Greek athletics or the Schliemanns. The death of Louis Thiers in September left a remarkable political and literary career to be written up for *Macmillan's Magazine*. Grove tried several people, including James Cotter Morrison, one who, according to Macmillan, 'had lived so long in Paris that he is almost a Frenchman in ideas, and sympathies'. Morrison had not long before contributed an impressive article on Taine's *Ancien Régime*. In the end Thiers was commemorated in an interesting personal portrait by the artist, Emily Crawford.

There was also correspondence over a new series of educational books which Grove was to superintend. Alexander Macmillan had questioned Grove's request to have his name shown on the books already issued in this series on the grounds that, since only two books had so far appeared,

[28] Ibid., f. 88.

[29] In a MS. book once the property of Grove and now in the possession of the author, 'Mr Ayrton, Cliffden, Saltburn' is noted on the endpaper. William Scrope Ayrton, son of William Ayrton (one of the founders of the Philharmonic Society), grandson of Edmund Ayrton, sometime Master of the Chapel Royal, and a cousin of the Chester Ayrton whom Grove had once known, was a retired Commissioner of the Leeds district Court of Bankruptcy. He lived near Edmund Grove at a house named 'Cliffden', where he died on 3 May 1885. The Ayrton family were connected with music in Yorkshire—particularly in Ripon—from the middle of the seventeenth century.

[30] He was much discomfited on having his attention drawn to a palpable act of piracy: someone in the U.S. had based a pedagogic tract on Grove's geography primer, and to his fury there was in Macmillan's opinion nothing that could be done.

it could seem somewhat pretentious. Grove wrote a long letter on 16 September at the end of which he made it quite clear what he thought:

> . . . I should very much like my name to appear on the cover of Taylor's Primer, and of Sullivan's.[31] It could be an advantage to my reputation and I hope no disadvantage to you; and seems to me to follow naturally from the fact that this class of primers was suggested by me; that I laid out the plans of the works with both S. and T. and that I have edited Taylor's book in the most complete and thorough sense of the word—We shall get Sullivan's in time, and I shall be prepared before long to propose one or two more to you with good prospect of success. I shall be very glad to hear that you approve of this; and in that case all that will have to be added to the cover will be a line at the top:—*Edited by George Grove*
>
> Yours ever affectionately
>
> G. Grove

Grove must have felt that he was Macmillan's anchor-man.

In the spring of 1878 Alexander Macmillan was once more abroad, this time with his son Malcolm (Kingsley's godson) and J. R. Green, who was deeply involved with his *History of the English People*. The party was in Italy, in search of good health. Alexander wrote to Grove from Florence saying that he had there met a clergyman, a Dr Robertson (the Revd Alexander Robertson, of San Remo?) who would be willing to write about Italian music for the *Dictionary*, if Grove so wished. Macmillan asked that the first two parts of the *Dictionary* (which was appearing sectionally) should be sent to Robertson, whose offer, however, seems never to have been taken seriously by Grove.

In the summer other developments that were to have consequence for Grove—although this was not to be appreciated at the time—were taking place. On 13 July the Prince of Wales, prodded by Henry Leslie, the famous choir director, convened a meeting at Marlborough House to reconsider a project previously put forward, and turned down; the establishment of a single national music conservatory. The idea of a merger of the two existing institutions, the Royal Academy and the National Training School, still appeared to make good sense. Support came from Prince Christian, brother-in-law of the Prince of Wales, and the Duke of Edinburgh, who was by far the most musical member of the Royal Family, as well as from the Prince of Wales. In the discussions that followed, George Macfarren, Principal of the Academy since the death of Sterndale Bennett in 1875, gave no hint of cooperation. The idea of a joint enterprise was therefore finally dropped, and the thoughts of the parties mainly interested turned towards the feasibility of a new

---

[31] The first of the works referred to was presumably Franklin Taylor's tutor on pianoforte playing; the second was aborted at an early stage.

and more ambitious school to replace the National Training School. Towards this end a committee of which Prince Christian was appointed chairman began seriously to work.

For some reasons the Victorians were aware that—as one of their poets said—death had all seasons for its own. Grove was continually reminded of this. On 6 March 1878 Luise Scott Russell, Grove's 'very dear friend' and once Sullivan's 'Little Woman', died. In the same month Walter Grove, who had left Marlborough three years previously, went to Australia on account of a 'weak chest' which had given his family cause for concern.

Grove was ready for a holiday, and as was often the case the opportunity came through the importunities of a friend who needed companionship. Not for the first time it was Stanley, who was just beginning to recover from the trauma caused by the death of his wife in 1874. In 1878 he hoped to be able to regain his sense of purpose, and to heal his hurt spirit by undertaking a tour in North America.

Stanley had for a long time harboured an ambition to bring the British and Americans into a close and understanding relationship. On Thanksgiving Day, 4 July 1875, he had preached on the theme of brotherhood (his text taken from Matthew 5:21, 22), reminding his congregation that in a year's time the centennial of Independence would be celebrated. He had already invited an eminent American divine to preach in the Abbey.[32] When the opportunity eventually came for Stanley to visit the United States he went with invitations to address not only Episcopalians, but also Presbyterians, Congregationalists, Baptists, Methodists and secular meetings.

No man was better suited to the ecumenical function. An exponent of the principle of unity in diversity, Stanley promoted it in his *Lectures on the Church of Scotland* (1872), *Lectures on the Jewish Church* (1876) and *Addresses and Sermons delivered at St Andrews* (1877), in which the importance of finding common ground between different faiths was stressed. In spite of an abundance of adverse criticism Stanley continued to maintain a liberal course.

When the Dean of Westminster crossed the Atlantic it was a matter of wide interest. Stanley was a divine with the highest credentials and

[32] Stanley had given the freedom of his pulpit to persons of diverse faiths and creeds long before it was fashionable to do so. The first layman to deliver an address in the Abbey was Grove's friend and a contributor to *Macmillan's*, Max Müller. A son of the German poet Wilhelm Müller (who provided Schubert with the text of the cycle *Die schöne Müllerin*), and an authority on Sanskrit, Müller spoke at Stanley's request on 'The Religions of the World'. In 1878 Müller (who had resigned his Oxford Chair of Comparative Philology in order to teach Sanskrit to Japanese Buddhist priests) delivered the first Hibbert Lecture in the Chapter House at Westminster, on 'The Origin and Growth of Religion'.

he had social recommendations. He had always been much respected by the Queen, and his wife before her marriage had been Victoria's favourite lady-in-waiting, while his brother-in-law had been British Minister in Washington. At the end of August 1878 Stanley wrote to the Queen as a matter of duty to inform her of his expedition to the United States, which inevitably would have some diplomatic overtones. He would, he said, be accompanied by his 'old and tried friend, Mr George Grove', and by a young doctor, Gerald Harper, recommended by his sister Catherine, wife of C. J. Vaughan, Master of the Temple.

The little party sailed out of Liverpool on the *Siberia* early on the morning of 5 September. Stanley gave a full description of the voyage to another of his sisters, Mary. Among their companions were a clerk from the War Office, a boy from Marlborough College, a professional philosopher, a tough settler from Natal, a tougher cattle man from the American West, and Bishop Arthur Cleveland Coxe and his wife. Stanley's cultural susceptibilities took something of a battering from the son of the 'wild west', who described a rough passage he had once endured in the Pacific. 'I was', he said, 'that sick that I almost brought up my knee-pads.' The Dean's liberal principles also came under assault from the pronouncements of Coxe, the dignified, bewhiskered, white-haired shepherd of the flock of western New York State Episcopalians, whose total opposition to any biblical revision and to propositions for which a scientific basis was claimed brought him into conflict with American theologians with whom Stanley was friendly. Grove meanwhile sat in his cabin making notes on the 'Eroica'.

Safely arrived in Boston on the afternoon of 16 September, the Stanley party settled into the Brunswick Hotel. When they began to take stock of their new surroundings they found Boston fascinating, in part Dutch or French in appearance, and with fine broad streets. A distinctly foreign feeling was underscored, reported Stanley, by the fact of being served at table by 'negro or mulatto' waiters. The respect in which a British church dignitary was then held was signified by the attentiveness of Governor Rice of Massachusetts, who took Stanley and his friends for a drive in his official carriage, drawn by two fine black horses. On the evening of that day, 19 September, on which they also met Longfellow, they attended a banquet at Salem to mark the 250th anniversary of the landing of John Endicott and his Puritan fellow settlers of the New England Company.

The weeks that followed would have been exhausting for any persons who were less intrepid slaves to duty than Stanley, Grove and Harper. The two latter were in supporting roles, but they were under a compulsion to fill any barren areas in their own experience with worthwhile knowledge. While Stanley was putting the final touches to his sermons Grove was considering musicology and the wider fields of education.

On Saturday 21 September he melancholically copied into his common-place book (RCM 2136) the melody of a march said to have been played at the execution of Marie Antoinette. The previous day he had visited Harvard College, to learn about the Harvard Musical Association.[33] In the following week he went to two other institutions of higher education, Wellesley—the women's college—and Yale.

In Boston the English party were looked after by Phillips Brooks, Rector of Trinity Church, a scholar of formidable accomplishments now approaching the zenith of his career. He published his first volume of sermons and was awarded the degree of Doctor of Sacred Theology at Harvard in that same year. His commanding authority in Boston, his ability to inspire, and his broad vision especially captured Stanley's regard, so that in 1880 Brooks was invited to preach in Westminster Abbey. A week after this occasion he preached before the Queen at Windsor—the first American divine to be honoured in this way. The themes of Stanley's addresses in Boston, 'The East and the West' and 'The Prospects of Liberal Theology', were thoroughly congenial to Brooks, who remained in correspondence both with Stanley and with Grove in later years.

From Boston the travellers moved to Philadelphia, where Stanley preached in St James's Church. For Grove this visit was made exceptional because he was able to attend a black Methodist service. The congregational singing in the enthusiastic manner derived from *Sacred Harp*, *The Southern Harmony* and the 'shape-note' books, with more or less extemporaneous part-singing, was strange to English ears. Stanley unchristianly referred to such a performance as a 'hideous exhibition'. Grove with more restraint remarked especially the violent contrasts of *forte* and *piano* in the congregational singing. He thought back, no doubt, to his previous experiences in ethnomusicology, especially among the Samaritans of Nábloos. 'Negro Music', with its reference to Black Methodism, was a subject in the first edition of the *Dictionary*.

In Philadelphia the party were guests of G. W. Childs, who ten years later was to present the Milton window to St Margaret's Church, Westminster. Next came an engagement at the new Johns Hopkins University in Baltimore, where their host was Daniel Coit Gilman, president of the University. Serenaded at his inauguration by the Peabody Orchestra, he was a friend of Sidney Lanier, the leading Baltimore musician. Gilman was so keen on music as to suggest to Lanier that a professor in the physics of music should be attached to the Peabody Library. While Grove enjoyed meeting Gilman, whose polytechnical interpretation of the role of a university he applauded, he was also pleased to meet Mrs Gilman, a poet and the author of children's books, at their house in Eutaw Place.

[33] See *Grove 1*, vol. I, p. 693, and vol. IV, p. 555.

From Washington the travellers made a pilgrimage to George Washington's house at Mount Vernon, and then down south into the charms of Virginia. Having arrived at Richmond Grove went on a private errand through, and 25 miles beyond, Lynchburg, to the Seneca district in Campbell County, where Arthur Bradley, Harriet's nephew, had in 1873 settled to farm. Two of his sisters were also living there.[34] Grove waxed lyrical over the pleasures of Southern life and the splendid landscapes amid the Blue Ridge Mountains. After that a train ride lasting a day and a night took him back north to rejoin Stanley, who had preached at the Calvary Church, New York, on 'The Perplexities of Life' and spent some time with Dr Adams, President of the Presbyterian Union Seminary, at Cyrus Field's house at Irvington, on the Hudson River.

After a Canadian intermission with engagements in Montreal and Quebec, between which cities the party travelled in the company of Lord Dufferin, the Governor-General, there was a final round-up of commitments in Massachusetts and New York. Meeting Emerson at Concord, Grove appreciated the sensitive and gracious philosophy of the New England group of which Emerson was the leading spirit. At the end of the month, in New York City, Stanley went into the most taxing phase of the visit. On 29 October he spoke on 'The Unity and Diversity of Christendom' in Trinity Church, Wall Street, and on John Wesley to a large gathering of Methodists in St Paul's Methodist Church. Next morning he attended a breakfast at the Century Club, and from his remarks there this tribute remains:

When in after-years you read at the end of some elaborate essay on the history of music or on Biblical geography the name of George Grove, you will recall with pleasure the incessant questionings, the eager desire for knowledge, the wise and varied capacity for all manner of instruction, which you experienced in your conversation with him here.[35]

After two final sermons in James Renwick's charming Grace Church, on Broadway at East 10th Street, and two addresses to Baptists and Episcopalians respectively, the travellers packed up and set sail for England on 6 November. Stanley said that he could not have carried through the tour without the help of his two companions.

There were three literary consequences of this tour. Arthur Bradley had given his Uncle George a paper entitled 'A Peep at the Southern Negro', which was published in *Macmillan's* in November. Bearing in mind that young Bradley came from a 'liberal background', this is a horrifying but truthful exposition of the principles of Southern society,

[34] A. G. Bradley, a pupil at Marlborough College 1862–7, remained in Virginia until 1884. On his return to England he wrote about the local history of Wiltshire, Wales, and the north, and published *The History of Marlborough College* in 1893.
[35] R. E. Prothero and G. Bradley, *Life and Correspondence . . .*, op. cit., vol. II, p. 533.

'which,' Bradley observed, 'in all matters except the exclusion of blacks, is eminently democratic.' On the following St Patrick's Day Stanley gave a lecture at Sion College on 'The Historical Aspect of the American Churches', the text of which was published in *Macmillan's Magazine* in June. And a year later another essay on an American subject appeared in *Macmillan's*; an intriguing account by Arthur Bradley of Herman Blennerhassett, the Irish-American lawyer-adventurer who gave his name to an island in the Ohio River.

CHAPTER EIGHT

Transitional Period

1878–1881

IN an age in which letter-writing was a common and inescapable discipline, friendships grew out of, and were nurtured by, the exercise. For Grove the act of writing letters was both occupational necessity and therapy, and it was nothing for him to write a dozen and more at a sitting. An early riser, he discharged some of his duties in this respect long before breakfast; alternatively, not being a long sleeper, he performed them late at night. The family was out of the way. He was alone. As he wrote he erased the accumulated anxieties of his professional routine, and the discouragements and disappointments of his private life. Coming towards late middle age he sometimes repined over the years in which he had experienced so little of the real intimacies and affections of life, and as far as might be possible, he prepared to make up for what had been lost. The death of Luise Scott Russell was a great shock, for with her going it was as if a door had been shut in his face. In his late years as more doors were closed he tried anxiously to find others to open.

The pursuit of his lexicographic ambitions was to Grove what mountaineering is to others. Here in the project of a *Dictionary of Music* was a high peak to scale. Success, however, could only come through a team effort. Grove built up his team judiciously, and set them severally to work. Already involved—and thus privileged to sit with Grove's party in the end gallery at the Crystal Palace concerts—was Dannreuther's promising pupil, young Hubert Parry, who had just escaped from a business career and who had been, as Grove later wrote, 'one of the first persons I asked to help me when I began the Dictionary'.[1] At an early stage William Barclay Squire and J. A. Fuller-Maitland also became associated with the project. In 1878 they were respectively twenty-three and twenty-two, with modest degrees from Cambridge—the one in history, the other in theology—and little idea of what profession to follow. Both were fortunate in having funds on which they could live until such time as they had found niches in the professional structure. They were passionate music-lovers, disciples of Stanford, and of that company of amateurs in the University Musical Society which helped to give a new impetus to British music.[2]

[1] Letter to F. G. Edwards, 4 June 1898; BL, Eg. MS. 3091, f. 237.
[2] This is even indicated by Squire's essay on Cambridge (see 'University Societies'), one of his first contributions to *Grove 1*.

Barclay Squire had been introduced to Grove while still an under-graduate, in the summer of 1877. At that time he was working on the musical holdings of the Fitzwilliam Museum,[3] and was only too glad to apprentice himself to musicology under the tutelage of Grove. Fuller-Maitland, connected with Grove fortuitously through being a grandson of Ebenezer Fuller-Maitland, a prominent member of the Clapham Sect, was also glad to become more closely associated. Squire quickly became Grove's confidant. Fuller-Maitland, who in 1885 was to marry Squire's elder sister Charlotte, was grateful for Grove's patronage, but less inclined to put himself in emotional thrall.

The constraints of Victorian family ethics irked Squire as much as they perplexed Grove. When the former was at home—at his father's house on Feltham Hill, aptly named 'The Grove'—he was a prisoner of convention and the frequent victim of misunderstanding, for City merchants did not normally see their sons into careers in musicology. Squire was looking for a sympathetic father-figure at a time when Grove's turn towards fields of affection wider than those allowed by suburban mores was becoming more obvious.

At the end of 1878 Grove wrote asking Squire to look at his description of the Fitzwilliam music, adding, 'I put in a bit of music paper as I remember the Museum destitute of that useful article.' By now Squire was also in the circle of those privileged to accompany Grove to the Crystal Palace concerts, and Stanford suggested to Grove that he should ask Squire to write the article for the *Dictionary* on 'Dance'. 'It has not been done at all well hitherto', remarked Grove, 'and I am anxious to amend.' (Certain people were anathema to Grove, and by now—surprisingly, in view of what he had said about him earlier to Bennett—Ebenezer Prout was high on the list. It was to Prout that the subject of Dance had been at first assigned.)

The integrity of the *Dictionary* was ensured by Grove's sense of purpose. He knew not only what ought to go in, but also what should not. So he asked Squire to cut down on 'Lyre'—'as we are not a *Dict.* of Ancient Music'—and to limit 'Luther' to the musical essentials. As for advice, Grove's contacts guaranteed that he could avail himself of the best that was available, as when he was reminded by Joachim in June 1879 that 'Spitta of Berlin'[4] would be at his disposal whenever needed.

In April 1879 the first volume of the *Dictionary*—Parts I–IV—was

---

[3] In 1879 he was joined by Fuller-Maitland, who took over the cataloguing of the Fitzwilliam music in association with him—a task lasting five years. Inspired by the thought that music was to be heard and not merely seen, this pair made a notable part of the Fitzwilliam collection, the so-called Fitzwilliam Virginal Book, generally available through its publication by Breitkopf & Härtel of Leipzig.

[4] Philipp Spitta (1841–94), German scholar, author of *J. S. Bach*, 2 vols. (1873, 1880).

published, the Editor's Preface being dated 1 April.[5] In May Richter's series of Orchestral Festival Concerts (from the following season known simply as the Richter Concerts) commenced in St James's Hall. The programme notes were dominated by Grove's magisterial supervision of the Beethoven territory.[6] On 14 June Grove attended a reception for Sarah Bernhardt, at which everybody who counted as anybody was to be seen. In July he went to visit his sister Ellen who lived at Sevenoaks.

Throughout the summer and autumn Grove and Squire exchanged information on the general subject of Dance, for since dance forms were now to be treated separately the comprehensive essay which had at first been intended needed redeployment in sections. In Squire's final articles details culled from Grove's letters are to be detected. In 'Polonaise', for instance, Moritz Karasowsky's *Chopin* (1878)—a book which Grove mentioned as having been recently acquired by him—is duly recorded.

Research took its toll. Fuller-Maitland was laid up with neuralgia, and one day in August Charlotte Squire sent a message to Grove that her brother was unwell. Grove wrote back hoping that he was not so poorly that he would have to withdraw from his dinner engagement at Sydenham on the following Saturday. Mrs Grove and Millie would be away, but, the domestic staff being in residence, there was a reasonable guarantee of a respectable meal. After that, weather permitting, they could sit out in the garden of which Grove was so proud. He advised Squire to take the 6.10 from Victoria or the 6.15 from London Bridge, with Sydenham Station on the Brighton line as the destination: 'Then walk down the hill from the Station until you come to the Prince Alfred on the right (my favourite Pub.). Keep the main straight road, and my house is the first after the Pub on the right—a white wooden house behind trees.—Dinner 7 sharp. No dress of course.'[7]

Unfortunately, to his chagrin, and Grove's disappointment, Squire was not recovered in time. He had wished to discuss another matter of some concern; not being able to do so in person he put it in writing. He was anxious to holiday in Spain, but his father was unfavourably disposed to the idea. Grove wrote back:

How odd your father's opposition to your going! I was trying to put myself in his place and I can find myself saying nothing to a son of mine in such a case

---

[5] Reviews of successive parts of the first volume appeared in the *Musical Times* XIX, in February, June and August 1878, and XX, in May 1879.

[6] In the book of the first concert, on 5 May, he recalled how William Ayrton had written of the first performance of the Seventh Symphony at a Philharmonic concert on 9 June 1817: 'All except the movement in A minor (the Andante) proved *caviare*; but other beauties by degrees became patent, though a curtailment of at least ten minutes would improve it.' In due course this reminder of the fact that Beethoven was once 'caviare to the general' was scooped into *Beethoven and his Nine Symphonies* (p. 269).

[7] Letter of 10 Aug 1879; BL, Add. MS. 39679, f. 24.

but go my boy and see all you can and be as happy as possible, and here is
£—— to help you on your way! However fathers differ.[8]

'Nearly at [his] last gasp with botheration and work', Grove himself
left England that year on 29 September for Berlin. Travelling with
J. R. Green and his wife, and other friends, he went by way of Cologne
and Hanover—where he saw *Fidelio*. The object of the journey was to
work on Mendelssohn material, and having seen what was available from
Paul and Ernst Mendelssohn, Sebastian Hensel (Mendelssohn's nephew)
and Joachim, he went on to Leipzig to see various members of the
Mendelssohn circle, including Charlotte, widow of Ignaz Moscheles;
the family of Conrad Schleinitz, Mendelssohn's friend who had been
director of the Leipzig Conservatorium; and Lili and Adolphe Wach. Lili
was Mendelssohn's youngest child, and her husband Professor of Law in
the University of Leipzig and personal adviser to the King of Saxony.

On 16 October, after breaking his journey in Magdeburg and Cologne,
Grove was back in England; and also back to the grindstone. Squire's
father invited him to visit the family at Feltham. Although he would
have been delighted to accept the invitation he had to reply:

I cannot at present spare the time—My work is so very hard that it takes up my
evenings as well as my days. Saturday is the only evening now that I give myself
and that I devote to my friends here. This horrid state of things will not last
always.[9]

Squire's associate Fuller-Maitland was able that year to sample Grove's
hospitality. One evening after a concert, Grove suggested that the young
man come back to the house with him to take 'pot-luck' for dinner.
Grove had forgotten, however, that other guests had been invited, and
Fuller Maitland did not know that dinner dress was *de rigueur* for formal
entertaining *chez* Grove. His sense of being conspicuous was not diminished when, in mid-dinner, Grove called out, 'Now, Maitland, we'll
have that good story of yours about the pig!' Harriet took alarm and called
down the table, 'George, I'll thank you not to bring young men to my
house to tell indecent stories.' The future Lady Grove's manner, commented the young man later, was 'perhaps more alarming than it need
have been'.[10] Fuller-Maitland, one might think, had noticed about her
something that few others had.

---

[8] Letter of 19 Aug 1879; ibid., f. 28.

[9] Letter of 29 Oct 1879; ibid., f. 35. Characteristically, Grove made a note at the time
that Squire senior, albeit not notable for his cultural aspirations, might prove useful at
some future time when no one else could. Two years later, he wrote to Barclay Squire
asking if his father's commercial interests included rosin, or if not whether he had
contacts with those whose did. The *Dictionary* article on this absorbing subject was by
E. J. Payne, barrister, historian and amateur violinist, who contributed also the fine
article on Stradivarius.

[10] J. A. Fuller-Maitland, *A Door-keeper of Music* (1929), p. 91.

Always running at the back of Grove's other activities was the editorial machinery of *Macmillan's*, looking after which gave opportunities for occasional literary dinner parties—at home and away. At the house of Frederick Macmillan, eldest son of Daniel, who had spent five years in New York, on 17 April 1879, he had met Henry James, then in his mid-thirties, whose *French Poets and Novelists* and *The American* had recently been taken on to the Macmillan list. Two days later James wrote to his father:

... I dined with Frederick Macmillan to meet Mr. Grove ... who had just been reading *The American* (these were the terms of the Macmillan invitation) 'with great delight'. There was also the estimable Craik (a partner in the firm), husband of Miss Mulock the novelist. Grove is a very jolly old fellow—one of those London men of letters who have done lots of unrecognized work. (He is sub-editor of Smith's Bible Dictionary and wrote much of it, etc.) He was very friendly, and I shall probably arrange with him before long for a serial in *Macmillan*—the obstruction being that the magazine is small, and, just now, overstocked.[11]

In 1880 James's *Portrait of a Lady* was published serially in the magazine.

At this time Grove was in correspondence with Charles Kingsley's widow concerning the fee for her son Maurice's 'Bisclaverat: A Breton Romance', which he feared might be rather inadequate. Appreciating Mrs Kingsley's sympathetic reference to his collie, Help, he remarked that it was 'just a year since the dear old fellow died in my arms'. He also soliloquized on the season of the year. 'I like the autumn,' he put in a postscript. 'I love the tints and the smells and the quiet decay—*promise of the burst of spring*.'[12]

An article published in the November 1879 issue of the magazine which crossed over various scholarly frontiers and was of special interest to Grove was on 'Gipsies'. This was by another remarkable polymath, C. G. Leland, whose *English Gypsies and the Language* (1873) was his prelude to several works on slang usage, to others on metal-chasing and wood-carving, and still others on will-power (and its development). On 13 September Grove had written to Leland about this article:

I have been reading the paper again this morning and venture to put two little questions—which I put out with all the diffidence that a tyro should feel in approaching such a master.
(1) Is not the name *Nats* (the tribe of singers and dancers) connected with Nautch? If so it might be as well to mention it.
(2) the word *Sukha* for a swan or pelican interests me extremely—because of

[11] Henry James, *Letters*, ed. Leon Edel, vol. 1 (1979), p. 167.
[12] Undated letter; BL, Add. MS. 42711, f. 20, 54793, f. 20. Maurice Kingsley's article was published in *Macmillan's* XLI, January 1880. (The preceding contribution, on the last page of the December 1879 number, was Stanley's 'Note on the American Church'.)

its likeness to the curious Hebrew (?) word *tukkiyim* which is translated 'peacocks' in the Authorised version of the passage in 1st Kings . . . the s and t are always convertible . . .
(P.S.) Others beside [Carl] Engel (a very small personage) have appretiated [*sic*] wild music—the gipsy element is strong in Schubert, Brahms, Chopin, Joachim, and a new man named Dvorak—and a lovely element it is. Liszt has written a book on the Hungarian music and 10 Ungarische Fantasie [*sic*] which are most characteristic.[13]

At the end of the year Grove's concern that collections of music should be adequately cared for led him to comment favourably on the interest shown by William Cusins, Master of the Queen's Music, in the priceless holdings then kept at Buckingham Palace. Cusins, whose pamphlet on *Messiah* sources (1874), was a helpful contribution to Handel research, was in process of preparing a complete catalogue, as indicated in Squire's article on 'Music Libraries' in *Grove 1* (p. 423). This intention, however, was never fulfilled. The last issue of *Macmillan's* for 1879 contained an article by Charles Sumner Maine, entitled 'A Conservatoire of Music for England, Report of Prince Christian's Executive Committee since its foundation by the Prince of Wales'. The ambition of Henry Cole to see a new school of music established had gone a stage further, and this was an intention that would be fulfilled.

On 30 December Grove wrote to Mrs Sullivan, who had sent him a letter from Arthur—now in the United States for the première of *The Pirates of Penzance*:

. . . I can sympathise with him on the loss of his sketches,[14] but I should not have been so brave and should have howled much louder. But then I am 59½ and he only 37½ which makes a difference. . . . I am going to write to Arthur on New Year's Day and shall ask him to try and bring in my *Dictionary* into some of the 'gag' in the Pirates of P. A good idea!—You might mention it too. . . .[15]

H.M.S. Pinafore is duly mentioned in the second volume of *Grove 1* which appeared in October 1880.

One day in April 1880 Grove met Renan, who both attracted and repelled him. The French historian was one of a party, which included Matthew Arnold, being taken round Westminster Abbey by Stanley. It was about this time that Grove met William Addis, formerly a member of the Oratory with Father Dalgairns, and sometime parish priest in Sydenham, whose religious doubts eventually took him into self-imposed exile. With Addis Grove formed a firm friendship.

The approach of Grove's sixtieth birthday brought together a company of 300 friends and well-wishers to present him with a gold chronometer

---

[13] BL., Add. MS. 42578, ff. 14–15v. Cf. Bible *Dictionary*, vol. II, p. 763.
[14] What the lost sketches were is not known.
[15] PML.

and a purse of 1000 guineas. The moving spirit in this event was Ernest von Glehn, who hired the banqueting room of St James's Hall for the ceremony and persuaded Archbishop Tait to make the presentation. The subscribers to the testimonial made a remarkable assemblage of talent from many fields, but no presence was more welcomed by Grove than that of Arthur Sullivan, not long back from the United States. He was preparing for the Leeds Festival at which, in October, he was to appear for the first time as conductor, and where his *Martyr of Antioch* was to receive its first performance.

Although the presentation to Grove was on account of his efforts on a broad front, it was his work at and in connection with the Crystal Palace that was uppermost in many minds. It was fitting (particularly in respect of a certain resentment which Manns had been feeling) that in the March following, preparations were made to honour Manns, to whom a testimonial and cheque for £800 were presented on 17 June 1882.

In September 1880 Grove went to Germany and Austria—his principal reason being the necessity of working on Schubert material for his *Dictionary* article. He met his daughter Millicent, who had been living in Frankfurt since April, and they went on together:

. . . We got to Linz at 12 o'clock at night and had to go in an hour by the train to Vienna. There had been a rifle shooting and the station was full of the competitors, more or less drunk, and in the big waiting room there was a brass band playing waltzes and other things. *You can't think what it was.* Such rhythm and *élan* I never heard—it was something quite new—something electrical—a new atmosphere altogether. I have never lost it since, and I have often wondered if the music of Mozart, Beethoven and Schubert was meant to be played in that extraordinary inspired style. *If so we have never heard their music.*[16]

The highlights of the visit were meetings with Brahms, then at work on the 'Academic Festival' and 'Tragic' overtures.

After this Grove went up to Leeds and, while not uncritical, was certain that Sullivan's new oratorio, performed on 15 October, was an important work. He ended a long letter to his 'dearest A.' with an apostrophe to the spirit of beauty:

Good bye old man. What can be better than to know that your last work is your best? and there can be no doubts about it in this case. In these days of ugliness, crudeness, and pretension, it is delightful to have a new work in which the words are fully expressed throughout, in which the feeling is as deep and as lofty as any one would wish, and yet in which there is not one ugly or inconsequent bar from beginning to end.[17]

Grove was displeased by the notices of the work in *The Times* and the *Telegraph*, whose critics were responsible for adopting 'a sort of bantering

[16] E.O., Feb 4 [1892]; in this letter Grove wrote 1884 but meant 1880.
[17] PML.

tone—only banter without any fun in it', quite unsuitable for a serious subject. He was particularly unhappy with Francis Hueffer, the new critic of *The Times*, who was, Grove suspected, being persuaded by Albert Visetti that Sullivan wanted to make use of him with regard to the National Training School.

At this time negotiations which had followed the report of Prince Christian's committee in 1879, and which were to culminate in the foundation of the Royal College of Music, had led to the completion of a draft Charter which the Prince of Wales was to lay before the Privy Council in June. The politics of higher musical education were becoming more and more complex, and Hueffer, according to Grove, was 'a queer fellow full of suspicions'.

At the end of the year Grove was in a melancholy state, induced by emotional discontent and overwork. Writing to Squire on 1 December he regretted having tried to dissuade him from involvement in church music:

When I was your age my religious flame burnt fiercely—I still remember the glow thereof. But alas, age and work deaden one sadly. How true (in that regard) are Wordsworth's lines:—

> The youth, who daily travels farther from the east
> Must travel, still is nature's priest,
> And by the vision splendid
> Is on his way attended;
> At length the man perceives it die away,
> And fade into the light of common day.

Thank God for the glimpses of it still, but oh dear, life is very hard somehow—I find it almost crushing.

Remarking on a beautiful performance of Schubert's Octet on the previous Thursday, 29 November, he wondered whether Squire would be coming to the Crystal Palace on 4 December for the performance of Goetz's 'lovely little' Symphony in F.[18] If so, Grove apologized that he could not invite him to dinner afterwards as the maids would be on holiday.

The next year, 1881, was marked by a sequence of deaths, which contributed to a heightening of Grove's tension, a quickening of his work rate, and consequent intervals of exhaustion. Agnes von Glehn died on 14 January at the age of sixty-six. She was—as Grove appreciated and as it was said in the local newspaper—'gifted with much of this world's goods which she used with a liberal hand for the benefit of those who were in less favoured circumstances'. At the funeral service at

[18] Grove's programme note on this work was thought by George Bernard Shaw to be insufferably patronizing; see *London Music in 1888–89* (1937), p. 242.

St Bartholomew's Church, Sydenham, the organist, William Westbrook, played an arrangement of the last chorus from the *St Matthew Passion* before the service, and of Mendelssohn's 'If with all your hearts' afterwards. The German character of the occasion was confirmed by the congregation singing what popularly was known as 'Luther's hymn'— 'Great God, what do I see and hear'.

In March Joseph Warren, one of the pioneers of English musical scholarship and of the Musical Antiquarian Society, died after years of paralysis and extreme poverty. And on 17 July Dr Gerald Harper, their companion on the American tour, called Hugh Pearson, brother of H. H. Pierson the composer and canon of Windsor, and Grove—two of Stanley's closest friends—to the Deanery at Westminster where the Dean lay dying. After they had taken their leave, Archbishop Tait, a Balliol contemporary, and C. J. Vaughan, an old friend from Rugby and now Dean of Llandaff, came to say farewell. Stanley died next day and on 25 July was buried beside his wife in the Abbey. As in the case of his wife, five years before, his final sickness was caused by the insanitary conditions of the Deanery, a sombre fact—'And deadly also his strength did undermine'—detailed by Matthew Arnold in his elegiac 'Westminster Abbey', the last of his poems.

A week before Stanley's death Grove wrote to Mrs Sullivan thanking her for having written to him:

It is a great drawback to my life that I am able to see so little of many of those to whom I am most bound; but the day is only 24 hours long, and my strength only a certain quantity; and after work is done there is very little left of either time or strength. . . . I am very sorry to hear of your illness. It seems to press around us. We are all in bad distress here at the illness of Miss Mimi von Glehn, born the same day as Arthur, and a very great friend of his and mine. She is dying of a galloping consumption. They are going to take her abroad but I fear it is of no use.[19]

Mimi was taken to Pontresina, as Grove informed Squire on 5 July, but she merely worsened and repined at being so far from home. There was one cheerful note in the letter to Mrs Sullivan: Walter Grove, who had gone to Australia in 1878 in the hope that his affected lung would benefit from the change of climate, was now thoroughly well, and on the way to becoming a sheep farmer.

In April of that year Grove had taken a fortnight off and gone to Italy in the company of J. S. Forbes, General Manager of the London, Chatham and Dover Railway, A. B. Gobold, the Continental Manager, and Harry Quilter, the art critic (uncle of the composer Roger Quilter), who had contributed to *Macmillan's Magazine* at the end of the previous year. As always Grove made the most of his time and saw everything there

[19] PML.

was opportunity to see in, among other places, Turin, Milan, Rome, Florence, Venice and Verona. He was immensely impressed by La Scala, but not by the performance he saw there of Verdi's *Simon Boccanegra*.

Back in England, he went to Cambridge to hear Parry's contentious *Prometheus Unbound* on 17 May, which was better performed and accorded a friendlier reception than in the previous year at Gloucester.[20] A week later, in a letter to F. G. Edwards, he drew the outline of one project which he was to bring to life in the years ahead:

Macmillan and Co. are certain not to publish the portion of the D[ictionary] instantly. It is hardly likely that after the *very large* outlay they have incurred they should take a step which would so seriously interfere with the rate of the whole work.

I have always contemplated enlarging my 3 or 4 biographies Beethoven, and FMB. [Mendelssohn], Schubert etc and making books of them but that may not come to pass. I feel so very fastidious towards anything which is to take an independent permanent shape; and can never satisfy myself. I have never re-printed the C.P. programmes. Every time I read I wish to rewrite them in a way more worthy of the works. I think that a good book on Beethoven's symphonies and perhaps a dozen other great works would be a good thing but—shall I ever do it?[21]

Meanwhile Sebastian Hensel's *The Mendelssohn Family* was in production with Sampson Low, and on 31 August Grove gave it his blessing in the form of a preliminary 'Notice'.

The careers of Parry and Stanford—the one thirty-three, the other four years younger, and both capturing the attention of audiences at home and even abroad—were being increasingly noticed by Grove, whose generosity to the young was one of his most engaging character-istics. Stanford's *The Veiled Prophet* (the libretto by Barclay Squire from Thomas Moore) was performed in February in Hanover, and Parry's F sharp minor Piano Concerto, launched by Dannreuther, and *Prometheus Unbound*, were taken as the harbingers of a new spring.[22]

With the *Dictionary* and other matters weighing heavily on him, Grove felt jaded and in need of relaxation. The Stanfords went off to Monte Generoso, the Parrys to County Tyrone. Grove stayed in England. But Stanford, on his travels, could be of service to him in looking up Schuber-tiana. The Schubert article had already been drafted as far as 1825, and

[20] Shelley, whose text Parry used, was still *persona non grata* for cathedral performance; and the music was thought too 'modern'.
[21] Letter of 25 May 1881; BL, Eg. MS. 3091, f. 3v.
[22] Grove was at the Birmingham Festival in September 1882 when Parry's Symphony in G and Stanford's Serenade in the same key were performed. He had previously written to Squire that he had 'heard both Parry's and Stanford's things and liked them very much. Parry's is the much the bigger, but Stanford's is the clearer and easier to make out;' 4 Sept 1881, BL, Add. MS. 39679, f. 58.

Stanford could, and did, consult Pohl, chase up the relative value of Viennese *Gulden* in Schubert's last years, and examine the evidence relating to what came to be known as the 'Gastein' Symphony.

Writing to Squire on 21 October about the nightingales of *Die gefangenen Sänger* (more nightingale references coming in the next letter to Squire in respect of *Ganymed*), Grove gave it as his opinion that in 1825 Schubert had written a Ninth—'Gmund-Gastein'—Symphony with an independent existence (although the score had been subsequently lost) so that the 'Great C Major' in truth was the Tenth.

Was not that Gastein a lucky find for me? It is plain that in 1829 when Bauernfeld wrote the Gastein Sym. and 1828 sym. were 2 distinct and known things. The *onus* of proving them to be one surely rests with the Viennese people and that must be my next point. I wish them joy.

G.[23]

Having written a paper—full of reminiscence—for the *Pall Mall Gazette* (25 October 1881), on the Palestine Exploration Fund's recently published map of the territory on the west bank of the Jordan, Grove, who had already written briefly to the press on the subject, prepared a paper for the *Athenaeum* of 19 November to justify the 'Gastein' Symphony. Within this period every Schubert trail was pursued. On 12 October he wrote to A. Dörfel in respect of Paul David's having informed him that when Mendelssohn conducted the 'Great' C Major at the Gewandhaus in 1839 he had made some cuts. Would Dörfel be able to look up the score or the parts to ascertain the nature and extent of any cuts?[24]

At the end of the year Grove appeared in better spirits; at least he could review his lexicographical tribulations more or less equably. 'Proud of Squire's friendship', as he put it, he unbuttoned himself over 'dear old Rockstro', whose excesses of generosity in treating of Sullivan, Stanford, Cowen, and others of the younger school, 'much too diffuse and laudatory', were a luxury in which 'no dictionary ought to indulge'.[25]

On 12 December Grove attended a 'grand soirée' at the Free Trade Hall, Manchester, at which the Duke of Albany, who was accompanied by the Duke of Edinburgh and Prince Christian, delivered an admirable address on music in general and the progress of music in England in particular. Grove, who had been approached during the summer with a view to his becoming a member of the committee to which the task of bringing the College into being was assigned, was the speech-writer. (No doubt he primed the other royal gentlemen, who also spoke, as well.)

[23] BL, Add. MS. 39679, ff. 62, 64. See *Grove 1*, vol. III, pp. 344f., and cf. O. E. Deutsch, *Schubert, A Documentary Biography* (1946), pp. 431, 757. The 'Gastein' theory in the end proved untenable.
[24] See *Grove 1*, vol. III, p. 357, n. 2. Grove also thanked Dörfel for the memoranda he had sent to him through Baron von Tauchnitz.
[25] Letter of 17 Dec 1881; BL, Add. MS. 39679, f. 65.

This was the first blow in the final battle to achieve the establishment of a new national College of Music.

Among the musicians invited to be present were Charles Hallé, John Stainer, Henry Leslie and Otto Goldschmidt. The programme of music played by Charles H. Fogg, on the Great Organ, comprised the 'Toccata et Fuga in D minor' [sic] (J. S. Bach), ballet music to *Henry VIII* (Sullivan), 'Nazareth' (Gounod), Coronation March, from *Le Prophète* (Meyerbeer), and the Overture to *William Tell* (Rossini). Since the Duke's object was to justify the need for a new national musical institution by emphasizing the general superiority of English [sic] music to all other, Grove, considering Fogg's choice, was obliged to suspend disbelief on the grounds, no doubt, that the ends justified the means. In his *tour d'horizon* the Duke arrived at the thirteenth century after having already spoken for a quarter of an hour:

It may not be generally known, but it is nevertheless admitted by the most learned and most hostile of our continental critics, that in the early discovery and practice of music England was in advance of all the nations of Europe by very many years.—(Applause). The round or glee, 'Summer is a-cummen in', . . . [sic], which is one of the musical treasures of the British Museum, is indeed accepted by the most learned antiquarians of England and Germany as the work of a monk of Reading in Berkshire in or about the year 1225. This is more than a century and a half before the admission of Dufoy [sic] to the Papal Chapel in 1380, which has hitherto been always taken as the earliest landmark in the history of modern music. We were a century and a half in advance of Flanders, Italy, or Germany.—(Renewed applause). Moreover this very early composition, instead of being grave and dull, is far more melodious and more attractive to the unlearned hearer than any music of the corresponding period in the foreign schools.—(Applause). In a word, this little glee, which is the germ of modern music, the direct and absolute progenitor to the oratorios of Handel, the symphonies of Beethoven, the operas of Wagner, is a purely English creation, dealing with English sights and sounds, and is animated in a very high degree by the truly English qualities of sense, fitness, proportion, and sweet, simple, domestic tunefulness.—(Applause). I am happy to say that you will have an opportunity of judging this for yourselves at the close (Renewed applause).[26]

The tone of the meeting, which was organized by the Manchester Athenaeum and attended by persons of distinction in every field,[27] was that of a party political conference, and the euphoria exuded had little to do with music. Though the royal Princes all spoke with guttural German accents, there was a regrettable air of chauvinism apparent that evening.

[26] *Manchester Guardian*, 13 Dec 1881.
[27] From the names of local worthies that of Alexander Ireland, editor of the *Manchester Examiner*, stands out; at home was his two-year-old son John, in due course to be a student at the Royal College of Music, and an important composer.

CHAPTER NINE

Sir George and an Irish Problem

1882–1886

AN article in the *Musical Times* on 1 January 1882 welcomed the royal initiative in respect of musical education, but not uncritically. In his Manchester speech the Duke of Albany had referred to the revolution of the seventeenth century—of which, the writer of the article suggested, certain moral and political vestiges remained. So, he said, it might well be that the students of the new College—if and when it came into being —would be kept away from the allurements of the theatre, to the detriment of any development in the field of opera. Further, a conservatory intended to resemble a continental *conservatoire* would be an indifferent institution unless it was backed—as was the Paris Conservatoire—by a government Department of Fine Arts. Remarkable in its prescience, the article called for 'a national institution, State-endowed, and under the control of Parliament'.

This, however, was not the way in which music was regarded at that time in Britain. As Sir Frederic Leighton (as he then was) expressed it, music was *sui generis*, with 'an awakening influence, an ethos of its own, a power of intensification, and a suggestiveness through association which aid those higher moods of contemplation that are as edifying in their way as direct moral teaching'.[1] While the Prince of Wales and the Dukes of Edinburgh and Albany were themselves music-lovers, music in a serious sense was regarded by them primarily as an agent for the celebration of the glories of Blood and State, and its lower-level practitioners as clients of a system of patronage which at Court level was by no means emancipated from the traditions of the petty German dukedoms with which the Royal Family maintained its connections. In Manchester, a city with strong German associations, the Duke of Albany had referred a little nostalgically to the value in former times of the resident court orchestras of Germany.

The National Training School had done a good job in that it had provided 'free musical education' to 180 pupils, thereby establishing a principle, but it was in no sense a 'national' institution. On 28 February 1882 the Prince of Wales convened a meeting of Lords-Lieutenant, Deputy-Lieutenants, Mayors and other interested persons, in the Banqueting Hall of St James's Palace, to consider the founding of such an

[1] *Musical Times* XXIII, 1882, p. 16.

institution. The Duke of Cambridge was among those present, and noted the speeches as being excellent. Grove, whose executive effectiveness at the Crystal Palace and in connection with the Palestine Exploration Fund was more respected by many than was his musical knowledge, was from now on much occupied in fund-raising.

To many people the enterprise must have seemed irrelevant. At the height—as it seemed—of Britain's imperial glory, of her technological ambition and military adventurousness,[2] shadows were once again darkening the western sky. Troops came from distant places and were sent far afield, to wars in Asia and Africa, while nearer home Irish discontent rumbled ever more menacingly. In 1881 almost 5000 agrarian offences had been committed in that country. The rate of conviction—about 10 per cent—was unpleasing to colonial authorities responsible for law and order. Helped by Irish-American sympathizers, the Land Leaguers were determined to make Ireland ungovernable by the British.[3] And on 6 May 1882 Frederick Cavendish and Thomas Burke were murdered in Phoenix Park.

For quite unexpected and somewhat bizarre reasons the Irish question was the one political matter on which in the course of the next few years Grove was to be required to express an opinion. Immediately, however, his duty was to collect funds for the national school of music to be.

The most urgent matter for consideration was the closure of the National Training School, the transfer of its assets and its hundred or so pupils to the new foundation.[4] This was formally done by the presentation of the building given by Freake, with its fixtures, instruments and funds, to the Prince of Wales. From the remaining funds the greater part was to be set aside for the 'private instruction' of the best scholars.

Speakers, at whose head rode Grove, travelled the country, canvassing support for the conservatory and manfully trying to promote the idea that what was best for every town in the country should be situated in London. When people in Bradford were approached they wondered, as did others, why the Royal Academy of Music could not be enlarged. And after the fifth Earl of Rosebery, acknowledging his ignorance of

---

[2] At the beginning of 1882 the Channel Tunnel—although not much liked by conservative minority opinion—seemed to be well under way, with more than 1000 yards ready for inspection. In March Tennyson's 'The Charge of the Light Brigade' was published in *Macmillan's Magazine*, for which Grove was still responsible.

[3] On 18 Mar 1882 the *Illustrated London News* asked: 'What can be done in a country where murder and outrage stalk abroad with impunity, and the people are under a system of abject terrorism that well nigh paralyses the arm of the law? There has arisen in some quarters a feeling that if Mr Parnell and his countrymen were to be returned, their influence would be used to repress outrages. . . .'

[4] See Sir Henry Cole, *Fifty Years of Public Work* . . . , op. cit., vol. I, pp. 376–7. Scholars of the National Training School, chosen by competitive examination, contracted 'to undergo a fixed term of two, three or more years' instruction'. The new institution therefore had to take over scholars with time still to run.

the subject and proving it by every word he spoke, had offered his support to the scheme, the *Musical Standard* cast further doubt on his credentials, as being one of 'a nation whose distinctive instrument is the bagpipes'.

Among those soliciting for funds there was not infrequently a touch of arrogance, as when the Prince of Wales expressed a wish that on the Sunday after Easter the Roman Catholic and Anglican churches of the country might consider contributing their collections to the cause of the College of Music. Cardinal Manning, an old acquaintance of Grove's from the Metaphysical Society and a frequenter of the Crystal Palace concerts, wrote to him asking that the Prince should be assured of his good will, but pointing out that Eastertide offerings were the main support of his clergy, who belonged to a body which, unlike the Church of England, had no State funds available for any purpose.[5] Manning did, however, promise to urge Catholic choirs to give concerts in aid of the College.

On 4 April Julius Benedict sent to Grove a list of 31 influential amateurs of good business standing in Liverpool,[6] with whom it would be beneficial to 'discuss and further the great undertaking of which the success seems to me beyond any doubt'. Liverpool figured prominently in Grove's calculations. On 20 June he wrote to Edward Samuelson, saying that during the past two weeks subscriptions had been coming in well, that there was now no doubt that 'the proposal will become a reality', and that the Prince was 'determined to carry out what he feels to be a good thing for the country':

. . . I return to my old argument:—Liverpool is sure to be one of the first places from which musical boys and girls will come knocking at our doors. Is it not therefore fair to help us to make some provision for them? If a musical school is a good thing you are sure to have one for Liverpool, and in Liverpool— ultimately. But that must take a long time; and meantime help us to establish one for your benefit in London.[7]

[5] 'Some of our dioceses', wrote Manning, 'are skeletons. One has only 6000 people scattered over 7 Counties: and they, of the poorest class . . . our whole population is about half a million: and of these nine tenths are working men and their families. Excepting the 20 or 22 Peers, and about 24 Baronets, we have very few families of the middle class. We are therefore convinced that a collection in Church would produce very little . . .'; RCM 2269.

[6] Among them were some whose names have some resonance still—Robertson Gladstone, F. R. Leyland, P. F. Cunliffe, H. F. Hornby, Samuel T. Hope and Fred H. Boult.

[7] Letter of 20 June 1882 to 'Mr Samuelson'; RCM 2270. Edward Samuelson (1823–96), son of an American father and German mother, was born in Hamburg and came to England as a child. So well educated in music that Jullien once offered him an engagement as solo violinist, he became a prosperous Liverpool tobacco factor. He had a deep interest in art and literature as well as music and helped considerably to establish Liverpool as a leading intellectual and artistic centre. See obituary notice, *Liverpool Courier*, 21 Dec 1896.

At the end of the year the Duke of Edinburgh visited Merseyside to open a Home for Aged Mariners. Accompanied by Grove, he addressed a meeting in the Town Hall at which, after speeches by both of them, and by the Lord Mayor, a 'Resolution in favour of this national undertaking, with a specific recommendation that one or two scholarships should be endowed for Liverpool students . . .' was passed. In the course of the afternoon speech the Duke mentioned that it was the fifty-sixth anniversary of Weber's death. At an evening concert in the Philharmonic Hall in aid of the College, the overture to *Der Freischütz* was the first item in a wide-ranging programme made memorable by the participation of the Duke as composer, conductor and violinist. He conducted his own 'Galatea' Waltz (according to a local critic, marked by 'neat melodic capacity and considerable knowledge of orchestral effects') and some other items. Towards Mme Roze's rendering of the Bach–Gounod *Ave Maria* he contributed the violin obbligato: a case of *noblesse oblige*.

In 1882 Grove's article on Schubert appeared in the fascicle of the *Dictionary* then issued, winning praise from, among others, John Addington Symonds, and a discordant rejection of his assessment of Schubert's status by H. Heathcote Statham, organist and writer on musical and artistic subjects.[8] The salient part of his demolition exercise on the Schubert cause, an essay in the *Edinburgh Review* on 'Schubert, Chopin, Liszt', ran:

But the admission of all that Sir G. Grove [*sic*] claims for Schubert as a composer would be tantamount to lowering very much the standards and requirements of instrumental music of the first class; and, without grudging him his private pleasure and satisfaction in the contemplation of his Schubert, I must candidly aver, not only that I do not share this enthusiasm to anything like the same extent, but that I think it desirable, in the interests of a true musical criticism, that musical readers generally should not share it, or at least that they should be admonished to think twice before doing so. . . .[9]

The reasons for this judgement are given at some length, culminating in its translation into moral obloquy: Schubert's works, concluded Statham, recalling what Garrick had once said of Adam Smith's conversation, were 'flabby, and therein reflect their author's whole life and character'.[10] Grove wrote a letter of complaint to Henry Reeve, editor

[8] Statham had written an account of the opening of Coutts Lindsay's Grosvenor Gallery for *Macmillan's* in 1877. Earlier he had legitimately taken exception to Grove's sometimes too colourful descriptions of Beethoven's working methods, in an article republished from the *Fortnightly Review* in *My Thoughts on Music and Musicians* (1892), pp. 307–8.

[9] Republished in ibid., pp. 316–17. Grove was not yet knighted at the time of the essay's original appearance; Statham evidently revised the mention of him on reprinting the piece.

[10] Ibid., p. 329.

of the *Edinburgh Review*, but received little satisfaction from him. Reeve indeed claimed that the offending article expressed his own views, and gratuitously added that Grove should have 'made more of Chopin'.[11]

Polemics aside, Grove concentrated most of his energy on the College of Music enterprise. Wherever he had contacts, like a cunning political operator he worked on them. He had such contacts at Marlborough College, where his brother-in-law George Bradley had been Master, and where his sons Walter and Arthur had been educated, the latter leaving in the summer of 1881. Grove became friendly with Bradley's successor, F. W. Farrar, and had begun to enjoy the acquaintance of G. C. Bell, who had followed Farrar. Grove was also connected with Marlborough through Harriet's sister Marian and her husband, Charles Bull, a master at the College from 1854 to 1893. C. M. Bull, a notable character, was long remembered at Marlborough for presenting the Bull Cup for proficiency in drop-kicking, and for his enthusiasm for the O.T.C. Marlborough was a hearty establishment and Grove wondered in a letter to Squire whether a summer-term concert featuring *Cox and Box* might be an occasion for fund-raising. If so, he asked if 'three fellows could be found to go down . . . for the accompaniment', and 'the gentry of the neighbourhood' persuaded to attend the performance. As for himself, he admitted, he was not 'wedded to Cox and Box'.[12]

His schedule was always tight. On 22 July he was in Macmillan's office until two o'clock, and off to Marlborough on the 3.30 train from Waterloo. From there he went to Exeter, Plymouth and Devonport, to solicit funds for the College. 'Hard work for me', he wrote, 'and still harder for my listeners'.[13] In December the college was so far in being as to have taken occupation of temporary headquarters in the office of the Duchy of Cornwall, at Buckingham Gate, and a public announcement that Grove was Director-designate appeared in *The Times* on 20 October indicating that his authority was supreme. Aspirants for professional posts began to solicit his good will.[14]

---

[11] Statham's complaints might have been thought rather more justified if applied to the 'completion' by J. F. Barnett of the E minor–major Symphony in Grove's possession, which was played at a Crystal Palace concert on 5 May 1883. Barnett's version, in pianoforte arrangement, was said to have been published by Breitkopf & Härtel in 1882. It is not in the firm's catalogue of that date, but may have been engraved by them privately, as was not uncommon. Brahms had been afraid that the music would be subjected to such treatment; see A. Einstein, *Schubert* (Panther Books, 1971), pp. 227, 229.

[12] Letter of 4 May 1882; BL, Add. MS. 39679, f. 72. *Cox and Box* was performed at Marlborough as the second part of the Prize Day concert in July 1883. 'The parts were sustained by Mr Charles Colnaghi as the hatter, Mr Quentin Twiss as the printer, and Mr R. G. Price as Sergeant Bouncer. The piece began well, but at the end was rather inaudible at the back of the room . . .'; *The Marlburian*, 3 Oct 1883.

[13] Letter to Barclay Squire, 21 July 1882; BL, Add. MS. 39679, f. 81.

[14] Among them was C. Armbruster, a friend of Robert Franz, who submitted a

At the end of May 1882 Sullivan's mother died. She had been in correspondence with Grove almost to the end of her life, and two late letters from him throw additional light on both himself and Arthur. The first carries no year but may be ascribed to 1880.

July 21 7 p.m.

My dear Friend:

I take it *very especially kind* of you to write to me as you have done—I see very little of Arthur, but I am bound up in him. He is to me always the same dear genial sympathetic boy that he was when I first knew him in 62, and when we ran together like two drops of water. I hear other people say he has changed —but to *me* never, and he *never will*.

Thank God for morphia, and chloral and all these other blessed things which enable us to bear our ills! I hope you will have good weather at Geneva and that he will be able to enjoy himself and get relief from this fiend. Give my love to him and take it yourself—a large share—

I am wonderfully well thank God—I often think what should I do if I broke down in health.

It is worry that kills me [:] as long as the work goes well, *and I don't lose letters and papers* I am all right—

G

During Arthur's travels—to Russia and to Egypt, it may be surmised— Mary Sullivan sent her son's letters to Grove to read. There came the day when he could give her some news:

. . . You have to congratulate me on being Head of the new Royal College of music: that is, I shall be head of it when the Charter and the money are obtained. I hope I shall be able to carry on the work which Arthur began so well at the Training school. How I could work *with him*!: Dear old fellow! I shall often have to ask his advice. I feel my own incompetence sadly, and am not able to behave at all like a *swell* as I suppose I ought to do . . .[15]

On 7 May 1883 Grove graduated as a 'swell' when the Royal College of Music—for the time being housed in the premises vacated by the National Training School—was officially opened by the Prince of Wales in the presence of (as is said) a distinguished gathering. The term had already been running for three weeks. The Prince and other royalty were received by the Trustees, the Duke of Westminster, Lord Charles Bruce, Sir Richard Wallace, and Sir John Rose and the Director. Others present included the Prime Minister, Gladstone, and his sister; the Archbishop of Canterbury; the Lord Mayor of London; Lady Folkestone—

---

testimonial from von Bülow (which he had previously used in respect of a post in Bath) supporting his application for a place as a piano teacher.
[15] Both Sullivan letters in PML.

a keen music-lover; and Lieutenant-General Sir Dighton Probyn V.C.[16] There were numerous musicians at the ceremony.

The Director went into the inaugural ceremony of the College as Dr Grove, but left as Sir George. That this would be the case had been conveyed to him by the Prime Minister on 3 May 1883, but it was felt proper that an announcement of the honour should be made by the Prince of Wales on the occasion most appropriate.[17]

After all the work that had been done by Grove and others the endowment fund of £110,000 seemed paltry:

There are, of course, abundant reasons for this apparent niggardliness. Some of the reasons are political, some religious, and others are only moral and even musical. But the main reason is that whilst the heart of the country is true to the project and to the Prince, the national intellectual bias is opposed to what it is pleased to consider non-essential. We are all honourable men, and lovers of music; but, to the ordinary educated Englishman, music is an abstraction until united with some essential, such as sectarian opinion, or utilised for charitable purposes, or made incarnate in a brass band ministering to the works of the flesh and of fashion.[18]

The philistine proclivities of the more prominent people in Britain had for long been a matter either of despair or of satisfaction, and this condition was to continue. The Prince of Wales, however, took a double risk in espousing the cause of the College. In his speech, he pointed out that among the first scholarship holders were 'a mill-girl, the daughter of a bricklayer, the son of a blacksmith, and the son of a farm labourer'. For at least one genteel parent, as will be seen, the reference to a mill girl was unwelcome. So far as the Prince was concerned, however, this was evidence of a social value in music. He spoke forcefully: 'The time has come when class can no longer stand aloof from class, and that man does his duty best who works most earnestly in bridging over the gulf between different classes which it is the tendency of increased wealth and increased civilisation to widen.'[19] No doubt the Prince felt the sentiments of the speech to be his own; whether or not that was the case, it is certain that in large measure they represented Grove's views. It was in his sympathy for students from modest backgrounds that he reflected

---

[16] The last-named, a warrior of the Indian campaigns and after his fighting days Comptroller of the Household of the Prince of Wales, belonged to a family long established in Gloucestershire; he was related to Alice Roberts, the future Lady Elgar.

[17] A lively account of the inception of the College is given by Stanford, who remarked on Grove's one conspicuous defect as the head of such an institution, that 'he never believed in the creative worth of the musicians of his own country'; H. Plunket Greene, *Charles Villiers Stanford* (1935), pp. 89f.

[18] *Musical Times* XXIV, 1 June 1883, pp. 309f.

[19] Ibid.

the radicalism he had admired in Maurice, Kingsley, Hughes and Arnold.[20]

Among the students of that first year's intake A. H. Brewer, Haydn Inwards, Emil Kreuz, Hamish MacCunn, W. H. Squire, Emily Stewart, Jasper Sutcliffe, S. P. Waddington and Charles Wood were to become at least relatively well known in musical affairs. Julie Albu became a social celebrity, through marriage with an American of substance named MacFarlane, with whom she emigrated to San Francisco. Sixty years after her admission the College was reminded through the publication of her will that she had been a student; she left the institution £8000. One student more than any other, however, was to have particular significance for Grove and exerted a singular influence on him throughout his remaining years. Edith Oldham, a girl of eighteen, was one of three students from the Royal Irish Academy of Music, in Dublin, who came to the College as scholars in 1883. The others were Louisa Kellett—like Edith a pianist—and Francis Bulkeley, a clarinettist. Edith had already distinguished herself in Ireland by winning the Lord O'Hagan Prize in the senior Pianoforte class of the Academy, where her teacher was the celebrated Margaret O'Hea.

The staff which Grove had assembled to teach this first intake contained some names which were also, or were to become, well known, consisted of the following (those marked with an asterisk being members of the first board of professors): Pianoforte—E. Pauer*, F. Taylor*, J. F. Barnett, Eaton Faning, Arabella Goddard; Violin—H. Holmes, R. Gompertz; Viola—A. Gibson; Violoncello—E. Howell; Double Bass—A. C. White; Flute—W. C. Barrett; Oboe—G. Horton; Clarinet—H. Lazarus; Bassoon—B. Wotton; Horn—T. E. Mann; Trumpet—T. Harper; Trombone—S. Miller; Harp—J. Thomas; Singing (female [sic])—H. C. Deacon*, Jenny Lind-Goldschmidt*, Eliza Mazzucato; [male? —A. Visetti*, R. Latter; Organ—W. Parratt*, G. C. Martin, J. F. Bridge*; Composition—C. H. H. Parry*, C. V. Stanford*; Choral—Eaton Faning; Orchestration—C. V. Stanford; Counterpoint—J. F. Bridge; Military Music—C. Godfrey; Musical History—C. H. H. Parry; Declamation (female)—Madge Kendall; Italian—G. A. Mazzucato.

Towards the end of his first term at the College Grove was requested to solicit the interest of the Prince of Wales for the National Eisteddfod to be held on 10 July 1883 in Cardiff. He wrote to Samuel Aitken, Secretary of the Eisteddfod and an amateur organist in Cardiff, to put him in touch with Lord Charles Bruce, who might be able to arrange an audience at Marlborough House. But soon he had to write to E. H. Turpin, conductor-elect of the Eisteddfod, that the Prince's engagements precluded his going to Cardiff. Which was as well, for the Eisteddfod—controlled by an Englishman and with all verbal communication in the

[20] See C. V. Stanford, *Pages from an Unwritten Diary* (1914), p. 218.

English language—was, in the event, by no means approved of by the Welsh people.

During this year Grove was also pushing on with his Mendelssohn researches; the composer's elder daughter Marie, wife of an Anglo-German businessman, Victor Benecke, and now living in Roehampton, supplied a great deal of fresh information, while the invaluable Squire —doing for Grove what Grove had once done for Stanley—was reading the proofs of his *Dictionary* and 'using the scalpel'.

In May Grove wrote for Rockstro's *Life of Handel*, published by Macmillan, an admirable 'Notice' in which he took a look at the existing biographical works on Handel.[21] Grove wrote to Squire on 23 July 1883 protesting against a review of the Rockstro book by Ebenezer Prout:

Why don't they notice Rockstro's Handel in the P[all] M[all] G[azette]? Have you seen Prout's pronunciamento in the Athenaeum? I wish I dared write to the Athenaeum and tell the story of Prout's calling him a *bloody fool* in Manns's room to me one day. It would make a rich scene and form a nice comment on the article.[22]

By now it is clear that Grove thoroughly disliked Prout (who had once been a teacher at the Crystal Palace School), which is one reason for his exclusion then and thereafter from the College.

For his summer holiday Grove went to his brother in Yorkshire for a fortnight, and then to Northumberland, where Mandell Creighton was nearing the end of a ten-year term as Vicar of Embleton. Grove was pleased to have an opportunity of calling on the Creightons, for he was busy supervising the official biography of Stanley which was ostensibly being prepared by R. E. Prothero but for which Grove had the ultimate responsibility, and on which Mandell's advice was valuable. But he was otherwise glad to be at Embleton. He had a great respect for Mandell and much affection for his wife, formerly Louise von Glehn, who as a girl had proclaimed her aesthetic loyalties by flaunting a yellow scarf. Her duties as a vicar's wife in the little community near the bleak north-east coast had in no way diminished Louise's vivacity or her interests in art and scholarship. The service Grove attended at Embleton was, he said, 'one of the nicest I ever took part in'.[23]

From the Creightons' fortified medieval vicarage he went to Ripon, and thence to Whitlingham on the river Yare, near Norwich, about which

[21] Grove's survey of Chrysander's torso of a biography has excellent advice, still worth setting before any prospective biographer. Chrysander's book, he suggests, has 'the defect of excessive length, and of stating every fact regarding its subject in equal proportions, mixing up the sources of information and the conclusions of the writer in one dense and difficult mass, without division into paragraphs, head-lines, marginal notes, or any other aid to a decipherment of the impenetrable page'.

[22] BL, Add. MS. 39679, f. 97.

[23] [L. Creighton], *Mandell Creighton* (1904), vol. I, p. 161.

he wrote enthusiastically to his daughter Millie. He was home again on
31 August. Although there were performances of Parry's 'The Glories
of our Blood and State', commissioned for the occasion, and Stanford's
'Elegiac' Symphony, and the sermon was preached by Stanley's old
friend Vaughan, now Dean of Llandaff, Grove did not go to the Gloucester Festival. 'I feel terribly tired and old, but always your loving G.', he
wrote to Squire just before Christmas.[24]

During the winter months Grove's official duties were punctuated by
bursts of academic grapeshot directed at the St James's and Pall Mall
Gazette, and The Times, concerning a variety of familiar —and some
unfamiliar—issues. In the spring of 1884 he went to Cambridge to hear
Joachim on 13 March, to Dannreuther's house in Orme Square six days
later to the first performance of Parry's String Quintet in E flat major, and
on 28 April to Drury Lane where Stanford's The Canterbury Pilgrims
was performed for the first time.[25] There was also a duty to whip up
support for the Lord Mayor's Fund for the Jubilee of Benedict, in order,
as the Neue Musik-Zeitung had put it, 'to keep the shadow of care far
from him in the evening of his life'.

Although he frequently felt anxious about his own prospects in the
approaching 'evening of his life', Grove's interest at this time was
concentrated neither on that, nor on the raising of funds for a deserving
cause, nor on new music, but increasingly on one of his pupils.

On 6 October 1883, soon after the new College term began, Grove had
written a dutiful letter to Edith Oldham on the death of her uncle
Wilton, a former Indian civil servant, later a clergyman, which had
taken place in Cheltenham:

Dear Miss Oldham

I am very sorry to hear of your trouble. I know what such losses are well, and
can feel keenly for you. When you have got over the first shock you will feel
what a blessing it is to recollect how good he was to you. May you be supported
under the heavy trial.

Yours very truly
G. Grove

The Oldhams were a Dublin family, well known in both trade and
scholarship. Edith's uncle Wilton Oldham had served as a magistrate at
Ghazipore in North-west India and published several works on Indian
affairs before returning to England, to be ordained in the Church of
England in 1878 and in this condition to enjoy retirement in Bristol.

[24] Letter of 'Dec [?] 26, '83'; BL, Add. MS. 39679, f. 100.
[25] The première of this, Stanford's third opera, took place at an unpropitious time,
the newspapers being still mainly concerned with the effects of the earthquake which
had occurred in Essex less than a week before, with the deaths of four people and damage
reported to a thousand buildings.

Thomas Oldham, another uncle, had been active in archaeological research for the British Government both in Ireland and in India, where he was Superintendent of the Geological Survey. Edith's father had been a principal in 'Samuel Oldham and Son, Linendrapers, outfitters, silk mercers, shawl and mantle warehouse', a business with a prime site at 12 Westmorland Street in Dublin, and one which her mother liked tŏ describe as qualifying them for membership of 'the élite of our class'. By the time Edith went to take up her scholarship at the Royal College in London, however, her father had died and the finances of the firm, in the hands of a not very competent brother (or half-brother), Eldred, were in a state of decline. In 1884 Samuel Oldham and Son was listed in Thom's Dublin Directory for the last time, and progressively the severest economies were forced on the family.

On the bright side, Edith's brother, Charles Hubert, who was five years her senior, was establishing himself as one of the leading young intellectuals of Ireland. Like his uncles a graduate of Trinity College, Charles Oldham had left the College with two gold medals—one for experimental physics, the other for mathematics—as well as a first-class degree, and burgeoning political and literary ambitions. Edith's sister, Alice, was also an intellectual, who took a good degree at Trinity and became a mistress at Alexandra College.

Edith had experienced life in England before coming to the RCM. In the summer of 1882 she had stayed with her uncle Wilton in Bristol, and when she announced her impending return to Dublin her sister Annie wrote a letter which indicates that Edith—as others later confirmed —'had a mind of her own':

And so at last we may look forward to your longed for return! Joy unspeakable! I hope it will be indeed the same Edith Oldham who went away that will come back, and not some knocked up with conceit young woman of English ideas and stupidity, for it is stupid to be conceited; and as (thanks to Alice and Hubert) you do happen to be more conversant with the facts of the living world than some others are.[26]

The Oldham family were delighted when Edith won the scholarship to the Royal College, and showered her with congratulations. But after the initial pleasure had worn off, Mrs Oldham, conscious of her responsibility to the rest of her talented children and the genteel poverty which was her affliction, worried on the one hand because Edith would have little on which to support herself in London, and on the other that she was a strong-minded girl whose willingness to take motherly advice was not to be counted on.

That in London her daughter was friendly with some girls whose origins were taken to be socially inferior to her own was another reason

[26] Letter of 17 Sept 1882; Oldham Letters, RCM.

for concern. Having settled in modest, student-crowded lodgings in Brixton, Edith was subjected to letters from home compounded of worry about the declining family fortunes and about the kind of company she was keeping. Mrs Oldham did not at all like her daughter having to 'be condemned to the society of Miss Kellett and the mill hands'. 'Louie' Kellett, the other Irish girl at the College on a scholarship, was from an impoverished background and conspicuous by her flaming red hair; she 'must be a very bad companion', wrote Edith's mother, adding that she was glad her daughter appeared to be steering clear of Miss Kellett; otherwise there was the danger of being 'deteriorated by her'. As for another Irish girl, Anna Russell, Mrs Oldham believed she came from a street which was 'one of the worst in Limerick'. So much for the policy of equality of opportunity in musical education formulated by the Prince of Wales and believed in by Grove.

But Mrs Oldham was not only worried about the impropriety of admitting the underprivileged to higher education, she was greatly concerned about the possible consequences of mixed concert-going and other unsegregated activities. On 17 November 1883 she wrote to Edith: 'You are very young and attractive at present but believe me if a girl once gets a reputation for being a flirt or what is called fast her attractions rapidly diminish. The very men who amuse themselves with her are the first to laugh at and ridicule her.'

At the beginning of 1884 Mrs Oldham was in deep distress. The firm had lost £700 in the previous half-year, and bankruptcy was imminent. Virtually moneyless, Mrs Oldham was forced to let two rooms to an old lady and her maid. Edith, requiring £1 pocket money every third week, which was more often than not left to Hubert to supply, was adjudged as extravagant. In the Easter holidays Grove, oblivious of the plight of the Oldhams, wrote on 24 April to Edith at home in Dublin, asking: 'What has become of you? I hoped to hear from you soon and to know how you found your friends, how Sir Robert Stewart[27] liked your [singing deleted] playing, and what prospect you had of a good holiday. But you are evidently faithless, and have forgotten my existence. . . .'

It seems she had written to him, for two days later he acknowledged a letter he had received from 'My dear Edith', who is given advice as to how to practise, is promised information concerning Stanford's Savonarola,[28] and advised of the 'nice music' of The Canterbury Pilgrims.

[27] Robert Prescott Stewart (1825–94), Professor of Music in Dublin University, and of Theory in the RIAM, and conductor of the Dublin Philharmonic Society.

[28] Savonarola was first performed in Hamburg on 18 Mar 1884 for the benefit of Kapellmeister Josef Sucher, and was appreciatively noticed in the May issue of the Neue Musik-Zeitung. The same journal, however, reporting in August on the Covent Garden performance by the German Opera Company managed by Hermann Franke, conducted by Richter, commented on the opera's lack of success there. Also see J. A. Fuller-Maitland, A Door-keeper of Music, op. cit., pp. 119–20.

Taking up from an observation of a more general nature delivered from her island, Grove drew on his reserves of native pride, remarking:

You are very hard on London and English scenery but let me tell you there is lovely scenery within 20 miles of town even Richmond and Windsor are beautiful and in Kent there are charming spots. So also Surrey at Guildford and Dorking.

Oh if we could all go there for a happy party some day! I will try to write again. Meantime thank you many times for your letter and for all the affection for your Director that it contains.

Yours in great haste
Very affectionately
G. Grove

I am so glad you have been idle and enjoying yourself so hard. I daresay Mr Parratt will give you an order for Windsor.[29]

It was three days after this that Sir Michael Costa died, and with him an epoch ended. Grove's supplement to the official obituaries, which he contributed to the *Pall Mall Gazette* (1 May 1884) under the guise of 'A correspondent', is valuable both historically and critically, and shows how firmly he kept his feet on the ground in respect of practical music:

None of the many biographies of Sir Michael Costa which have appeared in the papers since his death seem to have touched upon one important fact in his life. All have remarked his success, but no one has pointed out the means by which he attained it. His means may be summed up in three words—make yourself safe. Surround yourself by the best possible agents; have the best associates, the best players, the best assistants that you can obtain, quite regardless of expense, and success is certain. In the zenith of his career Sir Michael never moved without such men as Bowley to prepare the whole scheme of the transaction for him—Sainton, Blagrove, Hill, Lucas, Howell, Pratten, Lazarus, the Harpers, Chipp, and others of equal eminence at the principal desks, Peck and Henry Wright to distribute the parts. With the perfect organisation and efficient execution of such lieutenants, failure was impossible. And this was the secret of Costa's uniform success for a long series of years. Of course it was horribly expensive—so expensive that it crippled the Sacred Harmonic Society and at Covent Garden forced the proprietor entirely to alter the system; but it fulfilled its end, it ensured the triumph of the piece or the concert, and it brought applause and honour to the head organiser himself. Such a course shows how thoroughly astute Costa was, how full of 'practical wisdom almost amounting to genius'. But to do what we have seen done by Manns, Richter, and Carl Rosa—to take an orchestra composed mainly of second class materials, and by tact, knowledge, and perseverance produce the finest effects from it—that was entirely out of his power. Some of the biographers have mentioned his interpolations in great works. They were shameful; it is the only word! The additions to choruses in the 'Dettingen Te Deum' and 'Israel in Egypt', the prelude added to 'Wretched Lovers' in 'Acis and Galatea', are enough to make your hair

---

[29] Walter Parratt had begun in 1882 his long reign of 42 years as organist of St George's Chapel.

stand on end—so vulgar, so unnecessary, so out of keeping are they. The 'big drum'—'enormous' it should be called, for it was the biggest ever made—so freely laid on all through the Handel festivals, is not more inconsistent with Handel's score than it was brutal and monotonous. His ignorance was astounding. He once told me that 'Beethoven had no melody'; by which of course he meant that the long continuous flow of the Italians alone was melody; and on the same occasion he volunteered the statement that Mendelssohn was a plagiarist, 'for, do you know, none of the Psalm tunes in "St Paul" are his own composition. When I introduced a psalm tune in "Eli", I composed it myself'. Could anything show more egregious ignorance of the position of the chorale in the German school? . . . One more story. He was induced by a friend to put Beethoven's overture to 'Coriolan' into one of the concerts in the nave of the Crystal Palace in 1858, but that sublime work, which he then heard for the first time, so disgusted him that he could never play it again. 'It ends pianissimo', exclaimed he in his harshest voice, 'and you can never get any applause for it'. But still, even with these drawbacks, we owe Costa a debt. He was a splendid drill-sergeant; he brought the London orchestras into an order unknown before. He acted up to his lights, was thoroughly efficient as far as he went, and was eminently safe. An Englishman does not mind paying for his outing if he knows that the horses are sound, the vehicle in good repair, and the coachman able to drive.

Sometime in June Grove entertained a party of students at Sydenham and Mrs Oldham, amid the ruins of the family business, was glad that Edith had enjoyed herself, observing on 15 June that 'in the midst of our domestic troubles it was a good thing you had something to cheer you'. Soon after this Grove went off to Paris for a few days with his daughter Millie, partly to see the paintings at the Salon (about which a full account had appeared in *The Times* of 3 June). From the experience of viewing a large number of examples of 'flesh-painting' by Henner, Collin, Carolus-Duran, Giacomotti and many others Grove was to suffer a delayed moral shock which evinced itself years later (see p. 287). The Groves also went to the Opéra and to the Louvre.

Back home interest was concentrated on the first of the Students' Concerts at the College. For the first few years, until another room became available, these took place in the draughty area of the West Theatre in the Albert Hall. The first concert on 2 July included a performance of an otherwise unspecified String Quartet in E flat, by Haydn. The members of the quartet were Kreuz, Sutcliffe, Arnold Dolmetsch and Friend.

A week later Hubert Oldham, prospecting for work in England, called at the College and spoke with Grove and Pauer, who was Edith's pianoforte teacher. At this time it seems that Edith was asking herself questions about Grove's attitude; and she was not quite happy. Back from Dublin, and the desolation of the Westmorland Street premises, came her mother's sad counsel: 'You have been treated with exceptional kindness and attention by Sir George and it would be very unwise to lose his friendship for the sake [of] and resenting slights which may be more imaginary than real.' Eight days later, on 24 July, Mrs Oldham implored: 'whatever you do you must keep good friends with Sir George', who had again invited the girl to visit at Sydenham. It was advice which the mother was bitterly to regret having offered. Still keeping rigidly to the code which gave certain people entitlement to superiority of esteem, she threw in a warning against friendship with Kathy (Katy) Macdonald, from Chester.

Term over, Grove prepared for a holiday in Switzerland, after which he went to the Worcester Festival, principally for the performance of Dvořák's *Stabat Mater* and Symphony in D conducted by the composer. About this time the cathedral authorities at Worcester had gone so far as to allow performances of a 'Catholic' work in the cathedral; Grove noted with approval that his brother-in-law George Bradley, now Dean of Westminster, was adhering to the ecumenical principles of his predecessor, Stanley, as demonstrated by his reception in the Abbey of a group of Roman Catholics.

Since his appointment to the College, the circulation of interests and emotions in Grove's mind had led to a general concern for the young but also to a realization of faded time, of lost years, of impulses that would not remain dormant. Often in a state of exhaustion which he disguised from the public, always isolated within his domestic setting, he tried desperately to arrest the passage of time, even to reverse its flow.

In 1883 Squire had become a solicitor, from the bondage of which occupation he was one year later to extricate himself. His personal problems reminded Grove of his own, and on 21 November 1884, saying how distressed he was that Squire should be in trouble, but reminding him that he was fortunate to have an understanding family, Grove wrote:

To me 'water' has always been thicker than 'blood'. I have been driven outside my own family for affection and have often looked on with the keenest envy at brothers and sisters who, like you, are all in all to one another. No doubt the things that your sister's marriage [to Fuller-Maitland] brings with them are bad and leaving the old place is most afflicting—but cheer up, dear, after a little while alleviation will come and you will see that all is for the best. We had to do the same with our old home, where I was born and led a very full and happy life for 30 years. And now one of my saddest pleasures is to go over its ruins and now and then go into the old paddock and revive—as I can with the most singular completeness—the associations, nay the very feelings and emotions of nearly 60 years ago.[30]

A month later Grove wrote again. After commenting on the happy discovery of manuscripts at Durham Cathedral by Philip Armes, the organist, he advised Squire as to the course of action he should take in respect of his own career: 'I think you are right to go into the B.M. . . .

[30] BL, Add. MS. 39679, f. 106.

It is a definite career and one which may be made important—We want
a good musical archaeologist of the rank of Jahn or Nottebohm or Ambros
—and why should not you be he? (And a good deal better?)'[31] Squire
duly accepted the modest post of assistant in the Department of Printed
Books.

Meanwhile the students at the College were awaiting the results of
their end-of-term examinations. While all may be presumed to have been
anxious, some were more anxious than others. For one the period of
anxiety was sensibly diminished. Edith Oldham sent a Christmas card
to the Director, who wrote to her on Boxing Day that it was 'the best
I have had . . . so much of *yourself* in it . . .' He turned to the subject of
the examinations: 'I have not got back the Harmony papers yet but you
shall know directly I do. I should say you will certainly get through.
In History you did very well, notwithstanding your terrible fatigue.
(You quite frightened me I can tell you.)' The letter ended with a discussion of Shakespeare and a résumé of the progress of other students.

The relationship thus commenced settled into something resembling
normality for both parties. In February 1885 Grove was unwell and
obliged to spend a few days in bed, so that—

. . . there is no reason why you should go to the College at all. This is an *edict*,
and those who disobey it do so at their peril—

given at my court of South Kensington
this 20th day of February 1885
George

A week later Mrs Oldham reacted to a rumour which must have come
from Edith: 'I am sorry about Sir George. He would be a great loss to
you but perhaps a younger man might manage the College better.'
Among other matters disturbing Mrs Oldham were the reported crowded
bedroom conditions, which still obtained although Edith had moved to
new lodgings in Fulham.

In 1885 there were many reasons for feeling that the world was falling
apart. In February General Gordon was killed, and Khartoum fell.
In March incidents caused by Russian aggression on the Afghan border
brought about a further lack of confidence in Gladstone's administration,
which in turn, in June, led to the fall of the Government. Before this
happened, however, in order to bolster loyalty in Ireland the Prince
and Princess of Wales were sent to Dublin in April. This, thought
Grove, could provide an opportunity to promote Edith Oldham's interest.
He proposed, therefore, that she go home to Ireland with the hope that
she might be given opportunity to play the piano at some reception or
other given for the Princess of Wales and to be 'presented'. Edith, who

[31] Ibid., f. 108.

had otherwise been going to spend the Easter holidays with her aunt at Sydenham because it was too expensive to go home, was elated at the prospect; but her joy was short-lived. Her mother wrote on 19 March: 'I fear I shall displease you when I say that no matter whether Sir George is displeased or not I must say what I said before I cannot bring you home myself and I shall not ask Hubert to do so.' When Sir George offered to pay the travel costs, Mrs Oldham said that she could not 'put up any more opposition'. But the project never came off, and Mrs Oldham wearily observed: 'I daresay both you and he are much annoyed and blame me.' It must be said that Grove added to his general load of problems by involving himself in this manner.

Always feeling oppressed by overwork, Grove was glad to be able to find excuses to take days off, sometimes conveniently finding ways of combining business with pleasure. At Windsor, for instance, he could talk about College matters with Parratt while indulging himself in the contemplation of ancient buildings, which always excited him. A trip to Tenbury in April, at the invitation of Gore Ouseley—even if it was 'an immense way for only one day'—allowed him to indulge in railway nostalgia. All of this he recounted (on 1 May) to Edith, in whose absence in Ireland he took Louie Kellett to *The Mikado*—which had its first performance on 14 March. And then he told how the Palestine Exploration Fund had been in existence for twenty years, which was taken as a good reason for a dinner. This took place on 22 June, and Grove made a speech.

Among the few careers open to women at that time music—albeit offering meagre rewards—was the most alluring. That it was a lady-like pursuit was one of the more sacred tenets in a genteel philosophy attractive to parents whose daughters were not required to work for their living. For those who were under a necessity to do so, teaching the pianoforte in a select private school sometimes led to advancement in prospects, but matrimonial rather than professional. A college where the two sexes would study together (even if discouragement of social intercourse was enjoined) attracted the interest of girls who anticipated the opportunity to enjoy a new kind of freedom.

Grove was acquainted with many persons of distinction who were prodded by their offspring to find out what life would be like at the RCM. On 15 July he wrote to William Knight, the Wordsworth scholar, concerning the merits of his own institution, with guarded comment on the sister conservatory:

The advantage of coming here is that our teaching is systematic and broad. We do not form players only, but musicians, and—there is an amount of music in all sorts of shapes going on in the place which is very stimulating to the pupils.

Of the Royal Academy I prefer to say nothing. My opinion is not favourable in some respects, and if I expressed such an opinion it would naturally be put down to the ground that I belonged to a rival institution. Whereas we are *not rivals* and never should have been accused of it but for the absurd conduct of the R.A. themselves. . . . . To sum up if your daughter comes here she will find the ἦθος far beyond that of any other musical establishment that I know of— she can live in a good house under a quite satisfactory lady, but I myself should be constantly on the watch over her in every particular.[32]

The 'good house' was Alexandra House, where women students from the College as well as other establishments were lodged, and protected by a lady warden whose strictness in interpretation of her duties became somewhat irksome to Grove. It was at this time that he read *Music-Study in Germany*, a best-selling book by a lively and liberated American piano-forte teacher, Amy Fay. Grove recommended the book to Macmillan and when the firm accepted it for publication wrote a brief Preface.[33]

On the last day of 1885—a few days after writing his Preface—he went to a Millais exhibition at the Grosvenor Gallery, and the next day he wrote to the artist: ' . . . It was so delightful to see so many dear old friends all as familiar and as well-remembered as if one had seen them only yesterday. And all so sweet and kind—not a snarl, not one ugly word among the lot. Each one as harmonious and comforting as a bit of Mozart!'[34] The older he grew, inevitably the more Grove was pulled back into former times. His nostalgia was intensified in this case by re-cognition of Millais's genius. He looked at *The Carpenter's Shop*, *The Huguenot* and the 'dear old Knight on the river' (*Sir Isumbras at the Ford*) —works which had seemed startling in the 1850s—and expressed his pride in knowing what it was to be able to grasp the hand of the painter.

A week later two intimates of many years were carried away: Mimi von Glehn, a victim of consumption, whose father had died in the previous July, on 8 January, and James Fergusson the next day. But from certain other events in which Grove had a long-standing personal interest there was more encouragement. His old schoolmaster, Charles Pritchard, now well beyond the ordained span of three score years and ten, was not only as vigorous as ever, but brimful with academic originality. As Savilian Professor of Astronomy at Oxford he had lately published work con-cerning the use of photographic techniques in astronomical research. His *Uranometria Nova Oxoniensis* of 1885, which gained for him a half-share of the Astronomical Society's Gold Medal award, was, it may not unreasonably be said, one step towards man's progress to the moon. Elected an honorary Fellow of his old college at Cambridge in 1886, Pritchard was also honoured on 5 July by a banquet given by 100 of his old Clapham pupils. To his regret Grove's duties precluded his being present.

[32] PML.

[33] If he had not done so before, Grove met Miss Fay in London soon after the appear-ance of the English edition, as he informed Edith on 11 July 1886.

[34] PML.

Like his old master he was determined to keep going until he had realized his major ambition: to see the *Dictionary* completed, his book on Beethoven's symphonies written, and his College firmly established. He was sustained by youth—particularly by his daughter Millicent, the favourite of his family, by Edith Oldham, by his other students—and by the sociabilities that attended his daily round.

In the early part of 1885 Edith moved into new quarters, at 11 Hornton Street, Kensington, where—to Mrs Oldham's chagrin—Kathy Macdonald also lived. That summer, Edith found herself conscripted as the contralto in a vocal quartet, and an uncertain performance of 'Un di si ben' from *Rigoletto* was given. Having written home enthusiastically about the Director's appreciation of the performance, Edith received a cold douche from her mother on 17 July: 'Sir George seems determined to be pleased if he thought it so good when the tenor sang all wrong notes.' On 12 November Edith took part in another concert, partnering Bulkeley in a performance of *Two Fantasiestücke* (op. 43) by Gade. Mrs Oldham had a letter from Sir George, 'telling me how beautifully you played, and announcing that the board had unanimously recommended you for another year's extension of your scholarship'. But she was more concerned that Edith should come home, and earn some money.

Hubert Oldham, brilliant and unorthodox, without a firm appointment, was unable to contribute much to the household. But he was making his reputation. He had founded the Contemporary Club in Dublin, at which the best and ablest young men in the city assembled to discuss politics and literature. Collaterally he brought into being the *Dublin University Review*, into which he took Yeats's first significant poem—the verse drama *The Island of Statues*—for publication. But in a year in which J. B. Bury was the successful Fellowship candidate at Trinity College, none of this helped much to establish Hubert academically. So he thrust himself deep into politics: 'politics and nothing but politics', wrote his mother to Edith, 'is his ruling passion at present'.

In that by now a new site for a more adequate College building had been made available, on land in Kensington belonging to the 1851 Commissioners, and that it was going to be necessary to raise £50,000, it was well that some of the students of the RCM were beginning to attract favourable attention. Of them, among the pianists, were Kathy Macdonald, Atalanta Heap and Louie Kellett. The last of these demonstrated the supremacy of mind over matter by her performances. Conquering the frailness of her physique by an indomitable spirit, she commanded the respect of the most hardened of critics by her interpretation of the 'Emperor' and of Schumann's *Études symphoniques*. Early in 1886 Jasper Sutcliffe, a Lancashire boy, was noted as an orchestral leader of great promise. Zoë Pyne and Isabel Donkersley (the latter in due course to marry August Jaeger), pupils of Henry Holmes, were distinguishing themselves as solo violinists. Thanks to Parry's teaching, Charles Wood, a shy youth of twenty from Armagh, was showing himself as a composer of genuine talent; a pianoforte concerto and a setting of *O Salutaris Hostia*, for chorus and strings, were heard with approval in July 1886.

As so often Joachim, and the Joachim Quartet, took a good deal of Grove's interest and time. Beethoven, Schubert and Schumann kept him happy, while a new composer to arise in his firmament was J. S. Bach, whose 'Council Election' cantata of 1708, *Gott ist mein König*, was performed by the Bach Choir under Stanford, in St James's Hall, on 25 March of that year.

By now Grove's affection for Edith had grown into an obsession. Already on 15 February 1886, mindful, no doubt, of the information he had already conveyed to her concerning fellow students and members of the RCM teaching staff, he felt himself carried away by an impulse over which his self-discipline was beginning to prove ineffective, and he enjoined her not to 'repeat things' he had written to her. On 20 March convention trod on hope; but George allowed his imagination to wander:

Do you know that I am alone. My belongings have fled to Hastings. It would not be right to ask you both to come and *stay*, but how nice it would be if any chance thing were to direct you and Louie [Kellett] down here on Sunday afternoon. You could easily get back by the train. I am afraid this is all nonsense. . . .

Poor Edith was now the unhappy subject of an emotional tug-of-war, with neither of the contestants apprised of the feelings and motives of the other. She had not been home for Christmas. For a time it seemed she was not going to be home at Easter. On 23 March her mother wrote:

We, like yourself feel it a long time since you were home and I only wish you were coming home to stay as I had been so long looking forward to. I must say for many reasons I think it would have been the wisest course but when Sir George wrote I feared you might be giving up some real advantages and what weighed with me more than any thing else I thought you would be unhappy and disappointed if he refused to have you.

Edith was somewhat peevish. She had been asked by Franklin Taylor's wife to play for concerts which she arranged. Her mother berated her, expressing

surprise at the tone you have taken about playing at Mrs Taylor's concerts. So far from trying to get out of playing you ought to be glad of every opportunity of playing in public. Will you just for a moment ask yourself what you have been spending the last three years in London for, separated from your own family and giving your time exclusively to music, except you might be able to play in superior style both in public and private. . . . I think you should realise more fully the importance of these opportunities. You never can know what they may lead to. . . .

On the last Friday night of March Grove sat down once more in lyrical mood:

Dearest Edith:

I was sorry for you today. I hope you saw how I felt for you. It is the penalty, dear, you pay for your delicate feelings and highly strung nature. But depend on it in the end the possession outweighs the penalty—You suffer more, but your enjoyment is incalculably greater and purer. I scarcely ever see you for half a minute that I don't recognise some bit of unselfishness or delicate refinement that cannot be valued too highly. Thank God, dear, for having bestowed that nature on you. It is a special gift and—as I say—if it brings you troubles it also brings unutterable joys—I know by experience. . . .

Next day Edith went with Grove's party to the Beethoven concert at the Crystal Palace, when Joachim suffered the embarrassment of a broken string during the Violin Concerto. Edith wondered afterwards whether she had not seemed rather 'cross'. Grove assured her that she gave no such impression, and—somewhat illogically—that in any case he was glad that she sometimes showed him 'the seamy side as some one calls it'. All that worried him at the time was that Sophie von Glehn[35] might have been feeling that he had neglected her in favour of his pupil.

There was a heavy load for Grove to carry that spring. The impending departure from the teaching staff of Jenny Lind-Goldschmidt was a worry; not least because, on account of her knowledge and experience, she was able to help the able and deserving as perhaps no one else in the province of singing could. There was the case of H. C. Deacon, a teacher who was obliged to retire early on account of ill health. H. R. Haweis wrote soliciting Grove's help in setting up a Fund for Deacon, who, having been accustomed to living in some style, was now reduced to poverty. Haweis was another person who, like Prout, was *non grata* to Grove. In writing to him Haweis observed that Arthur Chappell 'knows very well that *we* have not been on cordial terms for years—but I said from my general knowledge of you that I did not believe that you would allow private feelings to interfere with any such proposal as I now make'.[36] Haweis concluded by saying that although he had had the opportunity for twenty years to belabour Grove in print, in *Truth*, he had never done so. Now his connection with that journal had ceased.

[35] The former Sophie Löwe, a soprano, niece of Johanna Sophie Loewe and a pupil of Stockhausen, came to London in 1871. Six years later she married William von Glehn and gave up the career of a virtuoso to concentrate on teaching (see p. 304).

[36] Letter of 30 Mar 1886; BL, Add. MS. 39680, f. 21.

In the Easter examinations at the College, the standard was not as high as could have been wished. Grove on the whole disliked singers and it was not altogether surprising that none of the vocal candidates was successful. Of the pianists there were, surprisingly, only four who reached the required standard: Max Pauer (son of Ernst), Annie Fry, Atalanta Heap and Adelaide Thomas, all of whom had started their careers at the National Training School.[37] While Grove was agitating himself over the examinations, the rest of musical London was for a memorable fortnight in a delirium of ecstasy on account of Liszt's visit— his last, as it turned out, for three months later he was dead. Grove naturally was involved, being at a Grosvenor Gallery reception arranged by Walter Bache on 8 April and, of course, at the Crystal Palace two days later.

Edith hovered helpfully in the background, and not always quite in the background. She paid visits to the Director's office to find a score for which she had asked, or on one occasion a note for which she had not asked, but which thrilled her when she found it. Grove was an animal-lover, and now it was Millie's terrier, Rusty, for whose welfare he was frequently anxious. If he was brought up to Kensington for the day, Edith was called on—as in this note of 12 April— to look after him.

In the Easter holidays she did in the end go back to Dublin, where on 20 April Grove wrote to her. 'I am glad you have settled down to your beloved poetry again—like a bee on the flowers! Nothing like it, dear, but remember that you at 20 and I at 120 *must* take different views and have different loves.' At the time Edith was going through a Shelley phase. George knew this poet, but— 'I am old you see and I cling to the mind of man and his hopes and loves and look at things from the human side and that is one reason I love Tennyson so.'

Having heard the Joachim Quartet play Schubert's D minor Quartet at a concert in St James's Hall—one of the Saturday Pops—Grove went to the Isle of Wight with the Franklin Taylors. In spite of the fact that on 30 April the University of Glasgow was to confer an honorary LL.D. on him for his services to music, he was irritable. Perhaps he was annoyed that Glasgow—with which his closest relationship was in engineering— had lost an opportunity of recognizing his contribution to technology. In any case he did not go to the University to receive the degree in person. Carisbrooke, which he did visit, was ruined by '*thousands* of excursionists'. Further annoyed that the Taylors were intellectually

---

[37] Atalanta Heap, of Walmer, Kent, together with a fellow student, Henriette Krüger, taught for a time at St Leonard's School, St Andrews. In one of his letters Grove asked Professor Knight, of St Andrews University, to pass on his greetings to his former pupils. Atalanta died on 23 June 1894. Adelaide Thomas was the first woman to pass the examinations for the Mus. B. degree at Oxford. Being a woman, however, she was disqualified from receiving the degree.

inadequate, unaccustomed to reading and conscious only of super-
ficialities, Grove settled down with the works of Longfellow—'far from
being a first-rate man', he grumbled—and Wordsworth. He at least was
'deep'. So too was Brahms, whose Fourth Symphony was introduced to
London by Richter on 10 May, on which day an unsigned article by Grove
on the composer's adoption of the chaconne form appeared in the
St James's Gazette. Two days later he wrote another article on the
Symphony for the same journal.

Always susceptible to climatic change, in the Isle of Wight Grove
felt his spirits reviving with improvement in the weather, which he
related to Schubert. On 18 May he wrote of *Ganymed*, 'it is the very
incarnation of spring'.

Sarasate, the famous virtuoso violinist, hero of many Philharmonic
and Crystal Palace concerts, and victim of a concerto written for him
for the Birmingham Festival of 1885 by Alexander Mackenzie, was in
London that spring for a series of concerts at St James's Hall. Since
people could flock in to all of his series of five London concerts, in
spite of the gloom then surrounding the nation's economy, one critic
opined that 'there must be money in the country'. The last of the series
was on 29 May, when the 'Birmingham' concerto would be played,
Cusins being the conductor. Also in the programme was the Liszt arrangement of Schubert's March in B minor, which Grove had once noted in
one of his commonplace books.[38]

Although it was an elaborate joke perpetrated by Sir George, Edith—
by then back from Ireland—was grateful to receive a note purporting
to be from Sarasate himself, in which she read: 'I am told by my friend
Sir George how that you are an extraoooooooordinary nice person,
fascinating beyond the power of man to conceive.' The envelope also
contained two tickets for Sarasate's concert.[39]

In June Edith fell ill with measles, and was confined to her room, now
at 5 Kensington Square. Grove was anxious, but not only for her. He
wrote a hurried note from his office: 'Goodbye dear. I can't come round
this afternoon but will be there by 10 tomorrow. It is such a comfort
to think of you as mending. What *will* happen to me when you go away?
No you must never go, but stay in London always.' Edith spent her
convalescence reading, and discovering she shared with Grove an interest
in the novels of Turgenev. Once or twice Grove could slip in to see her,
though most days he was, as he said, 'driven like a leaf every moment of
the day up to 6.30'.

Mrs Oldham heard some of what had been happening from Edith, and,
concerning an otherwise unrecorded gift, wrote on 16 June that 'it was
very kind of Sir George to give you such a handsome present'. But

[38] See p. 95.
[39] E.O., 29 May [1886].

gossip was filtering through, to the detriment of Mrs Oldham's punctuation:

Mrs Arundel was saying to Alice that you ought to stay in London but Alice said you did not know any one there except Sir George that he was very kind and often takes you to concerts. She was horrified at the idea of your going to concerts alone with him but Alice said you generally had some of the girls with you so as old as he is people will talk hoping soon to hear of your liberation.

Sir George meanwhile was composing his next letter—of 18 June—to Edith, which ended: 'Well goodbye my precious child—it was lovely to see you the other day—you looked really beautiful.'

On 23 and 24 June (at which time Edith was in a second phase of recuperation, at Royston) Stanford conducted student performances of Cherubini's *The Water Carriers*. On the second night the Prince and Princess of Wales, accompanied by their children, were present. So were Sullivan and D'Oyly Carte, and, said Grove, 'all sorts of strange musicians', including Albani, Blumenthal, Garcia, Goring Thomas, Macfarren, McGuckin, Randegger and Rockstro. The Prince wished for another performance 'for the colonials'.[40] On 26 June Grove was summoned to the Prince's presence but found him in an unusually puritanical mood, and 'dead against the opera as the most dangerous thing for the girls' morals —over exciting—discordant for the general plan of the College etc—such a hubbub! I assure you we walked about a large room and holloaed at one another till the whole place echoed.'[41] On 10 July there was a more decorous and formal royal engagement, when Grove attended the Buckingham Palace Garden Party.

Much was happening in respect of Irish affairs to put Edith's future in England much at risk. In February Gladstone had taken over the Government from Lord Salisbury, but with a divided Party, a divided country, and the temper of the Irish at flash-point, he persisted in his advice to the Queen that there should be another General Election, to determine the Home Rule issue. From Ireland in March, Edith had been told of the great excitement caused by the possibility of Home Rule. Hubert Oldham, of course, was all in favour of it; but as for Mrs Oldham, 'if [Gladstone's] plan were carried out I think there would be no money left in Ireland or the possibility of making it. Hubert is very sanguine and excited about it'. Later, as the result of a brilliant speech to the Home Rule Association, Hubert Oldham received a telegram from Parnell asking that he should put himself forward as a candidate. But, having no funds on which he could depend and having lost a temporary teaching job in Dublin, he felt that he could not accept the invitation.

[40] The Colonial and Indian Exhibition had opened on 4 May and brought many overseas visitors and official guests to London. Tennyson's Ode for the occasion was set to music by Sullivan.

[41] E.O., 26 June [1886].

Throughout that spring and summer Ireland was gripped by fear and apprehension. As a prelude to the Election the celebrations of the 12th of July in the north of Ireland, particularly in the Catholic districts of Belfast, led to violence. Three men were killed, and twenty seriously injured; the Mayor of Belfast by a Proclamation practically put the city under martial law. On 15 July the *Irish Times* remarked on 'the same miserable and shameful conflict of senseless mobs in Ulster towns, with where there is not loss of life, always a refreshing of malice and bitterness, and a further blow to the nation's welfare'.

Up to that time Hubert Oldham had been assisting Edith financially. Now it was no longer possible, Mrs Oldham wrote urging her to come home and find a job. She remarked that 'Sir George was writing to Hubert, and he said that you looked brilliantly when you returned from the country'. For a number of reasons, among which was anxiety concerning the girl's safety in Ireland, Sir George was determined that Edith should stay in London. But he overplayed his hand. On 23 July Mrs Oldham wrote furiously to her daughter:

I received today a letter from Sir George which hurt and annoyed me much. He threatens if I do not allow you to stay to charge me with your board and instruction for this last term. If he thought by this means to terrify an ignorant woman or to tyrannise over a poor one, I do not know but I consider his letter most ungentlemanly, and in the worst possible taste. I shall reply to him as civilly as I can bring myself to do for your sake but I sincerely hope he will never write to me again. I always detested his letters and now I hate them worse than ever. Mr Taylor writes in such a different tone that I feel a pleasure in answering him which I shall do today.

Sir George's letter was sent on to Alice Oldham at Coolcarrigan. She was no less angry, as the following letter to Edith, written on 28 July, shows: 'Mama sent me Sir George Grove's letter about you finishing your scholarship. It shows the kind of man he is. No one who was a thorough gentleman could have written it. If I were you I would not trust or think much of such a person.'

In August Jenny Lind-Goldschmidt generously offered to take two students to Italy to study, and Grove appointed five wind-instrument players to the staff of the College, primarily to strengthen the orchestra. Edith was invited to Sydenham to stay with the Groves, after which Grove wrote on 3 August:

It has been so nice having you; you are so pleasant and nice to talk to, and fit into me [*sic*] so perfectly that it's the greatest pleasure to have you. Also I am sure that my people like you immensely. I never saw my wife take to any body so easily.

On 28 August Grove wrote to Squire that he had as yet had no holiday.

He had, however, been to Sussex—where Edmund now lived in retirement—with Parratt, and the three of them had explored Winchelsea
and its two beautiful churches. They went also to Chichester, where
Grove 'found a progenitor in the shape of a Bishop! Robert Grove died
1696'. That Grove, whose library was sold at Tom's Coffee House in
1697, was one who was also busy with his pen; but his sentiments were
distinctly illiberal.[42]

After his Sussex visit George spent a few days with his brother Thomas
in Penn, and then came the Gloucester and Leeds Festivals. After a day
in town between these two events Grove, feeling lonely, wrote to Edith
on 25 September, informing her: 'I have got the most lovely dinner—
soup, fish, partridges—only wanting you. I am all by myself.'

Grove may well have felt bereft of sympathy just at this time. He had
been vigorous with his pen in all directions. On 27 September his 'A
Country Church' appeared in the St James's Gazette, and he was busy
with his serial study, 'The History of a Musical Phrase . . .', for the
Musical World. The former is one of the most charming pieces ever
written by Grove, recapturing much of the spirit of Addison, anecdotal,
and touched with a sense of sadness over a lost world and forsaken
ideals:

I stayed for a Sunday lately at Penn, the home of my ancestors for many
generations. A little Buckinghamshire village which has been practically un-
changed for the last two hundred years, . . . Penn proper consists of a street
about half a mile long, a school, a chapel, a few houses and cottages on each
side, and, at the further or eastern end, the church, the blacksmith's shop, and
the Institute, which is almost the only modern thing in the place. On either
side of the street are some of the most delightful fields in England, and thence
you may have unrivalled views.

It was in the church that I found my greatest pleasure. The chancel was
burned down many years ago, and was rebuilt (apparently on its ample old
foundations) in brick, without any attempt at architecture; but the nave, with
a south aisle, two large roomy porches, and low tower, massive with large
spreading buttresses, all of the fourteenth century at latest, remain pretty much
as they always were. . . .

The south aisle . . . was built later than the rest, and the two clerestory win-
dows which it covers, and which once lighted the nave, still remain there, above
the plain honest arches, without their glass, but otherwise sharp and firm,
exactly as they were at first. I sat in a large pew—square, with very narrow
seats, and with faded moreen curtains round it, which, if I were the squire,
I think I should remove. Opposite, in the end-wall of the aisle, was a monument,
a vase of oval Roman form, delicately sculptured in gray marble, and setting

---

[42] Robert Grove's memorial tablet on the west wall of the north transept of Chichester
Cathedral has now as neighbour that erected to honour Thomas Weelkes. On the pave-
ment below is a stone marking the burial place of the ashes of Gustav Holst, who was
one of the early students of the Royal College of Music.

forth that it was to the memory of 'Roger Mather, clerk, eleven years vicar of this parish, to whom Asheton Curzon, Esq., was pupil, patron, and friend'. How characteristic! The form of the monument, the character of the letters, the turn of the inscription, all spoke plainly of the eighteenth century. Curzon was one of the great people of the place, and he and Mather, like Walpole and Gray, probably travelled in Italy together. It is not 'whose pupil, patron, friend'—that would have imported a certain familiarity into the phrase; but 'to whom Asheton Curzon, Esq.', etc, thus giving all due pre-eminence to the great man! The music was unpretending and good, and the lovely hymn, 'The Saints of God', must have sunk into many a heart beside my own. At such times those whom one has lost, and those whom one is about to lose, take entire possession of the mind, and lift it into another and a higher sphere. . . .

In 'those whom one is about to lose' is a terrible prescience. Before the year was out Grove was to suffer the most grievous loss.

During September Edith stayed with her aunt—Wilton Oldham's widow —at 70 Avonmore Road, West Kensington, in which street a few years later the Elgars rented a house. While there she wrote a letter home in which she would seem to have extolled the virtues of her cousin Walter. On 6 October she heard what her mother had to say about what she had reported. Mrs Oldham clearly felt that her daughter told her less than everything about herself:

If ever we see him we will be sure to be disappointed. He should indeed be a marvel who could realise your 'Ideal Boy'. It is a safe thing to fall in love with him but you get so enthusiastic when you like a person that I am always afraid of hearing that you have fixed your affection on some one more dangerous than Walter but perhaps if you had we would not be told anything about it.

A few sentences later she asked, 'how are Sir George's son and daughter?'
   Meanwhile Mrs Oldham was in despair about where her family should live in Dublin. No longer was it possible to maintain the house in Waterloo Road, so a smaller house in a less desirable part of the city, in Marlborough Road, was taken. Hubert, however, was distinguishing himself as a spokesman on national affairs. In September he was selected by the Lord Mayor of Dublin to travel as part of a delegation to Holyhead, to meet a group of Indian and Colonial dignitaries who were to visit the Irish capital. He was also given an assignment by the *Manchester Guardian* to write a periodic 'Irish Letter', for a fee of two guineas a week. In November he went to Leeds, as a delegate from the Irish Home Rule Association, to address a Liberal meeting.
   Edith meanwhile had found herself a pupil, one Kathleen Cole, of 96 Philbeach Gardens, in order to help with her living expenses. She also moved her lodgings again, this time finding accommodation in Alexandra House, where—in an age when it seemed impossible to remain in good

health for long—she was soon in trouble again. So too, in other ways, was George, as indicated by this letter sent from Sydenham on 6 November:

My dear Edith:

I meant to come in and see you yesterday before I left; but I was told not to go to the girls' rooms and so that makes me cautious. This is a secret though. I hope your foot is better: also that you are looking on the Piano competition with due interest. Do you know either of the pieces already? We must have a talk over it, if we are ever to have a talk again! I have just been rudely awakened to the fact that my Dictionary is immensely behind hand and *must* be got on with—and the first few days of taking up again a task that one has allowed to drift—and of looking up papers that *were* to one's hand, and now are all moved and *tidied* by servants, is simply dreadful. I have been working today from 7 AM till (now) 4.30—without almost ceasing. . . . It has been a *horrid* day day [*sic*], blowing, black and rainy, and very cold. I hope you have been comfortable in your rooms, and not had to go out.

Isn't the enclosed a pretty drawing? done merely with common ink. It is by a friend of mine a Mrs. Brotherston [?] whose sad story I will one day tell you.

Now good bye—A happy Sunday to you—

Yours affectionately

G. Grove

Four days later, crossing the road in Knightsbridge, Grove was run down by a cab. Badly shaken, he took the next ten days recovering. But temporarily his own misfortune took second place to those of his old friend Alexander Thayer, who had sent him some material for the *Dictionary*. Having occasion to write to Squire on 26 November about another matter connected with the *Dictionary*, Grove brought up Thayer's sad state:

The poor fellow complains dreadfully of want of money. Don't you think it would be possible to get £50 together for him? His 3 Vols on Beethoven are far and away the best thing that has ever been done, and it is a great pity that he should not finish the 4th before he dies.[43]

Thayer, in fact, did not finish the last volume of his great work.

While Grove was thus concerned he was thrown into a deeper anxiety, by the fact that Millie was unwell and had been recommended to go to Italy. She arrived in Alassio on 22 November. A little more than two weeks later the Groves were summoned to her bedside, and found their daughter so grievously ill as to be virtually already beyond recovery. The full horror of their experience is contained in George's letter to Edith and Louie Kellett:

[43] BL, Add, MS. 39679, f. 138. See *Grove 1*, vol. IV, pp. 493-4, for Squire's reference to Thayer in his article on 'Yankee Doodle'.

Alassio, Italy
Hotel Mediterranee
Wedy morning

My dear friends Edith and Louie:

Till tomorrow night I know you will have your minds full of the competition, but after that you will have leisure to read this.—We are in dreadful trouble. We arrived here at 1 on Thursday aftn. and found our darling Milly at the point of death—Her pulse 160 temperature 105 (instead of 92). Her head and face swelled to nearly double its proper size, and deep red and her poor nose and lips and ears all covered with thick hard black scabs;—incessantly wandering—on her journey—at home—dressing her brother's baby etc. (most distressing to hear her). Friday was a *dreadful* day and that night we all thought she was going. However since that she had improved. Pulse this morning is 130, temperature 102·5 and though wandering she is less excited. The state of things is that the fever is devouring her, and that the 'waste' has to be kept up by giving her all the nourishment possible. She has a table spoon of brandy each hour, and at each half hour—milk or egg or the strongest beef tea and so on,—poured down her dear throat. If we can keep this up till the fever lulls she is saved, if not——[44]

I *daren't* say *I hope*—but still the fact that she is no worse than she was on Saturday is some encouragement. She is the most wonderful patient I ever saw or heard of. I have never heard one grumble: and every flower you bring her or thing you do for her is 'lovely', 'delightful', 'sweeter than she ever saw' etc.

We are close on the sea shore—a road and a strip of sand, and there are the breakers rolling in; a beautiful open sea before us with such sunrises and *such* moonlight.

The kindness of people is quite astonishing. We have brandy, wine, beef tea, fresh eggs—water proof sheets—everything—poured in upon us by people who know nothing of us and never heard our names before—but who have a loving heart given them by God. Bless them all. My poor wife is not strong, but she's as tough as steel and lies always on a sofa in Milly's room ready for anything. Fortunately we have got a real good nurse—a regular trained one 21 years old, daughter of the Doctor quite a 'treasure'—also our niece Fanny Bennett.[45]

Write me a letter please dears and tell me how the competition went. Tell me really all about it, and the Concert (Barton, Russell,—A Roberts, the music) tell me everything at length, and how things are looking.[46]

[44] Millie Grove travelled to Italy in a lowered state of health, and vulnerable to infection. The symptoms described in the letter indicate that in the first instance she had contracted pneumonia, with which was associated a progressive process of dehydration. It was not unusual for herpes to supervene on pneumonia, and the black scabs described indicate secondarily infected herpes, with which the swelling of the face is also consistent. The final stage, and the cause of death, was streptococcal septicaemia. The advice that Millie should travel to Alassio in order to regain her health, considering the state of public hygiene at such a place at that time, was tantamount to a death warrant. By the time her parents reached her there was nothing medical science could have done to save her.

[45] Fanny Bennett was the sister of Edmund Grove Bennett, of Salisbury. See below, p. 249.

[46] The programme of the last students' concert of the term, conducted by Stanford,

Good bye—my love to all my friends Daisy and Kathie and the others

Yours ever and ever

G. Grove

Has Atalanta [Heap] gone to St Andrews?

Next day Millie died, and on 17 December was buried in Alassio. Even in this distress Grove could not keep his mind long away from his commitments, and he sent a quick message to Squire two days after Christmas: 'Will you do Yonge (Musica Transalpina)?' But as the year died so his spirits sank into a black despair. This note shows that it was not only Millie's death that caused a hurt. There was an even harder blow to bear.

The grief is dreadful. We were very fond of one another; and yet when I read her letters to others it seems as if I had been a stranger to her. How am I to pass the remaining years I know not. . . . I am not irreligious—but I can't cast my problem on the Lord. It seems to me that all is so vague—years ago I had all that feeling, but the deaths, first of Lucy, and now of Milly, have altered everything.

At the end of Edith Oldham's College report were the Director's remarks: 'Good and encouraging reports. I hope that you will have good health and strength to take thorough advantage of your last term at College.'

---

included as 'test pieces', Mendelssohn, *Melusina* Overture; the duet between Elijah and the widow, in *Elijah* (Dan Price and Anna Russell); Beethoven, Fourth Pianoforte Concerto (Marmaduke Barton, cadenzas by J. F. Barnett); Mendelssohn, *Infelice* (Julie Albu); Schubert, Mass in F (Misses Himing, Rose Price, Annie Roberts, Messrs Houghton, Atkinson, Ridding).

CHAPTER TEN

The Royal College—Phase 2

1887–1889

LIKE many men of affairs whose marriages have endured on a foundation of convenience, Grove was greatly dependent on his daughters. Although he never recovered completely from the death of Lucy, the close companionship which developed with Millie was a source of warmth and serenity and it engendered the confidence he needed to fulfil his never-diminishing commitments. Her death was an immeasurable disaster, and—although just at that point mutual distress brought him closer to Harriet—emotionally it detached him from his family. His salvation lay in his College, and in the young people for whom he felt responsible. His attitude was paternalist, sometimes cloyingly so, as his general description of his students as his 'children' suggests. Sometimes his concern for girl students led him into a contemplation of aspects of personality and facets of their love-lives that bordered on prurience, and now and then left him on the edge of voyeurism. For the last seventeen years of his life his anchorage was Edith Oldham, substitute for daughters and wife, and if this relationship brought to both parties agonies of frustration, for Grove it meant the kind of understanding by which creativity is nourished. Grove, the good Victorian, inheritor of the principles of the 'holy village', was a slave to duty; the reverse of the medal was the licence he allowed himself in thought and word, if not in deed. The world saw in Grove, however, a model of normality, of moral probity, of resoluteness of principle.

In his New Year address to students in 1887 the Director spoke at first to the young men in somewhat chiding terms. Some of them had been guilty of rowdiness; some had torn down notices in the dining room; one had even gone so far as to dance a hornpipe on the landing before an audience of girl students. This part of his forty-minute speech over, Grove referred to the recent death of his daughter, and proceeded to outline the consequent relationship he hoped to establish between himself and the students. He would like each one, after leaving College, to write to him at least once a year.

There were students and students. Being in communication with Barclay Squire, now settled in his post in the British Museum, over the editing of the Supplement to the *Dictionary*,[1] Grove added this request:

[1] The need for the Supplement, or Appendix, was explained later by J. A. Fuller-Maitland, editor of *Grove 2*, in his Preface to that edition dated 1 Oct 1904:

Also can you tell me how I can get a man in as library attendant in the B.M.? He was a student at the College for 2 years, plays a little piano and organ and double bass (!) and is as good as gold—but is too stupid for music as a profession —I could get the Prince of Wales' nomination I think if I knew *where* to ask for it. Give me a little help. He would feed the pigeons splendidly, but aspires to handle books.[2]

The touch of hilarity was a hangover from the previous night when Grove had dined with Stanford at the Savile Club, where he was 'sure we were merrier than any two at the table'.

But often he felt himself at the opposite emotional pole. On 5 February, Edith, recovering from burns sustained in a domestic mishap, received a note marked 'Private'.

. . . there seems to be growing up a hedge between us because of the absurd rules of Alexandra House. And partly because of the increase in my work and somehow a loss of energy and determination to break through everything. But I *will* break through. I will not be conquered. Come in to me without going to those wretches opposite. *Come in tomorrow.* . . .

At the time Edith was excited by her brother Hubert's latest venture, *North and South*, the first issue of which came out on 16 February and drew a welcoming letter from Gladstone. Subtitled *An Irish Newspaper and Review*, it was, according to Hubert's advertisement,

a paper which, having in view the restoration to the Irish people of the control and management of their own affairs, will approach the consideration of the public questions incidental to any such change in constructive spirit, removed on the one hand from the bias due to connection with a particular class or creed and on the other hand from the distortion and narrowness commonly associated with a purely fighting and aggressive policy. . . .

These were ideas beyond Grove's range of thought, and the source of some tension in his relationship with Edith when she became in fact his *ferne Geliebte*.

When Sir George Grove projected the *Dictionary of Music and Musicians*, the first instalment of which appeared in 1878, he intended it, as he explained in his preface, for the general reader as much as for the musician, and it was in a great measure the fulfilment of this purpose which made the success of the book. Owners of the earlier copies of the old edition will remember that on the title page of the first volume are the words 'in two volumes', and the first of what eventually became four volumes includes the greater part of the letter I. It stands to reason, therefore, that the earlier letters of the alphabet were treated far more scantily than the later; as the work went on the scheme enlarged itself, as was indeed inevitable, and finally the more serious omissions under the earlier letters had to be supplied in an appendix, published in 1889.

[2] Letter of 21 Jan 1887; BL, Add. MS. 39679, f. 146.

Edith was then in the midst of preparing for a performance of Beethoven's E flat Piano Trio (op. 70, no. 2) with A. Bent and W. H. Squire, and for her final examination. The inmates of Alexandra House in general were agog with excitement at the forthcoming visit of the Princess of Wales officially to open the establishment, of which the concert hall was to replace the West Theatre of the Albert Hall for students' concerts. The ceremony took place on 14 March and was marked by performances of Schumann's A minor String Quartet and Brahms's A major Piano Quartet (in which Louisa Kellett played), and Charles Wood's *Song of Welcome*. Meanwhile Wood's composition teacher, weighed down with problems of pedagogy, was wrestling with a new work of his own. On 1 March the Bach Choir had seen for the first time as much as was finished of *Blest Pair of Sirens*, and as it went through the last stages of completion they rehearsed it with growing excitement. On 29 March a read-through of the entire work by chorus and orchestra according to the composer brought tears to Grove's eyes, as he jumped up to wring Parry's hand. The first performance took place on 17 May.

On 19 April the suspense under which the first lot of students at the College had lately lived was lifted with the publication of the list of the first holders of the ARCM diploma.[3] Edith, to whom Grove had written on 7 April, 'I could not wish for better reports or more satisfactory both to you and me' (the phrase he put into the official report), having been granted her diploma in Piano, took leave of Alexandra House and settled temporarily at her aunt's house at 70 Avonmore Road.

It was a remarkable spring and summer. Edith went down to Sydenham to visit the Groves at home and a few days later went with Sir George to the Grosvenor Gallery and then to the Prince's Hall for the first English performance of Brahms's new C minor String Trio (op. 101).[4] On 11 May Stanford's setting of Tennyson's *Carmen Saeculare* was performed at Buckingham Palace—the first of a number of musical offerings in respect of the Jubilee involving the College; and, if the number of performers exceeded that of the audience, Stanford considered himself no worse off than those in Bavaria who had on one occasion been compelled to present opera to an audience of one—King Ludwig. In June there were

---

[3] The complete list was as follows:

Theory: Kate E. Boundy, Exeter; Emily Daymond, Eastbourne; Augustus E. Tozer, W. Brighton. Piano: Emily Daymond; Frances M. E. Hine, Bradford; Mary C. Macdonald, Chester; Edith Oldham, Dublin. *Public singing:* Henry Cross, Willesden; Frederic W. Partridge, Beckenham. *Teaching singing:* Caroline O. Jannings, Doncaster; Henry Taylor, Bolton. *Flute:* Herbert Ivo Laubach [after November 1916, Bourne], Clapham.

The examiners were A. Blume, J. F. Bridge, Cowen, Mackenzie, Parratt, Parry, Carl Rosa, Stanford, Franklin Taylor, Albert Visetti and Grove. (Blume returned to Germany in 1896 where he became Königlicher Professor und Gesanglehrer in Berlin.)

[4] See C. Fuchs, op. cit., pp. 52–3.

7

three students' concerts: the Queen had commanded that one should also be given at Windsor; and preparations intensified for the production of *Der Freischütz* at the Savoy Theatre.

On 11 June Grove went down to Worthing for a week-end with Edmund: 'I am so knocked up I do think my head is cracking', he wrote to Edith, adding, 'A lady spoke to me of you yesterday, *in rapture*, she met you at our house and was "so much struck" by you.' To which— Edith being at Herne Bay—there was a postscript: 'I hope you will get well and fat and brown.' A few days later Grove felt things piling one on top of the other, saying, 'I have been fearfully busy and so disturbed in my mind that it is difficult to write.' He worried about the opera, and the problem of getting students home from Windsor after performing before the Queen, who Grove considered to have been 'rather thoughtless' in setting the starting time of the concert at ten o'clock. 'I am not at all happy—I am so overworked, and there is no chance of lessening it, and I find it more difficult every day to concentrate myself on things.'

But on 21 June the world looked different, as he took his place among the eminent of the realm for a Thanksgiving Service in Westminster Abbey. Next day he wrote to Edith:

I had a beautiful sight yesterday. I was in a gallery over Poets Corner looking right down on the centre dais where the Queen and all the royalties were assembled and could see every motion. Beyond them were the Speaker and the House of Commons but all the interest was in the centre part. The Queen was beautifully dignified and Queenly. The Prince Royal of Prussia the finest figure—a tall big man in white uniform with knots of riband—He and the Prince of Hesse kneeled in front of their chairs during prayers the others sat. I liked to see them. The Queen also sat but I fancy that she is very infirm. After all was over and the Blessing said, the children, children in law, and grandchildren, all came up to her and kissed her hand and cheek first the men and then the women—a most touching sight.

The students' concert at Windsor took place on 25 June in the Waterloo Gallery before an audience which a gratified Grove described as containing 'a Prussian Grand Duchess and on her left the Infanta of Spain, behind them the room was full of Kings, Popes [*sic*], Emperors, Princes, and all the magnificence of the world'. For the students the experience was harrowing. They had been unexpected by the Castle staff, mislaid in the kitchens, and kept waiting until the royals had dined and—more disastrously—wined. They performed in a fume-laden room to a somnolent assembly whose capacity for musical appreciation was at its lowest point. In the middle of the night, while the Queen's guests slept off their dissipations, the unfortunate students were trying to make their several ways home from Paddington Station. The *Pall Mall Gazette* was so forgetful of protocol actually to protest at the royal conduct of the affair. Eight years and several command performances later Grove harked

back to the event, commenting on how everything had been 'impromptu
and of the most slovenly kind'.[5]

Edith, of course, now had to find employment, and her job-hunting
caused more family controversies. Mrs Oldham was not keen that she
should teach at the RIAM, where 'Sir Robert Stewart is too lazy to do
much and they all seem so much behind the times'. Esposito, she added,
was 'the man most thought of'. Alice Oldham thought that her sister
should and could find a job with her at Alexandra College, which was a
most highly thought of seminary for the daughters of the gentry and
superior tradesmen of Dublin. But Edith was keen on taking over a
private teaching connection at Hagley in Worcestershire, which offered
as pupils members of the Lyttleton family, and those girls at Dudley
High School who wished to learn the pianoforte. Dudley, deplored
Mrs Oldham, was 'a horrible place all coal and iron'.

Whether Edith was enthusiastic about the situation in Worcestershire,
however, there is no doubt about the feelings of Sir George, and Franklin Taylor—who regretted her 'giving up a good chance for a great
uncertainty'. On 21 June Mrs Oldham wrote to her daughter angrily:
'Sir George and Mr Taylor I dare say hardly comprehend how people
are left so totally penniless as we are.' On 4 July she wrote in even more
angry terms to her daughter:

Sir George has written to Eldred to get him to use his influence to induce you
to accept the post, he seems to think there was no other place in the world where
you could earn your bread, just as he wrote in the same exaggerated style that
your prospects for life would be blighted if you did not come over to play for
the Princess,[6] but that is not all he proposes that I should go over to live with
you in Hagley. I suppose this is because he thinks it would not be quite right
for you to settle alone in a place where you had neither relative or friend, but
he words it in such a way, that you would think that I was some old woman
living in an almshouse and that it would be a great matter to me if you could
as he expresses it 'make a home for me'.

. . . I never got a letter from him yet but there was not something in it that
hurt and vexed me.

After some days on the Welsh coast at Barmouth, Edith went back to
Ireland, to holiday in County Wicklow. For his part Grove went sight-
seeing in Sussex with Parratt, and paid a visit to Edmund. Then he
moved on to Salisbury, where he attended some sessions of the 34th
General Meeting of the Wiltshire Archaeological and Natural History
Society, which took place during the first week of August.

Grove was pleased to be able to stay with his sister Anna and her husband at 27 New Canal, where they had lived for the past thirty years.

---

[5] E.O., Saturday March 2 [1895], when Grove was writing about the students'
performance of Delibes's Le roi s'amuse at Windsor.

[6] See pp. 176-7.

He was always at ease with William Wilkes, who moved easily in the world of books and the arts, and was, Grove once said, 'the nicest brother-in-law a man ever had'. Considering his wide selection of brothers-in-law, this was very flattering. Like her husband, Anna was deeply involved in the life of the town. It pleased Grove that she had been able to maintain her interest in music. She was an active member of the Sarum Choral Society, 'attending concerts and practices with unfailing zest and spirit, [and] helping for many years to sustain it through the fluctuating fortunes that often attend local musical societies'.[7]

After his stay in Salisbury—the end of which was marked by a sermon preached by Mandell Creighton—Grove was still avid for culture. He travelled to Peterborough, where he was just in time to see in the Becket Chapel in the Minster Precincts the Tercentenary Exhibition of Marian Relics, which closed on 9 August. This exhibition had opened on 22 July, when the Revd E. Bradley (not a relative of Harriet Grove), the celebrated author of *The Adventures of Mr Verdant Green at Oxford,* had given a somewhat prejudiced account of the historical circumstances which had led to the melancholy end of Mary Queen of Scots in nearby Fotheringay. Her remains had been laid to rest in Peterborough Cathedral, whence they were removed to London by James I. All of this was of great interest to Grove.

Back in London he was delighted to meet Raimund von Zur Mühlen, and to hear with admiration his interpretations of Schubert. Grove persuaded the singer to visit the College, where he met Charles Wood, whose settings of poems by Christina Rossetti and Tom Moore impressed him so much that he asked for copies of *Does the road wind up hill?* and *At the mid hour of night* to add to his repertoire.

But however full of interest his activities might seem, there was always for Grove an aching void, as he expressed to Edith in his letter of 24 July. He was also pulled by spasms of jealousy: 'How cold and dry it is talking to you in this way through the pen instead of with the lips! Let us try to keep our affection warm until that happy time comes again. Let me know *everything* that happens to you. Keep nothing from me. . . .'

---

[7] Anna Wilkes died on Easter Day 1917, aged ninety-one. At her funeral at Bemerton Julius and Arthur Grove were among the mourners. 'Mrs Wilkes will be very greatly missed in both city and social life,' wrote the *Salisbury and Winchester Journal and General Advertiser* (14 Apr 1917). 'Her ample gifts to numerous charities, her interest in social reforms, education, and the welfare of many varied classes of people all combine to make her loss deeply felt by those who no longer will receive her generous aid.'
A memorial tablet in the parish church of St Thomas of Canterbury reads: 'A generous supporter of all good works in accordance with whose intentions the sum of £3365 was devoted by four beneficiaries of her estate towards the purchase of a vicarage and the stipend of an assistant curate for the Parish of St Thomas.' In this church is recorded the marriage of Thomas Bennett—from whom James Bennett was descended—to Margaret Grove, of the Groves of Fern in Wiltshire, in the reign of Elizabeth I.

He saw Agnes Kitching into 'a nice place in the Chantry School at
Frome £60 a year with everything found', and Emily Daymond (who
became the first woman Mus. D. at Oxford in 1921) into a post at the
Holloway College for Women, now one year old. At the same time he
was saddened by news of the death of one of the first singing students,
Emily Stewart, and by the rapid deterioration of Louisa Kellett's
health.[8]

Anxious still about Edith finding a job, Grove promised that he would
write to Sir Robert Stewart and to Mahaffy[9] at Trinity College. Later
on in 1887 he wrote a recommendation for Edith also to A. J. Balfour,
newly appointed Chief Secretary for Ireland. But in the meantime she
found herself a job (despite what her mother had said) as 'assistant
professor of the pianoforte' at the RIAM.[10] On 8 October Grove wrote
that he had 'put the news up in the hall that everyone may know and
rejoice'.

Just prior to receiving this glad news he had, parenthetically, given
his former student early warning of an impending catastrophe at the
College. Jasper Sutcliffe, he said, was improving enormously, not only in
playing the violin but also in his general attitude. He was 'reading widely
and deeply and thinking about the best and greatest subjects'.[11] Grove
had been afraid of Henry Holmes's 'radical unbelieving views' and their
insidious influence, but now he considered the danger past. For Sutcliffe,
perhaps, it was; but not for other students. Holmes's alleged 'radical
unbelieving views', covering a wide area, came to crisis point when the
most fundamental of urges showed itself at their centre.

As the year ended Grove was concerned that Edith was condemned to
live in Ireland. Home Rule had been rejected; indignation against brutal
—often absentee—landlords had caused a fresh epidemic of violence;
this in train brought the introduction of the repressive Crimes Act and
the prosecution of William O'Brien. The English, torn between indolent
romanticism and nescient exasperation, for the most part comforted
themselves that they were not only not like other men, but superior to
them. In spite of his early mentors in sociology and political thought,

[8] In June he had noted how, a victim of tuberculosis, she was *'very bad'*, adding, 'with
her mother and sister on the road to starvation how can she help it?' During the summer
the Kellett family came over from Ireland and Grove liked them immediately. Louisa
lingered on into 1888. In the early part of that year she was moved to the Isle of Wight,
where she died in March.

[9] Mahaffy prided himself on both his knowledge of, and skill in, music, and when the
time came for him to receive an honorary degree (on the occasion of the tercentenary
of the College) he ordered—so to speak—a doctorate in music rather than in letters.
Grove, knowing Mahaffy as a contributor to *Macmillan's*, held him in the middle
reaches of his esteem, describing him as 'very clever and nice where his own interest
does not come in'.

[10] *Musical World*, 5 Nov 1887.

[11] E.O., Sept 25 [1887].

Grove in his later years proved no exception to this view. On 2 November he sent his prejudices to Edith:

I don't altogether like your picture of your Dublin life and I daresay that even the good people there—like Doyle[12] etc—are tainted with that absurd, inane [?], love of outsize show. It is only in a metropolis like London that people really shake together and find their own level in that shams of all kinds get torn off. But my darling you mustn't let that influence you. Keep up your own mind by reading and thinking on music and poetry and then you will always have your own position, and your own mind to retire into however many foolish people you will have to endure as a necessary part of life.

Absence certainly made the heart no less fond. At the beginning of 1888 Edith received this warrant of undying affection, albeit with a moderating phrase:

Bless you dear. I never was fonder of you, or loved you more tenderly. Never think anything else. I shall not alter—Of course the time will come when some one of your own age will step in between us and absorb you. That's Nature, and inevitable—but till then let me enjoy your affection!

At and in connection with the College much was happening. In the previous November Jenny Lind-Goldschmidt, who had done so much for so many students in the early years, had died. A day or two before this George Macfarren, Principal of the RAM, had also died. The College paid its tribute to a fine musician in a students' concert, of which the programme included works by Macfarren and also Beethoven's F minor Quartet (op. 95). It became apparent that the RAM, to which Alexander Mackenzie had been appointed as Principal, would go its own way and that all thought of alliance with the College was ended. Grove and his Council, whose hopes had been sustained thus far by the excellence of the work shown to the public by the students, and by numerous marks of royal favour, began the more earnestly to consider ways and means of obtaining new premises.

Appropriately enough in the shape of an engineer, a god appeared out of the machine. Grove's letter of 18 January to Edith took lyrical flight until coming to earth with this announcement:

I have just secured the money for building the new College. This day week I took a rich Yorkshireman to the Prince, and he promised H.R.H. £30,000 and if 30 was not enough 40 and if 40 was not enough, £50,000!—The magnificent donor is a certain Mr Samson Fox owner of the Leeds Forge—a self made man, but with a noble disposition, and not at all a slave to his business or his money-making. . . .

It was, perhaps, a sign of Victorian times that the edifice of the Royal

[12] Probably Henry Edward Doyle (1827–92), Director of the National Gallery of Ireland from 1869.

College of Music as it now is was created largely by two self-made men, both engineers. Samson Fox, born in Leeds in 1838, the son of a weaver, like his father was intended for the loom; but youthful ambition took him into mechanical engineering, to a meteoric rise in the firm of his apprenticeship, from which he moved into independent operation. He founded the Leeds Forge Company in 1874, invented and manufactured a 'corrugated flue' for boiler furnaces adopted by the Admiralty and shipping lines both British and foreign, and also processed pressed steel for railway rolling stock. In 1881 Fox acquired a residence in Harrogate, of which the appropriate name was 'Grove House'. He was invested with various municipal dignities; but, like many of his kind in the north, he had a passion for music. 'I felt', he said, 'I could not be as great a musician as I could be a mechanic.' He did the next best thing; he made it possible for others to become great musicians.[13]

Grove went to Yorkshire to see Fox, his enthusiasm from the visit transmuting all he saw on his homeward journey into gold:

I have seldom enjoyed anything more than my ride up from Leeds on Sunday week. It was a lovely afternoon, and from Doncaster to Grantham the line runs on top of the country, and the forms, and colours, and mist, and the pale wintry look, and the beautiful church towers every mile or two made me perfectly happy. I was by myself and studied some poetry to my heart's content.[14]

Grove's euphoria was heightened when he heard the student orchestra at the College play Schumann's Second Symphony on 17 January. In his letter of the next day to Edith, he informed her that the work 'has one of the finest slow movements in the world. Do you', he asked, 'recollect it with the long shakes in the fiddles? But indeed the whole work is Schumann's greatest.'

At the beginning of February Edith, having made an appearance at a concert in Dublin sponsored by the Medical Students' Loyal Orange Lodge (what did Hubert say?), was briefly in London. No sooner had she gone home than Grove went to bed for a day or two with rheumatism.

Musically it was a satisfactory year. Joachim and Clara Schumann were at the College when they were in London, and one student—Percy Sharman—was invited to have lessons with the former in Berlin, and two —Beatrice Hallett and Holden White—with the latter in Frankfurt. On 3 May, the day on which Grieg appeared at a Philharmonic concert to

---

[13] Fox's first offer of £30,000 was to meet the estimated costs of a new College building. As is not infrequently the case, revised estimates showed that the first costing was wrong, and that £45,000 was needed. At this point a 'London gentleman' promised half the extra money required. 'Nay', said Fox, 'we won't have two at the job.' Whereupon he came up not only with the extra £15,000 but also a supplementary £1,000 'for adornment of the vestibule'; obituary notice of Fox, *Harrogate Advertiser*, 31 Oct 1903.

[14] E.O., Jan 18 [1888].

introduce works of his own, Grove walked over to Clapham to meet him and his wife. (It was, he reported, a lovely day, warm as August, and he had wished that Edith were there to accompany him.) As was that of Grieg so too was Stanford's star in the ascendant in the European sky. His 'Irish' Symphony, first performed on 27 May 1887 in St James's Hall, by Richter, was played in Berlin and Hamburg under von Bülow.

Later that year Parry's *Judith*, commissioned for the Triennial Festival, was given its first performance in Birmingham. Out of loyalty to him and to Bridge, whose *Callirhoë* was also being performed for the first time, Grove went down to Birmingham in October on the line on which he had once worked as an engineer. It was a remarkable occasion. Dvořák's *Stabat Mater* inspired Cardinal Newman; Grieg's extravagances as a conductor—he took charge of his concert overture *In Autumn*—were contrasted with the dignified gestures of Richter; Robert Franz's edition of *Messiah* annoyed practically everybody, but since he was a friend of Richter it was useless to make a fuss; Sullivan's *Golden Legend* was received as a masterpiece; and Bridge's work was thought to be the last word in modernity.[15]

In the meantime Parry and Stanford were busy with works for the Leeds Festival of 1889, and George Henschel, a Professor of Singing at the College, had returned from Russia where he had undertaken a useful public-relations exercise in the form of a long '*tournée*'.

At the College the standard of the students' concerts was high, although Hallé, an external examiner, wondered whether sometimes they were not setting their sights too high. However, when in February Joachim, Robert Haussmann and Fanny Davies played Beethoven's Triple Concerto with the College orchestra, Joachim was so pleased that he insisted on playing the Brahms Violin Concerto with it on the following day.

In April a chamber music group was invited to play a Beethoven Quintet at the German Athenaeum in Mortimer Street. It was 'immensely applauded—the Germans having no notion that English boys could play so well'.[16] The tragic death from cancer of Friedrich III, the second Emperor of Germany and son-in-law of Queen Victoria, which took

[15] The theme from Pausanius, which was the basis of this work, was recommended to Bridge by T. B. Strong, a lecturer at Oxford who had been a pupil of the composer when a boy at Westminster School. The same T. B. Strong in the fullness of time became Dean of Christ Church and the first person to recognize the genius of the schoolboy Walton. Surprisingly it was not Parry but Bridge who was taken for an iconoclast; the *Musical Times* had no doubt that in *Callirhoë* 'the exercise of liberty approaches the frontiers of licence'.

[16] The next year the members of the German Athenaeum were again reminded of the musical interests of the British, and their lack of chauvinism in this respect, when Grove attended a meeting to promise support for the forthcoming third Beethoven Festival in Bonn, the purpose of which was to raise funds sufficient to maintain the composer's birthplace and establish a museum.

place on 15 June, only three months after his accession, was reflected in the programme of the next concert at the College, on 21 June, which began with Marmaduke Barton playing Chopin's Funeral March.

Parry meanwhile passed another milestone on the high road to respectability. He was elected to the other Athenaeum, after Grove—whose genial influence flowed in many directions—had helped forward his candidature by asking for Millais's support for 'an excellent fellow and a great musician'.[17]

As he had done in the previous year, Grove attended the Royal Academy dinner on 6 May. He was pleased to be with 'all the best men in London', even though it meant listening to speeches for four hours. The speeches were, however, interspersed with convivial music in the form of the latter-day madrigals and glees of Spofforth, Webbe, Horsley and Stevens. Moreover, he said, 'The pictures are very interesting, and it is really a lovely moment when the gas flames up and reveals the walls so full and so bright, when the Queen's health is drunk.' In reporting the occasion Grove told Edith that he had seen Doyle, Mahaffy and Lecky, and Leighton—who was 'pompous and graceful' at the same time. Luke Fildes, the painter, sat on one side of him, Edward Bond, the retiring Director of the British Museum, on the other; but they were 'not very interesting people'.

Andrew Clark, Gladstone's doctor, sat opposite, while Herkomer, Sullivan, Burnand, Layard, the Dean of Westminster, and various political personalities were within hailing distance. Herkomer—Bavarian-English, a painter of consummate technical skills, enormously popular, painter of portraits of Wagner, Joachim and other musicians, and given to eccentricities of one sort or another—put Grove off:

Talking of cheek I do think that Herkomer's late escapade is about the greatest. Writing an operetta, and actually asking all the musical men of London down [to his fantasy house at Bushey] to hear it. No doubt it's clever, but what *can* it be as performing music? I would like to know what he would say if Stanford or Mackenzie were to ask him to come and see a picture by them.[18]

Towards the end of 1888 Grove was surprised, to say the least, to hear of the defection from the Faith of an esteemed scholar and friend:

My great friend Addis suddenly left the Roman Church, and that not only distressed me very much—but obliged me to write and go about a good deal. He is going to be married (tomorrow) and then to go to Australia—I love him so dearly and esteem him so much that you may imagine how greatly all this concerns me.[19]

[17] Letter to J. E. Millais of 27 Apr 1888; PML.
[18] E.O., May 7 1888. The *Musical Times* for May 1888 mentions the 'Herkomer Stage Play' with 'music scored and conducted by Carl Armbruster' (p. 280).
[19] E.O., Nov 4 [1888].

That Grove should have been distressed at Addis's decision is surprising in view of a lack of sympathy with the Roman Catholic Church expressed elsewhere and his forward-looking suggestion that celibacy so far as priests are concerned would have to end.[20]

In his letter to Edith concerning Addis Grove also announced the death of one of his sisters. 'She had', he said, 'been separated from us for years and lived at a *maison de santé* in Staffordshire.'[21] On the outside of the envelope containing this letter Grove wrote: 'J'envoyais l'addresse de Sullivan—parce que il y a beaucoup de moi se dedans—vous le verrai'.

Grove was in bed for some days in January, and he complained of a nasty cough in February. He was distressed by news from Dublin of Mrs Oldham's death; and his convalescence was not helped by an article concerning Prout in the *Morning Herald*. He wrote to F. G. Edwards: 'I have a high regard for his abilities but (between ourselves) he is such a *snob* that I can never like him. He once accused me in print of having altered a quotation to make it suit my ends!—a terrible thing to hear!' Grove went on to describe Prout's 'myrmidons', W. A. Frost and J. S. Shedlock, as 'most 2nd class people', and to say that Prout's 'blows at me are directed by my having left him out of the staff at the College'.[22]

On the first Sunday in March Grove complained to Edith that he was forgetful, bewildered, full of worry:

I suppose it's the inevitable consequence of being so near three score and ten! I was reading the Psalm this morning at Prayers, and the impulse was to steal a look round the room, and see if Daisy Jenkins and Ethel Sharpe (here for today) and the maids and my wife were at all applying the passage to me!

Of these two favoured students Daisy Jenkins (who had lately played the Beethoven C minor Piano Concerto (op. 37) at a College concert) was the more chatty on this occasion, bringing Grove up to date with general gossip. In an age when £500 a year seemed a fortune, Nellie Marshall was reputed to be making £900; Lucie Johnstone, an Irish girl who was 'liée' (to use Grove's unusual word) with Charlotte Milligan, a soprano,

[20] See letter to Edmund Grove, Graves, pp. 401–2.
[21] Kezia, never mentioned by name by Grove in any letter, was buried in the same grave as her mother in West Norwood Cemetery. A private asylum (*maison de santé*) required licensing by a Court of Quarter Sessions, but registers of such institutions were not regularly kept. Until the 1850s there were three asylums in Staffordshire: Spring Vale, near Stone; the Moat House, Tamworth; and Oulton Retreat. Unless one of these was particularly recommended it is difficult to see why a sister of Grove should have been sent so far away from the family. It may be surmised that Augustus Legge, a Staffordshire man, a long-time friend of Grove when Vicar of St Bartholomew's, Sydenham, from 1867, and of Lewisham from 1879 until his appointment as Bishop of Lichfield in 1892, had something to do in the matter.
[22] Letter of 23 Jan 1889, marked 'Private'; BL, Eg. MS. 3091, f. 8.

from Belfast, was doing well. Annie Fry was in a position to charge as much as 15 shillings for some lessons. In Worcestershire (where Edith might have been) Ethel Knapp was earning £300; and Henrietta Krüger (who in 1915 found it expedient to change her name to Kingston) and Delia Tillott £200 each a year at the fashionable school of St Leonard's in St Andrews, where Atalanta Heap was also to teach.

It was a year of engagements and of marriages. Marion Osborn, a pianist, had become engaged to Arthur Leaf, ten years her senior, rich, and 'of very good family', Grove was pleased to know. 'But', he complained, 'our £700 is wasted, and a promising artist gone.' More disastrous, however, was the foolishness of Annie Roberts, who had thrown up her scholarship and herself into the arms of Augustus Harris, the Italian Opera manager, at the instigation of the man to whom she had become engaged. She was not prepared either for opera or for marriage, said Grove. To his fury, some months later he discovered that the girl was married:

. . . (if indeed she be married)—the whole thing a mass of lies and deception, such as I am very sorry to think of. I look on her as ruined now—a little whipper snapper of a worthless husband who has not a pound a week and nothing to make up for his poverty, who first ruined her and now can't keep her.[23]

In the summer of 1889 Grove decided to go to Bavaria, Switzerland and Austria. He thought that he would take his son, Julius Charles, with him, who had never been abroad as yet. 'I would', he wrote to Edith on 24 June, 'rather have a woman than a man, but there is none left to me. Would *you* like to go with me? Of course we can't do it, so we may please ourselves with thinking about it.' In the end he set out for Bayreuth with Manns. He was less than enthusiastic about the *Parsifal* he heard there, recalling the performance when he wrote to Edith on 2 October:

It was very astonishing and grand but the impression was so complex (made up of music, stage, and the strangeness of the circumstances) that one hearing is not enough. And I am not a Wagnerite and I rebel against these great archaic unnatural subjects—If I had heard the Meistersinger I should have found more human interest—but I could not stay; my heart was at Vienna and carried me on. No doubt this must seem strange to you. But much in 70 must seem strange to 23 and we must talk about it.

When he had arrived in Vienna on 13 August Grove set about visiting all the places in which Beethoven had lived. At Gneixendorf—where the composer had spent his last autumn, and caught the chill which led to his last illness—the house that had belonged to Johann Beethoven was now occupied by a Mrs Schweitzer, to whom Grove in due course wrote a

[23] E.O., Monday mg Nov 25 [1889].

204 GEORGE GROVE

letter of thanks.[24] The most exciting day of the pilgrimage took him and his companion Eusebius Mandyczewski, Keeper of the Archives of the Vienna Philharmonic Society, to

a valley called Brühl or Briehl near Mödling where [Beethoven] wrote the Pastoral Symphony, Op. 106 [sic] and the Mass in D is just as it was in 1815 and is (really) one of the most beautiful spots even now and the old taverns and houses are just as they were. We had our dinner at the Two Ravens, where the band used to play which he caricatured in the Scherzo of the Past. Symphony.[25]

From Vienna Grove went to Lucerne where he met his son. Next day he visited Mendelssohn's youngest daughter, Lili Wach (who had been 'awfully kind to me for years'), at Ringgenberg, above the Lake of Brienz. Here in the August of 1847 Mendelssohn had taken Henry Chorley and had played to him on the village church organ pieces by Bach as well as his own improvisations. These facts deeply moved Grove, always sensitive to atmosphere, both then and later.

Back in England Grove went up to Leeds for the Festival, which was distinguished rather by the work that was not composed for it than by those that were, for Brahms had declined an invitation to write a symphony on the grounds 'that his nervous state would not permit him to compose a new work'. Parry's *Ode on St Cecilia's Day* and Stanford's *The Voyage of Maeldune* were commissioned works; but the general impression was that because the chorus had been over-rehearsed—for twelve hours—on the Monday preceding the Festival, and for some time on the Tuesday also, the choral works came off rather badly. Grove's interest, however, was especially alerted by Sullivan's treatment of the Choral Symphony, in the slow movement of which he omitted the pause. This called for a letter to *The Times*.

But his true feelings and anxieties at this time are expressed in the following letter to Edith, who clearly is emotionally further entangled:

Oct. 17

My dear affectionate Edith,

Your letter was very good and pleasant to me. I was tired and out of heart, and it cured all my ills at once. Yes, I think I *am* constant—où je m'attache je meurs is the saying—I do not go that length, but I come very near to it. Some day I will tell you all about my life; it is a not uninteresting story, but it must be *told*, and can only be told to one with whom I am perfectly intimate. When shall it be, dear? I am getting fearfully old, and in a short time must look to go seriously down the hill—and that means loss of power and of keenness of sympathy, and all the other evils attendant on this terrible old age. So do make

[24] In January 1891 Grove still owed letters, 'the arrears of a whole year', to 'Heilpern in Vienna ... Mandyczewski ... Mad. Schweitzer, Mad. Wach etc ...'; E.O., Saturday night 10.30 [19 Jan 1891].
[25] E.O., Oct 2 [1889]. In Beethoven's day the Two Ravens had been Three (see *Beethoven and his Nine Symphonies*, p. 185).

a resolution to come over soon.—I am so very glad that your holiday set you up. You were wise in idling—I felt often that I was doing too much, but the sort of investigation on which I went to Vienna is more tempting and delightful to me than any other, and I could not stop. Still thank God I am very well; certainly stronger than I was—more able to face my work—and more able to see what is before me: and every day adds to my power of judgment. It's curious but I am now judging and feeling as most others judge & feel at 25 or 30. That no doubt gives freshness to life—but on the other hand it is surely wrong to have waited so long—But I must take things as they come. The College gives me great anxiety—I see evils, but don't know how to remedy them. I am sure it is too much a *school*—All those *students* who come for a year, who have no gift or intelligence, and who will never do anything in music—surely a College ought not to teach those sort of people—In answer to this:—they get better taught by us than elsewhere and therefore it is better they should come: but that merely means to say that there ought to be a preparatory school, so that College may be devoted to serious work on those who are likely to repay it, and then, in the College itself:—we have now been in existence 6 years and certain things are getting clear to me. We are too narrow in our circles. Take Holmes for example. There *cannot* be a better teacher, up to a certain line, but he shuts out the whole of the Belgian school of De Bériot & Vieuxtemps, and the Italian of Paganini, and the French of Lalo &c, and surely to state that fact is to condemn his teaching—Also I feel that he has no power of teaching a solo player. Such knowledge as how to stand, how to face an audience—is to him all worthless, but it's very important; and he has not the élan which a solo player wants—Look at Sutcliffe! I could cry when I see Cecile Elieson, once so saucy and so full of spirit, now gradually losing it all, and therefore ruined for a solo player for which she once bid fair. Then again look at Taylor & Pauer; it's the same story—the modern music of Liszt and Tausig is hateful to them and to me, but to a pupil it's absolutely necessary—the flood may be noxious, but one can't stop it; we can't dam everything back to Schumann or even to Brahms. The fact is we want some one within reach who is not only a good careful teacher but a famous *player*:—e.g. Bülow or D'Albert. I am sure that *life* can be kept in a teacher only by constantly playing in public and drawing thence constant new inspiration, new hints for expression & means of interesting the hearers. But then how all this is to be done I can't tell—the difficulties are enormous. Suppose that T. and P. and H. were to consent to remain with some one in effect over them, how are the functions of the new man & the old ones to be adjusted? Think of it and you will see the difficulties.

However, as I say, all this has to be talked about—and oh how I wish we could do it! The responsibility is terrible I can tell you.

Your description of 'Looking Backwards' doesn't tempt me. Every day I hate speculation more and more, and cling more closely to facts. A biography, a bit of history, a journey &c are more and more welcome. It is not that I love commonplace—for facts are the most poetic of all things—but it seems to me insupportable to be feeding on the possibilities of the intellect of a writer, when you can learn from what men have actually done. I am reading a curious book Le Journal de Marie Bashkirtseff a Russian, who at 12 thought & felt and wrote as maturely as most do at 2ce her age. She lived in Nice, Paris, Russia Italy &e

from 1872–1884, and of course saw a vast deal—I have read about 100 pages and am very much pleased & interested.

I am very much amused & interested also by your 'real difficulty'. I am quite prepared to hear it. It is what often happens, and what in your case was sure to happen. Do you know you dear child, that you are a most attractive person? It is hard to find a face so charming and so simple or a character at once so intelligent and clever and so sincere, as yours, and you are sure to be fallen in love with. You will have many more than five such troubles. But dear don't give way till you feel yourself in love—were you ever? tell me—If not you have got the greatest event of your life to come, but wait till then, and may the man be worthy of you! It will be hard to find him. How many millions of poor wretches have been told to turn their love into friendship!—It's simply impossible; the two things are as different as light and darkness: the one is an impulse, the other is a mode of life—the woman you love is an absolute part of yourself—you thrill with her emotions, you put all your own into your idea of her: but your friend is a separate person, apart from yourself, who now & then comes into your mind, pleasantly, beneficially—but oh how differently from the storm which accompanies *love*.

Experto crede me Roberto.

I know it, for I have felt it all, *no one ever more*, and the mockery of supposing that the one can be turned into the other is only too obvious.

I can understand a woman being driven by circumstances—health poverty etc. into taking refuge in marriage and often such marriages may be very happy —happier than a marriage of passion, but still nothing can really make up to a sensitive man or woman for the absence of passion, and when you think of the tremendous step that it is to surrender yourself (se donner) to another, it makes one hesitate to think of taking it on any other ground but that of real self sacrifice—& that only for passion['s] sake. Dear, I have just read over your letter. You are not now contemplating any such step are you?—Are you in difficulty? do you want money or rest? or anything which a devoted friend can give you, a friend who loves you dearly and devotedly & quite unselfishly? often and often have I repeated over & over all our interviews—I have you absolutely before me—your sweet dear face—your *precious* brogue your sensible valuable words. I have them all—Dear, trust to such a tried friend and tell me how I can help you, before you take any rash step.

Good bye dear let me hear at once. My love to Mr Bapty[26] and all possible congratulations I will try to write to him.

Good bye. I press you to my heart, dear

G.

I have so very much to write; but the nuisance of pen & ink is too great.

In the crop of autumn information given to Edith (whose emotions meanwhile had returned to the *status quo ante*) in subsequent letters,

---

[26] In 1892 Walter Bapty, a well-known Dublin tenor, was to be one of the quartet who sang verse passages in Blow's *I beheld and lo!* during the tercentenary service of Trinity College, in St Patrick's Cathedral; see *Musical Times* XXXIII, August 1892, p. 490.

Grove noted that S. P. Waddington, who had for some time been studying in Frankfurt, was now in Vienna, where he was staying with the Richters; that Charles Wood and Arnold Dolmetsch had won the first and second prizes respectively for their compositions in a competition sponsored by the Wind Instrument Society; and that Tertius Noble's setting of the Nicene Creed had gained for him a *Musical World* prize of 12 guineas. He was anxious about Hester Wallas, whose father, a clergyman, had lately died. Typically, Grove set about finding a job for her, and he had hopes of an excellent post in 'an endowed school in Leicester'.

The big news, however, concerned the engagement of Mary Beauchamp, an organ scholar, to the Count August Henning von Arnim, who was, as Grove proudly observed, 'a great nobleman, a member of one of the oldest families in Prussia'. The new Countess von Arnim transferred herself to the cold climate of Pomerania, where her husband maintained the Schloss Nassenheide; the rigours of Schlagenthin, near Brandenburg, where there was a second seat; and the formalities of Berlin, where there was a town house. Within a decade the Countess, the anonymous author of *Elizabeth and her German Garden*, was one of the writers on the Macmillan list most subjected to discussion.[27]

At the end of the year, after a performance of *L'Enfance du Christ*— 'a little kind of oratorio full of B[erlioz]'s merits and defects'—by his students, Grove went down to his brother Edmund at Brighton. From there he ended his letter of 20 December to Edith, 'Je t'embrasse, chérie, de tout mon âme et de tout mon corps'. Away in Venice on 12 December Robert Browning had died. The funeral took place in Westminster Abbey on the last day of the year and Grove was among the congregation:

Dearest Edith:

Thursday was a very impressive day. I *knew* Browning, but not to be an intimate friend, so that I could not say that I *grieved*; but it was very solemn and the music and the place beautiful. As we walked up the long nave the choir chanted all the first part of the service. The music was Crofts—old and solemn in style, all minor but with lovely major thirds at the close, a wonderfully beautiful feature. Then the coffin was brought through the choir to the intersection of the transepts and rested there while the lesson was read the Psalm sung and the Anthem performed. This could all be perfectly heard, and gave me great food for thought. Bridge had written what he called a meditation on a poem of Mrs Browning's, second verse ending 'so he giveth his beloved sleep'. A good choice, and set far beyond anything that I expected—quite an inspiration. Then the coffin moved on to the grave—close to Chaucer's. The two lie [*diagram*] so. Here the service was chanted to Purcell's music which though quaint strikes

[27] Mary Annette Beauchamp was born in Australia and was a cousin of Katherine Mansfield; see the latter's *Letters and Journals*, ed. C. K. Stead (1977), p. 225. Count von Arnim died in 1900, and six years later his widow married Francis, Earl Russell, from whom she was separated in 1919. Her literary career was one of ups and downs.

me as ambitious and more full of effect than the previous part. . . . After talking to Hallam Tennyson [I] went to the club and wrote his father a new year letter.

. . . K. Macdonald was here yesterday—older and more matured; and doing very well to all appearance. I can't say that I like her *very* much; but as a scholar of the college she will always be sure of my goodwill and best service. . . .[28]

[28] E.O., Jan 2 1890.

CHAPTER ELEVEN

'Too Late'

1890–1891

As the College increasingly made an impact on the musical life of the nation, its Director found himself being taken into areas in which he felt his critical competence limited. The result was the occasional exposition of somewhat negative attitudes. When he looked at the score of Charles Wood's *Ode to the West Wind* he did not 'like its look much—such twistings of rhythm and disregard of Shelley's emphasis'. As for Gluck's *Orfeo*, which Stanford was to produce at Cambridge, he considered it would prove 'too heavy for modern ears'. He was certain, however, that a primary function of the College was to supply good teachers (apparently of one sex), and he hoped that 'in a few years [it] will be recognised and then the girls can fight their own battles'.[1]

Restricted though life for a student then was, the College was a means of escape from even more restricted lives for many, particularly those from distant places. Gwendolyn Jones, 'a pretty very small Welsh girl', after previously having been beaten by the redoubtable Ethel Sharpe, was successful in gaining a scholarship in 1890. From Limerick arrived at the same time the son of a parson, 'a nice refined boy—an organist', rejoicing in the names of George Frederick Joseph Handel Haydn.[2] In that year Barton and Anna Russell were married. This drew from Grove—conscious of the fact that the investment in a musical career would pay no obvious dividend—the opinion that marriage was 'a terrible lottery'. He added this gloomy reflection: 'It really does seem to me that in the majority of cases marriages—viewed from any ideal—not a high ideal, but an ideal at all—are a failure—but oh dear I shan't go into that. . . .'[3]

The great excitement of 1890 was the laying of the foundation stone of the new building, designed by Sir Arthur Blomfield, on 8 July. Samson Fox, the munificent donor, had not only undertaken the whole cost of the building, but he brought his own works band—the Leeds Forge Brass Band—to show what ensemble playing could be, and why the north was entitled to its say in respect of the nation's music. To Grove, not the least interesting detail of the function was Fox's handing to the Prince of Wales a ceremonial trowel, made, said the donor,

[1] E.O., Sat morning May 3 '90.
[2] E.O., Mar 14 [1890].
[3] E.O., Sunday mg Nov 16 [1890].

from the metal of the corrugated boiler-flues of the troopship Praetoria, which, owing to her possessing those appliances to her boilers which I had then but recently invented, was enabled to convey the 91st Highlanders to Durban for the Zulu war, in 1879, with extraordinary speed. The boilers have now been broken up, after performing voyages of more than 600,000 miles.[4]

Edith Oldham, it seems, was present on this auspicious occasion, and after the end of term (which was marked by the firm of Brinsmead presenting one of their pianos to Ethel Sharpe) made excursions with Grove to Windsor and to Tewkesbury. On 1 August he was on the Isle of Wight, awaiting the arrival of Harriet that night. As he waited, he wrote to Edith:

I am so glad you liked our day at Windsor—I did immensely. I am very fond of Parratt as, thank God, he is of me:—but it was not that made me like the day—it was you. I can't tell you how inexpressibly I like being with you without words which I ought not to use to you—but so it is. I am very fond of talking and of talking intimately tho' I can rarely do it; and the pleasure of having you by me, able and willing to understand everything I say, and yielding to one's touch like the keys of a piano is delightful.

A few weeks later reading a book about Tewkesbury Abbey, in recollection of their recent trip, Grove complained to Edith that the 'wretched writer' failed to mention 'the lowering of the roof or the little brass plate about Edward Prince of Wales or any of the other things we liked so'.[5]

Edith suggested that Grove should go abroad for a holiday, but he replied that not only had he overspent on the previous year's holiday, but that he was obliged to pay more than might have been expected for that purpose to Arthur, who was getting married. Besides, 'there is no one to go with and I can't go myself.' However, after protesting his inability to go abroad he was soon on his way to Norway, in the company of his 'dear friend, [G.C.] Bell, the Headmaster of Marlborough'. He was hoping to see Grieg again, in Bergen. But life still had its imperfections. 'Even Bell's talk', he assured Edith, was 'insipid by the side of yours.'

When human companionship failed him, however, there were always animals. The affection of the literary for cats is notorious, and Grove was among those who turned to them for instruction and inspiration. At the beginning of October he slipped a humorous note into the *Spectator*, observing that—according to Max Müller and Archbishop Whateley—

---

[4] *Musical Times* XXXI, August 1890, pp. 475–6.

[5] E.O., Saturday afternoon [14 Sept 1890]. The timber roof of Tewkesbury Abbey was replaced by stone vaulting in the fourteenth century. The 'little brass plate' marking the supposed burial place of the eldest son of Henry VI is beneath the centre of the tower. Other matters likely to have caught Grove's interest were the fact that Mrs Craik's *John Halifax, Gentleman* was sited in Tewkesbury, and the presentation of the great organ in commemoration of the 1887 Jubilee by the Revd W. C. Grove.

the Sanskrit word for cat denoted an animal that was always cleaning itself, and that 'Puss' was a corruption of 'Pashta', the name of the Egyptian cat goddess.

During this autumn troubles began to pile up at the College. In particular there were tensions among the senior members of the teaching staff, and Stainer's dislike of Parratt made for a very frosty atmosphere at a Council meeting. Grove told Edith about this in the course of a 12-page letter; but another situation was causing him greater alarm. There could be a major scandal impending.

Isabel Donkersley, Holmes's most reliable pupil—'very good, but not destined to be great', according to Grove—had been much coached by him in recent months. In May she had led a performance of the Beethoven Septet. She was to give a performance of the Beethoven Violin Concerto —Holmes conducting—on 6 November. It was to be, indeed, a particularly meritorious performance. But Grove was past caring whether it was to be good or bad. What disturbed him was that it was going to take place at all. On 26 October he wrote to Edith:

Did I tell you about Holmes and Bell Donkersley? Early in the holidays I got an anonymous letter saying that I ought to notice Holmes's conduct with her; that they usually went across the park together; and hinting though very darkly at improprieties. I ought to ask the police near etc. Holmes is *very* foolish but wicked or dishonourable I don't think that he is. He was in France and there I sent him the letter begging him to stop at once any open intimacy that could lead to remarks etc. . . .

Sometimes Bell had been found alone with Holmes after having had an extra lesson. It came to Grove's ears that she had performed such intimate personal services as bringing his lunch to his room. To crown all, when Grove one day went to consult Holmes about a Junior Orchestra rehearsal, he found the two of them together.

As Grove worried about the adventurous Holmes, he busied himself with the *Life of Stanley*, which reminded him again of his own sense of deprivation in not having had an Oxford education; with a speech at the Lower Sydenham Institute; with a series of concerts; and with postal discussions with Edith on Newman, Mérimée, Caroline Fox, Wordsworth, Turgenev and Walter Scott.

Outstanding in the way of music that year was the playing of Leonard Borwick, a pupil of Clara Schumann, who had made his London début with the Schumann Piano Concerto in May at a Philharmonic Concert, and played a movement of the same work with the College orchestra at an afternoon concert in the summer.[6] It was also very much a Paderewski

---

[6] 'I like his playing very much indeed, and I liked himself almost more. I shall cultivate his friendship all I can'; Grove to Speyer, 4 July 1890; BL, Add. MS. 42233, f. 12.

year; the Polish pianist's interpretation of the Schumann concerto—with an orchestra raised by George Henschel, at the last of a series of four 'Paderewski concerts' in June, and at the Crystal Palace on 1 November—stimulated comparative critical assessment. Grove had expected something 'very loud and smashing'; what he heard, although very different from Clara Schumann's interpretation, was 'refined and delicate to a degree'.[7]

During that summer Grove's attention had been turned to the subject of the advantages accruing to Irish music students through the British connection, by a letter in the *Daily Graphic* from a well-known Dublin barrister, John MacMahon. To this he duly replied,[8] pointing out that—contrary to Dr MacMahon's supposition—Irish students were as eligible for places in the RCM as any other of the Queen's subjects. But soon he had to consider Irish affairs in a more painful manner. On 16 November Captain O'Shea was granted a divorce on the grounds of his wife's adultery with Parnell. The subsequent repudiation of the Irish leader by the Catholic bishops of Ireland and the splitting of the Irish Party put an end not only to Parnell's career but to the prospects of many of his supporters.

Among those who suffered deep disillusion was Hubert Oldham, who had in this year collaborated with Maud Gonne in publishing the Fenian Ellen O'Leary's posthumous *Lays of Country, Home, and Friends*. After the fateful and divisive meeting of the Irish members in Committee Room 15 of the House of Commons, Parnell tried to re-establish himself in Ireland. He addressed a meeting at the Rotunda in Dublin and went to gatherings in Mallow, Cork and Kilkenny. Edith wrote her perplexities to Grove, who answered her in incomprehension. He wrote late at night on 15 December that he was 'just over a chill on the liver', and continued:

I feel for you keenly in all this struggle—as far as I can—but it seems all topsy-turvy! The Irish party never can succeed in the way they want to. They are not fit to govern themselves, and until they are they must be governed by the English who are every day knowing better how to govern them and trying more earnestly. How can a country be governed by people who take an absolutely personal view of every affair, who have no reticence, no self control, no other quality which enables people to work together? Surely the 3 or 4 days which passed in the committee room of the H. of Commons shew what an Irish parliament would be like!—But perhaps the difference in the Irish and English temperaments is so irreconcilable that they never *will* get on—then I don't see what is to be done because England can never allow an island *moored* so close off her to be a garrison for enemies.

As for Parnell, I think I said it was not the adultery that seems to me the

[7] E.O., Tuesday morning [11 Nov 1890].
[8] See p. 311.

worst (tho' surely, Edith dear, that's as bad as anything can be) but the mean, cheating, and lying that was committed with it.

But indeed it is a hopeless question and I don't like going on with a matter where we are at difference—*I can't bear* differing from you. . . .

Less than a year later Parnell's agony was over. He died on 6 October 1891, and was buried five days later in Glasnevin Cemetery in Dublin. On 17 October Grove wrote to Edith:

. . . Your account of the Parnell affair was most interesting—so much so that I cut off the tail piece of your letter, and erased a few lines at the beginning and sent it off to the Editor of the St James's Gazette, as I thought it well worth printing—but he sent it back the next day saying that it was a very interesting letter but that he had printed so much about Parnell's funeral that he did not wish to give any more. I am sorry—as I thought it so good, and am sure it wd have been far better worth reading than the partisan descriptions of the regular newspaper correspondents which are often so dishonest—I don't feel the same interest in Parnell that you do, first because I have not followed his career as you naturally have, and next because I thought that some of the things that did come out at the O'Shea trial showed him to have acted in a very mean and false part—such love must always be false of course—but in some of his notions there was a meanness which was quite beneath a gentleman. But it is so difficult to judge of a person, as circumstances do alter cases as the lawyers say.

As the Parnell affair moved towards its dark conclusion, Grove, aware of still expanding ambitions and increasing responsibilities, became more and more dependent on friends and intimates for support. Most of January 1891 he spent in bed; but he was up and about in time to go to a rehearsal of Sullivan's *Ivanhoe*, reflecting that he had not seen Sullivan for about a year, and that it pleased him to see a handful of 'College boys' in the orchestra. He saw a performance of the opera in February but found D'Oyly Carte's 'wonderful theatre'—the Cambridge, built for this opera—distracted him from the music. When he did give his mind to this, he worried that it was not better than, and not perhaps as good as, *The Gondoliers* or *The Mikado*.[9]

Looking ahead at this time, Grove arranged for some of his books— '2 carts full'—to be transferred to the College, hoping that they might serve to keep his memory green. He also thought about his possible successor. 'Parry', he wrote to Edith on 7 February, 'is the only one who can carry on my work in my spirit; and I believe that he would do so well—while being a real musician he would in many respects be far

[9] None the less, he was delighted to be able to write to *The Times* at the end of February to draw attention to what appeared to be unique in the annals of English music. On Saturday 28 February Sullivan would have three major works being performed in London: *The Golden Legend* during the Lenten oratorio season (maintained since Handel's day) at Covent Garden; *Ivanhoe* at the Royal English Opera (as the Cambridge Circus Theatre was optimistically described); and *The Gondoliers* at the Savoy.

better than I.' Not being a 'real musician' was another of his obsessions. So, for example, he wrote a letter to William Shakespeare the singing teacher, introducing the Revd Brown-Borthwick as 'a compound of amateur and musician, somewhat in the manner of myself, but to a far better and more satisfactory pitch.'[10]

Crossing the road to Victoria Station one February day in a fog, Grove was again run down by a cab. For a few moments he had managed to hang on to the shaft, but weakened by the shock he could not continue to do so and dropped to the road. One of the wheels went over his left leg, just above the ankle, causing a nasty gash and severe bruising. He had some time before this mishap expressed to Speyer, now living in Frankfurt, the hope that Brahms's new Quintet in G major (op. 111) would be included in one of Joachim's chamber music concerts. He added, 'If you have an opportunity of seeing Brahms, will you recall me to his recollection as one of his most fervent admirers.'[11] When the work eventually was put into a programme—of a Monday Pop on 2 March— he was, as he wrote to Bennett that day, still on his back and therefore had to 'miss the new Quintet tonight'. Although his wound was healing, the process was not complete by the end of the week when, because of its initial success, the Quintet had to be repeated on Saturday. Instead of listening to Brahms Grove read Bennett's libretto for Mackenzie's *The Dream of Jubal*, and expressed his amazement at Bennett's flow of inspiration.

In May the serious illness of an old friend, Mrs Wodehouse (who lived at Farnborough, and had—he informed Edith—long fascinated him, though not stirred feelings deeper than an allowable affection, and who made the Index of the *Dictionary*), saddened him. At the end of a term in which Landon Ronald's playing of Schumann's Concert Allegro, and the performance of the College orchestra in Brahms's 'new' Fourth Symphony, pleased him greatly,[12] his sense of satisfaction with the College was somewhat marred by a display of bloody-mindedness at a Board meeting, 'where somehow the spirit of the d——l himself had been working in Stanford all the time—as it sometimes does, making him so nasty and quarrellsome [*sic*] and "contradictious"—as no one but he can be!' After that Grove heard that Jasper Sutcliffe was heading for disaster, being now on the point of marrying 'the sister of little Williams, a fatuous . . . moon-face who plays the cello'. He added to his letter to Edith, 'What a commentary on your tirade against marriage.'[13]

At Easter Grove had been to Paris, primarily to look over the library

[10] Letter of 4 May 1891, in the possession of Dr Chalmers Burns.
[11] Letter of 12 Jan 1891; BL, Add. MS. 42233, f. 16.
[12] 'The whole thing was so *big*, and loomed in my mind like St Paul's Cathedral'; E.O., Wed. [10 June 1891].
[13] E.O., Thursday [30 July 1891].

of the Conservatoire. In the summer he went to Switzerland for a fort-night, where he was disturbed by memories of time past spent there with Millie, and then to Berlin, 'to make a careful investigation of the Beethoven autographs, which are in Ernst Mendelssohn's possession and also look again through these in the public library.'[14]

Back from Germany, Grove went to the Festivals at Hereford—the first to be directed by G. R. Sinclair—and Birmingham, between which he went to his brother at Penn (where on Sunday he read one of the lessons in church) and his sister in Salisbury. At this time he was pursuing the idea ventilated in his latest letter to *The Times*, that facsimile editions of Beethoven's works should be published; and on 2 October he wrote to Speyer, informing him that he had 'received a very interesting letter from Breitkopf and Härtel on the subject. They propose that a committee should be formed with my name at the head.' When the matter was introduced to the Queen her response was less than whole-hearted: Grove was told that she would subscribe '£1 a year to your undertaking'. He was moved to express himself to Edith in what for him were revolu-tionary terms: 'isn't that mean. I call it *desperate*, for a woman rolling in wealth.'[15]

Across this period the intimacies of the relationship with Edith provide a perpetual, anguishing counterpoint to the professional and social pattern of life. One Thursday night (12 February) Grove stayed on in town after a students' concert, at rooms he used on such occasions in Henrietta Street, Cavendish Square. He wrote that night saying that he was tired of being isolated from his books and his papers: 'Only *home* is *home*,' and went on:

Also I find my wife does not care to come up; and when here, instead of having our London friends to dinner 2 & 2 grumbles at the smallness of the room—in fact is contumacious. I wanted to have had the College people whom I have so dreadfully neglected and kept aloof from (or *she* has) to dinner, and shewn them some little warmth of attention—but it is the same thing that has attended our life all through. She alas! has no interest in or sympathy with anything I like, do, or wish—not even any sensible desire to help me materially in the objects of life. By God, I often wonder how I bear it: how I don't get wild under it. For years I have borne it somehow, *always* trying to take the blame on myself. Many women do what they can to help their husbands, by being nice to their colleagues—pushing their husbands' interests etc. but no! not one grain of this have I ever known. All through my C. Palace work, my Bible dictionary work, investigation of Palestine, musical Dictionary, College—all the countless things

[14] Letter to Edward Speyer, 29 May 1891; BL, Add. MS. 42233, f. 18. Ernst von Mendelssohn, the son of Felix's brother Paul, was a director of the Mendelssohn banking house from 1871 to 1907.

[15] E.O., Nov 8 [1891].

I have tried—to everything she has been *absolutely cold*. At one time I violently rebelled by getting head over ears in love with another woman—a perfectly pure though *most passionate* attachment, which lasted for 20 years and only ended with her death.[16] But that's all past and I must not give in now. You must forgive my confession, though I know not why I should ask you to forgive my confidence, loving you as I do. If I could, I would ask you to marry me tomorrow, though it would be a hard lot to condemn even you to. But you are a dear—and I admire you—your face, your mind, your character, as I admire no one else. I am always thinking of you, and of how I can serve you.

Now dearie it is 12 and I must leave off. . . .

Later in the year Grove returned to the sad theme of alienation, when noticing how first editions of Tennyson and Browning, of which he possessed many, were fetching high prices. What would happen to his own treasures, as well as all his own notes and drafts, he did not know, for his sons were indifferent to literature. 'While Milly was alive,' he mused, 'I was all safe as she knew everything, but now my wife is utterly ignorant—never took the slightest interest in anything of mine and despises it all.' And from this general incompatibility came 'a general dissatisfied sense of nothingness'—a phrase used by Edith of herself at that time—and a disbelief in his own capacity. At College, he said, he sometimes found himself thinking that because he was truly an amateur he was 'a perfect imposter'.[17]

In March, as he often did, he wrote of two of his students in the half-moralistic, half-envious manner which was the consequence of his own unslaked desires: Sarah Berry

has never been in love, and if she has, what a passion it would be! how decorous and tame and provincial! and how can music be understood without! Pauline Cramer is at the opposite end of the scale. She and Armbruster I suppose must know all about what love is. Love of all sorts and kinds and proprieties . . .[18]

Next, Grove is exerting his influence on behalf of Edith's cousin, Ernest, helping him towards a tutorial post by writing a letter of commendation to Lord Aberdeen, sometime Lord Lieutenant of Ireland. After that he hears that Edith is not well. He sympathizes and on 22 April offers advice: 'The morning distress is dreadful. You must put some bread and butter and a cup of milk by your bed and devour it directly you wake. The real cause is that your inside is empty and wants some work.' In August, the matter still being under consideration, he quotes the advice of 'a great doctor' on the matter of early morning nausea, who was strong on the need for nourishment. What he recom-

[16] See above, p. 84 and below, p. 226.
[17] E.O., Fri. morning [31 July 1891].
[18] E.O., Monday evening [7 March 1891].

mended was Valentine's meat-juice, which, however, was apparently not always to hand when needed. For that very morning

I woke . . . at 5 in the most terrible fright—everything was black around me, in my mind. It was impossible to do what I had to do before starting [for Switzerland] on Thursday: I was a ruined man and was going down fast etc etc. I got out of my bed, lighted my gas burner, made myself a good cup of tea and ate some bread and butter, and at once my mental sun shone, and I was cheerful again. . . . Dear how I long to clasp your live beautiful little form in my arms and look into your sweet face and dear speaking eyes. . . .[19]

This echoed the phrasing of mid-May, in which Grove averred: 'Your darling letter has brought your precious image so very vividly before me—I could clasp you to my arms and say let us never part again.' Yet even after such an outburst of passion Grove could turn in the same letter to incomprehension of the behaviour of other people. Waldemar Meyer, a student, was living with the Franklin Taylors,

and I fear ere long there may be a catastrophe. I know that M. is dotingly fond of him and as she gets no kind of attention from her husband I am led to believe that there may be an explosion—But please dear this must be a dead secret. I have for long seen that something must happen—you know that I don't approve of Minna's ways. . . .[20]

In August Edith left the family home in Donnybrook, and moved with her sister Alice to a more agreeable neighbourhood. The house they took at 33 Upper Leeson Street, where Edith lived for 15 years, was convenient for Alice to Alexandra College. Sending his best wishes for the move, Grove burst out once more: 'Oh you dear friend I am so *dreadfully* in love with you and can think of nothing else, and am never happy but when I am writing to you. . . .' Early in September Edith came to England to stay with Mrs Wilton Oldham, now living in Cheltenham, and on 7 September she played the piano to Grove. 'You have made the Sonata of Beethoven a new and different thing to me!', he wrote two days later. 'I knew it before, as I thought; but on Friday it came with a fresh force to me: when shall I hear you play it again? Never perhaps.'

In November Grove noted that his eldest son Walter, in Australia, was marrying again, his first wife having died within a year of marriage, in childbirth. That Walter was about to come home would, Grove said in one of his gentler references to his wife, give great pleasure to Harriet, 'who dotes on him'. The way in which death then appeared to stalk the land was exemplified by the death in the near future of Walter's second wife, also within a year of marriage.

The end of the year was crowded with incident and memories. One

[19] E.O., [11 Aug 1891].
[20] E.O., [17 May 1891].

day there came a newsy letter from Polyxena Fletcher[21] in Vienna, detailing the Philharmonic concerts she had heard, at one of which Mozart's 'heavenly symphony in E flat' (K.543) was played. 'Dr Richter', she noted, 'took it slower than Dr Stanford.' She had also heard the most distinguished alumnus of the old National Training School, Eugen d'Albert, give 'an orchestral piano concert, that is to say, the programme consisted of a concerto in G [by] Beethoven, one in E minor by Chopin, and the E^b of Liszt. His technique and power were wonderful.' Polyxena, at least, was conscious of her duty to write a letter a year to her old Director.

Ethel Sharpe, with Hobday and Squire, gave a concert of chamber music in Prince's Hall. Grove was particularly moved by Schumann's D minor Violin Sonata, for this work was 'so charged with memories to me that it always would be dear, whoever played it, and however it was played. It used to be *beautifully* played by Wiener and Mimi von Glehn a girl with whom I was most desperately in love.'

The students' opera that year was Cornelius's *Barber of Baghdad*, of which the Queen subsequently commanded a performance at Windsor. At one of the concerts Clara Butt sang 'Che farò' from Gluck's *Orfeo*. Submerged by work and worry, and irritated by the presence of many people in the house, Grove wrote on 6 December:

But you don't need the assurance even of a dead tired man how deeply I long for our meeting and how earnestly I love you—I too don't need your previous letters to be convinced of your affection: but oh dear how sweet they are. What becomes of all the love there is? Is there some bank in which all the intense passion that is lavished in the world—often without coming to its legitimate result, and often apparently thrown away—some bank where it is stored up for a happy future? A sweet thought but I fear it's only a fancy. Do you remember Matt Arnold's verse:

> And sometimes, by too sad a fate
> The lovers meet and meet too late;
> 'Thy heart is mine' 'True, love, oh true'.
> 'Then, love, thy hand'—'Ah no, adieu.'[22]

[21] Miss Fletcher was one of the teachers of Elisabeth Lutyens; see the latter's *A Goldfish Bowl* (1972), pp. 17–18, 19, 21, 39.

[22] Grove did not remember this stanza of 'Too Late' quite accurately. The complete poem (1855 version) is:

> Each on his own strict line we move,
> And some find death ere they find love.
> So far apart their lives are thrown
> From the twin soul that halves their own.
>
> And sometimes, by still harder fate,
> The lovers meet, but meet too late.
> —Thy heart is mine!—*True, true! ah true!*
> —Then, love, thy hand!—*Ah no! adieu.*

The sentiment, in prose, went into the next letter five days later as: 'I think it very hard that we should be separated so far and love one another so much.'

CHAPTER TWELVE

Ideas of the Sublime

1892–1894

ONE of the unsung heroes in the Grove saga is Edmund, whose calm appreciation of his unpredictable brother's talents and defects was of inestimable value to the latter. Edmund's career was the reverse of George's, in that with him engineering took precedence over music; but he was sensitive and cultured in a way that the eldest brother, Tom, prosperous and pompous, was not. It was with Edmund that George saw in the New Year of 1892, and from his house he set out on 2 January to speak at the annual dinner of the Brighton Musical Fraternity. The dinner was good: the chairman was good; the speech by Franz Groenings on the subject of Performing Rights was good; everything was good—except the music. That, observed Grove, was 'atrocious', with a battered piano, vilely out of tune, its main support—'so characteristic of England'.

Back in London he was saddened by the condition of an old College girl as it was revealed to him. Grove knew that for many students higher education meant great sacrifice, with poor lodgings, too little to eat, and at the end, all too often, indifferent career prospects. There were, as has been seen, those who—literally—did not survive. The sad story of Louie Kellett always haunted Grove. And now there was the case of Elizabeth Fédarb, a Scholar of the College in 1888. A friend of hers told Grove that she was, as he reported,

a nice girl, but kept down by ill health (lungs) and by poverty, and ill health of her mother. Her father is a school-master in Westminster, the floor of the house being 2 or 3 feet only above the natural swamp at Westminster! in consequence B[essie] F. can't live at home but is obliged to have lodgings in Camden Town— and they have so little money![1]

Grove took what action he could. He found Elizabeth Fédarb a job in a girls' school in Eaton Square, though whether she could manage to put up with the drudgery without breaking down he doubted. Later in the year, when this girl was living in a healthier environment in Notting Hill, he went to see her; it was a sad report he gave to Edith: 'but, my dear,' he exclaimed, 'how she looks! it quite frightened me: *the look of death!*'[2]

[1] E.O., Jan 17 [1892].
[2] E.O., Sat. [11 June 1892].

Having suffered an attack of lumbago at the beginning of the year, Grove was considering the advisability of appointing an assistant at the College who could act as a link between his regime and that of his successor. He was also somewhat irked that, whereas he was quite unable to escape his duties, his brother-in-law, the Dean, was enjoying a ten-week holiday in Egypt—at the expense of a 'rich swell'—which would mean his returning to work with his 'nerves all in good order'.

The death of the Duke of Clarence from pneumonia following an attack of influenza also upset Grove, who had been at Marlborough on the day when the condition of the Duke—the eldest son of the Prince of Wales and lately betrothed to Princess Mary of Teck—was reported as 'critical'. He took it that that indicated the imminence of death.

... Somehow it quite paralysed me. The Prince and Princess have always been so good and so *just* to me that any thing that happens to them affects me very much. But indeed the feeling all over London has been very strong. At first one is inclined to think of the poor girl—but *quand on est jeune on se console*, both in love and in death and now I think much more of the poor father and mother. They are going down the hill and blows and wounds fall with terrible force in later life. And he was much superior to the second boy. True he was dull, but he was good, and a gentleman (what an example of that one has in Lord Hartington!) and you don't want brilliancy in a King. The blow to the Tecks must be tremendous. They are worldly people (nothing more I fear) and poor: and think what that trousseau must have cost them—I believe Princess Mary is really good and nice, and deserves to be fitted for higher constitutions; but to her father and mother it is enough to kill them.[3]

What is here said about the blows suffered in later life is intensified in a letter of a week later. Edith had reported the death of a man friend, and Grove's anxiety concerning her life in Dublin and his own state of mind led to another bout of religious disillusionment:

Tell me something about him and your intimacy with him—if you don't mind. . . . I, like you, often wish that I could look on the other world with that definite undoubting view that some of my friends (of the former generation) do. But I can't. I often try. I have not that happy simple faith; and if I could comfort myself with it, by tomorrow I should be all afraid again.[4]

As the winter went on Grove's health troubled him the more. After lumbago he complained of a hacking cough, but he refused to lay aside his routine. Apart from the College—which, to be truthful, was running itself tolerably well—he continued to write new programme notes and

---

[3] Ibid. Posterity has not endorsed Grove's opinion of the virtue of the Prince. The Marquis of Hartington, brother of one of the victims of the Phoenix Park murders of 1882, had just succeeded as eighth Duke of Devonshire. Although belonging to the Liberal Party he held conservative views and was firmly opposed to Home Rule.

[4] E.O., June 24 [1892].

revise old ones so that music societies all over Britain who asked for them should have them in up-dated form. He was regular in attendance at concerts, welcoming old and new friends into his 'dear old stuffy dark gallery', as he once described it to Edith.

Sometimes the conduct of the distinguished left something to be desired. At the concert at which he had played Bruch's Violin Concerto Joachim sat through the 'Great C Major' with Grove who remarked how it was 'delightful to nudge and be nudged continually'.[5] On another day, when Ethel Sharpe played Schumann's Introduction and Allegro in G and some Chopin pieces (on a bad Broadwood), Grove was with the Taylors, which gave him the opportunity once again to express his dislike of Mrs Taylor. Concerning what she had said at the concert, Grove wrote, 'You would think that she really knows something (or rather everything) about Pianoforte music; when she knows *nothing*.' Charles Wood was there too, and while the orchestra made its way through Beethoven's Fourth Symphony, 'we poked one another till we were sore'.[6]

On 28 March, Grove, Stanford, Parry and Holmes all went to the Monday Pop to hear Richard Mühlfeld in Brahms's new Clarinet Quintet (op. 115 in D), which Grove wrote of as 'such a beauty'. Later in the year he listened half-appreciatively to another new work which was to be recognized as a masterpiece of chamber music, Dvořák's Piano Quintet, the first two movements of which he described as commonplace, the last two as lovely.

At Easter Grove went to Paris, wondering whether he would go on to see Sullivan or not:

I ought to go to Monaco and see Arthur Sullivan—but I hate the atmosphere there, and I am not sure that the atmosphere of A.S.'s house quite suits me— 'morbid' you'll say, but still it's the fact. Still, he's my old friend, and we are very fond of one another and it *may* end in my going there.[7]

Before ending this letter Grove informed Edith, at the time staying with her sister Annie who now lived in Belfast,

I burned a great quantity of your letters last night. It's best I am sure. Such things as letters between those who love one another as you and I do, are so obvious to be misunderstood; and even if understood right why should other people be reading the burning words we have said to one another! I am just going solemnly to commit to the fire that most dear little note I got a day or two ago.

Grove did see Sullivan during his month's holiday. He also ran into an

[5] E.O., Sunday March 13 [1892].
[6] E.O., March 27 [1892].
[7] E.O., Sunday [10 Apr 1892].

old friend, the widow of Henry Wyndham Phillips, in Biarritz—where
he bought an inkstand for Edith.

He returned from Paris on 14 May. Next day he sent to Edith a
Turgenev novel[8] and Georges Ohnet's *Serge Panine* (1881), which, he
said, resembled Tolstoy's *Anna Karenina*, 'as clever as it can be and yet
there is not a person in the book for whom you care'. Around these works
and authors he discussed Barrie and Emily Lawless, whose *Little Minister*
(1891) and *Grania* (1892) respectively he was reading. *Grania*, a story of
the islands off Galway, led him to Lawless's earlier work, *Hurrish* (1886),
an acute and truthful narrative set in the turbulent Land League days.
But this for Grove was all 'rather common', and he could not see why
'the scenes and personages should be laid where so much that happens is
almost brutal'. He also thought that—in both Barrie and Lawless—
'excessive patois is a difficulty'.[9]

It is certain that Mahaffy would have supported this point of view, but
at the time Grove was having to conclude that in some respects Mahaffy's
judgement was open to doubt: 'I should like to know what Mahaffy
considers morbid in Beethoven. I should really, and even if there were
anything such in his first thoughts, yet the severe revision and purification
to which he subjected everything must have purged out any such faults.'[10]

Now and again Grove was carried out of his political depth as Edith
stirred freshly troubled waters on which the subject of Women's Suffrage
was now dangerously afloat. This subject was one which concerned
Parry, who lent his assistance wherever he could, but Grove was not
anxious to be too much involved:

Politically I don't like the movement, though I hardly know why for such a
woman has as much right to a vote and will exercise it as well (or far better) as
9/10[ths] of the wretched ignorant men who possess a vote at present. But I can't
go into that now and I frankly confess that with you as an antagonist I should
just lay down my arms![11]

At Sydenham the flow of people came and went, and Harriet undertook the statutory dinner- and tea-parties. When the sun shone on
summer afternoons the local clergy were encouraged to bring their
rackets and join in decorous sets of tennis in the Groves' garden. Among
them the most senior was Augustus Legge, Vicar of Sydenham and
latterly of Lewisham. Augustus, an old travelling companion of Grove's,
came that summer to bid the Grove family good-bye. He had lately
reached the top of his profession through the influence of his father, the
Earl of Dartmouth, who had pushed him into a sequence of family

[8] For Grove and Turgenev see below, p. 232.
[9] E.O., May 15 [1892].
[10] E.O., May 22 [1892].
[11] E.O., July 17 Sunday [1892].

livings and now into the Bishopric of Lichfield, in which diocese he was one of the prominent nobility.

In July there was a garden party at the Holloway College, where Grove threw himself contentedly into 'a tumult on the lawn with strawberries and tea' and congratulated Emily Daymond on having found such a fine place in which to work.[12]

The good weather departed and with rain came the return of rheumatism; but Grove was determined to go to Vienna again for the International Music Exhibition planned for the late summer. But in the last week of July he would rather have gone to Ballycastle in Antrim, where Edith was helping her sister to look after her three children. 'My dear Edith', he wrote, referring to the children, 'How I envy them their aunt. Yes dear I do. To be close to you and able to take your hand any moment, or "have (supposing me to be a child) a kiss" is a stretch of imagination that I nurse and nurse, but never hope to attain to. . . .'[13] A week later, in his next letter, he directed Edith's thoughts to Wordsworth and to Beethoven, comparing the last five lines of the third stanza of Wordsworth's *Intimations of Immortality* with 'the rough, jovial nature of the joy in the choruses of the 9th Symphony'.[14]

While considering Beethoven in the light of Wordsworth, Grove was independently examining different readings of at least one passage in the Ode and, with a professional precision, commenting on them in correspondence with William Knight. In 1890 Knight (supported at the time by Grove) had been an unsuccessful candidate for the Chair of English at Glasgow to which A. C. Bradley, who had not divulged his candidature to Grove, was elected.[15]

Grove went to Vienna by way of Bonn and stayed at the Ungarische Krone. He was in social mood, mixing with W. H. Cummings, the musicologist, who had his 'niceish slip of a daughter' with him; John Bergheim—at the time editing Schubert's songs; and the Heilperns, who—Grove did not fail to remark—were Jews. Mrs Heilpern had befriended Ellen Grove when she had lived in Vienna about 1860 and she was also a friend of the von Glehns. Eugen Heilpern was a photographer; his wife, 'a most beautiful person', as Grove noted, was clearly photogenic.[16] But it was very hot in Vienna:

[12] E.O., July 1 Friday [1892].
[13] E.O., July 22 [1982].
[14] Cf. *Beethoven and his Nine Symphonies*, p. 389.
[15] In a letter to Knight dated 'Feb 19' (without year), Grove wrote, '. . . I have just been saying over again Wordsworth's Ode and it occurred to me that the words "the sunshine is a glorious birth" (so printed in my edition—yours is not at hand) should be *sunrise* that is the *birth* not the *sunshine*. . . .'; PML.
[16] See *Grove 1*, vol. III, p. 381, 'Schubert'; acknowledgement to 'Herr Eugen Heilpern and the eminent photographers who act under the name of "Adèle" in Vienna'.

The paving stones in the streets at 4 in the afternoon are so hot that you can't keep the back of your hand on them; and the walls of the houses all along are like huge furnaces, enough to roast you. Still there is an alleviation:—A delightful park in the midst of the town with green bushy trees (not tall elms etc) always well watered, and benches everywhere. It is delightful to see the *common* people strolling about there and enjoying the evening in a way which no Englishmen and women of that class (or indeed of any other) can. . . .[17]

The Music Exhibition was intended to be comprehensive and most countries put on lavish displays. The British were represented by material from the Royal collection and several private collections. 'Unfortunately', commented the *Musical Times*, 'there are no Royal or State subsidies [in Britain], such as have helped other European countries to secure complete representation.'[18]

From Vienna Grove went by way of Salzburg to Interlaken, where he was hoping 'to take a real holiday and not bother my head for a little'. But meeting with Parratt, who had come from Nuremberg, it was not quite possible not to think along workaday lines. Together they went to Ringgenberg where Parratt played pieces by Bach and Mendelssohn on the organ on which Mendelssohn had played almost fifty years before.

At Thun Grove was delighted to meet the daughter of Wilkie Collins's 'Padrona', Nina Lehmann, herself the friend of Collins and George Eliot, who had married Sir Guy Campbell in 1887; Harriet's brother Herbert, whom he liked very much;[19] and Phillips Brooks, with whom he had kept up an epistolary relationship since 1878 but whom he now found he did not much like. Brooks, well over six feet, towered over Grove physically and dominated him conversationally. An honorary D.D. at Oxford, a recognized spiritual influence on the bankers of Wall Street, a bishop since 1891, Brooks disappointed Grove by 'an undisguised contempt and mockery of all things English in his talk', and a capacity for talking endlessly for the sake, it seemed, of admiring his own voice.

After the excitements of Europe came the tempered dignities of the Three Choirs Festival, at Gloucester. Grove had tried to persuade Edith to come over for this event, and—when she demurred on account of the expense—offered to send her £5. Pathetically, he noted, 'I can really do it without the faintest difficulty. I have always in the Savings Bank a fund, of the money I make by Programmes, articles etc., quite separate of house money, or my regular income.' But Edith (who became an Associate of the Royal Dublin Society that month) could not come.

[17] E.O., Sat. Aug 20 [1892].
[18] XXXIII, 1892, p. 281.
[19] 'Herbert is very handsome, very clever, very metaphysical, frantically in love with an American who won't have him (and isn't worthy of him) and the author of books which people buy but no one reads'; letter to E.O., 'Monday night' [April 1894]. Grove was proposing at that time to send a copy of Bradley's *Ethical Studies* to Edith to read.
8

The principal 'novelty' at Gloucester was Parry's *Job*, which, after a disastrous rehearsal, went splendidly and won such acclaim that it was performed in the sister cities at the next two festivals following.

Grove had numerous things on his mind at the time, all of which tended to send him into gloom. News had filtered through that Tennyson was seriously ill. There was a tiresome meeting of the professorial board of the College. He had an unpleasant interview with the father of a girl whom he found it necessary to expel. He had a bemusing letter from Edith to which he replied on 11 October. Edith herself was finding life on the emotional plane less than easy, which caused Grove to reflect on his own present and, once again, his past:

. . . I thought your letter most interesting: but my dear how early you have begun! the process you describe *I am going through now*. Literally every day some new light comes to me in music or poetry or the world. Just as I am losing all my power and going down into darkness, I find my insight sharpening and my judgment widening in a most interesting way. The first real moment in my life came when I was 43 years old, when my Lucy died, and I became madly in love with Mimi von Glehn. *There* was a passion! It lasted 20 years and more— till her death and with it came my first real insight into music, poetry, nature— everything. Now I am undergoing a similar further change, not the result of passion and with far less excitement than before—but very strong and real.

The conclusions to be drawn from this are clear. They were, it is to be assumed, also clear to Edith, who was well aware that if it was not 'passion' affecting Grove it was some very similar influence.

But the private man had to act as the public figure. Tennyson had died on 6 October, and Grove wrote for Edith a brief epitaph on the departed poet:

I shall go to the Abbey tomorrow—as one of the followers of the coffin I suppose. It's sure to be very solemn. Browning's was and Tennyson is far more to me and far greater than Browning. I can't regret his death (except for the simple and selfish reason that I should like to go and see him again as he told me to do in March), for he has died full of years and all the love and confidence of people, and has left a work behind him which surely no one has equalled but Shake-speare—not Milton—for except in L'Allegro Milton was not an *English* poet. Chaucer may be compared, but then Chaucer is not intelligible now.

At the funeral there was music from Stanford and Frederick Bridge in the form of settings of words by Tennyson for choir, and the well-known funeral music of Purcell, Beethoven (from the 'Eroica') and Chopin. 'My heart welled up', wrote Grove, 'as I thought how different and how in-ferior it would have been in France or Germany.' Amid the serried ranks of distinguished mourners was Fred Locker—now Locker-Lampson[20]—

[20] Locker-Lampson was a close friend of Tennyson, often spent holidays with him, and was godfather to Tennyson's son Lionel, who died in 1886.

who had been a fellow pupil with Grove at Elwell's School more than sixty years before. Grove was much moved to encounter him again, and 'hung on to his old arm with affection'.

The death of Tennyson frustrated another hope. Long ago, in the first flush of youthful zeal, Grove had gone to Farringford to request an Ode for the opening of the Crystal Palace.[21] In the last year of the poet's life he expressed the wish that Tennyson might compose some lines for the opening of the new College building, the business of which was from time to time taking him, often 'racked with pain',[22] to Marlborough House, to report to the Prince of Wales. From Tennyson he turned to Swinburne, who by mid-December had produced some lines which Grove described as 'mystical and poetical'.[23] 'I must', he added, 'adapt them of course.'

The College opera this year was Gluck's *Orfeo*. The show was stolen by Clara Butt, who, just out of her teens, was winning high praise from the critics. The *Musical Times*, reviewing the production, reported how she was giving 'signs of so much talent that her future career was spoken of as a matter of national rather than local importance'.[24] But the more he came to know her, the more Grove disliked her and the lower his regard for her musicianship became. Nor at the moment was he feeling too pleased with the Queen's latest show of philistinism. He had hoped that *Orfeo* might be performed at Windsor, but in response to his hints a signal came back from the Court: 'she does not like the opera of Orpheus very much'. Four days after *Orfeo*, his faith in people was restored by a splendid performance by the College orchestra of Brahms's Fourth Symphony.

Fiercely resolved to defy the process of ageing, Grove continued to do the work of two or three men, and, as he did, continued to suffer. Relying at the College on George Watson, the Secretary, he was thoroughly discomfited when, at the beginning of 1893, Watson was stricken with bronchitis. He told Edith on 2 January, 'my nerves are all shattered and broken and I feel quite forlorn and frightened'. Just then Sullivan invited his old friend to holiday with him in his villa on the Riviera. At first Grove resisted the idea, partly because he felt an 'incurable sense of shame and annoyance' at the prospect of missing the beginning of a term in which matters of urgency relating to the building work required constant attention, partly because of his unease at the thought of the amoral and bohemian habits into which Sullivan had now fallen.

[21] See above, p. 62.
[22] E.O., Dec 4 [1892].
[23] Swinburne's *Music—an Ode* was given to Charles Wood to set. Prior to its publication in *Astrophel and other Poems* (1894), the volume dedicated to William Morris, it was issued in brochure form.
[24] XXXIV, 1893, pp. 24-5.

But he fought back his reservations and when he met Sullivan he found him 'a *perfect* host—as simple and natural as when we first met 30 years ago; full of information about everything, and as affectionate to me as I could wish or require.'[25] Grove found himself being informed in areas of knowledge previously a closed book to him:

On Monday we went to Monte Carlo (5 miles off), and there I made my first acquaintance with gambling tables, never was more surprised; the saloons were dark and uninviting—and the play itself was the dreariest and most uninteresting thing imaginable. No one spoke, no one cried, or laughed. On the contrary all was so businesslike as a Bank and whatever the gamblers felt, they shewed no emotion—Monte Carlo itself is a very gay place—but surely very demoralising —full of cafés and saloons and other places for *pleasure*—all is pleasure and no one seems to care for anything else. Next afternoon we drove up to *Turbia* (find it in Tennyson's poem 'The Daisy') a ruined town, perhaps of roman times on the top of the heights.[26]

On another day there was a sight-seeing trip to Bordighera where they met two girls who were music students. One, Annie Fry, was a College student and Grove wrote to Edith how 'her Catholic soul [was] much excited by being so much in the arms of the Church'. He also noted how charmingly considerate Sullivan was to the girls.

For some days W. S. Gilbert, who had come to talk to Sullivan about *Utopia Limited*, was also a guest. Once or twice Grove went for a walk with Gilbert, but did not much take to him. He was, he wrote to Edith, 'a hard cynical man of the world . . . a bitter, narrow, selfish creature'. But as for the new libretto, Grove thought that a great improvement on its predecessors, being more real, and of a more truly critical character.

At the end of the month Grove was very restive. Having finished Macaulay's *History* there were no other books immediately available to him. He had none of the material he needed to proceed with the book on Beethoven which was now beginning to take shape. He could not walk in the hills too much for fear of tiring himself, neither could he rid himself of the exhaustion caused by trying to cope with the 'too abundant meals' served to him. He was 'literally without any occupation'; but Lord Charles Bruce, the most influential member of the College Council, was quite determined that he should stay where he was for a further period of rest.

On 28 January, after writing seven other letters which he himself described as long, Grove (in response to her latest 'beloved and interesting

[25] E.O., Sunday Jan 8 [1893].
[26] Ibid. Tennyson wrote 'The Daisy' after an Italian visit in 1851. The first two lines of the second stanza, which Grove notices in connection with La Turbie, are also recollected in Elgar's *In the South*, precisely at figure 20 in the score.

What Roman strength Turbia show'd
In ruin, by the mountain road.

words') opened his heart to Edith in a ten-page epistle. After three introductory pages he undertook another exercise in self-analysis, again searching out the present in the past:

Your letter is wonderfully interesting and you touch on a point which has often occupied me—When I first woke in the world to love, and music, and the sense of my fellow creatures (not till I was past 40) I used to look round me at dinner and say to myself 'What *tombs* we all are to one another!' I have often thought it, and it is to me a most painful and humiliating thought. Even the best friends: how little their words, the expression of their faces, really tells each other of their thoughts and meanings. I am thinking of *friends*—People in railway carriages dear, and still more these hateful, wicked, nasty creatures, at the play-tables, don't afford me with much desire or necessity to know their interiors. I do think Monte Carlo a most repulsive town, not only the gambling house— but the streets, the cafés, the promenades—every one you meet looks so *bad* and so sunk.

Edith had been reading a book by Edward Caird, the student of Kant and Hegel, and put into her letter some lines by Wordsworth quoted by Caird. Trying to identify the source of the quotation from memory, Grove was led towards the roots of his own philosophy:

How subtle are the influences of nature and things on me! and how often some apparently trifling little thing lifts one's mind to the contemplation of the greatest subjects, and makes an indelible impression! . . . Why should, on Tuesday last, an extraordinarily fine, warm, sunny, quiet day have seemed to wrap me in a mantle of good holy thought which I feel I shall never lose, but can always draw round me by recalling the time? These occasions were all independent of any other person or animate thing. They contained nothing like those many charms which bind me to the day when you and I went out for our drive at Cheltenham —and yet the impression produced could not be stronger or deeper or more permanent. That habit you speak of of always looking forward to the better time is, you know, embodied in the line of some poet—

> man never *is*
> But always *to be* blest.

—a line far inferior to the beautiful last line of your quotation.[27]

On Sunday morning Grove, having memorized the lines quoted to him by Edith, confirmed that they were by Wordsworth, and almost certainly from *Lines composed near Tintern Abbey*. In the context of the relationship between Grove and Edith the subject of this poem has poignant significance. He moved beyond the lines which he had memorized that morning, added a note on the workmanship of Tennyson and the magnificence of

[27] E.O., Jan 28 Sat. 1893; cf. Pope, *Essay on Man*, I, l. 95:
> Hope springs eternal in the human breast:
> Man never Is, but always To be blest.

Wordsworth, and—as evidence of the latter—gave the last part of *Intimations of Immortality*, with instructions to Edith that she should memorize them too. 'Poetry', he concluded, 'should always be learnt.'

Grove left the Riviera on the following day, called on Waddington in Paris en route, reached London on Wednesday, 1 February, in the morning, went to College, and was in Sydenham in time for dinner that night.

Soon he was reminded of the meaning the music of Beethoven held for him when at a students' concert he heard the Piano Trio in D major (op. 70, no. 1), of which the slow movement—one of the most telling episodes in Beethoven—he felt should be orchestrated: 'The piano wants the sustaining power necessary, and some of the passages will always sound vague and *half clothed*.'[28]

On 18 February Beethoven not only compelled Grove's attention at the Crystal Palace Saturday concert, but took complete possession of him. This was a remarkable—even a unique—spiritual experience, which he described next day to Edith and which certainly lies behind the sense of *afflatus divinus* in the apostrophe to the Fifth Symphony in *Beethoven and his Nine Symphonies*. The performance of this work, Grove said next day, was the most remarkable that he had ever heard:

I don't know that I can convey what I felt, but I will try. It was as if the music had vanished, and that I had got behind it—I don't remember noticing instruments or movements or subjects, or any technical things, but I seemed to realise the meaning—to feel that all through there was an incessant conflict going on between might and weakness; and now and then to be outside of everything and in presence of—I don't know how to say it—Reality, Eternity, spirit, space —I can't find the word.

Here he interjected his memory of the night at school more than sixty years before[29] and his feeling of being in the presence of some overwhelming force when hearing the 'Great C Major'. He observed himself as from outside himself and recorded the continuation of the mood of transcendence:

I must be in a susceptible condition just now for this morning after church something analogous came to me. Two College girls are here (children) and I took them to a church where the music is much better done than usual. They have a custom of singing a hymn after all is over as you walk out of church (walking during singing—'procession'—is always exciting). The hymn was one I am very fond of, words and tune—'and now O Father'. And *there* I found myself wonderfully affected, and almost out of my body: well, perhaps that was the sort of thing that the Apostles felt when they were with Christ when he was

[28] E.O., Sunday Feb 12 [1893].
[29] See p. 16.

transfigured . . . it was like going back to a lower state of existence altogether, when it was all over. . . . Why were you not with me yesterday? . . .

In the interchange of letters following the Riviera visit, Sullivan composed one to Lady Grove. Reminding Edith that long ago Sullivan had practically been a member of the household, Grove told her 'a funny thing':

Well in addressing her he began 'Dearest Harriet', and most natural—well it has given her the greatest annoyance—quite upset her. It does seem so odd to me that it should—but so it is! Isn't it strange that 2 people who have lived together for 41 years (since Xmas 1851) and know so little of one another as we do—be as you said such *tombs* to one another. I never can get her to *unbend*, to be really affectionate. I believe that the thing she likes best to say is 'no thank you'—to refuse something.[30]

In April Grove added a gloss to this sad summary:

The real man or woman is found after marriage to be sadly different to the image seen through the coloured glass or passion—What bad things some have to go through for that mistake! What hardships! and how easily avoided, even after marriage, with temper and patience. Alas![31]

On Sunday, 7 March, Grove had written to Edith saying he had had a visit from Henry Littleton, of Novello,

to ask me to publish my analyses of Beethoven symphonies among his Primers. I told him he was wrong to think they would make a *teaching* book (for one knows they were meant, and for amateurs they will always remain): and I stipulated that they should not be *improved* or edited by any one, or made to lose their character. . . . I had always looked forward to making a *lovely* book of them some day, as a kind of finale to my life.

By this time the beneficial effects of the holiday had already worn off. Bruce had been right in advising the extra month, although Grove may have felt that he was planning for him an easy path to retirement. The old symptoms returned, and were exacerbated by the unsatisfactory progress of Stanley's biography by Prothero. Grove's doctor could only hand him a 'tonic' and, without conviction, advise that the sovereign remedy for his much-tried patient was rest. However, Grove was diverted from his own troubles by those afflicting his former student Delia Tillott, now employed as a teacher at St Andrews. Poverty, under-nourishment, overwork, and anxiety had reduced her to a mental and physical wreck. Grove was deeply moved by compassion and a sense of helplessness: 'I fear she is doomed—she has got to sulphonal and all that sort of thing—

[30] E.O., Feb 12 [1893], op. cit. cf. p. 229 in respect of 'tombs' Grove is somewhat confused.
[31] E.O., Sat. April 22 [1893].

so poor that she *must* work ... but it won't be long before she must give
up that, and then——? It distresses me very much.'[32]

By now Grove had his contract for the Beethoven book, and Novello
had agreed that it should be, as he wished, compounded from the analyses
of the symphonies. Many people were delighted to know that such a book
would be available. Among them were Frederic Harrison, a versatile
author well known as a Positivist; the equally versatile Edward Pember,
a contributor to the *Dictionary*; Alfred Ainger, one of the royal chaplains;[33]
and Henry Silver, Douglas Jerrold's successor at the *Punch* Table, who
said that Grove had taught him all he knew of Beethoven. Enthusiasm for
the project, Grove wrote to Edith, came from amateurs; professional
musicians, he remarked unkindly, 'all turn up their sublime noses at
such things'. From this stricture he excluded Charles Wood, who was
busily checking all the musical examples for the book, and otherwise
lending aid.

Against this Grove was reading Turgenev's *Virgin Soil* in a recently
available French translation. When he had finished it he sent it to Edith,
pointedly drawing attention to 'the absurd attempts at Revolutionary
movements that have been made in Russia, and the ridiculous want of
experience, and preparation, and real insight, that has spoiled them all'.[34]
A week later he reflected on what might happen in Ireland: 'If Home Rule
or anything else drives you to this side, no doubt something can be
found for you without difficulty.' At the end of the ten-page letter
written (as so many to Edith, on a Sunday) on 14 May, Grove returns to
the subject. But before doing so he pays tribute to Harriet, suffering at
the time from neuralgia in the neck: 'She is really a wonderful person—
Any one else would lie slavishly in bed but no! though so bad that she can
hardly move, she is always getting up.' There was also a then familiar
problem—of a new housemaid settling in—and to make life even more
difficult the weather was behaving unnaturally. There was quite unseason-
able heat and even a threat of drought.

During that week Grove had been at the opening of the Imperial
Institute, having fitted himself into his 'court clothes' and girded on
his sword; three Indian Rajahs were in attendance and the Queen's
Escort included Indian and Colonial troops. Grove was accompanied by
a niece from Marlborough, who had some difficulty with her hat—which
kept falling off. As for the Queen, she 'looked *cross* (as she always does),
but spoke with wonderful force and dignity—"*my empire*" was quite

[32] E.O., Friday night, Mar 11 [1893].
[33] Ainger (1837–1904), a protégé of Maurice and Kingsley, was a friend of Alexander
Macmillan and a member of the von Glehn circle. A man of many gifts, he held important ecclesiastical posts. When he was made Canon of Bristol in 1887 Grove observed
to him that he would be able to purchase the complete works of Schubert.
[34] E.O., Thursday [2 Mar 1893].

thrilling'. It was, Grove considered, his Empire too; but Ireland—with the second Home Rule Bill having passed through its second reading in the Commons in April—was intensifying the threat to its serenity. Grove ended his letter with words that have been spoken by many on many subsequent occasions. Old questions abide.

You seem to treat Home Rule as certain to pass. But why? The House of Commons no doubt, but not the House of Lords! and much as one laments the 2 houses coming into collision, one only feels thankful here for the check. *Then* there will be a dissolution and then the majority against is sure to be overwhelming. It has been an unceasing wonder to me that though every one I speak to casually in train, omnibus or walking—is dead against H.R. yet that there is a majority in the house. But I can't think it will be so again. It's Gladstone['s] personal power and nothing else that does it.—Goodbye dearest always your fond, loving, grateful, devoted

G.

There followed, on 28 May, another letter which brought to the surface the bitterness that had festered within for years. Happiness came to him, Grove wrote, from 'the pursuit of certain aims and ends—my College, you, my Beethoven Book, B's music. . . . the beauty of the country or the sky or the trees . . .':

Other happiness I have somehow missed, through the unfortunate fact that my wife, on whom one must mainly depend, as the person who is most with one, and on whose treatment one's actual comfort hangs,—does not know or does not care—how to treat me. I am, as you know, immensely dependent on those in contact with me. I take great interest in them and like them to take interest in me; to know what I am doing, to sympathise in it, and be anxious about it. Now *she* is utterly and entirely devoid of anything of the kind—She is dead to music, dead to literature, dead to the College and to all my other concerns of life—*never* says a thing with the will to please me but as it seems to me rather the reverse. I always come down in the morning, or come home at night, with strong *intention* to be nice and sweet, and give my fate one more chance—and I am as regularly disappointed—that, I grant, *is* unhappiness—no! it is discomfort. It is an unpleasant thing which annoys and hurts me as a blow would—but then, thank God, there is the *immense* alleviation of one's *pursuits*—of music, poetry, one's business, one's friends, what one can do to help forward the progress of the good and the beautiful etc. But as to thinking of all this in the light of one's own happiness surely it very seldom happens—it may now and then drive one into one's bedroom to storm and rage for a few moments—and the folly of such a proceeding soon becomes apparent, and it stops. . . .

In June Grove went with Anna and Ellen, Edmund and Tom, to the funeral of his eldest surviving sister, Bithiah. His spirits were at rock bottom and at the beginning of July his doctor gave him an injection of morphia. 'Don't be frightened, darling,' he wrote to Edith, 'I have had them before when in great pain; and *one* cannot set up a habit.' The presence of Polyxena Fletcher and Gertrude King, both promising young pianists, cheered him up one week-end and he led them through Kinglake's *Eōthen*, one of his favourite books, and, at 'Plex's' request, Browning's 'Love among the Ruins' and 'Karshish', from *Men and Women*. Grove was also cheered by a message from the Queen's Equerry, Major A. J. Bigge, that Ethel Sharpe had covered herself with glory when playing before the Queen at Osborne.

At the end of July Edith came to London for a brief visit, and her departure was the cause of a minor catastrophe and a major disappointment. Armed with a 'nice basket of greengages' Grove set out on 27 July to see her on to the Irish Mail. He went, alas, not to Euston, but to Paddington. On her way to Holyhead Edith sent a note from Chester, which awakened old memories. While the train was, as he calculated, rushing through Rugby Station Grove was writing regretfully, 'The greengages *were* so good. I got the best, and better could not be!'

In his letter of 29 July, Grove reminded Edith of the unpleasant realities of the present, referring to the feelings aroused by the Home Rule Bill, on which something like 80 days had already been spent. To carry this through the Commons Gladstone introduced the 'guillotine' procedure. On 1 September the Bill passed its third reading in the Commons. A week later it was rejected by the Lords by an overwhelming majority of more than 300.

By this time Edith had gone to Newcastle in County Down for a holiday, and Grove to Ragatz in Switzerland in search of effective alleviation of what was now diagnosed by his family practitioner as sciatica. At Ragatz hot mineral water poured in and out of 90 baths disposed in four bathhouses. When the rheumatic hordes had luxuriated in these reputedly healing waters they were led, or pushed, into the Kurgarten, where, three times each day, a band provided further therapy. On 15 September Grove claimed to have written 193 letters in Ragatz to date, '*and not one could have been spared*'. On the way home he stayed briefly at the Hotel Rigi beside the lake at Lucerne, where he had stayed on his first visit in 1866. In Mulhouse he was delighted to meet a brother and sister-in-law of Mimi von Glehn.

For at least a year Grove had concentrated his attention on his Beethoven book. Not the least valuable part of it—as of the preceding analytical essays and the *Dictionary* article—comes from the fact that when Grove was a boy Beethoven was a new composer, but that as Grove came to maturity so too did Beethoven's reputation. About all Grove's writing on Beethoven there is a sense of actuality, which was enhanced by the kind of anecdotes that came his way.

In his essay on Beethoven for *Chambers's Cyclopaedia*, for example, he introduced the generative motif of the first movement of the Violin

Concerto in this casual manner: 'These four notes, which haunted
Beethoven so persistently through his first movement, are said to have
been suggested to him by his hearing, while lying awake at night, a person
who was shut out of a neighbouring house, and who kept on knocking
for admission, four strokes at a time. . . .' With proper scepticism, Grove
suggests that this is ridiculous. But, assuming the mantle of common
sense, he continues, 'To some this story may appear apocryphal, absurd,
below the dignity of the subject. But surely without reason. Its very
triviality is in favour of its genuineness.' And then he seizes on a profound truth, unconsciously precipitating the answer to his own questions
concerning the sublime: 'The four knocks were to Beethoven what the
hulk of the "old Temeraire" was to Turner, or the Daffodils to Wordsworth, commonplace objects in themselves, but transmuted by the fire
of genius into imperishable monuments.'[35]

Sometimes one is brought to earth by recollections of impious behaviour. Even musicology benefits from the occasional gust of ribaldry.
Time after time one becomes aware that modern music raises someone's
hackles. Once it was Beethoven, and Grove lets us know that he had to
fight for his place in the sun, and that his works were once viewed with
mistrust and incomprehension: 'It was at the first [English] performance
of the Pastoral that old Mr [William] Horsley and someone else are said
to have walked out in the slow movement, muttering as they went,
"call that music".'[36] Regarding the same symphony, Grove remembered
how at one early performance in England Handel's 'Hush ye pretty
warbling choirs', from *Acis and Galatea*, was inserted between the second
and third movements.

I wonder was it at Mr Vaughan's Concert that the 'warbling choir' was brought
in? One would like to know too what Dr Crotch did 'at the organ' on the
occasion? A propos to the organ I see that Moscheles was so proud of his use
of it in the 9th Symphony that it was announced beforehand; see Mus World
May 1838, p. 40 (and praised!).[37]

'How queer it is,' Grove concluded, 'looking back to those dim old
times.'

In the summer of 1893 Grove was interested in peripheral areas of
Beethoven research: in the studies of Cramer to which he refers in the
book (p. 111)—but which, in respect of his particular research, he found
less helpful than he would have thought; and in the MS. of a libretto on
the subject of Prometheus by the Duke of Wellington, which the Duke

[35] The story is made use of again—somewhat reduced in bulk—in the chapter on the
Fifth Symphony in *Beethoven and his Nine Symphonies* (pp. 147–8).
[36] Letter to F. G. Edwards of 4 Nov 1892; BL, Eg. MS. 3091, f. 34.
[37] Letter to Edwards of 16 Jan 1895; ibid., f. 78. Thomas Vaughan (1782–*c*. 1845)
was a singer in the choirs of Westminster Abbey, St Paul's Cathedral and the Chapel
Royal, and organized annual benefit concerts.

had handed to Costa with instructions that he should set it to music. But on 27 July Grove wrote to Edith that the Fifth Symphony was 'always tearing away at my vitals'.

On 15 September, in what was probably his 194th letter from Ragatz, Grove wrote:

The first movement of no 5 seems to me to be intended primarily to be a picture of B. himself.

and of the Countess Theresa—with whom he was then violently in love—and who is

the two phrases are exact portraits, and the behaviour is just what Beethoven was accustomed to shew for every body.[38]

Ragatz was particularly associated with Beethoven criticism in Grove's mind. When near the end of his work on the book, he informed Edith (in slightly ambiguous terms) that he had 'practically finished the Pastoral Symphony' when he was there in 1864. (He remembered inaccurately, and wrote 1863.) But the big issue—one which could only in that age have been of fundamental concern—was stated in these disarming terms: 'I wish', he wrote to Edith on 1 September, 'you wd tell me what your ideas are about the sublime.' He invited comment from other correspondents, including A. C. Bradley who was professionally qualified to respond, his old friend Mrs Wodehouse, and his brother Edmund. Fortunately, sublimity is discussed in the *Nine Symphonies* with some discretion.[39]

At the 1893 Gloucester Festival a performance of the work brought Grove back to the Fifth Symphony which he now found to be 'delicate and romantic in the extreme', and he praised Lee Williams's interpretation in a letter to *The Times*. He did not find such appellatives applicable, however, to the Second Symphony of Frederic Cliffe (a Leeds Festival commission of 1892), of which he heard a rehearsal and for which he needed to write a note for the Crystal Palace concert of 22 October. It was the composer—an alumnus of the old National Training School and a piano professor at the RCM—rather than the music which called for adverse comment. Cliffe, a Yorkshireman, was

a strange compound of ability and commonness. His first symphony was very able and full of matter very well expressed—but he has had little or no education

[38] Cf. *Beethoven and his Nine Symphonies*, p. 155, where some of the words are as in the letter.

[39] Ibid., pp. 146 and 217.

and has not supplemented it by any literary study; but his American friend, his fondness for rollicking society, and his frantic passion for Nordica have acted on him so much that he can now never change.[40]

During the autumn private grief once more supervened on public duty. The deaths of Jowett, whose works he had for so long zealously read and recommended, and Sir William Smith—to whom in one sense he owed everything—saddened him. Meanwhile technical problems attendant on the preparations for occupation of the new College building needed his attention. Sometimes they perplexed him. In view of his own knowledge of engineering it is surprising that he showed such diffidence in discussing the relative merits of central heating and open fireplaces. He had referred to Barclay Squire, hoping that his experience of the heating system of the British Museum might help him to come to a decision.

My own feeling and that of the board of professors is a disinclination to throw themselves into the arms of a vast system which, with the finest construction, may get out of order and may persist in making a noise, in being hotter than can be borne or not hot enough etc. and that it would be better to have the control of your own room, which is got by an ordinary fireplace. Some people also question the healthiness of the air warmed by hot water pipes.[41]

On Sunday 10 December Grove sent news, and a gift, to Edith. He had spoken about her cousin Ernest, now a curate in Wolverhampton, to his bishop, who was well satisfied with his progress. He agreed with Sir Robert Stewart's criticism of the Index to the *Dictionary*, but Mrs Wodehouse, its author, was gravely ill and not likely to be able to return

---

[40] E.O., Sept 25 [1892]. Nordica, *née* Lillian Norton (1859–1914), an American soprano (and at this time a widow) sang in *The Golden Legend* in Dublin in 1891. The next year she visited the city on 22 February, for a concert promoted by the Railway Benevolent Institution, and again on 24 May for another performance of *The Golden Legend*. When Edith reported her reactions to Nordica Grove responded (25 Nov [1892]):

> I am glad you liked Nordica. I have a great dislike to her personally (too long to tell) but it prevents my enjoying her;—and then she is such a very poor musician! If she got through the concert without coming in wrong etc it was more than she does elsewhere. Her sweet voice and pretty face I grant you, but what credit are they to her? She is not engaged to Cliffe—that is one of the things I quarrel with her for: Cliffe has been madly in love with her for years, has been her slave, her dog, her doormat and she keeps him dangling on, wasting his life! Well she has certainly been the cause of his writing a very fine [first] Symphony. But, for *her*, I wish she would go back to America and never let us see her again.

Between 1888 and 1893 Nordica sang in every season of opera at Covent Garden; in 1893 she sang the part of Zelica in Stanford's *The Veiled Prophet*. Three years later she married a Hungarian tenor, from whom she was later divorced.

[41] Letter of 25 Nov 1892; BL, Add. MS. 34679, f. 155.

to this project soon, if ever. The great shadow, however, was cast by *l'affaire* Holmes:

I am afraid a horrid row is impending over us on account of Holmes—I have just found out that he lectures his girl pupils not only on Atheism and Socialism —but on other matters which no man ought to talk to any woman about—I am trying to get some evidence, and tell them, it must be kept *most secret*. I think he is fool enough for anything; but I can't practically see how such things as I am warned of can be done in the presence of several girls!

Goodbye darling write again as soon as you can. Where do you go for Christmas? Stop at home? How I wish I were that ring! Good bye. Always your most loving

G.

The blow fell next day, as reported in the letter written on the following Sunday evening, 17 December:

Deadly private

. . . I am in a horrible hole. Last Monday aft^n I heard from the guardian of one of my girl violin scholars that Holmes was in the habit of committing and enticing to committ [*sic*] the grossest immorality with his female pupils—It was given me in such a form that I could have no alternative—so I at once wrote a letter to him forbidding him to enter College again till I had laid the matter before the Council. This I did on Wednesday aft^n and he was then formally deprived of his position and appointments at College—meantime I had had to find out 3 of the girls whom he had tried (ineffectually) to seduce, and take their evidence—Meantime he wrote—not denying—but saying that he thought it expedient to resign! thus admitting the charge . . .

I know you will be thinking about me. If you were here to help me!—to influence the girls!—for many of them I know will stick to him, not realising what it is he is turned away for! He seems to have attempted 3 (and probably many more) and to have actually succeeded in ruining 4. Those I know of but there may be dozens. His wife and children are all in the same way of thinking!

The postscript to the letter epitomizes the philosophy of permissiveness as then preached and practised by Henry Holmes: 'He used to represent it as a necessary accompaniment to music and art, and to freedom in Politics and everything else.'

This incident signalled the beginning of the end of Grove's Directorship. Through the first part of 1894 he prepared for a smooth transfer of authority. First, there was the matter of a successor to Holmes (who had silently fled to San Francisco). Not unnaturally, Grove wanted 'a gentleman, and a man of culture, and personally agreeable'. So he wrote to Speyer whose acquaintance with Frankfurt qualified him to speak of the merits of Hugo Heermann, director of the Museum Concerts and professor in the Conservatorium of the city, and one of the soloists in the 1890 Beethoven Festival at Bonn. Although Henschel and Ludwig Straus recommended Heermann, and—after reviewing the claims of Willy

Hess, who did not then wish to leave Manchester—Grove interviewed him, the appointment went to Fernández Arbós, although he had at first expressed such reservations that Grove felt him to be 'too tied to the Spanish Court'. During these negotiations there had been an undercurrent of xenophobia, some professors protesting against the selection of 'a fresh foreigner'.[42]

Just as the time for occupying the new building was near Grove was hit by a bombshell from Manchester. There was talk not only of a College, but of a Royal College, of Music in that city, and this for Grove—for whom it was always a case of London *aut praeterea nihil*—was a gesture of impudence that was insufferable. 'Cheek! isn't it,' he wrote to Edith on 4 March; 'the R.A.M. and we are going together to oppose this and oh! the work that that gives.' The sudden rapprochement between Academy and College at this late date has an ironic tinge.

Despite whatever machinations were taking place in Manchester, the new building of the R.C.M. was duly opened on 2 May. A fortnight later, George Watson, the faithful Secretary, who had silently carried a considerable administrative load, suffered a stroke.

One of Grove's less attractive traits was that, conscious all his life of his father's cultural deficiencies, he tended to work out his own sense of inherited inferiority on those who had also made their own way towards the top. Thus, reporting the opening to Edith, he told her that the ceremony went without what 'Mr Samson Fox would call "an 'itch, your Royal 'Ighness" '.[43] At the beginning of March 1894 there had been a letter from Edith which put him in mind of another notable offender in this particular.

Have you got a photograph of yourself as Night? I long to see it. I can't tell you how I should like to have it. I never wore a disguise but once. Did I ever tell you about it? I was at a great masked party given by old H. Littleton at his house in Upper Sydenham. I have an African chief's robe—very full, dark blue, with lovely embroidery on the front. I put on also a red fez with a turban round it, and you may imagine it made me rather unrecognizable. Well, I wandered out about 10 o'clock shielding myself from inquisitive [cads?] and the police by an umbrella. I found old L. (one of the vulgarest old snobs imaginable) sitting in his hall to receive his guests, with a large visitors' book on the table by him. I walked up to him and began, 'O great sage I have come from the ends of the earth to enjoy your hospitality and taste the flavour of your wisdom, deign to utter a few words of welcome to your slave'. I never saw a man look so bewildered. 'Oh shut up, shut up', said he, 'tell us 'oo you are' on which I took up the pen and fortunately recollected Persian enough to write a long name in the book. Then of course I revealed myself.[44]

[42] E.O., Jan 14 [1894].
[43] E.O., Wed. night May 2 [1894].
[44] E.O., Mar 4 [1894].

There had been an instance of this obsession two years earlier.[45] When Clement Spurling went to Oundle School he replaced a man with limited powers of discipline. What, in Grove's view, was worse, 'somehow he was not a gentleman and made odd slips—Once a boy named Hall, in a harmony class, misbehaved, and the master wishing to signalise him said " 'All stand up" on which all the class stood up, and he did not see it, and got furious and thought they were ridiculing him.'[46]

In his last year as Director—during which Sir George Donaldson presented his collection of instruments to the College—Grove took pleasure in the achievements of those of his students who had set out to become composers and had been given the opportunity to prove themselves at the College concerts. Of the Grove dispensation those who survived to make reputations were Hamish MacCunn, Arnold Dolmetsch, W. E. Duncan, Walford Davies, Charles Wood, Samuel Coleridge-Taylor, S. P. Waddington and W. Y. Hurlstone. It was on 5 July, having heard Coleridge-Taylor's Nonet, that Grove, who praised the work in general, is reported to have said: 'He will never write a good slow movement until he had been in love. No man can who has not been in love.'[47] In respect of this it must be concluded that Grove was at some stage overruled in the design of the College building, where the sexes were segregated as much as possible. To this fact the two staircases, the one male, the other female, are a lasting memorial.

Almost exactly in the middle of that summer—to be precise, on 22 June—and almost exactly a year after the composer had been in England, Grove heard Tchaikovsky's last symphony. In it he found something akin to sublimity; and in its pessimism, it would seem, something akin to his own. Indeed, in the letter he wrote to Edith at half-past six on the morning of 28 June, one senses a kind of beatification of pessimism:

. . . the last symphony made an extraordinary impression. I don't remember having been so, or so much, affected since the early days of the great Schubert in C. It is very difficult, and was played splendidly, but I am thinking of the work itself. It is called Pathetic and was his last; and pathetic it is, most wonderfully so! but it is also *noble* and *beautiful* and poetical in the most extraordinary degree. I have never before heard anything of his that I cared for and it was quite overwhelming. . . .

[45] When Edith had written to Grove in 1892 about the Brahms Horn Trio, he responded thus: 'I like you having been so happy over the Trio—the first movement I know (and don't you remember it at College in early days, (Joseph) Smith playing what he called the 'orn, or the 'and 'orn)'; E.O., Tuesday 11 p.m. [22 June 1892]. In the end Smith was, in Grove's ears, redeemed. In reporting on the College performance of *The Flying Dutchman* in 1898 (see p. 265), he commented on the fine playing of 'Horn Smith'.
[46] E.O., Thursday 21 Jan [1892].
[47] W. C. Berwick Sayers, *Samuel Coleridge-Taylor—Musician* (1915), p. 23.

As 1894 moved on, the front runners for the Directorship, according to Grove, were Parry, whose health was none too good; Parratt, for long considered the favourite, but lately showing personality defects that seemed to reduce his chances; and Frederick Bridge, who was rising in esteem. As for Stanford, he was in another race for which the bookmakers were laying odds. Robert Stewart had died and Edith was keen on Stanford succeeding him at Trinity. Grove reminded her that Stanford—her 'ideal', as he somewhat caustically remarked—was 'tiresome'. For Dublin he would put forward the name of G. R. Sinclair, of Hereford, 'an Irishman, and certainly very clever—young and vigorous, without being rough or extravagant'.[48] If Sinclair had gone to Dublin the content of the 'Enigma' Variations would have been different—and dog-less. It was Prout who in the end was chosen to succeed Stewart, and when the intimation came to Grove that he probably would be the successful candidate, he commented tersely and unenthusiastically, 'I see Prout mentioned as Stewart's successor—clever, accurate, grumbling—not a gentleman—not a player—anti-Hibernian in every sense'.[49] The last comment might be thought to have been somewhat gratuitous.

On Monday 5 November the Council of the College, with Prince Christian in the chair, had before them five names, of which one was to be selected for recommendation to the Prince of Wales for the post of Director. The five were Bridge, Parratt, Parry, Stanford and Taylor. The Council unanimously chose Parry. 'He', wrote Grove, 'is the best, but o my dear—in many things he will be very poor—no backbone no power of saying no, or of resisting those whom he likes.'[50] After his election Parry was asked to comment on the situation by the editor of a Scottish journal. He responded as follows: 'I cannot say the appointment makes me in any degree jubilant, for the loss of such a friend as Sir George Grove, and the irreparable gap his retirement will make at the College, makes every one connected with the place feel depressed.'[51]

Leave-taking was nervously exhausting for Grove. Visetti burst into tears and kissed him; Parratt, silent 'à l'anglaise', twisted Grove's hands; Pauer, characteristically, said no word 'of sentiment or affection (tho' he felt it I am sure)', but inquired whether with the Director's going he should not also go. Stanford rushed home after a period of reflection, to put on paper what he had been too full of emotion to speak.

[48] E.O., Monday night [13 Apr 1894].
[49] E.O., Thursday morning 6.30 June 28 '94.
[50] E.O., Saturday Nov 10 [1894].
[51] 'Dr Hubert Parry', Scottish Musical Monthly, vol. II, no. 16 (January 1895), p. 75.

50 Holland Street, Kensington W.,
Nov. 23, 1894

My dear old G:

I could not say anything before fuzzy headed Pauer today, but now that it's all over I must just write you one line of the most heartfelt gratitude for all the love and kindness you've shown me all these years at the College and for making the last 10 years the happiest I ever spent. Any good I have done has all been from your loyal help and splendid initiative, and the effect of that will last longer than you or I. I've always felt somehow as if your influence was like Arnold's at Rugby, and certainly he was not loved and honoured more than you. You dear, bless you.

We'll try to keep up to your standard if it is only for your sake and for what you have done. And forgive me for having often been a hot-headed and worrying chap always turning up at your busiest moments, and making your life a burden to you generally.

And do preach to Hubert, to be methodical, and not to wear himself out and to keep some of his time always for his own works. . . . Goodbye, my dear dear G, till Monday. We must all, as Parratt says, keep a special armchair in our rooms for you to drop into at any hour of the day or night.

Yr loving
C.V.S.[52]

The end of term opera was Delibes's *Le Roi l'a dit*, in which Louisa Kirkby Lunn appeared as the Marquise de Moncontour, and it went off, Grove said, 'with extraordinary spirit'. His last day in College was Friday, 21 December 1894, and all that remained over were the Reports which would come to him for signature in the morning. After that—

I have got to think only about myself. No necessity to hurry out of bed in the dead of night to put down a memorandum of some thing which must be remembered in the day; no necessity to get up before the sun in order to get off by the 8.30 train: no constant worry and anxiety: no hundred other things which now make up the warp and woof of the day. . . .

He was writing to Edith late that night, from home: 'An odd thing, this is the only house I am connected with in which I get no sympathy and no help—so it is: things are absolutely unnoticed.' What would he do? Maybe he would voyage to the Cape of Good Hope, there being the possibility of a free voyage. He would like to help Thackeray's daughter, Mrs Ritchie, with whom he had at one time been friendly, in preparing a corrected text for a projected new edition of her father's works.

Edith was off to the Fosters in Belfast, to a house called Clonmilla, in the Antrim Road. Grove was carried away into his world of dreams:

[52] From a copy of the letter made by E.O. and kept by her with a letter from Grove of 25 Nov 1894.

. . . the words are most musical and magical to me, I *love* them. I always think of you with the children round you, laughing, and worshipping their darling aunt. I know an old child who would love to be there too only he would shew his feelings too unmistakeably. Send him a message, dear. I will convey it. God bless you and yours—How long have I loved you, darling!

G.[53]

[53] E.O., Friday night. Dec 21 [1894].

CHAPTER THIRTEEN

'There will be no one quite like him again'

1894–1900

His last year as Director of the Royal College was trying for Grove in more ways than one. 'I have', he wrote to Speyer on 17 November 1894, 'all but broken down; but thank God I have escaped a "stroke" or any other blow that might have incapacitated me.'[1] As he prepared for retirement with the hope of greater leisure to come, he became more aware of strains within the family, of Harriet's louder discontent with modern times and habits, and of the marking of the passage of time by reports of the infirmities and the deaths of old friends.

At the beginning of the year Grove found himself at cross-purposes with one of his daughters-in-law and one of his sons. His second son, Julius Charles—known familiarly as 'Tundy'—was saddled with a 'tiresome, provoking, little wife, with no heart, and [an] extraordinary means of making you angry'.[2] 'Tundy' himself, his father said, was never out of humour. As for the youngest son, Arthur, an electrical engineer, he was said to be very clever, fascinating and amusing, but, 'I am told, talks to his wife with quite alarming freedom; swears, and uses the most dreadful expressions'. Arthur's wife, Grove testified, was 'not that sort'. Despite having some reservations about her—'She is not quite congenial to me, but she is very fond of me, and is musical enough to sit by, and appreciate things'[3]—he was glad to have her company for one day of the Handel Festival. A few days before this event news had come from Australia of the death of Walter's second wife at the age of twenty-three.

Ethel Sharpe's career in 1894 had now become a relentlessly triumphant progress. She had played in Vienna, where she was praised by Hanslick, had become friendly with Brahms, and had made a successful *tournée* with Albani through Bohemia, Austria and Italy.[4] In June she paid a visit to the Groves, and unwittingly became the cause of a family row. On 28 June Grove wrote to Edith, saying:

My wife would be very glad to take you in here if it would come in with your

[1] BL, Add. MS. 42233, f. 37.
[2] E.O., Jan 14 [1894].
[3] E.O., 22 June [1894].
[4] See the *Musical Times* XXXV, February 1894, p. 116.

plans. Poor woman she is so outraged by the want of manners of some of the College girls. Ethel Sharpe was here on Sat. and Sunday (playing beautifully) but she offended her Ladyship sadly—'so dreadfully common'—while two others—L[ouie] Heath from Middlesborough [*sic*] and M[arie] Busch a singer— found more favour.[5]

On 25 May 1894 Grove wrote to his brother Tom that Lord Rosebery had that very morning offered him a C.B. 'at the desire of the Queen . . . in recognition of the eminent services which you have rendered to the public in connection with the Royal College of Music'. Hearing of the honour, an old friend from the earliest Crystal Palace days who was also in at the beginning of the Palestine Exploration Fund re-emerged. A letter came from Sir Henry Layard, and Grove was duly grateful:

Your congratulations are immensely gratifying. . . . I am sadly knocked up at present. The fact is I have worked too hard and am now paying the penalty. I fear I shall have to give up all, or a great deal of my work. I am sorry to hear so poor a report of you. I should like dearly to meet again, though we can't hope ever again to buy *roasted chestnuts* together, as we did once on a time at the corner of Suffolk Street and Pall Mall! That must have been about 1854!![6]

A chance remark of Edith's that summer concerning a trip of hers sent him still further back in recollection, to a time when, clearly, his mind had been set by his teacher in the ways of prejudice in respect of British history: 'Drogheda was a great place in Cromwell's time, I think, and he always spells it Tredagh—even now the name is only 2 syllables, is it? though at school I was always told Draggeda—I remember Lough Neagh was always called "Low (like cow) Nay".'[7]

In September there was a brief holiday in Scotland—to the Highlands, to St Andrews, where he saw the school in which a number of girls from the College had gone to teach; and to Edinburgh, which he described as a 'beautiful city', but with qualifications, as being 'perhaps a little conscious of her good looks and good manners, but very interesting—so many fine streets, fine buildings, spacious squares, showing public statues, and a castle more picturesque I think than any one I ever saw.'[8]

In the following month Grove's response to visual effect was aroused by the autumn woods of Buckinghamshire, and as was so often the case the experience set up sympathetic vibrations in his memory. The occasion was a sad one: Grove had gone to Great Marlow for the funeral of his old friend and chief, Edwin Clark, of the Britannia Bridge engineering team.

[5] Louie Heath came not from Middlesbrough but from Broughty Ferry, near Dundee. The next year Ethel Sharpe's career was diverted by her marriage to Alfred Hobday, the viola player; she left the international field to her husband, and with him devoted herself to the promotion of chamber music.

[6] Letter of 30 May 1894; BL, Add. MS. 39100, f. 309.

[7] E.O., 13 June [1894].

[8] E.O., 2 September [1894].

There was, he wrote, 'nothing special about it except the lovely autumn colours of the woods on the Thames, not so vivid as those in America but wonderfully rich and imposing'.[9]

When at last he was freed from the College, Grove continued to hark back to former times. A bundle of Louie Kellett's letters turned up, and naturally he confided in Edith: 'I ought to burn them but confess I can't—May I send them to you?—as a rule I never shew a woman's letters—it's so impossible for an outsider to understand them! But these are different; she was only a child and never let herself go.'[10]

At about this time Grove encountered Mrs Ritchie—with whom he had 'a good talk'—at the Winter Exhibition of the Royal Academy. He otherwise found this occasion significant on account of Romney's *Lady Hamilton as 'Sensibility'* (loaned by the brewer, Lord Burton), which he apostrophized as 'the most lovely, life-like, delicate, speaking thing I ever saw'. Another portrait of musical interest in that exhibition was Gainsborough's fine study of Carl Friedrich Abel.

On 12 January he went to the Saturday Pop, remarking in his next day's bulletin of news to Edith that 'Brahms's string sestett in G [op. 36] [was] *very fine*—logical and continuous and full of the subjects—quite in the Beethoven school'. At the same concert he heard Borwick play Beethoven's Sonata in C minor (op. 111). It was, he said, 'very grandly played . . . but perhaps wanting in a shade of dreaminess or mysticism'.

The retirement of Grove stimulated the Sydenham local newspaper to feature him in its 'Brief Sketches of Local Men'. The writer—one W.J.R.—referred to Grove one day meeting a man who had voyaged to Jamaica, and would have perished in a gale off Morant Point but for its 'friendly lighthouse'. There was also a story from H. R. Haweis concerning a dinner party at the Groves, at which he had been present with Browning and Anton Rubinstein. After dinner, while the company sat in the drawing room with the doors open to the garden and the scent of flowers and the moonlight flooding in, Rubinstein played Liszt's arrangement of Schubert's *Erlkönig*, 'as only he and Liszt could'. After the great pianist had departed, Grove discovered that there were six broken hammers in the piano.

It was cold at the beginning of 1895. As Grove sat at home—dealing with an average daily intake of 20 and outflow of 15 letters, the 'symphonies', and untruthfully assuring Edith in one of his postscripts, 'I do *not* keep your letters'—he thought, unscientifically, how much colder it must be in Ireland. If Edith, of whom Stainer brought news after a trip to Dublin, did not possess a fur-lined cloak, he asked to be allowed to buy one for

<hr>

[9] E.O., Monday evening [30 Oct 1894].
[10] E.O., Thursday 2 p.m. [3 Jan 1895].

her. With more than £100 in his Savings Account he considered himself well able to afford this privilege.

Although worried in February and March by a bronchitic cough (partly the result of smoking cheap cigars) which, he said, reduced him to the 'very lowest depths of depression and weakness', Grove took much interest in observing the musical world from a more independent, if not more detached, standpoint. On 12 February he attended a meeting of the Musical Association, of which he was a vice-president, and read his paper on the Ninth Symphony.[11] During the subsequent discussion Grove related the story of Beethoven being turned round after the first performance to *see* the enthusiastic applause.[12]

In March Grove noted wryly that the College finances were in a state of disorder which would not have been possible in former times. The expenses of moving into the new building and the necessity of enlarging the domestic staff having wiped out the nest-egg of more than £7000 which Grove and Watson had accumulated, there was now need for a period of cutting back. Not perhaps for the last time, the administration was compelled to look round for areas in which economies might be effected. Instead of holding terminal examinations, therefore, it was determined to have only annual examinations, to the intense mortification of Taylor and Bridge. 'Also', wrote Grove to Edith on Saturday, 2 March, 'they will have to cramp Stanford's expenses with his opera—and that will want all Parry's resolution and tact, god help him!'

Bridge, meanwhile, was excited to have discovered what he took to be the autograph of Purcell's *Te Deum*.[13] With a bicentenary imminent he was conducting his Purcell researches in a manner agreeable to Grove, pushing them forward into a commemorative service in the Abbey (of which Bridge was organist), his own paper in the November 1895 issue of the *Musical Times*, and a general renascence of interest in Purcell. Bridge, said Grove, 'has really developed quite a capacity as an investigator and lecturer and is throwing it all in the English direction'.[14]

On 20 November the first performance of *Dido and Aeneas* in modern times was given by RCM students, conducted by Stanford, at the

[11] See 'A Few Words on the Successive Editions of Beethoven's Ninth Symphony', *Proceedings of the Musical Association* XXI, 1894–5, p. 65.

[12] He had had this story direct from Caroline Unger-Sabatier, who had sung at that performance and had herself helped Beethoven to face his audience; she had come to London in 1869 and had been among Grove's gallery party at a Crystal Palace concert. See 'Beethoven', *Grove 1*, vol. I, p. 197; vol. IV, p. 202; and *Beethoven and his Nine Symphonies*, p. 335.

[13] In fact it was not an autograph but a copy, of sufficient authority, however, to allow Bridge to appreciate the extent of Boyce's rewriting of the work in his published edition. In his autobiography, *A Westminster Pilgrim* (1918), p. 274, Bridge gives an amusing account of his acquisition of this manuscript, which is detailed in Alan Gray's Purcell Society edition of the *Te Deum*.

[14] E.O., Saturday March 2 [1895].

Lyceum.[15] Grove was surprised that some of the music was 'much more advanced' than he had expected; but this may have been due to the additional wind parts supplied for the occasion by Charles Wood. In his next letter to Edith, on 29 November, Grove wrote:

As to Dido and Aeneas I found it interesting, and no more—I am less and less an antiquarian in music; and feel nothing but *historical* interest in many of the old compositions. Beethoven and Schumann spoil me for all that comes before except in the restricted sense. People now go in crowds to hear Dolmetsch play J. S. Bach and other ancients on the *original instruments*—I confess I don't care more for it than I do for the poetry of that time. Pope and Dryden are to me dead except historically, and so are the composers. Their choruses are an exception— but the mass of instrumental works—no!

Although the thought that English music was worth special attention was a new one to him, and despite what would now be regarded as a reactionary indifference to what was considered archaic, Grove applauded exactness. If a composer gave instructions, he saw no reason for not taking notice of them. Bridge was in a position to advertise this moral, and Grove asked him if, in his capacity as newly appointed conductor of the Royal Choral Society, he would consider dispensing with Mozart's additional accompaniments for the annual Albert Hall *Messiah*. Bridge took the point, and dropped Mozart. In presenting his case, Grove characteristically fell back on a precedent from what was to him a more familiar field: 'Suppose too Wagner had been able to force on us his proposed addition to the score of the scherzo of No. 9:—

wouldn't it be a very nice thing to have it as B. wrote it.'[16]

Grove was again seeing more of Sullivan—outside whose house one day in March 1895 he ran into one of his old clerks from the Crystal Palace, in which his interest was still high. On 30 March Sullivan conducted a concert which included the Beethoven Violin Concerto with Joachim, and the Bach Concerto for two violins in which Joachim was partnered by Emily Shinner, a pupil. Sullivan, Grove noted, was 'an excellent conductor'. He particularly admired his slower than usual tempi for the Violin Concerto and for Schumann's Fourth Symphony, which, in the opinion of the *Musical Times*, however, went 'carefully

[15] The principals were: Dido, Agnes Nicholls; Aeneas, Eva Bedford; Belinda, Helen Jackson; Sorceress, Emlyn Davies; Sailor, Thomas Thomas; Witches, Morfydd Williams and Jeannie Appleby. (Ralph Vaughan Williams was one of the chorus basses.)
[16] Letter of 19 Sept 1896; F. Bridge, op. cit., p. 274.

rather than impressively'. After he had finished playing, Joachim, as usual, joined Grove in his gallery and was 'as nice as nice'.

On Easter Saturday, 12 April, Grove went to Victoria Station in the morning to say good-bye to Joachim, and to the afternoon concert at Sydenham to hear Ethel Sharpe play d'Albert's Second Piano Concerto in E. Afterwards he took Hermann Kretzschmar, a leading musicologist from Leipzig, home to dinner, where the Waddingtons were also guests.

In March Parry arranged a special Schubert concert at the College for Grove. In that month Grove had been down to Brighton to stay with Edmund, and to present prizes at a girls' school. While he was there a series of calamities befell the Bennetts in Salisbury, as Grove related to Edith on 25 March:

I have there a nephew the son of my eldest sister a man of 50 the father of a large family. This day fortnight, as he, his wife and daughter were sitting in the drawing room waiting for the dinner bell to ring—he suddenly fell off his chair on to the floor and *died* in an instant! The funeral was fixed for Friday and her sister whose husband was a well known solicitor arrived in Salisbury for it. On the Friday morning she [the sister] went out of her bedroom into his room, to see if he was ready to go down to breakfast, when she found him stretched on the floor dead! I think I never heard of so complete a tragedy—did you? I can't say that they are interesting people—but that is no fault of theirs and does [not] make their suffering less. The eldest girl—very nice—was on the point of being married—one of the boys is an Engineer another a lawyer etc., etc.[17]

Although Grove had spent a few days in bed with a cold, which prevented his attendance at the funeral of his nephew, he was well enough to undertake a local commitment at the beginning of April. On 6 April the *Sydenham Gazette* reported how on the previous Thursday he had distributed the prizes at the local High School. The advice he gave to the girls, as summarized in one epigram, would serve well as his own epitaph: 'Accuracy is far better than brilliance.'

A few days later James Maxtone Graham, a Scottish laird, of the estate of Cultoquhey, near Crieff, in Perthshire, sent to Grove a newspaper

[17] Edmund Grove Bennett took over the family business of printing and publishing on the death of his father and ran it with one of his brothers. In 1895 he was—to be more exact than his uncle in this respect—fifty-three years of age. When on 12 March he suffered a lethal heart attack, the family doctor, Grove's brother-in-law William Wilkes, was summoned but could do no more than merely confirm his death. B. G. Wilkinson, Bennett's brother-in-law, whose fate was as told by Grove, was a solicitor in Reigate.

Bennett's funeral was quite a civic affair, with music provided by the Cathedral choir and organist, Charles South. The *Salisbury Journal* of 16 Mar 1895 not only reported who were present, but also those of significance who were not. Miss F. S. Bennett (Fanny), who had been at Millie Grove's deathbed in Alassio, was prevented from coming because she was abroad; Sir George and his brothers 'by infirm health or other causes'.

account of a lecture on music he had given. True to form, and flattered somewhat by the approach to him from a prominent commercial and political figure, Grove responded with a warmly appreciative letter, which Graham promptly had printed in the local paper.

On 30 April there was a reception for Manns, on the occasion of his seventieth birthday, at the Grafton Galleries. Grove was one of the organizing committee.[18] The Duke of Saxe-Coburg-Gotha—the former Duke of Edinburgh who had succeeded his uncle as ruler of this pocket State in 1893—was present, and Grove was the principal speaker. A public occasion, especially when royal persons were present, stimulated him.

But nowadays he was quicker in falling into depression, and at the beginning of May, complaining of lumbago, he went back to Brighton. One evening he found himself in mystical mood, within which echoed Caribbean memories of long ago:

My brothers and I strolled out after dinner up a sloping road—to look at the stars coming out—My dear, how solemn—how infinitely touching the scene is! the long line of departing day on the top of the downs opposite us—the stars coming out so mysteriously out of the sky, are speaking to me as of something 'about to be'.[19]

In the same letter, responding to news of a performance of the work in Dublin, Grove observed:

As to Sullivan I don't care for Ivanhoe—but I do like the Golden Legend. I have heard it 6 or 7 times and every time I like it better. Take it as it is meant to be and don't compare it with Bach or Beethoven or Schubert and it is *lovely*— the duet always makes me weep, and so does the point of imitation where the chorus comes in 'the night is clear'. . . .

All this time, Grove was 'living with Beethoven', as he put it, and this too induced a particular kind of reverence. But there was the practical aspect of his contemplation of the great theme. So, before turning to the mysteries of the heavens and the music of Sullivan, he had given a brisk assessment of his own creative energies of the past in order to revitalize them for the task in hand: 'Happened just now to look at one of my articles in Smith's Dictionary of the Bible—written when I was nearer the time I was talking of [1863]—and really I am *astonished* at the style of the writing and the extraordinary go and force of it all. . . .'

With the coming into operation of the new Stranraer–Larne ferry service Grove reminded himself that Edith sometimes stayed in Larne with the Fosters, and also of his uncompromising views. 'It would be a blessing to some people who fear the sea', he said, 'but how I wish some

---

[18] The other members were Sullivan, Barnby, Mackenzie, Parry and Stanford. *Allgemeine Musikalische Zeitung* XXII, 1895, p. 142.
[19] E.O., Monday night, 6 May [1895].

convulsion would come and fill up the Channel and make the 2 countries one as England and Scotland are.'

A number of old pupils at this time commissioned Alfred Gilbert to make a bust of Grove, and the professors of the College asked Charles Furse to paint a portrait. The former was for the College, the latter to be presented to the subject himself. Gilbert was the son of a musician, Furse was the son of a Canon of Westminster; so in both cases there were points of potential compatibility. Grove enjoyed chatting during the sittings, and Furse subsequently remarked on the pleasure he received from his commission because of the encouragement which Grove gave to him.

On 12 July an Address was to be presented to him at the College; before the great day, Grove tried to expel his rheumatism by the renunciation of sugar—in tea and coffee—and wine; by taking a trip with Edmund to Winchester, Romsey and Christchurch; and by sitting in the garden at home. He 'never saw the flowers better [and there are] heaps of peas and strawberries, and everything is delightful'.[20] There were exciting musical happenings too, to encourage him. On 27 May Borwick played Stanford's new Piano Concerto in G at a Richter concert; on 10 June Richter conducted the Pastoral Symphony; and at St James's Hall on 24 June, at a Fanny Davies concert, Mühlfeld played the two new clarinet sonatas (op. 120 in F minor and E flat) by Brahms. That day Wood came to lunch, and Grove regretted that he found him delighting in criticism apparently for its own sake. He supposed this complaint to be due to college life in Cambridge and to 'want of women's society'. Franklin Taylor had just been to Chester and a letter from Kathy Macdonald from Abbey Square—where Grove had had rooms almost fifty years before—told him all about it. Kathy was now the senior music teacher in the Queen's School for Girls.[21]

At the presentation on the 12th, as Grove wrote to Edith the next day, 'I wore my Order of the Bath an oval gold medal thing suspended by a red riband beautiful to look at. I was tremendously cheered and I did long for you so!' However, 'The signed book was very nice—far better than I expected,' he went on. 'I looked wildly for your signature but among the thousands could not see it, but the book's coming down to me at once and then I shall be able to "kiss you on the spot" . . . .'[22]

This letter contained an invitation to Edith to stay at Sydenham:

[20] E.O., 25 June [1895] Thursday evening.

[21] Offering only music as a subject, and adequately qualified academically, Kathy (listed in the Chester City Directory as a Professor and Teacher of Music) was the only specialist on the staff of the school; another mistress taught 'Drill, Singing, and English subjects'; Fräulein Blütte, the German mistress, who also offered some music, was taken to be qualified on grounds of nationality; another lady came in to teach solo singing, and the Cathedral organist, J. C. Bridge (brother of Frederick), took Class Singing.

[22] E.O., Friday night 10 p.m. [13 July 1895].

'Lady G. would be delighted to have you, and would be very nice to you I am sure.' Edith went with her aunt in August to Chamonix and Montreux, and her visit inevitably reminded Grove of his Swiss tour of 1874. On 15 September she did come down to Sydenham for Sunday lunch, and was able to learn that only a few days previously Grove had sent to the publisher the section of his book on the Ninth Symphony, which meant that the book was virtually completed. After what was an all too brief—and all too formal—visit, Grove wrote on the following Wednesday that he was 'greatly pleased with Lady G's attention to you. But in such cases I never know how much is feeling and how much is due to her good manners—which she has a great deal of.' There is a terrible sense of detachment about this, Harriet—not for the first time—being seen as a creature under examination.

In the early part of the same letter Grove told how his old pupil Zoë Pyne had become engaged to Francis Hueffer (junior).

His mother was a daughter of [Ford] Madox Brown, the oldest of the band of Pre-Raphaelites. I am told that both the boys[23] are clever, in an erratic sort of way. This one is younger, I fear a good deal younger, than Zoë, and I rather fear the result, but that's my way. His father was a coarse selfish creature.

She is wildly happy just now. I always connect first love with the grass in the early morning with a whitish dew upon it, and the sunshine flooding everything. The G minor Concerto of Mendelssohn (one of the very youngest, purest, works in the world) comes into my mind too when I see the lawn so—which I do very often as I am generally prowling about before six.[24]

In the same autumn in a laudable attempt to popularize the great operas, the impresario E. C. Hedmondt organized a speculative season at Covent Garden at reasonable prices and in English. In order to cut costs he was obliged to go outside the normal tariff of artists' fees, and so it was that Lillian Tree, a former pupil of the College, appeared as 'a diminutive Brünnhilde' in The Valkyrie. Characteristically Grove asked Bennett to give her a helping word. With his tongue in his cheek, no doubt, he told Bennett, 'How hard you work! I sometimes think I work hard; but Lord bless you I'm a babby to you!'

In the same letter he stated his intention (in terms similar to those used by Elgar of Gerontius) to finish his book by Christmas: 'I have put all my heart and self into it, and good or bad it will at least contain that. How I long for old Jemmy [Davison?] to read it, dear old cove! I hope he has got a good bed up there and is able to lie abed till 12 o'clock.'[25] On 9 November Grove reported to F. G. Edwards that he had almost completed the book, but that he was concerned to present it with a

[23] Francis Hueffer junior, son of Francis Hueffer, music critic, and Catherine Hueffer, was brother of Ford Madox (Hueffer) Ford (1873-1939).
[24] E.O., Wed[nesday]. 18 September [1895].
[25] Letter to Joseph Bennett of 14 Oct 1895; PML.

proper introduction. 'The Preface', he said, 'will be very difficult because I must make it evident that I don't write for musicians; and yet I want to do this in a modest and conciliatory manner.'[26]

In October Taylor and Grove had discussed the possibility of Edith Oldham filling a post in a new preparatory school. But since it contained the duties of housekeeper and matron it was not thought to be suited to her talents, even though she was expressing some discontent with the state of affairs at the RIAM. December came and a present of a particularly personal character was sent to Dublin. It was gratefully received: 'I am so glad you liked the ring; but say a little more about it. Can you find a finger to fit it? or do you wear it round your neck? Please tell me— Just before I sent it off its size seemed to me *enormous*.'[27]

At home the Grove family was again sorely troubled during the autumn by the state of Arthur's marriage, which seemed rapidly to be falling apart. His father acknowledged first that it was Arthur's fault, and second that he couldn't himself do anything about it. But it was not a situation that was agreeable to one who had (as he considered) endured the burden of uncongenial matrimony for more than forty years.

Grove did not seem to be at all well to his doctor, who tried to persuade him to voyage to the idyllic islands of his youth. But since Edmund was not keen to go to the West Indies and there was no other companion to be found, this exercise in recuperation was not undertaken. There was, however, a trip to Paris.

The most talked-of young singer in England at the time was Clara Butt, and the Queen proposed to pay for a course of lessons in France. One Saturday at the end of November Grove took this formidable young woman—she was 6 feet 2 inches tall—to Madame Marie Trélat, a celebrated singing teacher in Paris, and a friend of Fauré. Mme Trélat declared herself delighted with the girl's voice, though expressing reservations about an incipient tremolo. But when he heard the singing at the Paris Opéra, where *Lohengrin* was being performed, Grove thought Butt's tremolo practically unnoticeable. So far as the girl herself was

[26] During this year Grove was much in correspondence with Edwards, not only about his own book but also about Edwards's *The History of Mendelssohn's Oratorio 'Elijah'* . . ., to be published early in the next year by Novello. On 21 Apr 1895 he had written to Edwards of the latter:

> [it] will be sure to be received by the Press, or certain members of it, with the smears they always give—and would utter *ore rotondo* if they dared—both for the Messiah and Elijah but I don't think the public share these sentiments. . . . I also hope that the gentlemen you mention won't be allowed to *paw* your work all over—in fact I think that should be a stipulation. I am quite happy to help you in any way in my power—*my name not appearing*. . . . Don't give it to any so-called 'literary man'. . . . BL, Eg. MS. 3091, f. 86.

[27] E.O., 3 Dec [1895]. See p. 238 for another reference to a ring, about which Edith apparently had written.

concerned, however, while ready to help her at this juncture out of a sense of duty and national pride, he still did not like her:

I found out from her mother that she is very wilful and independent. Her mother knows *nothing* of her, nor has seen any of her money! She is engaged to be married! and seeing her name as 'Madame Clara Butt', the horrid thought struck me that she is *married*! I must see her soon and put the question.[28]

The presentation of Furse's portrait was duly made by Parry in December, and it was 'quite a family party'. About sixty people were present, including girls from the kitchen and Mrs Gee, the cook. After this occasion, Grove looked forward with some apprehension to Christmas. Four days after Christmas he reported to Edith that there had been a crowd of people bustling around—'5 grandchildren, 2 parents, and 2 nurses all crammed into this little house'. Such anniversaries meant less to him, he said, with advancing age, and he sank into an Elian reverie, thinking on the 'dream children' in Belfast and their favourite aunt from the south.

Meanwhile death took further toll. On 25 October Charles Hallé had died. At the beginning of 1896 Alexander Macmillan and George Watson died. And when Grove's Beethoven book came out in March, Alexander Thayer, too ill to write, was only able with difficulty to dictate a brief message of congratulation.

The book's appearance was a major event, whose immediate impact was far greater than Grove could ever have imagined. Inevitably there was some initial carping, not least from Fuller-Maitland in *The Times*. Thanking Bennett for a kindly notice in the *Daily Telegraph*, Grove commented on the manner in which it contrasted 'with my friend of the Times in his poor little "short notice" yesterday (save me from *some* of my friends?) However I know he detests my C.P. analyses so perhaps I may be grateful.'[29]

Grove had other reasons for complaint, in particular the lack of enterprise on the part of the publisher. On 17 May he wrote to Edith:

Very busy over the 2nd edition, correcting blunders and making an Index. An order came from New York on Friday and there are not enough copies left [from] the first 1000 to supply it. That's good! though if those beasts the Novellos had advertised it they might have sold 2000.

Michele Esposito wrote from Dublin approving the book, but he wondered why there was no mention of Wagner's suggestions for revised scoring of

[28] Ibid.
[29] Letter of 17 Apr 1896; PML. In *The Times* of 16 Apr the 'short notice' indicated that since the analyses from which the book was made were well known, there was little that needed saying.

the Ninth Symphony.[30] In June Edith sent a notice of *Beethoven and his Nine Symphonies* (by J. C. Culwick, organist of the Chapel Royal in Dublin) from a Dublin paper, and on 28 August the *Allgemeine musikalische Zeitung* published a long and complimentary review which emphasized the thoroughness of the author's treatment of the subject, the stimulating quality of his writing, and the total absence of any kind of 'dryness'.

Meanwhile on 6 March, in St James's Hall, the College orchestra played two works by composers for whom Grove had a special regard. One was Hurlstone's Piano Concerto in D major, the other Coleridge-Taylor's Symphony in A minor (three movements).[31] The concert was otherwise remarkable for the fact that Gustav von Holst played the trombone, and Vaughan Williams (as printed on the programme) the triangle. A frequent visitor at College concerts at this time was August Jaeger— Elgar's 'Nimrod'.[32] It was due to Jaeger, a member of Novello's editorial staff, that Coleridge-Taylor was taken on to the Novello list.

Coleridge-Taylor introduced a new element into British music, already indicating that narrowly English views on ethnic relationships were under assault from unexpected quarters. In Ireland meanwhile the political movement that was causing increasing alarm in England was flowing across wide areas of cultural aspiration. Musically, the Irish had been treated as a colonial people to the second degree; that is, the Europeans who had dominated British music in part had come to dominate Irish music almost entirely, although the admirable Esposito was rapidly trying to turn himself into a nationalist Irish composer by a preference for basing his original works on Irish ideas and by making arrangements of Irish folk-songs.

On 8 December 1894 a letter from Thomas O'Neill Russell had appeared in the *Dublin Evening Telegraph* protesting about the general neglect of Irish music, and suggesting the institution of a Feis Ceoil— thought of as roughly an Irish counterpart to the Welsh Eisteddfod. The result was the formation of a committee, drawn from members of the Irish National Literary Society and the Gaelic League, to indicate what steps should be taken to remedy the situation. First, it was decided,

---

[30] The consequence of this was the footnote to p. 357 in the second edition (see above, p. 248).

[31] Coleridge-Taylor was to record his lasting gratitude to Grove in the dedication of *Hiawatha's Wedding Feast*, which was given its first performance at the College on 11 Nov 1898 under Stanford. Other Coleridge-Taylor works given first performances at College concerts were the Nonet (5 July 1894), *Zara's Ear-rings* (6 Feb 1895), *Fantasiestücke*, for string quartet (13 Mar 1895), Clarinet Quintet (10 July 1895), *Lament* and *Merry making*, for violin and piano (22 Jan 1896), String Quartet in D minor (25 June 1896), *Legend*, for violin and orchestra (15 Feb 1897).

[32] Jaeger in 1897 was to marry Isabel Donkersley, Holmes's erstwhile pupil (see above, p. 211), who had taken a leading part in College concerts for a number of years.

an educational programme should be undertaken. This consisted at the outset of lectures given in various parts of the country by Annie Patterson and A. P. Graves. Word of this got through to Grove, who wrote an afterthought to one of his letters to Edith of May 1896 on the outside of the envelope: 'Qui est ce Monsieur A.P.G.? le père de C.L.G. et fils du vieux évêque?'[33]

Meanwhile the shape of the Feis was beginning to emerge, and was communicated to Grove. Improbably, but conveniently, having encountered an influential peer of Irish extraction on a London bus, Grove got up early on the morning of 3 June and at six o'clock wrote to Edith:

Dear E.O.

I am at home again. I saw Lord Monteagle in an omnibus yesterday and he asked me if I knew anything about your project. I told him it was in good hands—yours—and he might write quite openly to you about it—also that I thought Miss [Alice] Balfour was interested in it. He said he was afraid there were all sorts of difficulties from jealousies and intrigues etc.

He found the plan of an Irish orchestra would not answer at first; there would (for instance) be no wind.

But why should you not be content to have as many Irish as possible in the orchestra? And why should the conductor necessarily be a Celt? Manns is conducting the South Wales Festival, and I don't think that the Eisteddfods are (or were) so exclusive.

The great point surely is to start the festival—get it into working order—and then the Celtic element will increase every year. This is very strongly borne in upon me after I left Monteagle and I thought I would tell you.

Thank you very much for the paper with Culwick's article. Isn't it good? There is also a cheery one in the Monthly Musical record for June.[34]

Good bye no time for more

Yours always
G. Grove

Persuading himself that he would not go to Switzerland for a holiday that summer, Grove happily went to Scotland, visiting among other places St Andrews and Edinburgh. Mrs Lehmann, Robert Chambers's eldest

---

[33] Alfred Perceval Graves (1846–1931), second son of Charles Graves, Bishop of Limerick, was Inspector of Schools in England, but best known through his studies of Irish literature and music. He was a member of the London Irish Literary Society. Charles Larcom Graves (1856–1944), fourth son of the Bishop and an old Marlburian, was assistant editor of the *Spectator* and *Punch*, and biographer of Grove and Parry.

For interim reports on the progress of the Feis Ceoil at this time see the *Musical Times* XXXVII, July, 1896, p. 478, and October 1896, p. 663.

[34] For Culwick's article see above, p. 255. The 'cheery' article in the *Monthly Musical Record* (1 June 1896, pp. 125–7) was not uncritical of Grove's book, but it was warm in its appreciation of its main virtues: '. . . we are spared the patronising criticism which makes so much that is written by the pedantic school utterly impossible to read. Sir George Grove is always readable: you may pick him up at any page, and you rarely want to lay him down until you have reached the last one.'

daughter and a friend of almost forty years, was his hostess at Portobello, while various members of her family were glad to welcome him on his Scottish tour.[35] Grove was in a reminiscent frame of mind. Old times came to life in the company of old friends. Bennett, who had been to Rouen that year, reminded him of once having been in the city. Edith went to Abbeville, which brought back memories of Boucher de Perthes, his discoveries, and the excitement which these had caused.[36]

In Edinburgh almost every day Grove was glad to be able to talk with William Addis, now returned from Australia. But recollection of old times brought on melancholia:

I am afraid that I don't think that I have got much relief to my pain or my spirits —but the point is I must take that part of life as it comes and realise the fact that I shall not have any relief until Death comes and ends it for me.

Also I am afraid that I shan't do anything more of importance. I want to complete the life of Beethoven—but that I can't do unless I can have a clerk to write letters for me.[37]

In September Grove went to the Hovingham Music Festival in York-shire, in October to that at Bristol. On 15 November he wrote to Edith concerning 'an article on me in the Saturday Review of last Sat. by a certain G. B. Shaw—but the Saturday review is so *wicked* and so nasty that I am not very anxious to see the article'. More often than not Shaw had been graceful in his recognition of Grove's services to music. In 1892 he had written, for instance, that his 'life-work [had] been of more value than that of all the Prime Ministers of this century'.[38] Now, in respect of Grove's book, he surpassed himself in paying a long tribute of marked generosity but not without characteristic and quotable Shavian-isms. The essence is contained in these two sentences: 'But though it is possible thus to differ here and there from "G", he is never on the wrong lines. He is always the true musician: that is, the man the professors call "no musician"—just what they called Beethoven himself.'[39]

Soon after this Grove received a prospectus for the Feis Ceoil, of which Edith was joint honorary secretary with Joseph Seymour. Wishing that he could have given a more handsome subscription—'but I am poor'— Grove commented that he thought the book[40] well done, and he especially liked 'the girl with the harp. She is very pretty indeed'.[41] He sent

[35] See R. C. Lehmann, *Memories of Half a Century* (1908), p. 237.
[36] Letter to Bennett of 17 Apr 1896, PML; E.O., 19 Aug 1896; and see above, p. 46.
[37] E.O., Aug 13 [1896].
[38] G. B. Shaw, *Music in London 1890–94*, vol. II (1932), p. 214.
[39] *Saturday Review*, 14 Nov 1896, p. 517; see Appendix B.
[40] *First . . . Feis Ceoil. Irish Music Festival, Dublin 1897. Syllabus of Prize Compositions etc.* (Dublin, 1897).
[41] E.O., 13 December [1896].

9

Christmas greetings to Edith on 17 December, wondering whether they would ever meet again, and recalling once more 'that delightful time, when we had that long ride in Cheltenham'. Manns, meanwhile, fit and spry, was making preparations, Grove had noted, for a commemorative Schubert concert on 31 January and for his third marriage, 'to a nice person about 31 . . . with £600 a year of her own.'[42]

In the year of the Diamond Jubilee it seemed on the one hand that the English social structure was unalterable and unassailable, on the other that the age of Victoria had already passed, and that a new dispensation had already begun. The perfect Victorian in so many ways, Grove had effectively brought his life's work to an end with the publication the year before of *Beethoven and his Nine Symphonies*, and his relinquishing responsibility for the Crystal Palace programme notes. In the world of letters, the dignified standards which had been maintained in the principal magazines were being replaced as more strident voices, expressing to the old a diversity of less than congenial thoughts, became audible. In the *Savoy*, edited by Arthur Symons, for instance, Shaw, Havelock Ellis, Edward Carpenter, Joseph Conrad and Aubrey Beardsley were the arbiters of opinion and taste. In music, in Grove's view, composers were doing what the Pre-Raphaelites had done in art, by giving themselves 'to the worship of ugliness'.[43]

Among composers heard in 1897 who were previously less than familiar to London audiences were Busoni, Grieg, Moszkowski, and Strauss whose *Tod und Verklärung* and *Till Eulenspiegel* for many proved shattering blows. As Manns began to lay aside some of his responsibilities for promoting new music, a young conductor named Henry Wood seemed to be ready to take on his mantle. Among the new composers there was one whom Grove welcomed almost without reservation. This was Edward Elgar, whose *King Olaf* was performed at the Crystal Palace on 3 April.

On 31 March Grove had braved the rain in order to call on the Elgars, but 'the maid, wreathed in smiles, promptly announced that you were out!'[44] He would like to have talked about Malvern, with which, he wrote, he had hitherto connected '*one* musical person'—Jenny Lind-Goldschmidt. He also asked for news of the Acworths—Grove had known the parents of H. A. Acworth, librettist of *King Olaf* (from Longfellow) and *Caractacus*, who were friends of the Elgars in Malvern.

In Grove's appreciation of Elgar's music there is a particular significance. The old man felt himself to be far down the road, with little of

[42] Ibid.
[43] E.O., Friday Jan 8 [1897].
[44] Grove to Elgar, 24 Mar 1897; Hereford and Worcester County Record Office [H. & W. C.R.O.], Letter no. 1765.

8

life left to him. In a letter written to Edith on St Patrick's Day he gave this *cri de cœur*:

Goodbye beloved It is a joy to me to know that I have one friend who clings to me as you do Good bye—whether we meet or not—here or elsewhere—we shall love one another to the end
Bless you my darling

Always your fond and loving
G.

On 7 May he was more pessimistic. After all, there was no future to anticipate: 'I fear however we shall never meet again, either here or *there*—all that idea of another life as a complement to this gets vaguer and more unpractical every day.' To such melancholy thoughts the music of Elgar was prophylactic, giving some kind of assurance that life was worth living.

The Songs *From the Bavarian Highlands*—all filled with *joie de vivre*—were performed on 23 October. Next day Grove wrote to Elgar:

Sunday
Dear Elgar

I was very unfortunate in missing you yesterday, and missing Mrs Elgar both days. I could not find your former address in town.

I hope you were pleased and will do some more dances at once—so pert and spirited and tuneful I confess (though I hope I don't hurt you) I liked them better than 'King Olaf'. I find it very hard to bring my mind to Siegfried and Olaf and hoc genus omne—I welcome so warmly the scenes and feelings of our own times—and get out of the solemnity which these antient heroes carry about with them.

I have got Mrs Elgar's copy of the Bavarian Highlands and shall have it carefully packed and sent down to her by post tomorrow. I take it for granted that the verses are hers!

Believe me to be
Yours very sincerely
G. Grove[45]

On Monday Grove returned Mrs Elgar's book on 'Oberammergau and District', which recalled to him his own visit of 1860. He wondered incidentally whether the Elgars happened to know his brother-in-law, Herbert Bradley, who was then living in Malvern. Finally, he hoped to hear more of 'that lively heartfelt music'.[46]

In respect of older music, shifts of emphasis were becoming perceptible, for musicologists were beginning to wield influence. The works of Bach (somewhat to Grove's chagrin) were coming more and more to the fore, and reports of the Bach Festival at Meiningen in the summer of

[45] Letter of 24 Oct 1897; H.&W.C.R.O., Letter no. 7389.
[46] Letter of 25 Oct 1897; ibid., Letter no. 7388.

1895 had encouraged Stanford to move towards authenticity of performing practice with the Bach Choir. On 6 and 10 April 1897 (a miscellaneous Bach programme intervening on 8 April) the *St Matthew Passion* was sung in German—to the dismay of the *Musical Times*—with oboe d'amore, viola da gamba, and cembalo (played by Fuller Maitland) for the recitatives, among the accompanying instruments.[47] Even in the popularization of this work Grove, through his note on an early English performance (see p. 299), had played a part.

Arnold Dolmetsch, now turned from his student ambition to be a composer towards his mission of the revivification of antiquity, was already promulgating his ideas with sufficient confidence later that year to present a programme of Tomkins, Domenico Scarlatti, Bach, Ariosti and English lutenist composers. At the Victorian Era Exhibition at Earl's Court a section devoted to music was presided over by Barclay Squire. Among the portraits there exhibited was one of Grove, whose career was epitomized in the October issue of the *Musical Times*.

Some institutions remained stable. The prestige of choral societies—so valuable in hymning the praises of the Queen—was at its zenith, and the manner in which the great northern choirs functioned never failed to awaken the admiration of southerners. When Mottl conducted the Ninth Symphony on 13 April during the Jubilee year the Leeds Festival Choir was engaged. Travelling to London on the morning of the performance, this intrepid body rehearsed all the afternoon, but at night—to the amazement of one German critic—sounded '*frisch und unermüdet*'.

On 8 July the Leeds Choir came to London again, to be joined by the Orchestra of the RCM in a 'Festival Concert' with a suitable programme for the International Congress of Naval Architects and Marine Engineers then taking place. Stanford was the conductor, and the occasion was altogether one particularly to interest Grove and Samson Fox.

But the biggest choral event had taken place a month earlier when singers poured into Sydenham from all over the country for the 14th Handel Festival at the Crystal Palace. Since 1857 more than a million people had attended these festivals; in this year the attendance was 67,378, including Grove.[48]

If Sydenham provided a power-house for Handel the classics were as firmly established there as anywhere in the world. So long as Joachim (whose career in England began before Paxton had even thought of the

---

[47] *Allgemeine Musikalische Zeitung*, 12 Apr 1897.

[48] In this connection, in spite of his distaste for singers and his conviction that music of the Baroque era was not to be understood in days of enlightenment, Grove showed himself to be a victim of the English disease of Handelolatry. He gave himself away in his article on the composer in *Chambers's Cyclopaedia*. 'There is', he wrote, 'something expressly English in Handel's characteristics. His size, his large appetite, his great writing, his domineering temper, his humour, his power of business, are all our own. So was his eye to the main chance.'

Crystal Palace) was still playing, Grove struggled to get to the concerts. But he was beginning to fail. He was afflicted with deafness; his arthritic condition made movement difficult and painful; he was becoming increasingly forgetful, and obliged to apologize for what he termed his stupidity. He would have liked to go to a Chamber Music Festival in Bonn, but there was no one to take him. Nor was it possible to fulfil another wish, to go to Dublin. For this, however, there was something in the way of a substitute in a recital in London by Esposito.

Grove had been sanguine that the South Wales Music Festival would prove a great success, despite the total absence from the choral music of anything in the Welsh language and the domination of the whole affair by foreigners. The Festival was a complete fiasco. The performers sang and played to rows of empty benches. The Feis Ceoil, on the other hand— which took place between 17 and 22 May 1897, with works by Field, Wallace, Culwick, Stanford, Esposito and others, excellent competitions which brought in amateur performers from all over the country, demonstrations of harps and harp music, recitals of folk-songs, and heart-warming speeches—had been a great success. After the Countess Plunkett had given away the prizes—no prize-winners being more heartily cheered than the City of Belfast Madrigal Choir—everyone went away happy, beginning to prepare for the next Feis.

In August Grove wrote a neat little letter to *The Times*, linking the bird-songs in *The Winter's Tale* (IV, ii) and *As You Like It* (II, v) with Tennyson's 'The Throstle'. In every case it was the same rhythmic pattern, with 'each foot being sharply accented on the second syllable . . . the exact effect of the short phrases which are so noticeable in the thrush's song'. Later that month he went to Woodhall Spa in Lincolnshire where he critically read through *Vanity Fair* preparatory to examining Thackeray's other novels in anticipation of the forthcoming edition. As so many years before, while in Lincolnshire Grove visited churches, including the splendid examples of medieval art in Boston and Heckington, as well as the city churches of Lincoln.

On 28 October Marie Benecke, one of Grove's oldest friends and a strong personal link not only with her father but also with the whole German classical tradition, died after a short illness. In November Tom Grove died. So far forgetting himself as to address her as 'My dearest Ethel', George wrote to Edith:

Sunday after Nov 21 97
to Wed 24

. . . My eldest brother died on the 9th inst and was buried on Monday last at Penn near High Wycombe in Buckinghamshire. He was 8 years older than I— we were on very good terms—but had little in common, he cared little for literature and still less for music. I think he was proud of me, and he was *much* bound to the *place* where our family had lived for a long, though uncertain period. My father's father was the last 'yeoman' of the county and—if my brother was to be believed—quite as I think without ground—the Groves came over with William the Conqueror and had been in the spot ever since. Tom had bought a quantity of land and owned an estate worth £500 a year. But beside that he had money to the tune of £100,000. This is all divided among his brothers and sisters. I have got the Penn property for my life (entailed on my sons) and about £10,000 of money. But it puts me in a difficulty. I am so infirm that I can't do my duty, and have put it off on one of my sons [Walter] and it makes me sadly anxious and depressed. . . .

He also wrote to Sullivan, his 'dearest old Arturo' on 21 December:

. . . I am groaning under the bequest of my old brother's estate in Buckinghamshire, which produces nothing to speak of, and has been spoiled by his absurd generosity to the tenants, to whom he gave whatever they asked to such a degree that he has kept up every charity, school, church, organist etc etc. Easy for him who had a big income behind him but impossible for me who have only £700 a year!

I should like to see your handwriting once more. I came on an old note of yours the other day and found the old *smart* come into my eyes at once.

Good bye and God bless

Ever your affectionate old friend

G. Grove

In 1895 Grove had sold off the biblical and geographical part of his library; a year later he gave his pictures of Fanny, Rebecca, Felix and Paul Mendelssohn to F. G. Edwards, to whom, in 1897, went a treasured portrait of Paul Mendelssohn dated '2 Oct. 1871' and inscribed by the subject, 'Many thanks for all your kindness'. Now Grove was advised that it would be prudent for him to rid himself of more of his effects, taking into account the possible consequences of the Estates Duty Act of 1894. Thus the College acquired still more valuable material. But Grove found no corresponding diminution in his financial problems, for legal delays prevented any settlement of his brother's affairs until after his own death.

The year 1897 ended with Edith in England again. She had travelled to London with Esposito for the annual conference of the Incorporated Society of Musicians, held at the Hotel Cecil. On Boxing Day, which was Sunday, Grove wrote to her at 30 Seymour Street, Portman Square, to advise her of the trains from Victoria to Sydenham. She was expected to lunch one day that week and the best train would be the 11.50, arriving at 12.26, after which the comfortable half-hour walk would bring her conveniently for lunch at 1 o'clock. 'So don't fail', he implored, at the same time warning her that she would find that he had become more deaf. At the following week-end there was a flurry of notes and postcards, in which Grove expressed the hope that he might be able to come up to town to see Edith.

On 4 January 1898 the Conference opened and in the evening Joseph Seymour, Edith's partner in the enterprise, read a paper on 'The Irish Feis Ceoil'. Despite suffering 'an attack'—as he termed it—on that night, which prevented him travelling on Wednesday, Grove managed to go to the Cecil on Thursday, 6 January. He also called on Novello to talk about the book. Next morning he wrote: 'I was talking to some man before going away with you yesterday (while on that sofa), and mentioned Hadow's book on Haydn and "a Croatian composer".[49] Who was he?' Edith left the next day and on Sunday, 16 January, Grove wrote to her in Dublin: 'It was such a pleasure to see you, and find you so exactly what I believed you to be, and what I liked of all things. Bless you dear always be as nice.'

In February Esposito's *Deirdre*, which had won the first prize for composition at the first Feis Ceoil, was performed at a Saturday Symphony Concert in the Queen's Hall. The *Musical Times* 'could not help wondering what the other works were like which were *not* considered worthy of the prize'. Grove did his best for the work, observing to Edith that it was 'not great music but it was extremely graceful and interesting, full of heart and often *very* touching and there was an unmistakable Celtic, Irish, character about it. I was in *close relation* to it the whole time.'[50]

After the concert Grove saw Esposito, who spoke to him of his intention to stimulate further the musical life of Dublin. He had, he said, played almost all the pianoforte sonatas of Beethoven at recitals there, and he now planned to form an orchestra with the primary purpose of providing opportunity for the Dubliners to hear Beethoven's symphonies and overtures.[51] Persuaded by Edith to put faith in Grove in all matters, Esposito asked Grove's permission to send him a score of his 'piano and Cello Sonata [*sic*] for an opinion'.[52]

In August 1897 Edith had been present at the Welsh National Eisteddfod at Newport, Monmouthshire, which inspired her to write a paper, 'The Eisteddfod and the Feis Ceoil', which she read to a meeting of the Irish branch of the Incorporated Society of Musicians. Not the least interesting part of this paper, which was published in the February 1898

[49] W. H. Hadow's book on Haydn, *A Croatian Composer*, was published in 1897.
[50] E.O., Feb 28, '98.
[51] A visit to Dublin by the Hallé Orchestra showed that there was a demand for orchestral music on a permanent basis, and Esposito—modelling a Constitution on that of the Milanese orchestra in his homeland—brought the Dublin Orchestral Society into being at the beginning of 1899. The leader was Adolf Wilhelmj. See the *Musical Times* XL, February 1899, pp. 89–90, and J. F. Larchet, 'Commendatore Michele Esposito', in *The Royal Irish Academy of Music 1856–1956* (Dublin, 1956), pp. 19ff.
[52] Esposito's sonata was published in 1899 by Breitkopf & Härtel (Leipzig).

issue of the *New Ireland Review*, contained her impressions of the attitude
of the mining communities of the Welsh valleys to music and her appreciation of the famous miners' leader, William Abraham. Such sentiments
were unlikely to arouse the enthusiasm of the personages who were
made aware of the article by Grove, who wrote to its author on 24 February:

Dear Edith:

I have sent off a copy of the new Ireland Review to Col. Bigge the Queen's
Private Secretary (an old acquaintance of mine): à propos to the concert of
Welch [*sic*] music which H.M. heard on Tuesday.

I think he will read it and perhaps shew it to the Q. though of *that* I can't be
sure. I thought the concert was to be given before the Prince of Wales, and,
having to write H.R.H. on Saturday I mentioned the article to him, and tried
to interest him in it. But now I find it was sung to the Q. Well, mother or son,
I hope it will some how do you good.

I have no more time today or you should have a nice letter; but I lost my way
in the Crystal Palace grounds after dark yesterday and only escaped with my
life, after walking about 7 miles! and today I am none the better for the
adventure.

Good bye dear
How I long to see you again.

G.

Also in 1897 Alexander Thayer had died, leaving his *magnum opus*
on Beethoven unfinished. H. E. Krehbiel (whose own popular *How to
Listen to Music* had just come into Grove's possession) suggested that
Grove should complete Thayer's project. It was a flattering proposal,
but it was too late. Grove did, none the less, take the matter up with
Speyer, with whom he also discussed the placing of an article by Speyer
on Thayer.

Beethoven was never far from Grove's thoughts, and on 26 March
1898 there were commemorative concerts at both the Crystal Palace and
St James's Hall. At the former (at which the attendance was adversely
affected by the Boat Race) Lady Hallé played the Romance in F and the
Violin Concerto, and Marie Berg, from Berlin, sang Clärchen's songs from
Egmont, of which the overture, together with that of *Fidelio* and the
Pastoral Symphony, completed the programme. At St James's Hall there
was a chamber music programme provided by the Joachim Quartet
(augmented for the Opus 29 Quintet by Alfred Hobday) and Lillian
Henschel, who contributed *Lieder*.

Grove tried to keep his interests alive, but he was up and down. In
May he was noting with pleasure the steps being taken in Dublin to ensure
the continuation of the Feis Ceoil, and he wrote to F. G. Edwards, in
his capacity as editor of the *Musical Times*, to ensure that credit went
where credit was due:

The Feis Ceoil seems really to have entered on a so far solid existence. Whatever is done is due to Miss Oldham, who has worked her honorary secretaryship in a splendid manner and as *wisely* as *well*. The day after your account was in the Times, I wrote a letter calling attention to the fact that Miss Oldham was not only a 'student' at the College, but that she was one of the very first 'Scholars' elected at the start in 1883. But they did not put it in.

Do not lose an opportunity of blowing her trumpet whenever you can, for she richly deserves it.[53]

In June he went to Bristol, but he described the visit as 'rather a failure'.[54] In July, however, he was in lively mood, exchanging witticisms of Sydney Smith with Edwards, and complaining of the difficulties being put in the way of French and German translations of *Beethoven and his Nine Symphonies*. Less than a month later, however, he was continuing a valediction, which had been part of his letters to Edith for some time past, in increasingly poignant terms. On 5 August he wrote to her in County Donegal:

. . . You and I have been *such* friends. We must look to the next world for comfort. Go on and prosper. You have begun right well, and perhaps I have helped you; but I should not unless you had been able to help yourself. You have helped me, I know, much and often.

Don't say I shall get better. I shall never get better.—I see a constant deterioration.

> Good bye Dearest
> > Your very affectionate and, as always,
> > > loving friend.
> > > > G.

At the beginning of October, although he had recently suffered two or three 'attacks', Grove was well enough to go to St James's Hall for the rehearsals for the Leeds Festival—the last to be directed by Sullivan. In December, the students of the College gave a performance of *The Flying Dutchman* at the Lyceum, in which Muriel Foster played the part of Mary. Grove heard the performance with relish and confessed that he had previously been guilty of underestimating this work. He went so far as to describe it as a 'masterpiece', with 'so many lovely tender airs all of the same cast, and yet all different . . . and *such* instrumentation, thin, but each part a long melody'.[55]

On 18 January 1899 the last phase of Grove's life was ushered in by this sad, brave, and in parts hardly legible, letter:

[53] Letter of 18 May 1898; BL, Eg. MS. 3091, f. 237.

[54] Letter to F. G. Edwards of 6 June 1898, in which Grove also recollects how 'my acquaintance with Parry began, if I remember right, in the end gallery of the Crystal Palace, and he was one of the first persons I asked to help me when I began the Dictionary . . .'; ibid., f. 237.

[55] E.O., 11 December [1898].

My dear Edith

Your letter of the 17th has just come and I answer at once, that I may not again be disappointed. It finds me in a bad way. At last the blow has come! This day fortnight I was knocked over by a—it is really a paralytic stroke in one of the muscles of my mouth. Very small to do so much. At first it took away my speech, but now that has returned but I shall always be liable, though it will probably improve. Thank you for your dear letter.

I wish I could give you a longer, or more sensible one. When you come I can always—well what can I always do? I hardly know: at present I can't find words, so I had better not speculate till the time arrives.

That is good news that Stanford brings henceforth a friend. I am very glad to hear it. I have heard his Te Deum long ago at Richter's rehearsal but forget it all myself and as to its being badly or lightly scored I can remember nothing— you are where I was when the College was started—what an expanse lay before us! and how bright it shone too! well I certainly worked my hardest. It was what I was accustomed to, and I thought it would go on and never stop.

Well dear, you *were* good and if more had been like you I should have been pleased. I don't mean that there were cases who were not good, but I mean that [if] there had [been] more of you the result would have been better. I can't say what I mean exactly so I will only give you my love and ask you to think of me as well to the end. My wife makes a very good fight.

Ever yours and ever,
G. Grove

[Margin] Come here when you arrive in the summer.

On Saturday, 11 February, another letter was written:

My dearest Edith:

How can I thank you for your answer to my last question? more than an answer? I was thinking of the 'Dear Irish girl', of which I have now a very good character [in the] Spectator somewhere else; and, notwithstanding your strictures, think I shall try it. I am sorry she has allied herself with Moore—for I don't like him— at least the [flavour?] which has spread round him I can't think what there is attractive in immoral tastes!

Well dear! I am very much obliged to you for your last letter—so many and so long! You have repaid and more than repaid anything that I have given you. Certainly I have tried to give you the best I could, and you certainly have given it me back.

I am afraid that I can give you no more: so I will send you my best love and thanks for all that has come this way. I hope we may meet in the next world. How different it will be from anything we can conceive!

Good bye my

best, kindest, most natural friend. I *may* live for *months*, but I may die very soon: may you come to a more consistent and useful end than I have. Many opportunities I have had and hardly come up to one of them!

Your very affectionate admiring, grateful, friend
G. Grove

On 3 March Grove promised a guinea for Joseph Robinson's testimonial (which he sent four days later) and, valiantly trying to keep up with the achievements of his protégé, asked Edith, of Stanford's 1896 Norwich Festival piece, 'What do the words Phaudrig Crohoore mean?'

As the light of life became increasingly dim, the old man grasped at fragments of activity, even though the result most often was an apology for non-attendance at some gathering. There were proposals for a monument to Brahms, who had died in 1897, and the committee formed to consider them was headed by Joachim. Speyer was brought into the deliberations and it was to him, on 27 June, that Grove sent his apology for not being able to accept the invitation to attend. On 1 July he thanked Speyer for informing him of what had transpired at the meeting. He closed his note sombrely: ' . . . I am so poor that I can only promise you a small amount—a guinea or so. I have not already given it to you have I? I don't think I am going to get better, at least I see no prospect of it.'[56]

Two other brief missives to Speyer survive, and two more to Edith. On 5 July he said that he had been seriously ill, and apologized for the *Spectator* only being sent spasmodically. (He had long been in the habit of supplying her regularly with this journal.) On 10 July he asked that she should come to see him if she could, and her forgiveness for 'this shaky letter'.

On 3 October Lady Grove wrote a postcard to Miss Oldham:

I know how sorry you will be to hear that Sir G. has been for over a month almost unconscious, hovering between life and death. I did not know your address and therefore could not send the Spectator.

H. Grove

Four days after Harriet's card was written the Brahms memorial was unveiled in the 'English Garden' in Meiningen. If he could have understood this Grove would have been pleased. He would also have been pleased that Leonard Borwick, whose artistry always impressed him, played Mozart's A major concerto (K. 488) at the ceremony.

For much of that winter Grove was oblivious to what was happening around him. He lived through the spring—sometimes being wheeled out into the garden; after a few weeks in bed he died on 28 May 1900.

Next day, at its morning rehearsal, the College orchestra played the Funeral March from the 'Eroica' and Parry spoke briefly to the students about his predecessor. The obituary notice in *The Times* on the same day was unfortunately inaccurate, stating that George was the son of Thomas and Harriet, daughter of the Rev C. Bradley.

The funeral service took place on 31 May in St Bartholomew's Church, Sydenham, and was conducted by the Dean of Westminster, assisted by

[56] BL, Add. MS. 42233, f. 44.

the Bishop of Southwark, the Sub-dean of the Chapel Royal and the
Vicar. Among the mourners were Charles Morley, M.P., an old friend of
the College; Frank Pownall, an Oxford friend of Parry who succeeded
Watson as Registrar; Gerald Harper, Stanley's doctor; Mackenzie,
representing the RAM; W. H. Cummings, representing the Guildhall
School of Music; Walford Davies, Barclay Squire, Stanford, and Parry,
who had suffered a mishap on his way through the overturning of a
carriage. Lady Grove was not present. Family mourners were Walter
Grove, Mr and Mrs J. C. Grove, Mr and Mrs Arthur Grove, Edmund
Grove, and Mrs E. Long Fox.[57] The grave is in the Ladywell Cemetery,
Lewisham, marked by a marble cross with the text, 'Everyone that loveth
is born of God and knoweth God'. Behind is a tiny headstone, signifying
the burial place of Grove's daughter Lucy Penrose, who had died so
many years before.

There were many tributes to Grove. One of the most telling, for it
came from the nation for whose music he had done so much, was in the
Allgemeine Musikalische Zeitung of 8 June, which concluded:

Grove's articles on Beethoven and Schubert in his Dictionary are of particular
value, for they were based on original source material. After his retirement he
published an interesting study of *Beethoven and his Nine Symphonies*. He was a
man of many parts, thorough in what he did, and of a kindly disposition.

One of the most wide-ranging was in the *City News*, Manchester, of 2
June. Balancing his talents in the caption 'Engineer, Musician, and
Editor' and in a generous text, the writer remarked how Taine, 'in his
book on England and English life, instances Sir George Grove as the type
of the busy Englishman'. With an awareness that initiative in musical
matters could be found outside the metropolis the writer stated:

No concerts have ever been given in England [London?] precisely of the same
character as those of the Crystal Palace. Instead of being addressed to the public
at large—with perpetual repetitions of ultra-popular works—they were arranged
to give subscribers a complete idea of the genius of this or that composer.

The effective word, surely, is 'complete'.

On 22 June the College orchestra gave a concert in St James's Hall,
at which the first item, *in memoriam* Grove, was an arrangement of
a Beethoven-inspired *Trauermarsch* by Schubert (Op. 55 or 66). Also
included in the programme were Beethoven's overture 'Leonora no. 1'
and Brahms's Double Concerto (Op. 102). Grove would have approved
these works for such an occasion and would have been gratified also by
the fact that on 25 June there was a State Concert at Buckingham Palace
given by students of the College.

[57] Presumably the Miss Edith Fox named by Graves as Grove's amanuensis in the
last years.

The life of Grove is full of poignancy, but nothing is more poignant than the unseen life of Harriet Grove, which emerges at the end in a proud flourish of dignified loyalty. Harriet was a true daughter of the 'holy village'; it was a woman of character who wrote the following letter:

Lower Sydenham/Friday [29 June 1900]

Dear Miss Oldham:

Thanks so much for your letter. I have been tearing up heaps of your letters which I felt you would not wish to be read by a publisher if such a person should appear.

For the last year my dear husband was almost unconscious of anything and knew no one and lived the life of a baby—What a blessed waking up in the next world after such a long time of ignorance here. This thought reconciles me very much to his departure. There will be no one quite like him again.

Believe me

Yours very sincerely
Harriet Grove

The will was proved on 13 August. Grove left £31,744, which—except for small sums to his executors (one of whom was his son Julius Charles)—went in trust to his widow for life and then to his three sons. On 1 September there was a resolution of the Council of the Royal College that a 'George Grove Memorial Scholarship' for the study of composition should be founded.

Harriet Grove died on 31 March 1914, on the same day as the artist von Herkomer.[58] It was in a way fitting that at the Royal Philharmonic Concert on the previous night Mengelberg had conducted the 'Eroica'. That, at least, would have pleased George Grove. *The Times* summarized Harriet's career judiciously, so that it is possible to read into the obituary the causes of her husband's discontents:

. . . She assisted Grove in the earlier stages of his Biblical Studies, helping him to make a complete index of every proper name in the Old Testament, the New Testament, and the Apocrypha; but her talents were practical rather than literary or artistic, and her sterling common sense made her an excellent helpmate for her versatile and vivacious husband. For many years she had helped him to dispense hospitality in their picturesque old wooden house in Lower Sydenham, where friends, men of letters, and musicians, met on Saturday evenings at the table of the editor of *Macmillan's Magazine* and Secretary to the Crystal Palace.

Finally, said the writer, she was 'shrewd, unaffected, and sincere . . . a woman of fine character'. Her funeral took place at All Saints' Church,

[58] See above, p. 201.

Sydenham, and she was buried with her husband. In her will, published on 23 May 1914, she left £5,560.

In 1906 Novello published the German edition of *Beethoven and his Nine Symphonies*, in a sensible translation by Max Hehemann in which the translator corrected some minor points according to information to which Grove himself had not had access.[59] The German edition also carried information about recent English choral works available in German versions. They included all of Elgar up to *The Apostles* in the Novello catalogue, Parry's *Blest Pair of Sirens*, Stanford's *The Revenge*, and Coleridge-Taylor's *Hiawatha's Wedding Feast*. Somewhere in these works resides also some part of the genius of Grove, who gave counsel to their composers at crucial points in their several careers.

In the year in which *Beethoven und seine neun Symphonien* was published Edith Oldham, then forty-three, married Dr Richard A. Best, who was eight years her junior. One of the foremost scholars in the field of Irish philology and literature and from 1904 Assistant Director of the National Library of Ireland,[60] Best in 1924 became Director of the Library, and for three years from 1943 he was President of the Royal Irish Academy.

Edith Best continued to teach the pianoforte at the RIAM until 1932, and she remained in close contact with this institution, of which she became an honorary Fellow in 1938, until the end of her life. She also maintained her links with Alexandra College, to which in 1926 she presented a bookcase in memory of her sister Alice and her brother Hubert. After the departure of Esposito for Italy in 1927 Mrs Best undertook the duties of director of music at Alexandra College, and stimulated the pupils not only through her playing and teaching, but also through her lectures on the broader aspects of musical history, the music club which she founded, and her insistence on cultural experience in many fields. She remained a loyal pupil of her master.

The Bests were familiar figures in the cultural life of Dublin and benefactors to the National Gallery. Edith Best died in 1950, her husband in 1959, after which the cache of letters from Grove—which Best had zealously guarded, and from which in his last years he is reported to have derived a tangential pleasure—came back to the College from which they had gone forth.

[59] See *Beethoven und seine neun Symphonien* (London and New York, 1906); cf. Vorwort, pp. vi–vii, with pp. 131–5 of the English edition.
[60] Best is one of the participants in the long Platonic dialogue set in the National Library on 16 June 1904, which forms the *Scylla and Charybdis* episode of James Joyce's *Ulysses* (1921).

CHAPTER FOURTEEN

'G'

THE issue of yet another edition of the *Dictionary* that still bears his name, a hundred years after the appearance of the original, is a reminder that Grove himself has passed into mythology. Thus *Grove 6*—shorthand for the formal title—contains virtually none of the substance of *Grove 1*, but all of the intention and ideal of its founder. It is, perhaps, too obvious to propose that without *Grove 1* there would have been no *Grove 6*; but what is obvious not infrequently fails to capture attention. *Grove 1* (even though it was only one of Grove's claims to fame) was one of the great achievements of the Victorian era. It goes alongside the engineering masterpieces of the age and Grove with those who, having designed and executed them, were, in the words of Samuel Smiles, 'entitled to be regarded in a great measure as the founders of modern England'.[1] This is the more apposite in that the only professional training Grove received was in engineering. Another whose career began as a civil engineer—also on the London–Birmingham Railway and as assistant to Moorsom —was Herbert Spencer, with whose career that of Grove may be seen to show a number of parallels.

Grove 1 differed from previous musical lexicons in that it contained a considerable diversity of interest within singleness of purpose. It was created by one who, having already led a full life, accomplished this task at the centre point of a multifarious career. From this centre there were various radii. Grove was the first notable popular writer on music in England; but he was also the first effective and methodological musicolo-gist. By means of a singular ability for combining boyish enthusiasm with administrative efficiency and tact, in partnership with Manns he made possible the provision of concerts of the widest range and greatest intrinsic interest for the general public. No doubt it will be said that, if he had not persuaded the directors of the Crystal Palace to put their investments where their hearts often were not, someone else would have done so. But this is speculative. In one sense (as Henry James indicated) Grove was a back-room worker, but he knew how a back room can also be an engine room. In the world of letters Grove would now be reckoned by most as a specialist. He was, however, exactly the opposite. He specialized in the general, so that, adding together his analytical faculty, his poetic feeling, his never-diminishing zest for exploration and his

[1] Samuel Smiles, *James Brindley and the Early Engineers* (1864), p. 1.

conviction that writers should express themselves with precision and simplicity, he became a great editor and literary adviser. His fingerprints are on many pages of nineteenth-century literature, not least in the department of pedagogy.

Within each area of Grove's involvement there were nodal points. Within that of pedagogy, for example, was the study of geography, from which Grove's competence extended to the science of archaeology and the establishment of the Palestine Exploration Fund. Also from within the same general area came the inspiration for the institution and direction of the Royal College of Music. Here Grove not only made higher education in music nearly respectable, but—almost imperceptibly—he created conditions in which British music could flourish. It was said that Grove's respect for the German classics rendered him indifferent to British composers (although in respect of this charge his vigour in championing Sullivan against German detractors must be put among extenuating circumstances). But under his stewardship students and former students of the College produced a flood of works which have often been used as evidence for a new state of national creative excellence. Not less important was Grove's insistence on fundamental conditions being met; he believed that a main purpose of a teaching institution was to provide teachers. And because teachers of music should be more than music teachers, he was insistent that a good musical education was not a substitute for a good education, but part of it.

There, one is back at the beginning, at Pritchard's school in Clapham. What Grove did was to live out the sketch plan presented to him as a schoolboy. But he was only able to do this because of his temperament. That he was able to accomplish so much was due to his fortitude, his inability to renege on any public commitment, his extraordinary sense of obligation to the exigencies of time and his particular form of egotism. Great men—among whom Grove was not the least—are more often than not notoriously unhappy, and—sometimes oblivious of the fact—the cause of unhappiness in others. Friends and acquaintances tended to see Grove as though he were one of Dickens's Cheeryble Brothers, and the image of the merry little dinner companion (of the awful association of Muttonians) is what was often projected. In truth he was subject to bouts of anxiety-neurosis whose symptoms are laid out in his more intimate correspondence, which may be taken to support the Freudian thesis of sexual basis for such a condition and its somatic consequences. This is even more patently supported by Grove's relationships with his girl students[2] and his attitude to certain male friends, in particular Sullivan

---

[2] Cf. M. Kelly, 'Classroom Sex', *New Society*, 20 Nov 1975: '. . . life, even in educational institutions, is more complex, more plural, more fraught, emotionally different than the clichés of behavioural principles still bandied about in popular stereotypes and behavioural prejudices.' This certainly applies to life in the RCM in Grove's day.

and Barclay Squire. In public Grove was able to disguise himself, and the manner in which he accepted virtually every invitation—to dine out, to distribute prizes, to speak—shows how much he felt the need to do so. The pattern that emerges is not unfamiliar. It is that of an 'eminent Victorian'. Of his time and of his society Grove was typical if not indeed prototypical. In the end he felt that he had worked, but that he had not lived.

The era in which Grove's career lay was one of technological development that brought unprecedented changes, in the structure of society and the mechanisms necessary to maintain it, and in the philosophical and political principles which were both cause and effect of change. When he was a boy John Dalton's 'atomic theory', concerning the properties of gases, was in the van of scientific research. When he was an old man Ernest Rutherford was already engaged in the study of radioactivity. In the year of his death Sigmund Freud published *Die Träumdeutung*—his famous theory of dreams. When John Keble preached the 'Assize Sermon' which was the commencement of the Oxford Movement, Grove was a boy of thirteen. When he was eighty, William Temple was an undergraduate at Oxford and already preparing to fit Christianity for a new role in secularized society.

The shock waves that marked the progress of theology in England affected Grove particularly. His own spiritual pilgrimage through the hazardous regions marked out by radicalism and liberalism is tolerably well told in his own words. In other areas of literary expression Grove moved from the world of Jane Austen to that of George Eliot and Mrs Humphry Ward, from that of Tennyson to that of Clough and Arnold. In a record of increasing uncertainty culminating in an implicit disbelief in the more sanctified tenets of middle-class and suburban protocol, there is a feeling of tragedy. In the field of which he made himself master, however, there was a sense of permanence, of which the music of Beethoven, Schubert and Mendelssohn was the main assurance.

Grove felt the familiar world to be perpetually in a state of alteration—sometimes of disintegration—because of the conflict between his way of life and his mode of thought. The way of life was based on the premise that while men worked—to which activity a special grace attached—women wept, or otherwise surrendered themselves to masculine prerogatives. Grove was quite explicit on this point. At a time of intense sexual frustration in his middle years he wrote his essay, 'On a Song in "The Princess" ' (quoted above, p. 86f), of which the third stanza is interpreted by him with a degree of hysteria. The girl 'yields', because, says Grove, 'she is forced to admit how right as well as how powerful her lover has been in his obstinate perseverance; because she finds herself too feeble, and is compelled to give herself up to an influence which is too strong for her weak will to combat'. Finally, there is 'silence and fondness, and unutterable union of hands to hands, and lips to lips, and heart to heart, and being to being'.

Although Grove recognized and regretted that his sister Bithiah, in particular, had suffered from the tribal sex conventions, and although he was sad at the manner in which these same conventions led to the sacrifice of one girl student after another to meaningless drudgery, he could only express alarm when it seemed that John Stuart Mill's views regarding women's suffrage might be realized. It is not surprising that Grove required that the domestic arrangements in Sydenham should be precisely and unquestioningly adjusted to his wishes. This requirement consolidated as his inner life (within which was hidden a memory of Elizabeth Blackwell and her son) was more and more afflicted with a sense of desolation caused by death and disillusion. Grief moved Grove far away from the principles of faith once promoted in the 'holy village' of Clapham.

If there is a future life, then the dead are there, going on in their upward progress —if there is none: they are saved from probable failure—Meantime those that they have left are bereft of their love and friendship and their actual help and presence. I can't tell you in how many ways I feel every day the absence of my Milly. Her death has added quite twice to the burdens of my life. It is a selfish view, but it was a great part of our common life—the care which she took of me, to make matters easier for me and to be an extra pair of eyes and hands to me: and then our intercourse! She was always there for me to shew a bit of poetry to, or to advise as to this or that, or to look over some translation for her—and so on. My wife is a dear wife—but she has never taken interest in any of my pursuits public or private—[3]

But loneliness, as F. L. Lucas remembered of Matthew Arnold, in respect of 'Morality' (a poem with much meaning for Grove), 'is not only the doom of man, it is the price of man's greatness'.[4]

Amid a psychological maelstrom Grove built the lasting structure of his *Dictionary* and its satellite works, which give us the image of Grove the artist. This appellation he deserved more than many who were quicker to describe themselves so because, in the old meaning, he was a 'maker'. In his literary works his qualities as an engineer can be understood by inference. The responsibilities which he undertook in his early twenties and the successes of the enterprises with which he was associated speak for themselves. From experience in engineering Grove carried into other spheres the principle, better understood now than formerly, that teamwork is the basis of effective production method. By operating according to this principle Grove became an outstanding literary editor— whose qualities as such have been hitherto lost sight of—and the creator of the work by which he is universally known. Fergusson was responsible

[3] E.O., Monday mg Nov 25 [1889].
[4] *Eight Victorian Poets* (1930), p. 46.

for the major article on Jerusalem in the Bible *Dictionary*, but here as elsewhere the presence of Grove is felt. Referring to a detail of the architecture of the Temple, Fergusson politely added a footnote: 'This fact the Writer owes, with many other valuable rectifications, to the observation of his friend Mr G. Grove.'

Graves, for whom Grove was a man apart, apologizes for the fact that in respect of specialist study of music Grove was an amateur, about which Grove also tended to be apologetic. But this was the consequence of a misconception: that the techniques required of a composer or an executant were those necessary to the historian-cum-analyst. In that in regard to biography he sought to record verifiable facts rather than unsubstantiated anecdotes, or merely prejudices, and in respect of the study of music itself he endeavoured to subject a wide range of specimens to microscopic examination, he established guide-lines for future research. In so doing he must take a prominent place among the founding fathers of the separate faculty of musicology. At the same time, inspired by a synoptic sense, he rarely failed to imbue his writing with vitality, nor to abnegate the duty of a writer to establish stylistic coherence on the one hand and a balanced relationship with the reader on the other. There is, in short, a kind of simplicity about him which, despite his scholarship, keeps him on the reader's level. This is the virtue within his amateur status—as he called it—and was so well recognized by Shaw in his review of *Beethoven and his Nine Symphonies*.

Grove was projected into biblical scholarship by his upbringing and his sense of curiosity. The Bible was fundamental to the culture of Clapham, and with sisters named Bithiah and Kezia, it was impossible not to set speculation as to origins at work. Later association with liberal theologians refined early intentions and gradually Grove passed from the respect due to the Good Book to the greater respect due to good books created by critical appreciation. He became a scholar and his training ground was the *Dictionary of the Bible*.

To understand the magisterial quality of his scholarly writing one may turn to the great essay on Palestine (vol. II, p. 672). This noble piece begins in the grand manner, with reference to *Paradise Lost* and the *Ode on the Morning of Christ's Nativity*. But Grove easily modulates into a more familiar mood. Noticing Mary Eliza Rogers's *Domestic Life in Palestine*, he again takes the opportunity of paying tribute to her brother, who had not only enabled Miss Rogers to write so well of life in Jewish and Arab households (which no one previously had done with such intimacy and humour) but also had so much helped him in former times. The article also contains a warm recommendation of Stanley's *Sinai and Palestine*, in which, Grove points out, Stanley did not so much try to 'make fresh discoveries, as to apply those already made, the structure of the country and the peculiarities of the scenery, to the elucidation of the history'. The facts have been garnered and scrutinized, opinions sieved and discussed, and authorities cited; but the land of which Grove writes is one with which he shows himself to be acquainted in a physical sense, and into which he invites the reader to share his traveller's reflections on the views: 'Great as is this charm when viewed as mere landscapes, their deep and abiding interest lies in their intimate connexion with the history and the remarkable manner in which they corroborate its statements.'

In another monumental essay, on Elijah, Grove writes graphically of the countryside of Gilead—with 'chase and pasture, tent-villages, and mountain-castles'—of people conspicuous for backwardness and for conflict with neighbouring societies.

To an Israelite of the tribes west of Jordan the title 'Gileadite' must have conveyed a similar impression, though in a far stronger degree, to that which the title 'Celt' does to us. What the Highlands were a century ago to the towns in the lowlands of Scotland, that, and more than that, must Gilead have been to Samaria or Jerusalem.

In a footnote Grove refers the reader to a relevant passage in Scott's *Rob Roy* (ch. XIX). In another important article, on Moab (vol. II, p. 391), he again evokes a kaleidoscope of landscapes and discusses their influence on people.

Regarding persons there are entries which build the recorded events of some lives into dramatic episodes worthy of a larger setting. Grove wrote about Merab and Michal, daughters of Saul, while the essays on Saul and David (with whom the two women were involved) were by Stanley, and it is notable that out of the collaboration between Grove and Stanley grew the idea of a *Life of David*,[5] which also took in his own experience. Concerning David he wrote to his sister-in-law Marian:

I take him to be the great instance of a man who waits till mature life before he has his 'grand passion'. Abigail and Ahinoam and Eglah, etc. were only women he picked up in the villages 'to make his establishment'. Michal was his first love, but when she came back to him they were both so altered and all the circumstances so cruelly against Michal, that it was impossible for it to end except as it did—and then came the grand event of his life, and poor fellow, it wrecked him. Ah! how many a man has been wrecked on the same reef.[6]

In his contributions to the *Dictionary of the Bible* Grove was scrupulous in giving etymological derivations and bibliographical references. But he rarely lost an opportunity of showing the past in the present—as in

---

[5] See Graves, pp. 150–3; it is stated that Grove made this entry in a notebook: 'Saul was like Mr Tennyson, Absalom . . . [Giovanni Matteo] Mario [Italian tenor], Benjamin and Judah . . . Saxons and Normans.'

[6] Letter of 10 Aug 1867; ibid., p. 151.

his little note on Eglah, in which he writes that the name was one given
to Arab women in his own day. In the essay on Elijah, Grove excuses his
referring to Mendelssohn's oratorio, which, he says, 'may seem out of
place in a work of this nature'. But, he avers, it is 'one of the most
forcible commentaries existing on the history of the prophet.' For good
measure he goes on to assist the biblical scholar's musical education by
observing: 'The scene in which the occurrences at Beersheba are embodied is perhaps the most dramatic and affecting in the whole work.'

On whatever subject he wrote, Grove looked at every detail. His attitude
was exemplified in the Report he made to the British Association in 1866
on the Palestine Exploration Fund:

> Mr Grove announced the intention of the Association to persevere until every
> square mile in Palestine has been properly and accurately surveyed and mapped;
> till every mound of ruins has been examined and sifted; the name of every
> village ascertained, recorded, and compared with the lists in the Bible; till all
> the ancient roads have been traced; the geology made out; the natural history
> and botany fully known.

The same disciplined yet imaginative method is conspicuous in his
work in the area of musicology. While it is true that the experience
gained in biblical research was invaluable in his later lexicographical
undertaking, it is also true that the rigorous process of self-education of
his youth—especially among the manuscripts of the British Museum—
was indispensable in developing the faculties of analysis and synthesis
evident in the earlier as well as in the later Dictionary.

The commonplace books which contain Grove's researches and which
were his companions in many parts of the world are not only filled with
excerpts displaying an astonishing range of score-reading, but also a
determination to distinguish fundamental principles in structure and
design. Apart from careful annotation of individual passages—in which
practice Vincent Novello was his particular exemplar—he brought
together assimilations of ideas, as instanced by the reiteration of certain
germinal note-formations in different structures by different composers
of different periods. He was alive to the broader issues of musical expression and understanding, as when he considered the nature of the music of
the Yom Kippur ceremonies of the Samaritans or the singing of the black
Methodists of Philadelphia. He was concerned with minutiae, so that
he followed these motifs

up hill and down dale, from Certon to Sullivan, from Morley to Mendelssohn, from Corelli to Beethoven.[7]

But Grove was no mere pathologist; musical phrases had organic significance and it was their vitality in function that captured his attention. He did not only look at music; he listened to it. Edith Oldham wrote to him in June 1892 about Brahms's Horn Trio (op. 40), which she had just heard. She recalled something from her student days and reminded Grove of one of his basic motifs. He replied, 'Fancy you noting the old phrase in the Scherzo! He is tremendously fond of it and uses it often— *most* beautifully in the opening notes of the Song of Destiny, where it is quite *unearthly*.' The opening bars of the work follow.[8]

Since all roads led to Beethoven, it is instructive to compare the analysis of one of the symphonies in an early programme note with the parallel section in the book of 1896. Grove never allowed his notes to be reprinted as they had at first appeared; like Handel, his ideas concerning any of his works were always in process of development. In the course of time he tried to bring his prose nearer to his readers in order to compensate for a missing dimension. For whereas the Crystal Palace notes went with the music, the essays in the later book were intended as aids to reflection in tranquillity. The early note on the Pastoral Symphony—drafted at Ragatz in 1864—began the analysis proper as follows:

1. The Symphony opens without introduction or other preliminary, with the principal theme in the violins, commencing as follows:

This phrase may be almost said to contain in its own bosom the whole of this wonderful movement (512 bars long). As the piece proceeds, each joint (so to speak) of the theme germinates, and throws off phrases all but identical with itself in rhythm or interval. It would be difficult to find in Art a greater amount of confidence, not to say audacity, than Beethoven has here furnished by his incessant repetition of the same, or similar, short phrases throughout this long movement; and yet the effect is such, that when the end arrives, we would gladly hear it all over again. As instance of this boldness in repetition, we may quote a phrase of five notes—

[7] Tracing the history of the so-called 'Jupiter theme', Grove cited its appearance in works by Certon, Tye, Purcell, Croft, Scarlatti, Bach, Mozart, Schubert, Mendelssohn and Sullivan. See his 'The History of a Musical Phrase attempted', *Musical World*, 1886, serially from p. 627 (October issue). Grove was not only interested in collecting the material. In many cases he copied episodes to show how the material was used. For a recent study of the same subject, see Susan Wollenberg, 'The Jupiter Theme: New Light on its Creation', *Musical Times* CXVI, Sept. 1975, pp. 781ff.

[8] E.O., Tuesday 11 p.m. [22 June 1892]. See above, p. 240.

formed out of the theme, which first occurs at the 16th bar, and is at once repeated no less than ten times.

In the book (after a longer historical and biographical prologue) the corresponding passage reads:

The Symphony opens without other introduction or preliminary than a double pedal on F and C in the violas and cellos—with the principal theme in the violins, as sweet and soft as the air of May itself, with buds and blossoms and new-mown grass:—

This beautiful subject may almost be said to contain in its own bosom the whole of the wonderful movement which it starts, and which is 512 bars long. As the piece proceeds each joint, so to speak, of the theme germinates, and throws off phrases closely related to the parent stem in rhythm or interval. It would be difficult to find in Art a greater amount of confidence, not to say audacity, than Beethoven has furnished by his incessant repetition of the same or similar short phrases throughout this long movement, and yet the effect is such that when the end arrives, we would gladly hear it all, over again. The Violin Concerto gives another example of the same practice. As an instance of this boldness in repetition in the Symphony, we may quote a phrase of five notes, formed out of theme No. 1:

A *locus classicus* in this symphony is the passage at the end of the slow movement incorporating the sounds of nightingale, quail and cuckoo. The heat that was once generated over the propriety of such a breach with the 'absolute' is no longer to be felt; indeed, since Messiaen's use of such material recourse to birdsong may be thought to have some statutory authority. In the early Crystal Palace note the matter is thus introduced:

At the close of the *Andante* occurs the only example of direct imitation of natural sounds which we have yet encountered—the well-known passage in which the notes of the nightingale, quail, and cuckoo, are imitated by the flute, oboe, and clarinet, respectively. The passage, which is four bars in length, is repeated with half a bar interval, and Beethoven has taken off the rawness which it would inevitably have had if left to itself by introducing between and after it the lovely phrase quoted above in the first violin—a consummate device very analogous to the methods by which the Gothic and Moorish architects employed the forms of birds, or flowers, and made them harmonize with the 'pure music' of the surrounding conventional ornament.

In the book Grove extends his reflection, from which this passage overlaps the citation from the programme note:

How completely are the raw travesties of nightingale, quail, and cuckoo atoned for and brought into keeping by the lovely phrase 12a

with which Beethoven has bound them together, and made them one with the music which comes before and after them—

Just so in the equally anomalous arabesque of Oriental and Renaissance art do the feet and tails of the birds and dragons and children, which play among the leaves, run off into lovely tendrils, curving gracefully round, and connecting the too-definite forms from which they spring with the vaguer foliage all round.[9]

It is typical that Grove precisely notices the containment of the birds within four bars of music, by which discipline the balance of the structure of the movement remains unimpaired. It is characteristic of Donald Tovey that he throws a heavy punch at those 'superior persons' who did not trouble to notice this essential fact while complaining of Beethoven's violation of the 'absoluteness' of music. In his essay on this work, regarding this movement Tovey delivers one phrase which has the ring of Grove: 'Thus the air is full of tiny sounds which no one can tell to be less vast and distant than the stars of the Milky Way.'[10]

Grove agreed with the principle of the Enlightenment enunciated so

[9] In 1873-4 Grove contemplated writing a handbook on Chinese porcelain, of details of which he had made numerous drawings. A draft for an introduction to such a handbook commenced:

This little book is concerned with blue and white Oriental china only. It is little more than a translation of a portion of the great work of M. Stanislas Julien on China porcelain—itself chiefly a translation from a Chinese treatise—and was provoked by the pretension inaccuracy and incompetence of the existing works on the subject with which the writer came in contact.

See Graves, p. 202.

[10] D. F. Tovey, *Essays in Musical Analysis*, vol. I: *Symphonies* (1935), p. 51.

often by Burney, that it was only in 'modern times' that artistic expression came to its full potency; so that the record of a motif, implicitly at least, is an account of continuing improvement. The ultimate in excellence, so far as Grove was concerned, was represented by the music of Beethoven. This conviction—hostile, of course, to the proper objectivity which the scientist is expected to practise—had two unfortunate consequences. On the one hand singers were invariably written down as an inferior race; on the other, music beyond a certain point, because of its age, was archaic and outside common understanding.

Regarding singers Grove could be singularly uncharitable. As he wrote to Edith Oldham:

. . . Singers as a rule (of course there are exceptions) are thoughtless empty uneducated persons given up to the admiration of themselves and their own sweet voices. Patti, Nilsson, Grisi, Mario—what are or were all these and hundreds like them, but mere machines for producing sweet sounds, which the public values for their own sweetness, overlooking entirely with what intelligence or study they are regulated. These people never read and unless you flirt or talk more personal rubbish they have no communication. E. Lloyd *never* reads— not ever a newspaper nor does Reeves or ever will. Of course there are exceptions, Lind, Santley, Malibran, but you may count them on your fingers. Compare them with Joachim, Mad. Schumann, Liszt, von Bülow, etc. etc. etc. You may thank God dear that you belong to the modern class, and therefore cherish that sense and act upon it as you do. Yes my dear be an *artist* and never get mercenary. It's easy for me to talk, because tho' never a rich man, I have always, thank God, been in such a position that I never had to think about the value of money. . . .[11]

Fortified by his own musical experience, his familiar personal contacts, and the prejudices arising therefrom, Grove was not afraid to go against the changing tide of advanced opinion:

I found out that same day that Mendelssohn has taken the subject of 'It is enough' from 'It is finished' near the end of Bach's St John Passion, and recollecting what you said about the Passion I had the two airs carefully sung to me. The spirit is the same in both, but *how much finer* Mendelssohn's is than Bach's! There's so much more in it, so much colour, and it's far more dramatic without losing any of the religious feelings or tenderness that is so long in the

[11] E.O., 20 April 1888. Cf. N. Temperley, 'Sterndale Bennett and the Lied—2,' *Musical Times* CXVI, Dec 1975, pp. 1060f.:

Potter was a pupil of Attwood, Woelfl and Förster, and an ardent disciple of Haydn, Mozart and Beethoven. He made modern instrumental forms the basis of his teaching, an innovation as far as English musical education was concerned. It is not surprising that the generation of Academy pupils that emerged in the 1830s, including J. W. Davison, G. A. Macfarren and T. M. Mudie as well as Bennett, tended to regard instrumental music as the most important medium of composition (an opinion shared by Schumann among others).

Bach. Bach produces the same effect on me as Sandro Botticelli, Ghirlandaio,
Sodomo, among painters—I love the sentiments but the effect is so imperfect
compared to what it might be with the advance of modern art.*

* Bad clumsy attitudes imperfect hands and feet ill drawn postures.[12]

Edith apparently took her old master to task for his lack of perception
(or, rather, his change of heart) in the matter of Bach. But he was un-
repentant and, recognizing that reality for him had first been defined in
terms of civil engineering, reiterated his belief that the best of all possible
music was the music of Beethoven. In the letter in *The Times* in 1886,
Grove recalled an ancient battle that had not yet been won. People, he
said, did not go to church as much as might be thought desirable. He
suggested 'Sunday music'—afternoon performances given in parish
churches, arranged not by incumbents but by laymen. In due course,
he boldly speculated, a Rate might be levied for this purpose. In any case
scanty congregations would be mightily boosted by Mendelssohn's
oratorios, or Beethoven's symphonies—'as truly religious as any oratorio',
he added. To Edith he wrote:

I did not say a word to you about Bach—you wrote a glowing two pages about
him with much of which I agreed. Perfect workmanship and finish, and tender
sentiment he surely has; religion, and grandeur, and a calmness seldom heard in
the modern world—but still he is an *ancient*, and much as one respects these
ancients they can't be to us as the moderns are—In the matter of finish and
sentiment surely he has never matched the slow movement of that same sonata
in D minor [op. 31, no. 2] which you played me the first movement of—while
what an intimate interest—a width as well as a depth of meaning, a flavour of
our own times and questions, that piece of Beethoven has what Bach *could*
never reach through the formality that encompassed everything 2 centuries ago.
No! I always think that painting, poetry, music—great, immeasurably great as
the works of the old school were, they are *necessarily* divided from us by their
distance, and by the inevitable change of circumstances; and are by their very
remoteness much less interesting. To me the greatest difference between a work
produced on the other side of the Fr[ench] Revolution and another on this side
—the whole world (not mine only) seems traversed by an enormous trench like
a Railway cutting—on that side lies the old world—on this side ours with its
new hopes and interests and feelings of knowledge. Oh dear while I think too of
the many orchestral movements of Beethoven—the Leonora overtures, the
Eroica, the Adagio and Scherzo of the 9th Sym. Oh dear! how far more human
and everything else they seem than the simple calm heart of old Bach! and that
being so how can one cling to the one and not give one self up to the other.
What is it Tennyson says:—'I *must* have loved the loftiest that I know' or
something like that.[13]

[12] E.O., Monday [after 17 Oct 1891]. In respect of Mendelssohn's air having 'so much
more in it', reference may be made to J. Werner's account of the Jewish element in the
music; see *Mendelssohn's 'Elijah'* (1965), Appendix A, p. 84.
[13] E.O., Monday [9 Nov 1891]. See *The Idylls of the King*, 'Guinevere', ll. 652f.;
Tennyson's word is 'highest'.

Grove's odd valuation of Bach—in view of the enthusiasm which he displayed in the old pioneering days before the world had woken up to the master—and general reservations about 'the old school' are one thing; but, by the example of his scholarly rigour in examining any musical work as a thing in itself in respect of structure, he helped others in general to appreciate what he himself could not come to terms with in particular. Grove's concern for artefacts necessarily included concern for the artist. Just as in attempting to understand and then to elucidate the nature of musical phenomena he brought together all available evidence, so in respect of the artist's life he followed the same practice. He was an acknowledged master of biography, and the principles which inspired him are defined in the letter to William Knight of 24 June 1889 in which he promised to support Knight's candidature for the Chair of English at Glasgow.

... When I look at your long and valuable labours in the cause of Wordsworth and his friends, I hardly know how to express my admiration of them sufficiently. Your chronological edition of W.'s poems seems to me a pattern of what ought to be done for every poet. My own attempts at the same things in the case of Beethoven and Schubert in my dictionary of music—shew how *essential* such a treatment is in my opinion—it is impossible in any other way to trace the progress of an author's mind.

Your delightful Coleorton book[14] is invaluable to every student of these great men and it is curious that only yesterday I wrote you to S. Andrew's a long note from Sydenham, endeavouring to set forth my appretiation [*sic*] of vol 1 of your Wordsworth's Life which I have just finished. In that note I tried to shew why I thought the book a model biography, based on the soundest principles—principles which have guided me in my humble attempts at the lives of the three great musicians Beethoven, Mendelssohn, Schubert, and which after a quarter of a century of study, I have gradually become convinced are the true principles to guide a biographer—namely to find out all the facts of the lives in which the works were produced, and which must have the closest connexion with them, and to leave criticism alone. The world settles that: and biographers have nothing to do with it.[15]

There is a nice compliment to Grove's exactness as a biographer in a sentence in a letter from Marie Benecke to F. G. Edwards, who was anxious to have details of the first performance of the *Hymn of Praise*. 'It seems to me', she wrote, 'that you cannot do better than adopt Sir George Grove's account of the [Birmingham 1840] festival.'[16]

[14] *Memorials of Coleorton: Letters from Coleridge, Dorothy and William Wordsworth, Southey, and Scott, to Sir George and Lady Beaumont of Coleorton, Leicestershire* (Edinburgh, 1887).
[15] PML.
[16] Letter of 31 July 1882; BL, Add. MS. 41573, f. 13.

The earnest manner in which Grove advised his students (and anyone else within earshot) to read was the result not only of his love of reading but also of his dependence on books. Music was one sort of reality, literature another; both were aids to, and sometimes also substitutes for living. Grove's eventual reluctant rejection of a Christian philosophy meant the loss of certitude, and turning more to the poetry of Clough and Matthew Arnold. In 1891 he wrote to Mrs Wodehouse that he had been learning 'To Marguerite, in returning a Volume of the Letters to Ortis'—a cry from the sense of eternal loneliness:

> Dotting the shoreless watery wild
> We mortal millions live *alone*.

At the same time he was memorizing 'The Future' and 'Morality'. 'Don't cry as you read it', he wrote to his friend about the first, 'but I am hardly able to help it.'[17]

The old-time method of 'learning by heart' is not so much now in favour as once it was; but there is no doubt that for many it had a particular value. It mattered what was learned, and Grove was fortunate in the encouragement he received early in life to explore the broad acres of English—and a good deal of foreign—literature. In continuing the practice of 'committing to memory' (the phrase came to him from Macaulay) what moved him, he assembled his own secret library. Released from the printed word he was able to look at literature in a different way from most, and he was able to convert poetical into musical values. This is immediately to be appreciated from the references given in the Index to *Beethoven and his Nine Symphonies*. Wordsworth and Tennyson were his favourite companions, but Browning had a special place in his esteem. He was glad one day to hear that Edith was reading Browning:

I don't know very much of him but what I do know I know well. It is confined to Men and Women Christmas Day and Easter Eve and a few of the earlier poems outside these books . . . in 'Men and Women' my favourites are 'Love among the ruins', Two in the Campagna, Karshish (your friend) *In a balcony*. But the gem of all is the last poem *One word more*. It wants browsing, like a piece by Beethoven. . . .[18]

It was always back to Beethoven. In a programme note on the Violin Concerto, preparatory to a Joachim performance, Grove manages to convey not only a relationship between the composer and Tennyson—as perceived by him—but also even something redolent of Joachim's interpretation of the slow movement:

[17] Letter of 11 July 1891; see Graves, pp. 373-5.
[18] E.O., 15 Sept [1887].

... The lovely melody, with its beseeching, yearning tone, the soft sustained accompaniment of the strings, and the mellow monotonous reiterated call of the horns, suggest (at least they suggest inevitably to the mind of the writer) the 'calm and deep peace' of a lovely still autumn day, in a land like that of the lotus-eaters [*sic*] of the Poet,

'A land
In which it seemed always afternoon'; where
'The charmed sunset linger'd low adown' ...

In a passage in one of his later letters—in which the last movement of the Ninth Symphony is shown in parallel with passages from the *Ode on the Intimations of Immortality*, Grove links together his interests and his feelings into a challenging episode of combined narrative and (in spite of his reservations about the biographer as critic) criticism:

... but the vocal part is mostly redolent of the beer garden—and therein is very different to the first 3 movements, in which there is not one vulgar or common bar. I have been living a good deal with Beethoven lately, through a very good book written by a man (Gerhard von Breuning) whose father was one of his oldest and dearest friends, the author himself having been about 16 when Beethoven died, and having been accustomed to see him every day all his life: and the conviction is forced upon me that he must have been an extraordinary *queer* person:—a man who habitually spoke at the top of his voice, who walked through the streets humming and singing and throwing his arms about and perfectly unconscious of time or place or persons; who generally called everyone by a nickname, and was always ready for a practical joke, however rough— must have been very trying, and very disappointing to those who knew him by his works. The 8th symphony (in F) is a most characteristic portrait of himself, written when he was very well, very happy, in the society of his best friends, deeply, (and boisterously) in love with a lady who he had just encountered— and it is astonishingly full of jokes and rough horseplay. Of course all this does not affect his music—but it raises one's wonder, and makes one feel that that kind of artist is gone for ever. Brahms is something like it, and in Germany Tennyson would probably be so, but they are the last of the old men. Is this so? or is the force of art so great that if a new Beethoven were to appear he would set society at defiance?[19]

This, more or less, is a free rendering of a passage in the *Dictionary* (vol. I, p. 198). It is an important passage, for Beethoven in demeanour was everything that a man should not be—in Sydenham. But his greatness was undeniable, and here Grove was able to fall back on lessons he had been taught about Handel. Beethoven therefore becomes a moral preceptor—an honorary Victorian. In his article on the composer in *Chambers's Cyclopaedia* Grove rather goes over the top:

Living in a profligate city, and in a time of the loosest morals, and himself

[19] E.O., 24 July [1892].
[20] *Grove 1*, vol. I, p. 202.

singularly attractive to women, his name is not connected with a single *liaison* or scandal. 'It is one of my first principles', says he, 'never to stand in any relations but those of friendship with another man's wife'.

Earlier in life Grove had thought it prudent similarly to cover Mozart's reputation with a modest coat of whitewash (see p. 66). But more important is the moral didacticism with which Beethoven is endowed for the pulpit:

All the sentiment and earnestness of Schumann, all the grace and individuality of Schubert, are there; with an intensity, breadth, and completeness, which these masters might perhaps have attained if they had bestowed the time and pains on their work which Beethoven did. In this ['middle'] period he passes from being the greatest musician to be a great teacher, and in a manner in which no one ever did before and possibly no one will ever do again, conveys lessons which by their intense suggestiveness have almost the force of moral teaching.[20]

It will be seen that Schubert and Schumann were castigated for their comparative inability to understand that work was an end in itself. Even so, at the end Grove found himself a little unsure of his moral stance on the nonconforming Beethoven, and had to introduce 'almost' as a brake on impetuosity.

It sometimes appears that Grove had read everything. Even taking into account that a considerable part of his professional life was devoted to editorship—in which he was meticulous in operation—the range of his experience in books is remarkable. He did, of course, make the best use of his time. He never boarded a train without reading material. If there was any possibility of his being kept waiting he secreted a volume in his pocket. For instance, in 1887 he took his newly acquired copy of Victor Hugo's *Choses vues* (it having just been posthumously published), to Westminster Abbey to use the time before the beginning of the Jubilee Service.

A writer particularly high on his list of favourite reading was Turgenev. 'I do so like your being fond of Tourguenoff', he wrote to Edith on 18 June 1886, 'because I am too. They are lovely books—so little padding and so much like real life'. Five years later he was interested to hear of Edith's cousins' 'reception of Tourguenef. Those charming, good, books must do them good.'[21] He offered to lend Edith any of Turgenev's works

---

[21] E.O., Oct 17 1891. There was a personal reason for Grove being especially interested in this author. Turgenev paid frequent visits to Britain between 1847 and 1881 and Grove had hardly taken up the reins of office as editor of *Macmillan's Magazine* before he tried to obtain from Turgenev (through the singer Pauline Viardot) a short story, in translation, for publication in the magazine. Turgenev was willing, but the intention was never fulfilled. See Graves, p. 158, where part of a letter from Turgenev to Grove, in French, is quoted. On p. 424 of the same book, in a letter to an unnamed friend, Grove expresses dislike of a 'brutal' quality in Tolstoy, while describing Turgenev as 'one of the greatest artists of our time'.

which he had and she had not. In recommending Pushkin's *Prose Tales* to Edith, Grove crossed over into music by way of Turgenev:

P. you know is the great Russian poet to whom Turguenief is constantly referring; and his tales are not only interesting in themselves, but most interesting as the forerunners of T.'s. They have much the same relation to T.'s smaller stories that Zumsteeg's songs have to Schubert.[22]

This letter was one accompanying a copy of Mérimée's *Lettres à une inconnue*.

With French writers Grove had a love-hate relationship, of which his own definition gives a clear insight into the conflicts in his personality. He was always rather conceited about his knowledge of the French language (in which he tended ostentatiously to address Edith on the outside of envelopes), but scandalized by the use to which it was put by many French writers. He was, however, never deterred from avidly reading their more licentious works. For example, from a literary point of view, he found Mérimée's letters 'delightful'. From a moral standpoint, however, he strongly objected to them:

I suppose a Frenchman will always look on the relation between himself and a woman in a different way to what we do, and certainly Mérimée says and hints things to his correspondent which are most incredible; but I won't suggest them to you. Otherwise they are very charming. . . .[23]

Many of his most intensely felt letters (as this last) were written on Sunday evenings, when, for a regular church-goer, the old inhibitions of Clapham theology and recollections of the old Adam, were certain to be revived. Zola's *Le Docteur Pascal*, which he read almost immediately after its publication, impressed him by the veracity of its descriptive force; 'but we can't live on psychology, especially when it all tends to filth—so I think je le jetterai au feu.'[24] That he could even imagine a burning of books shows to what extent Grove was disturbed by the collision of convention and frustration.

It was Renan, however, whose works most exercised his conscience. With Renan—who belonged to the same generation—Grove had a good deal in common, especially in the history of religion and its associated disciplines; and both men could be described, in Owen Chadwick's phrase, as 'martyrs for true scholarship'. In both cases the search for truth and academic probity led to alienation from Christianity. But Grove was forever haunted by the siren voices of Victorian respectability. In the end those who had raised objections to the Sunday opening of the Crystal Palace, even more those who had demanded mutilation of the

22 E.O., Sat. 14 July 1894.
23 E.O., 28 Sept 1890.
24 E.O., Aug 6 [1893].

statuary proposed for the building, won a battle for the soul of George Grove. Renan was the real *casus belli*. As Grove wrote to Edith:

I did not know that Rénan [*sic*] was so unknown to you before. He has been a good deal connected with Palestine and the Bible and I have known his books well (and himself a little) for very long. The interesting part in the *Souvenirs* was the description of the Breton village, and his early days there—so very strange and *outre tombe*. Also his own changes of belief and attitude were full of interest. I don't admire his tone or taste. I would rather cut my hand off than crack the joke which he [makes?] about the lady who kept the hotel near the Sorbonne—'point de scandale'—or some vile nasty thought of that sort and close to the very word there is an expression which jarred on me, where he speaks of that varied serious life of his as '*une belle promenade*'. In his Vie de Jesus, describing our Lord's Agony in the Garden and endeavouring to account for it, he suggests that the failure of His Life may have been partly the cause, and enquires if the thought of 'les jeunes filles qui auraient peut être consenti à l'aimer', if he had asked them had anything to do with it! Isn't it horrid? The French mind completely puzzles me. Nothing struck me as much in Paris last time I was there as the frightful indecency that reigned everywhere in pictures, and in books. Things forbidden to us seem to be quite permissible to them. For instance. In the Exposition there was a picture of the last moments of a mother. She was lying in bed at the point of death. But her daughter who was closing her eyes was—stark naked! Another picture—and a lovely one—was a meadow of high luxuriant grass; and through it, crashing down towards you, was a splendid bull, who was being pulled back by a young peasant girl, who was stark naked!![25] The Charivari—their Punch—wonderfully witty is now so frightfully immoral that no woman can look at it. . . .[26]

In his retreat from the principles of liberalism with which he had been acquainted in the pioneer days of the Working Men's College, Grove took on some Podsnap characteristics—disliking George Eliot because of Tom Tulliver's bullying of Maggie, and deploring *Robert Elsmere* because of Mrs Ward's having trodden 'the paths of display and pretension'. Partly this was due to his own misfortune in being treated, albeit in a modest manner, as a hero. A man who comes to be regarded as a proper subject for painter and sculptor is thereby denoted heroic and worthy of recommendation to posterity. For the self-made man, the autodidact, even if happiness is not the final reward, this is true fulfilment. Neither in portrait nor in bust does Grove quite look the hero. Furse and Gilbert —each flattered by the friendly attentions of a companionable man of distinction who had time and courtesy to spare for those who still had

[25] The Paris Salon of 1884, to which Grove refers, had more than its share of 'flesh-painting' that shocked not only him but also 'A British Matron' whose letter to *The Times* set off J. C. Horsley to protest against such depravity and to express concern over the effect on British art. Never guilty himself of painting a nude, he was known among fellow artists as 'Clothes' Horsley.

[26] E.O., 2 March 1890. Renan's *Souvenirs d'enfance et de jeunesse* was published in 1883, his *Vie de Jésus* in 1862.

their way to make in the world—represented only what they saw before them.

Nevertheless Grove was in the class of those of whom it might be said —and more than most he would have recognized the source of the quotation—'I do know but one that unassailable holds on his rank'. He was an idealist; but he was pragmatic. He loved others; but was afraid of himself. He was a savant; but not an intellectual. He believed in free access to knowledge; but doubted man's ability profitably or sensibly to use knowledge gained. He was a religious man who understood the lure of mammon.

Not only that without money there is no existence, but there is a close connexion between work and gain. Even poetry and music. Shakespeare and Tennyson both distinctly wrote for money, and profited largely; and Beethoven, great as he was, was hungry after gains. Schubert not—most certainly—but if he had been would it have been worse for him to have regular dinners and a proper house, and so on![27]

He worshipped one god, to whom all his life he paid his dues in the manner prescribed by Ralph Waldo Emerson, in *The Conduct of Life*: 'There is no way to success in our art but to take off your coat, grind paint, and work like a digger on the railroad, all day and every day.' Led back in this way to the beginnings of the creative life of George Grove, as a pupil of Alexander Gordon, a builder of lighthouses in distant lands, and an agent in the improvement of transport at home, a consistency of development is to be seen. Towards the end of his life, in a letter to Maxtone Graham, of Cultoquhey, of 22 April 1895, Grove sensed this consistency, and also a unity of human purpose which it was his principal aim to promote. He wrote: 'Did you ever notice that at the first enumeration of the inhabitants of the world (Gen. IV, 20, 21, 22) they are divided into three great sections—herdsmen, *musicians*, and engineers? It struck me as very interesting when I first observed it.'[28]

---

[27] E.O., Jan 18 [1888].
[28] Letter published by Graham in the *Strathearn Herald*, 27 Apr 1895.

10

Appendixes

Bibliography

General Index

Sir George Grove, 1894

C. H. H. Parry

An address to the Students of the Royal College of Music,
delivered on 7 January 1895

I cannot help being conscious that the strongest feeling which is present in our minds at this moment is the sense of the great loss we have sustained in the absence of our dear old first Director, Sir George Grove. It is the first serious loss our College has sustained, and it is one we shall inevitably feel the results of for a long while. But the energy and ability of our professors and the goodwill and honourable conduct of all you scholars, exhibitioners, and students may carry our College through the crisis; and it is rather as the loss of a personal friend who made a part almost of our daily lives that we shall feel his absence most severely.

There are few of you here present who have not felt the influence of his personality and realised the whole-hearted enthusiasm for whatever is really good which was his most marked characteristic. And we unluckily older people, who could call him friend even in the days before many of you were born, can recall an even more lively phase of his vital and energetic delight in the best art, and the best literature, and the best music, as well as in the loveliest scenes of landscape or of sea, and even in the joyous impressions of mountain and of forest which rested in his lively imagination. You who have only known him for years can have no such idea of him as we who have known him for tens of years.

It makes me often smile inwardly when I recall the jolly times he and I had together some twenty years ago, when I had the privilege and good fortune to work with him as a sort of sub-editor on his well-known *Dictionary of Music*. We had some uncommonly dreary and tiresome work to do. If you could have seen the state in which some of the articles were sent in you would wonder how they were ever got into shape. I remember we not only had to recast the details of the language of many of them, but to turn the articles inside out and upside down, to put the end at the beginning and the middle at the end, and to cut out whole paragraphs of rigmarole, till we were driven nearly distracted.

But all the while our dear old friend was sandwiching in stories of his many experiences, such as the memories of his boyhood, when he was a clerk in Whitehall, and remembered such ancient incidents as the first appearance of lucifer matches, and hearing and seeing boys in the streets selling bits of stick with sulphur at the end to make it easier to get a light from flint and steel; and at another time he would tell me of his adventures when he was building the first lighthouse in Jamaica, and nearly got killed by tumbling through a hole down the middle of the building; and at another time of the strange and wonderful relics of the ancient work and manners of men which he came across when he was in Palestine as Secretary of the Palestine Exploration Fund; and of the interesting men like Dean Stanley; and of the thrilling artistic excitements of the time when he went to Vienna with Sir Arthur Sullivan, and found buried under the accumulated dust of years the priceless products of Schubert's genius, which had been hidden in old cupboards and forgotten since the days when the composer had last laid his hand upon them. And you can imagine yourselves how he was always ready with some humorous quotation from Dickens, or some deep thought from Browning, or some beautiful musical phrase of Tennyson, or some happy and pathetic fragment from an out-of-the-way poet, whose very name we hardly remember.

When did any of us meet with a man so alive to everything that was honourably delightful, whether as beauty of thought, or grace of language, or noble dignity of sentiment, or vivacity of humour? What mind so well stocked or so cosmopolitan? But, alas, all human things are transient in a sense—and in a sense we lose him.

But it is the happy outcome of an honourable life that things that belong to it are not so transient as they seem. It is true we lose the immediate influence of his personality. But the influence of his work may last long beyond the limited vista of the lives even of the youngest of us. For not only the fruits of his actual organisation will still subsist with us, in the system and plan of our College, but the example of his high-minded, whole-hearted devotion may inspire us constantly, not only to develop such talents as we have to the highest we can, and to put them to the most honourable uses, but also to go forward unfalteringly, never yielding to the shallow sophisms of a vulgar, greedy, vain, and money-grubbing world, but clinging steadfastly to high ideals; seeking to serve and to help all our fellow-creatures whenever occasion offers, and doing our best to develop our own selves into honourable and refined men and women.

Let our old Director be as it were our patron saint. If we can but live and act as he would have us, truly this College will be an honour to our country, a very beacon set on a hill, and will help to make our art to be held in such honour as has not been paid to it for hundreds of years. . . . I look forward to the day when many of you here present will be winning honours for honourable achievements, and giving the world assurance that the College is a worthy mother of worthy children—a place where all may learn to love what is best and purest and noblest—both in music and in other products of human skill and devotion; so that in the days to come we may all look back to having taken our part in making our College a centre from which light and enlightenment may radiate through all the country.

Beethoven's Symphonies

Article in the *Saturday Review*, 14 November 1896

"Beethoven and his Nine Symphonies." By George Grove, C.B. London and New York: Novello, Ewer & Co. 1896.

On cold Saturday afternoons in winter, as I sit in the theatrical desert, making my bread with great bitterness by chronicling insignificant plays and criticizing incompetent players, it sometimes comes upon me that I have forgotten something—omitted something—missed some all-important appointment. This is a legacy from my old occupation of musical critic. All my old occupations leave me such legacies. When I was in my teens I had certain official duties to perform, which involved every day the very strict and punctual discharge of certain annual payments, which were set down in a perpetual diary. I sometimes dream now that I am back at those duties again, but with an amazed consciousness of having allowed them to fall into ruinous arrear for a long time past. My Saturday afternoon misgivings are just like that. They mean that for several years I passed those afternoons in that section of the gallery of the Crystal Palace concert-room which is sacred to Sir George Grove and to the Press. There were two people there who never grew older—Beethoven and Sir George. August Manns's hair changed from raven black to swan white as the years passed; young critics grew middle-aged and middle-aged critics grew old; Rossini lost caste and was shouldered into the promenade; the fire-new overture to Tannhäuser began to wear as threadbare as "William Tell"; Arabella Goddard went and Sophie Menter came; Joachim, Hallé, Norman Neruda and Santley no longer struck the rising generations with the old sense of belonging to to-morrow, like Isaye, Paderewski and Bispham; the men whom I had shocked as an iconoclastic upstart Wagnerian, braying derisively when they observed that "the second subject, appearing in the key of the dominant, contrasts effectively with its predecessor, not only in tonality, but by its suave, melodious character," lived to see me shocked and wounded in my turn by the audacities of J.F.R.; new evening papers launched into musical criticism, and were read publicly by Mr Smith, the eminent drummer, whenever he had fifty bars rest; a hundred trifles marked the flight of time; but Sir George Grove fed on Beethoven's symphonies as the gods in "Das Rheingold" fed on the apples of Freia, and grew no older. Sometimes, when Mendelssohn's Scotch symphony, or Schubert's Ninth in C, were in the program, he got positively younger, clearing ten years backward in as many minutes when Manns and the band were at their best. I remonstrated with him more than once on this unnatural conduct; and he was always extremely apologetic, assuring me that he was getting on as fast as he could. He even succeeded in producing a wrinkle or two under stress of Berlioz and Raff, Liszt and Wagner; but presently some pianist would come along with the concerto in E flat; and then, if I sat next him, strangers would say to me "Your son, sir, appears to be a very enthusiastic musician." And I could not very well explain that the real bond between us was the fact that Beethoven never ceased to grow on us. In my personality, my views, and my style of criticism there was so much to forgive that many highly amiable persons never quite succeeded in doing it. To Sir George I must have been a positively obnoxious person, not in the least because I was on the extreme left in politics and other matters, but because I openly declared that the finale of Schubert's symphony in C could have been done at half the length and with twice the effect by Rossini. But I knew Beethoven's symphonies from the opening bar of the first to the final chord of the ninth, and yet made new discoveries about them at every fresh performance. And I am convinced that "G" regarded this as evidence of a fundamental rectitude in me which would bear any quantity of superficial aberrations. Which is quite my own opinion too.

It may be asked why I have just permitted myself to write of so eminent a man as Sir George Grove by his initial. That question would not have been asked thirty years ago, when "G", the rhapsodist who wrote the Crystal Palace programs, was one of the best ridiculed men in London. At that time the average programmist would unblushingly write, "Here the composer, by one of those licenses which are, perhaps, permissible under exceptional circumstances to men of genius, but which cannot be too carefully avoided by students desirous of forming a legitimate style, has abruptly introduced the dominant seventh of the key of C major into the key of A flat, in order to recover, by a forced modulation, the key relationship proper to the second subject of a movement in F—an awkward device which he might have spared himself by simply introducing his second subject in its true key of C." "G," who was "no musician," cultivated this style in vain. His most conscientious attempts at it never brought him any nearer than "The lovely melody then passes, by a transition of remarkable beauty, into the key of C major, in which it seems to go straight up to heaven." Naturally the average Englishman was profoundly impressed by the inscrutable learning of the first style (which I could teach to a poodle in two hours), and thought "G's" obvious sentimentality idiotic. It did not occur to the average Englishman that perhaps Beethoven's symphonies were an affair of sentiment and nothing else. This, of course, was the whole secret of them. Beethoven was the first man who used music with absolute integrity as the expression of his own emotional life. Others had shown how it could be done—had done it themselves as a curiosity of their art in rare, self-indulgent, *unprofessional* moments—but Beethoven made this, and nothing else, his business. Stupendous as the resultant difference was between his music and any other ever heard in the world before his time, the distinction is not clearly apprehended to this day, because there was nothing new in the musical expression of emotion: every progression in Bach is sanctified by emotion; and Mozart's subtlety, delicacy, and exquisite tender touch and noble feeling were the despair of all the musical world. But Bach's theme was not himself, but his religion; and Mozart was always the dramatist and story-teller, making the men and women of his imagination speak, and dramatizing even the instruments in his orchestra, so that you know their very sex the moment their voices reach you. Haydn really came nearer to Beethoven, for he is neither the praiser of God nor the dramatist, but, always within the limits of good manners and of his primary function as a purveyor of formal decorative music, a man of moods. This is how he created the symphony and put it ready-made into Beethoven's hand. The revolutionary giant at once seized it, and, throwing supernatural religion, conventional good manners, dramatic fiction, and all external standards and objects into the lumber room, took his own humanity as the material of his music, and expressed it all without compromise, from his roughest jocularity to his holiest aspiration after that purely human reign of intense life—of "Freude"—when

"Alle Menschen werden Brüder
Wo dein sanfter Flügel weilt."

In thus fearlessly expressing himself, he has, by his common humanity, expressed us as well, and shown us how beautifully, how strongly, how trustworthily we can build with our own real selves. This is what is proved by the immense superiority of the Beethoven symphony to any oratorio or opera.

In this light all Beethoven's work becomes clear and simple; and the old nonsense about his obscurity and eccentricity and stage sublimity and so on explains itself as pure misunderstanding. His criticisms, too, become quite consistent and inevitable: for instance, one is no longer tempted to resent his declaration that Mozart wrote nothing worth considering but parts of "Die Zauberflöte" (those parts, perhaps, in which the beat of "dein sanfter Flügel" is heard), and to retort upon him by silly comparisons of his tunes with "Non più andrai" and "Deh vieni alla finestra." The man who wrote the Eighth symphony has a right to rebuke the man who put his raptures of elation, tenderness, and nobility into the mouths of a drunken libertine, a silly peasant girl, and a conventional fine lady, instead of confessing them to himself, glorying in them, and uttering them without motley as the universal inheritance.

I must not make "G" responsible for my own opinions; but I leave it to his old readers whether his huge success as a program writer was not due to the perfect simplicity with which he seized and followed up this clue to the intention of Beethoven's symphonies. He seeks always for the mood, and is not only delighted at every step by the result of his search, but escapes quite easily and unconsciously from the boggling and blundering of the men who are always wondering why Beethoven did not do what any professor would have done. He is always joyous, always successful, always busy and interesting, never tedious even when he is superfluous (not that the adepts ever found him so), and always as pleased as Punch when he is not too deeply touched. Sometimes, of course, I do not agree with him. Where he detects anger in the Eighth symphony, I find nothing but boundless, thundering elation. In his right insistence on the jocular element in the symphonies, I think he is occasionally led by his personal sense that octave skips on the bassoon and drum are funny to conclude too hastily that Beethoven was always joking when he used them. And I will fight with him to the death on the trio of the Eighth symphony, maintaining passionately against him and against all creation that those cello arpeggios which steal on tiptoe round the theme so as not to disturb its beauty are only "fidgety" when they are played "à la Mendelssohn," and that they are perfectly tender and inevitable when they are played "à la Wagner." The passage on this point in Wagner's essay on Conducting is really not half strong enough; and when "G" puts it down to "personal bias" and Wagner's "poor opinion of Mendelssohn," it is almost as if some one had accounted in the same way for Beethoven's opinion of Mozart. Wagner was almost as fond of Mendelssohn's music as "G" is; but he had suffered unbearably, as we all have, from the tradition established by Mendelssohn's conducting of Beethoven's symphonies. Mendelssohn's music is all nervous music: his allegros, expressing only excitement and impetuosity without any ground, have fire and motion without substance. Therefore the conductor must, above all things, *keep them going*; if he breaks their lambent flight to dwell on any moment of them, he is lost. With Beethoven the longer you dwell on any moment the more you will find in it. Provided only you do not sacrifice his splendid energetic rhythm and masterly self-possessed emphasis to a maudlin pre-occupation with his feeling, you cannot possibly play him too sentimentally; for Beethoven is no reserved gentleman, but a man proclaiming the realities of life. Consequently, when for generations they played Beethoven's allegros exactly as it is necessary to play the overture to "Ruy Blas," or "Stone him to death"—a practice which went on until Wagner's righteous ragings stopped it—our performances of the symphonies simply spoiled the tempers of those who really understood them. For the sake of redeeming that lovely trio from "fidgetiness," "G" must let us face this fact even at the cost of admitting that Wagner was right where Mendelssohn was wrong.

But though it is possible thus to differ here and there from "G," he is never on the wrong lines. He is always the true musician: that is, the man the professors call "no musician"—just what they called Beethoven himself. It is delightful to have all the old programs bound into a volume, with the quotations from the score all complete, and the information brought up to date, and largely supplemented. It is altogether the right sort of book about the symphonies, made for practical use in the concert-room under the stimulus of a heartfelt need for bringing the public to Beethoven. I hope it will be followed by another volume or two dealing with the pianoforte concertos—or say with the G, the E flat, the choral fantasia and the three classical violin concertos: Beethoven, Mendelssohn, and Brahms. And then a Schubert-Mendelssohn-Schumann volume. Why, dear G, should these things be hidden away in old concert programs which never circulate beyond Sydenham?   G. B. S.

Index of Works

Place of publication London unless otherwise indicated

I   Major engineering schemes with which Grove was associated:

Morant Point Lighthouse, Jamaica, 1841–2
Gibb's Hill Lighthouse, Bermuda, 1843–6
London and Birmingham Railway, 1846
Joint Railway Station, Chester, 1847–8
Britannia Tubular Bridge, Menai Straits, 1848–50

II   Books:

Geography, No. 4 of *History Primers*, ed. J. R. Green (1875)

Beethoven and his Nine Symphonies (1896); 2nd ed, 1896; 3rd ed, 1898; reprint London–New York, 1962

Beethoven und seine neun Symphonien, trans. Max Hehemann (London–New York 1906)

The Story of David's Early Life, Preface by W. Addis, privately printed after 1900[1]

Unfulfilled intentions included *A Dictionary of Persons* (1860); *Chinese Porcelain* (1873–4); *Handbook to the Bible* (1863); *Geography—a Class Book* (1877); biographies of Beethoven, Mendelssohn and Schubert, based on *Dictionary* articles (1887)[2]

III   Articles, lectures, miscellaneous contributions:

'On the floating of the Tubes of the Britannia Bridge', by 'A Correspondent', *The Spectator*, 23 June 1849

'Mathematical Principles exemplified in Common Things'; lecture at the Hall of Association, 18 Apr. 1853 (text not extant)

Analytical Notes, Crystal Palace Concerts 1856–96[3]

Preface to programme of the *St Matthew Passion* (Bach), 'Contributed by a Member of the [Bach] Society', for the 'second public performance', 'It is to be hoped that the Performance of the Passion will do something to disabuse the minds of our hearers of the notion which is but too prevalent, that Sebastian Bach was a mere manufacturer of mechanical difficulties—a writer for the eye and not for the ear.'[4]

---

[1] See p. 276, and Graves, p. 153.
[2] Dates indicate when these projects appear to have been in mind.
[3] Many of these Notes were revised and reissued in programmes of various musical organizations; see Richter Concerts.
[4] Detached from a programme, with no date remaining, in BL, 7898.o.12; 'G. Grove',

'Nábloos and the Samaritans', in F. Galton, *Vacation Tourists and Notes of Travel in 1861* (Cambridge, 1862)

articles in *A Dictionary of the Bible* (1863)

'On the Exploration of the Holy Land, as proposed by the Palestine Exploration Fund'; Report for the Geography and Ethnology Section of the British Association for the Advancement of Science; Birmingham Meeting commencing 6 Sept 1865

'On a Song in "The Princess",' *Shilling Magazine* III, February 1866

'Palestine Exploration Fund: A report on the Topographical Results of the First Expedition sent out by that Association, towards which, at the last Meeting, a grant of £100 had been sent by the General Committee'; Nottingham Meeting commencing 22 Aug 1866

'Tears, idle Tears', *Macmillan's Magazine* XV, November 1866

Miscellaneous items, undated, previous to 1867:

Two poems, MS.[5]

   (a) 'Across this Heart, Time, softly pass'
   (b) 'In the train'

'Palestine: Church of the Holy Sepulchre', with an Appeal from the Empress Eugénie 'to the Princesses of Europe' in the original French, with translation and commentary[6]

Syrian Legends: I, 'The Ant's Rock, and the Fisherman who thought he was wiser than God'; II, 'The Grapes of Darâya'[7]

Notice of a contribution by a Mr Mills on the general subject of the Samaritans, with reference to Nábloos[8]

'Recollections of Mendelssohn: by Professor [J.C.] Lobe, of Vienna' [?][9]

'Exploration of Jerusalem and the Holy Land'; lecture at the Institute of British Architects, Conduit Street, London, 17 February 1868[10]

'The New Testament under a New Aspect', *Macmillan's Magazine* XX, September 1869

---

in author's hand, appended. The Bach Society gave a first English performance, under Sterndale Bennett, in Hanover Square Rooms on 6 Apr 1854. A second performance, also under Bennett, took place in St Martin's Hall on 23 Mar 1858. See *Grove 1*, vol. I, p. 118; cf. 'Sebastian Bach's Music', p. 306.

[5] In commonplace book dated 22 Feb 1865 (RCM 2134, f.2v, f.6v).

[6] 'G. Grove' written in at end of unsigned article; no location given (BL, 7898.o.12).

[7] No location (BL, 7898.o.12).

[8] No location (BL, 7898.o.12).

[9] See *Grove 1*, vol. II, p. 310. Lobe was active in Weimar and Leipzig—not in Vienna—as journalist and critic. These 'Recollections', from Lobe's *Fliegende Blätter* (Leipzig, 1853), in unacknowledged English translation with no location given in BL, 7898.o.12, may have been the work of Mimi von Glehn.

[10] Reported in *The Times*, 18 Feb 1868.

'Mr Deutsch and the "Edinburgh Review",' *Macmillan's Magazine* XXVIII, August 1873

articles in *A Dictionary of Music and Musicians* (1879–89)

Analytical Notes, Richter Concerts, St James's Hall, May 1879

'Beethoven's Symphonies', Introduction to the performance of the nine symphonies during the series commencing 10 May 1880

Daily News, 27 Sept 1881, unsigned contribution on the opening of the fifth season of the Sacred Harmonic Society. 'The society restored and fully established the practice of giving complete oratorios instead of selections made up of fragments detached from the several works to which they belonged'. The Society also 'exhibited the wealth of our English cathedral music', superintended nine Handel Festivals, provided music for International Exhibitions, and gave the first London performance of the *St Matthew Passion* in its entirety

'Western Palestine', *Pall Mall Gazette*, 25 Oct 1881. Concerning the issue of a map by the Palestine Exploration Fund, embodying the work of Wilson, Warren, Conder, Kitchener and others on the west bank of the Jordan

The Times, 10 June 1882; obituary notice of J. Scott Russell (unsigned)

St James's Gazette, 6 Oct 1883. On the derivation of Phoenix Park, Dublin, from the Gaelic fionn-uski (clear water) a spring so named in the environs of Dublin[11]

Pall Mall Gazette: 16 Oct 1883. A critic, noticing the Leeds Festival (*The Times*, 13 Oct), regretted Sullivan's departure from 'serious music'. Grove pointed out how Mozart showed that music could be both 'light' and 'masterly', and that Sullivan did the same, as, for example, in the Lord Chancellor's song in *Iolanthe* (Act II)

Pall Mall Gazette:

The Times critic remarked on the performance of a duet from *Kenilworth*, 'which made me regret two things – first that the conductor of the Leeds Festival has included so little of his own music in the programme; second, that of late he has afforded so few opportunities for serious and appreciative criticism'.

30 Nov 1883. Concerning a 'complete and trustworthy edition of Schubert'[12]

4 December 1883. Concerning the error contained in the A.V. of Proverbs 1:17, and corrected by a Cambridge scholar to accord with the likely practice of Solomon, who was, Grove suggested, an experienced bird-watcher

---

[11] Unless otherwise stated, contributions by Grove to the *St James's* and the *Pall Mall Gazette* were anonymous and appeared in the section in each journal entitled 'Occasional Notes'.

[12] Cf. *The Times*, 6 Nov 1883.

1 May 1884. 'The Secret of Sir Michael Costa's Success', by 'A Correspondent'

St James's Gazette:
At this period Grove was indefatigable in contributing material to this journal. Graves (p. 312) identifies some contributions as positively by Grove, but states that more were written. The most likely contributions from Grove are listed below. Where there is confirmation in Graves the item is marked*

10 May 1886. Brahms's use of chaconne form in the Fourth Symphony; ' . . .we are told that at some of the performances in the German towns, where the symphony has been already heard, and where "analytical notes" are at a discount, a good deal of embarrassment was caused by the structure of the finale not being quickly recognised'*

12 May, after Richter's performance of the symphony; ' . . . how overwhelming is the effect of the enormous power of Brahms's genius. He is like Carlyle's favourite Indian, who had fire enough in his belly to burn up every one else.' Because of the difficulty of the work and also of having opportunity of hearing it in the near future, the writer suggests: 'Music has now grown so full of contrivance and thought, that even practised musicians require more than one hearing before they can take it in'*[13]

17 May, Sarasate concerts[14]

19 May, Rubinstein's 'Historical Concerts'

21 May, Saint-Saëns's cadenzas for Beethoven's Fourth Pianoforte Concerto, Philharmonic Concert (cond. Sullivan)

1 June, Carl Rosa performance of *Figaro*

2 June, political implications of music at Dinners of City Companies

4 June, comment on German reactions to *The Mikado* production in Berlin

7 June, parody of 'The Analytical Programme' (letter signed 'T'.), for or against Grove, as the reader wishes

10 June, response to commuter's comment on 5 June that suburban railway travel was indescribably bad; 'these things', wrote Grove, 'are enough to lash a quiet man, regularly travelling on this trying line [Brighton], to madness, but for the thick spirit of stolid forbearance which seems to distinguish every Englishman'*

11 June, brain drain of musicians from Germany exemplified by the departure from Berlin of Lilli Lehmann

14 June, poor attendance at Hallé–Neruda concert on 12 June blamed on there being too many concerts; Stanley's regret at never having had one of his works in the Tauchnitz Edition, and his envy of the Revd F. W. Robertson of Trinity Chapel, Brighton, who had*

[13] Cf. C. L. Graves, *Hubert Parry* (1926), vol. I, p. 267.
[14] See p. 183.

15 June, comment on account in *The Times* (14 June) of 'opening' of a new organ, which was not once played at the ceremony*

26 June, article on 'Russian Music', on ethnicity in music

St James's Gazette, 2 Aug 1886: A Japanese visitor went to *The Mikado* in Hamburg, expecting to see a Japanese national production. He wrote to a newspaper to 'expose' the work as fraudulent

'A Blunder in "The Spectator",' *St James's Gazette*, 5 Aug 1886. On 31 July the *Spectator* printed a piece on the vagaries of Heidelberg professors. Grove discusses the vagaries of the writer of the article. One professor, for instance, 'did not disdain to attire himself in the dress of a street-musician and amuse an evening party with his "improvised organ-grinding". Improvisation by the handle of the barrel-organ! This is really too funny. It beats even George Eliot's famous description of the "sweet series of descending fifths"'

'A Country Church', *St James's Gazette*, 27 Sept 1886

'The History of a Musical Phrase attempted', *Musical World*, serially from 2 Oct 1886 (pp. 627–821 passim)

St James Gazette:

8 Oct 1886. The performance of Sullivan's *Golden Legend* leads Grove to consider the importance of libretti and to call for a closer alliance between poetry and music

8 Feb 1887, praise for H. E. Thorndike's singing of Schubert's *Waldesnacht* at Popular Concert on previous day

23 Feb, concerning Schubert's *Ganymed* performed at the Henschels' concert of previous day

23 April. 'There ought not to be much difficulty, writes a correspondent [Grove], in accounting for the treatment of Sir Arthur Sullivan's music by the Berlin newspapers, on which some new facts are given in the *Daily Telegraph*. It may all be summed up in the word Retaliation. Sir Arthur has never made any secret of his wish to have music in England performed by Englishmen. He delivered himself unmistakeably on the point some three years ago, in answer to an interviewer; and he has acted on the principle in the choice of the Philharmonic Band which he leads so magnificently. Whether he is right or wrong is not the question; but it is certain that the unfair and absurd judgements passed on the "Golden Legend" at Berlin, form the method which the persons who write the musical criticisms for the German papers have taken to shew their dislike of his opinion. They are no verdict on the merits of his work. The only wonder is that, with his cleverness and common sense, he did not foresee what was sure to happen'

The Times, 11 May 1887; obituary of C. F. Pohl (unsigned)

'Beethoven', *Musical Times* XXVIII, June 1887; unsigned review of *Zweite Beethoveniana, Nachgelassene Aufsätze von Gustav Nottebohm* (Leipzig, 1887)

Address to the College of Organists, reported in the *Musical World*, 10 Sept 1887: ' . . . Nothing is more remarked on by the German musicians who visit England than the prevalence of organists. They say it has coloured our national music. So it may have done, but I do not see that the colour need necessarily be an unpleasant one. Sebastian Bach was an organist'

'The C minor Symphony [Beethoven]', *Musical World*, 3 Nov 1888. Its possible connection with Count Oppersdorf

'Canon by Mendelssohn', *Musical World*, 1 Dec 1888.[15] About an enigmatic canon written as a thank-offering for Paul David and C. Weisse, who had sent Mendelssohn a delicacy from their dinner table. Having quoted the music, Grove observes: 'I commend it to the ingenuity of your readers. They will notice that the 12 bars, from the signature $\frac{3}{4}$ (which apparently abolishes the B flat) are from the Trio to Beethoven's Quartet in E flat, op. 74. Whether the mysterious minims which stand under the first three bars are a continuation of the minim phrase which ends the canon or not, I do not presume to judge. I have given the whole as it stands on the autograph. I am sometimes tempted to fancy it may be a mere hoax.' Grove also quotes a canon 2 in 1 for two violins, 'written by Mendelssohn in the book of Mr Parry, Birmingham 1846', also to be found in commonplace book RCM 2136, where there is an end-note: 'see *Mus. World* 1848 p. 534'. Cf. *Grove* 1, vol. II, p. 300

'Beethoven's Marches', *Musical World*, 29 Dec. 1888

'A Letter of Beethoven's', *Musical World*, 19 Oct 1889. Concerning a letter to C. Pleyel (26 Apr 1807) on exhibition in Paris

'Orlando Gibbons', 'Beethoven', and 'Handel', *Chambers' Cyclopaedia*, 1890[16]

'Royal College of Music Scholarships', *Musical Herald*, Apr 1891. For the benefit of future candidates in answer to a request from the Editor after the examinations recently held

'Madame Sophie Löwe's Concert', *Pall Mall Gazette*, 6 May 1891. Sophie Löwe had mainly devoted herself to teaching since her marriage (see p. 181). A concert arranged by her in the Prince's Hall on 5 May was primarily for her pupils of whom Louisa Dale, a soprano, created a favourable impression (*Musical Times* XXXII, June 1891). Grove drew attention to Mme Löwe's artistry in songs by Sullivan, Bizet and Krüger. She was accompanied by Henry Bird, and Agnes Zimmermann contributed pianoforte solos

'The Birds in the "Pastoral Symphony" ', *Musical Times* XXXIII, Dec 1892

Address at Dinner of College of Organists, 8 May 1893: 'Last Monday I was Chairman at the dinner of the College of Organists and I assure you I made quite a nice speech—was quite at my ease and let myself go and had quite a nice time. The report is very poor (in the Musical News)

---

[15] Unsigned, copy in BL, 7898.o.12, 'G.' added by hand.
[16] Copies in BL, 7898.o.12; only the last acknowledged by addition of 'G.'.

I corrected it all carefully, but somehow the printer neglected my proof, and I am quite ashamed of it'; E.O., Sunday May 14 [1893]

'English Music', *Strand Musical Magazine*, Feb 1895

'A Few Words on the Successive Editions of Beethoven's Ninth Symphony', *P.M.A.* XXI, 1894–5: paper read on 12 Feb 1895

Address at Sydenham High School for Girls, 4 Apr 1895; report in the *Sydenham, Forest Hill, and Penge Gazette*, 6 Apr 1895

The Times, 18 Jan 1896; obituary of G. Watson (unsigned)[17]

'Madame Schumann', by a 'Special Contributor', the *Scottish Musical Record*, June 1896

'Explanatory Notes by Sir George Grove, C.B.', for a performance of *Israel in Egypt* (Handel), at Windsor, 26 Mar 1896

Musical Times XXXIX, Apr 1898; brief appreciation of Joachim

IV Edited, or translated:

The Fine Arts, their Nature and Relations (trans of F. Guizot, *Etudes sur les beaux arts en général*, Paris, 1852) (1853)

A. P. Stanley, *Sinai and Palestine* (1865)

W. Smith, *A Dictionary of the Bible* (1863)

S. Clark, Rector of Eaton Bishop, *The Bible Atlas of Maps and Plans to illustrate the Geography and Topography of the Old and New Testaments and the Apocrypha with Explanatory Notes . . .* and *Complete Index of the Geographical Names in the English Bible by George Grove* (1868/1900)

Macmillan's Magazine, 1868–83

An Atlas of Ancient Geography, Biblical and Classical (1874)

[W.] Franklin Taylor, *Primer of Pianoforte Playing* (1877, 1890, 1906)

A Dictionary of Music and Musicians (*A.D. 1450–1889*), 4 vols., 1879, 1880, 1883, 1889; Index by Mrs Edmond Wodehouse separately issued 1890; with Appendix, edited by J. A. Fuller Maitland, and Index (London/New York, 1898); Second Edition, ed. J. A. Fuller Maitland, 5 vols. (Appendix) (London/New York, 1904–10); Third Edition, ed. H. C. Colles, 5 vols. (London/New York, 1927); Fourth Edition, ed. H. C. Colles, 5 vols. (with Supplement) (London/New York, 1940); Fifth Edition, ed. E. Blom, 9 vols., 1954 (Supplement, ed. D. Stevens, 1961); Sixth Edition (*The New Grove*), ed. S. Sadie (London/Washington, 1980)

L. H. Berlioz, *Autobiography*, trans. Rachel Scott Russell Holmes and Eleanor Holmes, 2 vols. (1884)[18]

[17] Copy in BL, 7898.o.12, with 'G' and wrong date (18 Feb 1895) written in.

[18] In December 1881 the *Athenaeum* announced that the *Mémoires* of Berlioz, translated by Mrs W. H. Holmes, and edited 'with such notes as may be desirable from the 2 volumes of Berlioz's letters and other sources' by Grove, would be published by Macmillan. This edition had a long life and was the basis for E. Newman's 1932 edition.

V   Prefaces and appendixes:

Kreissle von Hellborn, *Life of Schubert*, trans. A. D. Coleridge (1869), Appendix.

F. Hiller, Mendelssohn: *Letters and Recollections*, trans. M. E. von Glehn (1874); Preface, 24 June

S. Hensel, *The Mendelssohn Family*, trans. C. Klingemann and an American collaborator, 2 vols. (1881); Advertisement, 31 Aug

O. Jahn, *Life of Mozart*, trans. P. D. Townsend, 3 vols. (1882); Preface

W. S. Rockstro, *The Life of George Frederick Handel* (1883); Notice, 23 May

A. Fay, *Music-Study in Germany* (Chicago, 1880; London, 1885); Preface, Dec 1885

A Short History of Cheap Music (1887); Preface 14 June

Early Letters of R. Schumann, originally published by his Wife (Jugendbriefe, trans. M. Herbert) (1888); Preface, 14 Oct 1887

F. G. Edwards, *The History of Mendelssohn's Oratorio 'Elijah'* (1896); Introduction

VI Letters to the Editor:

'Sebastian Bach's Music' (signed 'Constant Reader'), *Spectator*, 11 June 1853

'The Holy Plays in Bavaria' (Munich, 28 Aug, signed 'G.G.'), *The Times*, 5 Sept 1860

'Jerusalem explored', *The Times*, 7 Mar 1864

'Pierotti's Jerusalem', *The Times*, 21 Mar 1864

'Palestine Exploration', *The Times*, 3 Jan 1865

'The Crystal Palace Concerts', *The Times*, 21 Feb 1865

'Palestine Exploration Fund', *The Times*, 17 Jan, 12, 21 Feb, 3, 9, 23 Apr, 21 May 1866; 5 Aug, 26 Sept, 14 Nov, 4 Dec 1867

'Titian's "Peter Martyr" ', *The Times*, 3 Sept 1867. One of 131 water-colour copies of pictures in continental churches and museums available from the Crystal Palace. (It is probable that this was selected not least on account of Mendelssohn, who saw the original in the Franciscan Church, Venice, as he wrote to C. F. Zelter on 16 Oct 1830)

'A Renewed Eruption of Vesuvius' ('Naples, 4 April'), *Pall Mall Gazette*, 13 Apr 1868

'A Discovery in Jerusalem', *The Times*, 7 Jan 1869. Lt C. Warren's findings concerning the north wall platform of the Mosque of Omar; request for donations to be sent to W. Besant, W. Morrison, M.P., or J. Abel-Smith M.P.

'On the Moabitish Antiquities', *The Times*, 10 Feb, 24 Mar 1870. The claims of Warren, Clermont Ganneau, and 'Mr. Klein of the Prussian community in Jerusalem' in respect of the discovery of the 'Moabite Stone'. Cf. *Illustrated London News* LVI, p. 505

'A Conscientious Parish Clerk' (submitted by 'G.G.'), *Pall Mall Gazette*, 18 Apr 1870. A letter (with a touch of Sterne in its style) said to have been sent to his incumbent by a parish clerk in Yorkshire, taken from the *Whitehaven Herald*. The clerk, dissatisfied with his wages, threatened to leave; but relented—concluding his letter, 'Now Sir, I shall go on, with my fees the same as I found them, and will make no more trouble about them; but I will not—I cannot—leave you nor my delightful duties'

'The Survey of Palestine', *The Times*, 10 Nov 1871. Announcing that the autumn expedition had set out

'The Palestine Exploration Fund', *The Times*, 15 Aug 1873. A tribute to Clermont Ganneau, a fine scholar, speaking Arabic like a native, given sabbatical leave by the French Consulate in Jerusalem to assist in exploration

'Palestine Exploration', *The Times*, 14, 19 Oct, 2, 17 Dec 1874. Inscriptions in Hebrew discovered by Ganneau and Conder cut into rock, likely to interest Adolf Neubauer, the chief Talmudic scholar in England since the death of Deutsch; Ganneau at Gaza; Conder and Kitchener at Hebron; support for the Fund from London City Companies

'The Palestine Exploration', *The Times*, 5 Aug 1875. Conder's party of 15 attacked by Muslim tribesmen on account of being Christians; after infliction of casualties on explorers and loss of equipment attackers driven off by Turkish soldiers

'Mr Manns and Flamingo', *Musical World*, 19 Feb 1876. Letter dated 15 Feb about 'Flamingo's' [nom de plume of a contributor] attempt to credit Grove instead of Manns in a letter published on 12 Feb

'Palestine Exploration', *The Times*, 28 Mar 1877

'Welsh Nomenclature', *The Times*, 8 Jan 1878

' "La Marseillaise" and "God save the Queen" ', *The Times*, 4 Feb 1878. Lord Houghton had ascribed the latter to Lully; letter from Grove to T. L. Southgate published

'St. Mark's, Venice', *The Times*, 27 June 1881. Suggests publication of a book detailing its sculptures and inscriptions for the benefit of tourists

'Another Unknown Symphony by Schubert', *Daily News*, 27 Sept, *The Times*, 28 Sept 1881. The so-called 'Gastein' Symphony; recollection of previous works by Schubert thought to have been lost, but found; reference to Vienna excursion of Grove and Sullivan in 1867[19]

'A Musical Explorer', *The Times*, 21 Nov 1882. Complaining of inadequate notices of G. Nottebohm (d. 29 Oct)

'The Sacred Harmonic Society Library', *The Times*, 25 Nov 1882. Correction of report that the RCM (which had no funds for the purpose) had purchased a collection, which had, however, been 'secured for its use'

'An Incident for the Psychic Society', *The Times*, 21 May 1883. On 6 Sept 1874 Pape, principal clarinettist of the Crystal Palace Orchestra, died.

[19] See O. E. Deutsch, *Schubert* (1946), p. 131.

On 8 Sept Grove wrote to Manns asking for the time of the funeral so that he could attend. The letter reached Manns on 1 May 1883. It had stuck in the letterbox to be discovered when, nine years later, the box was removed for repairs to the lock. Three hours after the letter had come to light, but unaware of the fact, Grove remarked to Manns how Pape would have enjoyed a clarinet passage in the Schubert symphony being played. He did not learn of the arrival of his letter until after the rehearsal

'Imagery of the Psalms', *The Times*, 14 Aug 1883. Different translations of the Hebrew word *tsinnor* in 2 Samuel 5:8, and Psalm XLII ('water-brooks')

'The Songs of Schubert', *The Times*, 6 Nov 1883. Appeal for material likely to be useful to M. Friedländer in preparing a new edition for Peters, for which M. Müller had promised a Preface

'September Primroses', *The Times*, 10 Sept 1885. A correspondent's query answered by Grove's quoting the last stanza of Canto LXXXV, *In Memoriam*:

> Ah, take the imperfect gift I bring,
> Knowing the primrose yet is dear,
> The Primrose of the later year,
> As not unlike to that of Spring.

'A Concerto by Beethoven', *The Times*, 10 Dec 1885. Quoting from a German source, on 8 Dec *The Times* stated that M. Friedländer had found the MS. of a Sixth Pianoforte Concerto by Beethoven in a Carinthian village. Grove mentioned how he had once written about one movement of a concerto discovered by Nottebohm in a Crystal Palace note[20]

'Sunday Music', *The Times*, 22 Mar 1886

'The Dream of St Jerome', *The Times*, 16 June 1886. How Thackeray, in *Philip*, invents a piece by Beethoven—the 'Dream of St Jerome'—having misinterpreted a title of Thomas Moore, 'Who is the Maid? St Jerome's Love—Air Beethoven [from op. 26]'[21]

'Tom Moore', *Irish Times*[22]

'New Musical Publications', *The Times*, 6 Sept 1886. Written from Saltburn; about the Beethoven and Schubert editions, and the Centenary Edition of music by Friedrich II of Prussia, in preparation by Breitkopf & Härtel, Leipzig

'The Gastein Symphony', *Musical World*, Oct 1886

[20] See L. Lockwood, 'Beethoven's Unfinished Piano Concerto of 1815', *The Creative World of Beethoven*, ed. P. H. Lang (New York, 1971), p. 122.

[21] 'Lovers of two of the very greatest names in literature and music will be grateful to Sir George Grove for his letter [on the *Dream of St Jerome*]', *St James's Gazette*, 16 June 1886.

[22] This letter is indicated by Graves (p. 313) as having appeared in the *Irish Times* of 16 July 1886, but it does not seem to have been published there on that or any other day in July.

'Brahms and Beethoven', *St James's Gazette*, 2 Nov 1886; written on
1 Nov in respect of an article in the *Daily Telegraph* of that day. Grove
signed himself 'P'

> ... it is surely not the sober and learned writer who usually reports
> for the *Telegraph*, but some Phaeton of the moment. Brahms is advised
> 'not to write in his study', but 'to go into the largeness of the world;
> let the generous sights and sounds of nature work upon him, as
> Beethoven did, and catch their spirit', etc. What 'largeness of the
> world' did Beethoven enjoy, who worked in his room for six or seven
> hours daily; whose recreation was a run round the ramparts of Vienna
> in the afternoon, stopping every now and then to drop a thought into
> his sketch-book; whose dinner was taken in a stuffy little pot-house,
> where his absence of mind and deafness cut him off from all com-
> munication with 'the world' but such as could be got by shouting at
> him? True, he spent his holidays in the country; but it is notorious
> that Brahms is an insatiable lover of the open air. This very year the
> beautiful country on the lake of Thun was his summer resting-place
> for months. In conversation, too, he is one of the most genial and
> humorous of men.
>
> Such criticisms as those I allude to are more than foolish: they
> show an ignorance of the history of music as well as of the principles
> on which it should be judged

Grove also pointed out that it had taken half a century for Beethoven's
works to find general acceptance, and that those of Schumann were
'still occasionally sneered at'

'The Performance of Oratorios', *The Times*, 7 Dec 1886. Having heard
Sullivan's *Golden Legend* on 4 Dec Grove contrasted its conventional
manner of performance with that of Schumann's *Faust* in Bonn in 1873,
in which Stockhausen introduced dramatic gestures. Approving such
an aid to interpretation Grove also asked whether oratorio performances
would not be further improved by sinking orchestra and conductor in
Wagnerian manner, and by using a smaller chorus. He was thinking
along lines which in due course led to dramatization of Handelian oratorio.
Commenting on this letter in the *Musical Times* XXVIII, Jan 1887,
a writer touched the subject with facetiousness: 'By the way, a part of the
"Golden Legend" is supposed to be sung on horseback. How would
Sir George convey that idea in a realistic manner?'

'The Crystal Palace', *The Times*, 9 Feb 1887. Issuing their Annual Report,
the Directors warned that because of an unfavourable financial situation
they would need to 'review their position'. In interest the Company
was obliged to pay £27,000 annually to its Shareholders. In 1886 the
income fell short of this sum by £10,000. Anticipating that the orchestral
concerts, as well as other cultural events, might fall victim to panic
economy measures, Grove asked that the directors should remember the
great potential of the institution, quoting Kingsley and Lord Shaftesbury
on its importance in the lives of the 'poor', and Cardinal Manning's
description of it as 'the largest and best place of rational recreation in

the kingdom'. On 19 Feb a public meeting was held in Norwood, when various ideas for maintaining the Palace were put forward. These included the novel idea of a 'subvention from the nation'

'Persian Hyperbole', *St James's Gazette*, 21 Feb 1887. Mention of the Thames Tunnel reminds Grove of a group of Persian princes who were in England in 1837, soon after the completion of the tunnel, which they described 'with inimitable naiveté, as a contrivance "for making ships pass over the heads of the people" '. He continues to draw attention to oddities of expression in general among 'Oriental' people

'A Symphony by Richard Wagner', *The Times*, 4 Oct 1887. The C major symphony of 1832 was played under Henschel to an almost empty St James's Hall on 29 Nov. Although in anticipation of this performance Grove regarded it as of equal importance with the first Palace performance of the 'Unfinished' in 1867, he was angry at an evident lack of idealism.

'I cannot close this letter', he wrote,

without expressing my deep regret at the commercial spirit in which the interesting discovery is being treated by Wagner's representatives, who have sold the right of performance at a price so enormous as to make it almost prohibitory. . . . Such action is a serious blow to those who, like myself, are striving to raise music in this country from the dependent position into which it has been thrown by our extreme devotion to business and politics. But how is this to be done when the maxims of the shop are thus carried into the purest of the arts by those from whom we should least expect it—by the countrymen of the great composer, who have set us such bright examples of indifference to gain. It really looks as if money is destined to reign everywhere and over everything.

'The Royal College of Music', *The Times*, 30 Jan 1888. Concerning Samson Fox's offer announced on 27 Jan

'Warning about a Person calling himself Dr Heinrich Pauer', *The Times*, 29 June 1889. An impostor claiming the name Pauer, and connection with the RCM, where Ernst was a professor and his son Max had been a student

'Grattan Cooke and Mendelssohn', *The Times*, 18 Sept 1889. Grattan Cooke, oboist, after the first rehearsal of *Elijah* complained that he had no solo in the work, whereupon the composer took the score and inserted the long-held C against the boy's 'There is nothing . . .' (no. 19)

'The Schubert Monument at Vienna', *The Times*, 2 Oct 1889. ' . . . an unhappy monument . . . so incorrect and inadequate a representation'

'Leeds Festival', *The Times*, 28 Oct 1889. The substance of this letter is repeated in *Beethoven and his Nine Symphonies*, p. 370

'The Encore Nuisance', *St James's Gazette*, 29 Jan 1890. Sims Reeves had written to the *Daily Graphic*, complaining that encores were out of place at musical performances. On 28 Jan 'A Singer' put the case for encores, and Grove, on the same day, wrote to approve of that letter, observing that Mozart, Mendelssohn and Beethoven all welcomed a show of audience enthusiasm

'Madame Arabella Goddard', *The Times*, 4, 15 Mar 1890. As Mme Goddard was ill and unable either to perform or to teach, Grove appealed for subscriptions. Her son, Henry Davison, was displeased, accusing Grove of putting out misleading statements. Grove replied that what he had written was correct, and implying that the family of Mme Goddard were doing more talking than anything else to assist her

'The Arabella Goddard Concert', *The Times*, 27 Mar 1890. A 'Benefit Concert' realized almost £600 and there was a donation from well-wishers in Belfast through Charlotte Milligan, the old RCM student

'Education in Music in Ireland', *Daily Graphic*, 31 July 1890. John H. MacMahon, M.A., LL.D., a sardonic bachelor and barrister, and brother of Ella MacMahon, author of Irish tales and novels (contributor to *Blackwood's*), complained in a letter to this paper that Irish students were debarred from studying in the RCM. Grove, with special interest in Irish students, corrected him: 'Ireland is, fortunately, still a part of the United Kingdom, and, therefore, the advantages of the College being offered to all her Majesty's subjects indiscriminately, are open to the natives of the Green Isle. . . .' He listed eleven scholars and seven paying students who had come to the College from Ireland. He also observed: 'Miss Oldham is carrying out the principles which she was taught in the College as a professor of the piano in the Royal Irish Academy and elsewhere in Dublin'

'The Cat's Toilette', *Spectator*, 4 Oct 1890

'An Interesting Event in English Musical History', *The Times*, 26 Feb 1891

'Beethoven's Orchestra', *Musical News*, 27 Mar 1891

'Examples of $\frac{5}{4}$ time in German popular Song', *Musical News*, 1 May 1891. In particular, 'Zelte, Poste, Wera-tu-fu' and C. Löwe, 'Prinz Eugen der edle Ritter'

'The Autographs of Beethoven's Manuscripts', *The Times*, 15 Sept 1891. Concerning the autographs of Symphonies 4, 5, and 7, owned by Ernst von Mendelssohn, and of the orchestral parts of nos. 8 and 9 in the Royal Library, Berlin, all of which Grove had examined. A suggestion that facsimiles should be produced

'Lord Rodney', *Spectator*, 21 Oct 1891

'Facsimiles of Beethoven's Works', *The Times*, 22 Dec 1891. Breitkopf & Härtel to undertake production. Patrons include the Queen, the Prince of Wales, Prince Christian, Parry, Herkomer, A. J. Balfour, E. W. Hamilton, and Spencer Lyttelton

'The Gloucester Festival Band' (signed 'Old Concert Goer'), *The Times*, 12 Sept 1892. Arising out of a comment by *The Times* critic that it was not until the playing of the 'Pastoral Symphony' (*Messiah*) on the last day that a pianissimo was heard. Grove disputed this, drawing attention to the previous day's performance of Beethoven's Fifth Symphony, which was distinguished by beautiful *pp* effects enhanced by the acoustics of the building

'Timbuctoo' and 'Jehoshaphat', *The Times*, 14, 22 Oct 1892. Contributions to typical *Times* correspondence, in this case concerning comic rhymes on these and other names

'The Royal College of Music', *Manchester Guardian*, 15 Oct 1892. Rebuking Hallé for saying that RCM students heard no music except what they themselves made

'Crossing the Bar', *Spectator*, 5 Nov 1892. About the epilogue of Tennyson's 'Tiresias' (*Tiresias and other Poems*, 1885) to E. Fitzgerald

'Beethoven's Letter to a Child' (signed 'G'), *Musical News*, 30 Dec 1892

'St Mary's Oxford', *The Times*, 17 Jan 1893. Stanley once held a conversation with Pope Pius IX, who declared his belief in the miraculous powers of one of the statues on the church

'Beethoven', *Spectator*, 27 May 1893. Protest against a sonnet by William Watson in which Beethoven is portrayed 'as though grief was his only characteristic'. On 10 June A. P. Graves defended Watson and drew attention to the verses of John Todhunter on music of a generation earlier, which anticipated Watson's sentiments

'Links with the Past', *Spectator*, 3 Feb 1894. Grove had known a lady who had once visited Joshua Reynolds's studio, and on other occasions had seen Nelson and Napoleon; a Sydenham postman whose grandfather's grandfather had been in Whitehall on the day of the execution of Charles I; and other persons with interesting connections with historical events and people

'Declaration on the Inspiration of the Scriptures', *Spectator*, 30 June 1894. On 23 June a statement under the above title had been issued by a group of Anglican clergymen led by William Bright, Professor of Ecclesiastical History in Oxford University. This was intended as guidance for those caught between theological liberals and fundamentalists. Grove pointed out that the Evangelists were 'ordinary orientals', untrained in research methods, and that it was reasonable to ask whether the sayings of Jesus represented precisely what he had said

'Mendelssohn and Schumann', *The Times*, 11 Sept 1894. Quotation of a letter from Mendelssohn to a London publisher (27 Jan 1844) pleading the cause of Schumann who wished to come to London for a performance of *Paradise and the Peri*, to rebut suggestions of animosity between the two composers

'A French Whittaker', *Spectator*, 19 Jan 1895. In a review of the *Almanach Hachette* (12 Jan) it was suggested that Frenchmen were not well informed in current affairs. Among examples of Frenchmen who provided evidence to the contrary Grove cited the Curé of Dijon with whom he had travelled in the Mediterranean in 1861 and who, said Grove, 'made me ashamed of my own ignorance of parallel matters at home'

Letter to J. Maxtone Graham, 22 Apr 1895, published by Graham in the *Strathearn Herald*, 27 Apr 1895:

I got the copy of the paper, and have read your lecture carefully, and congratulate you on having got through a very *difficult* task most successfully—wonderfully, indeed; and with an amount of tact and practical ability for which I envy you. It may interest you to know that Beethoven had a print of H.'s father's cottage hanging on his walls, and that he was delighted to show it. 'Fancy', he used to say, 'that great man was born in this mean cottage'. One of the last things that disturbed his death was that in putting a new frame on the print the frame maker had spelt the name 'Hayden': and blockhead was the smallest term he bestowed on him.

I am glad that you left out Bach; it would have been impossible to make him accessible to your audience. Handel, on the other hand, everyone has heard of. One hardly realises how familiar he is to the masses of England—I often think quite as much as Shakespeare. . . .

'Priestism', [journal uncertain] (signed 'Reader'), 14 May 1895.[23] High Church priests claimed the right 'to interfere between God and his creatures' in their 'power to absolve sin . . . which no orthodox Dissenter does'

'The Lamoureux Concerts', *Sunday Times*, 26 Apr 1896. Annoyed by a critic making comparisons too favourable to the French orchestra, Grove drew attention to the Crystal Palace Orchestra as one 'which [also] has played for years under the same conductor of the highest rank'.

Grove also pays tribute to his 'old friend', Mr Sturgeon of the Crystal Palace printing office, for his 'eminent services as music compositor'

'The Normal Diapason Pitch', *Leeds Mercury*, 12 Oct 1896. A letter, dated 7 Oct, from Grove to F. H. Spark, supporting adoption of 'normal diapason pitch' for the Leeds Town Hall organ, which was printed with similar messages from Mackenzie, Parry, Cummings, Stanford, Stainer, Parratt and Guilmant

'Shakespeare and the Thrush's Song', *The Times*, 2 Aug 1897

'Some Sydenham Disappearances', *Sydenham, Forest Hill, and Penge Gazette*, 25 Sept, 4 Oct 1897

'Rossini and Beethoven', *Spectator*, 16 Oct 1897. About a detail in a review of *Beethoven and his Nine Symphonies* by C. Bellaigue in the *Revue des deux mondes* (15 Aug)

---

[23] Cutting in BL, 7898.o.12, described as from the *St James's Gazette*, where, however, it is not to be found on that date.

Bibliography

The place of publication London unless otherwise stated

Allen, R., *Sir Arthur Sullivan, Composer and Personage* (New York, 1975)
Arnold, M., *Essays in Criticism* I, II (1865, 1888)

Banister, H. C., *Sir George Macfarren* (1891)[1]
Battley, J. R., *Clapham old yet ever new* (1937)
Baughan, P. E., *The Chester and Holyhead Railway* (Newton Abbot, 1972)
Beaver, P., *The Crystal Palace 1851–1936: A Victorian Portrait* (1970)
Bennett, J., *Forty Years of Music 1865–1905* (1908)
Bradley, C., *A Selection from the Sermons preached at High Wycombe, Glasbury and Clapham*, ed. G. J. Davies (1884)
Bradley, G. G., *Recollections of Arthur Penrhyn Stanley* (1883)
Breuning, G. von, *Aus dem Schwarzspanierhause* (Vienna, 1874)[2]
Bridge, F., *A Westminster Pilgrim* (1918)

Chadwick, O., *The Secularization of the European Mind in the Nineteenth Century* (Cambridge, 1975)
Chambers, W., *Memoirs of Robert Chambers with Autobiographic Reminiscences of William Chambers* (Edinburgh/London, 1872)
Chantel, F., *Biography of a Colonial Town—Hamilton, Bermuda* (Hamilton, 1961)
Chitty, S., *The Beast and the Monk: a Life of Charles Kingsley* (1974)
Cole, Sir Henry, K.G.B., *Fifty Years of Public Work of*, 2 vols. (1884)
Colloms, B., *Charles Kingsley: the Lion of Eversley* (1974)
Creighton, L., *Mandell Creighton: Life and Letters* 2 vols. (1904)
Cruse, A., *The Englishman and his Books in the Early Nineteenth Century* (1930)
Cundall, F., *Catalogue of the Portraits in the Jamaica History Gallery of the Institute of Jamaica* (Kingston, 1914)

Davison, H., *From Mendelssohn to Wagner: Memoirs of J. W. Davison* (1912)
Dayot, A., *Salon de 1884* (Paris, 1884)
Dealtry, W., *An Address at the Opening of the Clapham Literary and Scientific Institution, Tuesday, November 9, 1841* (Clapham, 1841)
Deutsch, O. E., *Schubert: a Documentary Biography* (1946)
Dickens, Charles, *Letters of, 1842–3*, ed. M. House, G. Storey, K. Tillotson, vol. III (Oxford, 1974)
Dickson, W. E., *Fifty Years of Church Music* (1894)[3]

---

[1] From Grove's Library (in Parry Room, RCM): 'G. Grove, Jan 28 1891'.
[2] From Grove's Library: 'Sept 19, 91'.
[3] From Grove's Library: 'G. Grove from the author'.

Edwards, D., *Leaders of the Church of England, 1828–1944* (1971)
Edwards, F. G., *The History of Mendelssohn's Oratorio 'Elijah'* (1896)[4]
——— 'Sir George Grove, C.B.', *Musical Times* XXXCIII, 1897, p. 657
Einstein, A., *Schubert* (1951, 1971)

Fay, A., *Music-Study in Germany* (Chicago, 1880; London, 1885)
Flood, W. H. G., 'Sir George Grove, a Centenary Appreciation', *Musical Times* LXI, 1920, p. 603
Fuchs, C., *Musical and other Recollections of Carl Fuchs, 'Cellist* (Manchester, 1937)

Gordon, A., M.Inst.C.E., *Lighthouses of the British Colonies and Possessions abroad, being a Letter to Joseph Hume, Esq., Chairman of the Lighthouse Committee of the House of Commons, 1845* (1847)
Graeme, E., *Beethoven, A Memoir*, with an Essay—Quasi Fantasia—on the hundredth year of his birth, by F. Hiller (1876)[5]
Graves, C. L., *The Life and Letters of Sir George Grove, C.B.* (1903)
——— *Post-Victorian Music, with other Studies and Sketches* (1911)
——— *Hubert Parry, His Life and Works*, 2 vols. (1926)
Greene, H. P., 'Leonard Borwick' in *From Blue Danube to Shannon* (1934)
——— *Charles Villiers Stanford* (1935)
Grove, J. W., *Old Clapham* (1887)

Hadow, W. H., 'Sir Hubert Parry' in *Collected Essays* (1928)
Haight, G. S., *George Eliot: a Biography* (Oxford, 1968)
Hammond, B. and J. L., *The Bleak Age* (1934)
Hellborn, K. von, *Franz Schubert* (Vienna, 1865)[6]
Hewitt, J. F., *The Building of the Railways in Cheshire down to 1860* (Manchester, 1972)
Hogarth, G., *The Philharmonic Society of London* (1862)
Howarth, P., *The Year is 1851* (1951)
Hughes, T., *The Stranger's Handbook to Chester and its Environs* (Chester, 1856)
Hutchinson, N., *The Reformed Presbyterian Church in Scotland, 1680–1876* (Paisley, 1893)

Jahn, O., *Wolfgang Amadeus Mozart*, 2nd edn, 4 vols. (Leipzig, 1867)[7]
James, H., *Letters*, ed. L. Edel, vol. I (1976)

Keefer, L., *Baltimore's Music* (Baltimore, Md., 1962)
King, A. H., *Some British Collectors of Music* (1963)
Kingsley, C., *Letters and Memoirs of his Life*, ed. F. Kingsley (1877)

[4] From Grove's Library: with MS. notes by Grove.

[5] 'A book *ludicrous* full of mistakes of all kinds'; Grove—who corrected some of them. Copy contains a report of a Joachim concert at the Crystal Palace (*The Times*, 20 Mar 1876).

[6] Occasional pencil notes in text; one sheet of notes, printed notice of death of K. von Hellborn, and part of autograph letter from C. F. Pohl inserted.

[7] Pencil notes: 'A precious long yarn, Baden Oct 1 1867'.

Krehbiel, H. E., *The Philharmonic Society of New York: A Memorial* (New York, 1892)[8]

Landau, H. T., *Erstes poetisches Beethoven-Album* (Prague, 1872)[9]
Larchet, J. F., *The Royal Irish Academy of Music 1856–1956* (Dublin, 1956)
Lehmann, R., *Men and Women of the Century: Portraits and Sketches* (1896)
Lehmann, R. C., *Memories of Half a Century* (1908)
Lenz, W. von, *Beethoven et ses trois styles*, 2 vols. (St Petersburg, 1852)[10]
Locker-Lampson, F., *My Confidences* (1896)

Mackenzie-Greave, A., *Clara Novello, 1818–1908* (1955)
Maitland, J. A. Fuller, *Joseph Joachim* (1905)
—— *A Doorkeeper of Music* (1929)
Mendelssohn-Bartholdy, J. L. F., *Briefe aus den Jahren 1830–1847*, 2 vols. (Leipzig, 1861, 1863)[11]
Miller, E., *That Noble Cabinet: A History of the British Museum* (1973)
Monk, E. W., *The Journal of Caroline Fox, 1835–1876* (1972)

Napier, J., *Life of Robert Napier* (Edinburgh, 1904)
Nowell-Smith, S., ed., *Letters to Macmillan* (1967)

Oliphant, M. E. (afterward Graham, M. E. Maxtone), *The Maxtones of Cultoquhey* (Edinburgh/London, 1935)
Ormond, L. and R., *Lord Leighton* (Newhaven, 1975)
Orr, S., *A Handbook to the Works of Robert Browning* (1896)
Overton, C., *The Crystal Palace; or, the Half not Told* (Hull, 1851)

Palgrave, F. T., ed., *The Golden Treasury* (1867)[12]
Parry, E., *The Railway Companies from Chester to Shrewsbury* (Chester, 1849, 1884)
Parry, C. H. H., *College Addresses Delivered to Pupils of the Royal College of Music by*, ed. H. C. Colles (1920)
Parry, J., *An Account of the Royal Musical Festival . . . in Westminster Abbey, 1834* (1834)
Paston, G. (pseud.), *At John Murray's—Records of a Literary Circle 1843–1892* (1932)
Paton, H., *Genealogy of the Symington Family* (1908)
Petitpierre, J., *The Romance of the Mendelssohns* (1947)
Phillips, J., *Jamaica: its Past and Present State* (1843)
Pierotti, E., *Jerusalem explored . . .*, trans. T. G. Bonney, 2 vols. (1864)
Polko, E., *Erinnerungen an Felix Mendelssohn-Bartholdy, etc.* (Leipzig, 1868)[13]

[8] On front board: 'Sir George Grove from the author Feb 1895 Lower Sydenham S.E.'.
[9] Pencil signature: 'Sept 1892' on fly-leaf.
[10] Pencil signature on endpaper verso, and notes.
[11] Note on vol. I: 'my Palestine journey 1861'.
[12] Inscribed to Charles Wood: 'Nov 1884'.
[13] 'G. Grove Rome 1868' in pencil.

Poole, L. and G., *One Passion, Two Loves: The Story of Heinrich and Sophia Schliemann* (New York, 1966)

Pritchard, A., *The Life and Work of Charles Pritchard* (1897)

Pritchard, C., *An Address at the Opening of a Proprietary Grammar School, June 9, 1840* (1840)

Prothero, R. E. and Bradley, G., *Life and Correspondence of Arthur Penrhyn Stanley, D.D.*, 2 vols. (1893)

Punshon, W., 'Macaulay' from *Lectures delivered before the Y.M.C.A. in Exeter Hall, November 1861–February 1862* (1862)

Richards, R., *Two Bridges over Menai* (Cardiff, 1945)

Ritter, C., *Ritter's Geographisch-statistisches Lexikon , , ,* (Leipzig, 1855): 5th edn (1864–5)[14]

Robinson, E., *Biblical Researches in Palestine, Mount Sinai, and Arabia Petraea: A Journal of Travels in the Year 1838*, by E. Robinson and E. Smith. Drawn from the original Diaries, with Historical Illustrations, by E. Robinson, 3 vols. (1841)

Robinson, K., *Wilkie Collins* (1951)

Rogers, M. E., *Domestic Life in Palestine* (1862); 2nd edn (1863)[15]

Rowse, A. L., *Matthew Arnold, Poet and Prophet* (1976)

Saintsbury, G., *A History of Nineteenth Century Literature (1780–1900)* (1896/1912)

Schumann, E., *Memoirs*, trans. M. Busch (1927)

Scott, H., *Fasti Ecclesiae Scoticanae: III Synod of Glasgow and Ayr* (Edinburgh, 1910)

Shaw, G. B., 'Sir George Grove', *Saturday Review*, 14 Nov 1896

—— *London Music in 1888–89* (1937)

—— *Music in London 1890–94*, 3 vols. (1932)

Simpson, F., *Chester Free Public Library* (Chester 1930–1)

Smith, E., *Clapham: an Historical Town* (Clapham [1968])

Smith, W., *An Atlas of Ancient Geography, Biblical and Classical* (1874)

—— *A Dictionary of the Bible* (1863/1893)

Speyer, E., *My Life and Friends* (1937)

Stanford, C. V., *Pages from an Unwritten Diary* (1914)

Stanford, W. B. and McDowell, R. B., *Mahaffy: a Biography of an Anglo-Irishman* (1971)

Stanley, T. P., *Addresses and Sermons . . . U.S.A., 1878* (1883)

—— *Sinai and Palestine* (1856, 1864, 1868)

—— *The Life and Correspondence of Thomas Arnold, D.D.* (1844)

Statham, H., *My Thoughts on Music and Musicians* (1892)

Stoppard, E., *George, Duke of Cambridge*, 2 vols. (1906)

Strachey, L., *Eminent Victorians* (1918)

Tennyson, C., *Alfred Tennyson* (1949)

---

[14] 'Presented by Sir George Grove', 21 September 1883 (not in Grove's hand).

[15] The author gives her address: 21 Soho Square, London; dedication: Wm. Holman Hunt.

Thomson, D., *England in the Nineteenth Century* (1950)
Tovey, D. F., *Essays in Musical Analysis I* (1935)
Tovey, D. F., and Parratt, G., *Walter Parratt, Master of the Music* (Oxford, 1941)
Trevelyan, G., *Life and Letters of Lord Macaulay* (1876)
Turnbull, R., 'Musical Glasgow' in *Old Glasgow Clubs, Transactions* (Glasgow, 1913–18)
Tynan, K., *Twenty-five Years* (1918)
—— *Memories* (1924)

Wakefield, G , *Layard of Nineveh* (1963)
Walker, C., *Thomas Brassey, Railway Builder* (1969)
Waugh, A., *Alfred, Lord Tennyson* (1892/1902)
Wilkinson, H., *Bermuda from Sail to Steam: A History, 1784–1901*, 2 vols. (1973)
Wyndham, H. Saxe, *August Manns and the Saturday Concerts* (1909)

Yeats, W. B., *Reveries over Childhood and Youth* (1915)

Alexandra College Magazine (Dublin), 1931, '33, '40, '50
Athenaeum, The, 1821–
Allgemeine Musikalische Zeitung (Leipzig), 1867, 1875

Birmingham, History of, ed. C. Gill, A. Briggs, 2 vols. (1952)
Black's Picturesque Guide to Glasgow and the West Coast (Edinburgh, 1852)
Bradshaw's Railway Manual, Shareholders' Guide and Directory, 1848–1923
British Association for the Advancement of Science, with Transactions of the Sections, 1865, '66
Buckingham, The Victorian History of the County of, vol. III (1925)
Burlington House—The Royal Academy of Arts Anniversary Dinner, Programmes of, 1884, '85, '86, '89

Cheap Music, A Short History of (1887)
Chambers's Journal, 1854–
Chester Chronicle, The, 1848
Chester Courier, The, 1848
Chester, Journal of the Architectural, Archaeological and Historic Society of, 1849–1855 (Chester, 1857)
Chester, Mechanics' Institution of, Annual Reports 1847
Chester, Philipson and Golder's Directory for, 1893, '94
Chester, Williams's Commercial Directory of the City and Borough of (Liverpool, 1846)
Chester and Holyhead Railway, General Description of the Britannia and Conway Tubular Bridges on the, [by] A Resident Engineer [E. Clarke] (1850)
Civil Engineers, Proceedings of the Institution of, 1837–
Clapham, with its Common and Environs (Clapham), 1827, '28, '41
Clapham Grammar School, Prospectus of the Regulations of the, *c*. 1840
Clapham Grammar School, Reports of the Committee of the Subscribers to (Clapham), 1835, '37, '39

Crystal Palace, The Removal of the (1852)

[*Crystal Palace, The*] *in 1853: a Dialogue between Lady Fanny Seymour and Miss Caroline Howard* (1853)

Crystal Palace, The: Why it should not be open on the Afternoon of Sundays (1855)

[Crystal Palace, The] *Why not open the Crystal Palace and Park on Sunday Afternoons*, by A Clergyman of the Church of England (1855)

[Crystal Palace, The] *Catalogue of the Principal Instrumental and Vocal Works performed at the Saturday Concerts from 1855–1872* (Crystal Palace, 1872)

Daily News, The, 1881

Dublin, Thom's Directory of (Dublin), 1867–

Early Victorian England, 1830–65, 2 vols. (1934)

Edinburgh Review (Edinburgh) 1882

Engineer, The, 1900 ('Sir George Grove', p. 567)

Engineering, 27 Dec 1867 ('Mr. Robert Napier: Engineer and Shipbuilder')

First etc. Feis Ceoil. Irish Music Festival (Dublin, 1897) ('Programme Syllabus of Prize Compositions, etc.')

Grove, George, Sale Catalogue of, 4 November 1895

Harrogate Advertiser, The (Harrogate), 1903

Illustrated London News, The, 1842–

Irish Times, The (Dublin), 1886

Liverpool Courier, The (Liverpool), 1896

Liverpool Museum, The (Liverpool), 1848–9

Music in England: The Proposed Royal College of Music (Three addresses delivered by HRH The Duke of Edinburgh, HRH The Duke of Albany, and HRH The Prince Christian [at Manchester]) (1882)

Musical Examiner, The, 1842–4

Musical Herald and Tonic Sol-fa Reporter, ed. J. S. Curwen, 1889–1920

Musical Times, The, 1844–

Musical World, The, 1836–91

Neue Musik-Zeitung, Die (Stuttgart), 1880–1928

New Ireland Review, The, vols. I, VIII, IX (Dublin, 1895, 1898)

North Wales Chronicle, The (Bangor), 1849

Norwood Review and Crystal Palace Reporter, The (Sydenham), 1881

Novello, The History of: A Century and a Half in Soho (1961)

Picture of Glasgow: Strangers' Guide, 3rd edn (Glasgow, 1878)

Sacred Harmonic Society, Annual Reports of The, 1832–1880

Salisbury and Winchester Journal and General Advertiser, The (Salisbury), 1887, 1895
Salisbury Times, The (Salisbury), 1895
Saturday Review, The (1896)
Schumann, Gedächtnissfeier für Robert, 17, 18, 19 Aug 1873 (Düsseldorf, 1873)
Scottish Musical Monthly (Glasgow), 1895
Strand Magazine, 1 June, 1895 (biography of George Grove),
Sunday Times, The, 1896
Sydenham, Forest Hill, and Penge Gazette, 'Brief Sketches of Local men: Sir George Grove' by W.J.R. (Sydenham), 11 Jan 1895

Times, The, 16 Apr 1896 ('Beethoven and his Nine Symphonies')
———— 29 May 1900 (obituary notice of Grove)
———— 1 June 1900 (account of funeral)
———— 1 Apr 1914 (obituary notice of Lady Grove)

Windsor Magazine, The, 1891–1904 ('Chronicles of Our Time: Vanity Fair')

General Index

attitude to, 56, 60, 71, 212, 213, 223,
232, 233, 238; relatives, involvement
with, 95, 151, 195, 220, 244, 249, 253,
262; religion, views on, 64, 68, 71, 76,
77, 90, 111, 123, 124, 156, 259; stoical
qualities, 67, 85; war, opposition to,
119; work, obsession with, 30, 32, 70,
104, 115, 131, 194; complexity of
character, 271–5; quality of scholarship, 275–8; style of presentation, 278–
283; critical faculty, 283f
PRINCIPAL WORKS: *Atlas of Ancient
Geography*, 88, 91, 122; *Beethoven and
his Nine Symphonies*, 204, 224, 233,
234, 235, 236, 247, 254, 255, 256, 257,
258, 270, 275, 278, 279, 280, 284, 285,
286; *Dictionary of the Bible*, 72–4, 75,
77–8, 82, 87, 124, 154 n13, 215, 250,
274, 275–7; *Dictionary of Music*, 30, 33,
40, 47, 94, 97, 99 n14, 112, 124, 126,
127–48 *passim*, 149–52 *passim*, 154,
158, 159, 164, 179, 188, 190, 191, 214,
215, 224 n16, 234, 237, 265 n54, 268,
271, 274, 283, 285; MS. Commonplace
Books, 30, 39, 86, 94, 98, 111, 136–7,
146
Grove, Georgiana, 24
Grove, Harriet (Bradley): marriage, 54;
hostess, 70, 152, 223, 252; kindness to
A. Sullivan, 85; younger brothers of,
117, 225; absence from home, 151;
strength of character in adversity, 189,
232, 267; marital difficulties, 191, 215,
216; feeling for eldest son, 217; discontents in later life, 231, 244; not
present at Grove's funeral, 268; death
of, 269
Grove, John, 15
Grove, Julius Charles, 74, 203, 244, 268,
269
Grove, Kezia, 13 n1, 35–6 n14, 54, 202,
275
Grove, Lucy Penrose, 57, 81, 84, 191, 226,
268
Grove, Margaret (of Fern), 196 n7
Grove, Mary Bithiah, 13 n1, 24 n19; *see*
Bennett
Grove, Mary (Blades), 13, 15, 23, 36 n15,
54
Grove, Millicent, 81, 151, 155, 160, 170,
174, 179, 188–90, 191, 216, 274
Grove, Bishop Robert, 186
Grove, Thomas, 13, 15, 17, 54, 59 n16
Grove, Thomas Blades: youth, 13 n1, 16;
accompanies George to Scotland, 30;
house at Charing Cross above the business, 36 n15; Master Fishmonger, 54;
letter to *The Times*, 93 n41; a pillar of
society in Penn, 133 n11; George
visits his rich brother, 186, 215; at

Bithiah's funeral, 233; letter to, 245;
death of, 261–2
Grove, Walter Maurice, 14 n3, 70, 131
n9, 144, 157, 165, 217, 244
Grove, Revd W. C., 210 n5
Gruneison, Charles Lewis, 102
Guardian, The, 19 n11
Guizot, François, 57
Gunton, Frederick, 44

Hackett, Maria, 28
Hadow, Sir William Henry, 126 n32; *A
Croatian Composer*, 263
Hagley, opportunity for Edith Oldham
with the Lyttletons, 195
Haifa, 73
Halberstadt, 95
Hallam, Henry, 31
Hallé, Charles, 160, 200, 254; Lady Hallé
(Wilma Neruda), 264; Orchestra, *see*
Manchester
Hallett, Beatrice, 199
Hamburg, 172 n28, 200
Handel, George Frideric, 23, 40, 45, 160,
278, 285; *Acis and Galatea*, 60, 101,
128–9, 235; *Athalia*, 39; *Esther*, 32;
Funeral Anthem, 24; 'Hallelujah'
chorus, 32, 63; *Hercules*, 135; *Messiah*,
23, 24, 25, 26, 28, 31, 32, 37, 79, 154,
253 n26; edition of R. Franz, 200; *Ode
for St Cecilia's Day*, 102; *Samson*, 39;
Saul, 39; VI Fugues, 32; operas, 79;
additional accompaniments, 173–4, 248;
Handel Festivals, 24, 68, 78–9, 244, 260
Hanover, 158
Hansard, Revd Septimus, 55, 76 n13
Hanslick, Edouard, 244
Hardy, Thomas: *The Poor Man and the
Lady, Desperate Remedies*, 116
Harmonicon, The, 25
Harper, Dr Gerald, 145, 157, 268
Harper, Thomas, 168, 173
Harris, Augustus, 203
Harrison, Bithiah (Grove), 233, 274, 275
Harrison, Frederic, 106 n24, 232
Harrison, Revd Joshua Clarkson, 36
Harrison, Samuel, 24
Harrogate, Grove House, home of Samson
Fox, 199
Harrogate Advertiser, 199 n13
Harrow School, 72 n6, 129
Hartington, Spencer Compton Cavendish,
Marquis of, 221
Harvard College, 146; Musical Associa-
tion, 146
Harvey, Admiral Sir Thomas, and Light-
house Commissioners, 34
Hausmann, Robert, 200
Haweis, Revd Hugh Reginald, 132, 181,
246

INDEX 339

Pye, Kellow J., 131
Pyne, Zoë, 179, 252

Quarterly Musical Magazine and Review, 25
Quarterly Review, 124, 125
Quebec, 147
Quilter, Harry, 157
Quilter, Roger, 157

Raff, Joachim, 106
Ragatz, 84, 234
Railway Companies: Birkenhead, Lancashire and Cheshire Junction, 43; Chester and Birkenhead, 43; Chester and Holyhead, 43; Conway and Holyhead, 42; Eastern Bengal, 74 n9; Grand Junction, 29; London and Birmingham, 28–9, 42, 48, 53, 200, 271; London and North Western, 42; London, Chatham and Dover, 157; London and Southampton, 29; Manchester, Sheffield and Lincolnshire, 53; Shrewsbury and Chester, 43
Ramsay, Andrew, 90
Randall, William, 24
Randegger, Alberto, 184
Rausch, Count, 83 n23
Reed, W. F., 65
Reeve, Henry, 164–5
Reeves, John Sims, 281
Reform Bill, 20, 55
Reid, Sir William (Governor of Bermuda), 37
Religious Tract Society, 55
Renan, Ernest, 77 n15, 154; *Souvenirs, Vie de Jésus*, 287–8
Renwick, James, 147
Rice, Alexander Hamilton, 145
Richards, Mrs Elizabeth (murder of), 16
Richmond (Va), 147
Richter, Hans, 151, 172 n28, 173, 183, 200, 207, 218, 251, 266
Ridding (R.C.M. student), 189 n46
Ries, Ferdinand, 137
Rietz, Julius, 100
Rimbault, Edward Francis, 33
Ringgenberg, 204, 225
Ripon, 44, 169
Ritchie, Lady Anne Isabella (Thackeray), 242, 246
Roberts, Annie, 189, 203
Robertson, Revd Alexander(?), 143
Robinson, Dr Edward (American archaeologist), 123
Robinson, Joseph, 267
Rockstro, William Smith, 159, 184; *Life of Handel*, 169
Rogers, Benjamin, 32, 39

Rogers, Edward Thomas, 73, 76, 91 n38, 275
Rogers, Mary Eliza, 73; *Domestic Life in Palestine*, 73 n7, 277
Rome, 105, 106, 107, 158
Romney, George, 246
Romsey, 251
Ronald, Sir Landon, 214
Rosa, Carl, 173, 193 n3
Rose, Sir John, 166
Rosebery, Archibald Philip, Fifth Earl of, 162, 245
Rossetti, Daniel Gabriel, 114
Rossetti, Christina, 196
Rossini, Gioacchino, 39, 59, 160; *William Tell*, 66
Rouen, 257
Royal College of Music; 156, 159, 160, 161–90 *passim*, 209–19, 220, 221, 228, 230, 233, 236, 244, 245, 246, 247, 265, 271; new building for, 198, 209–10, 227, 237, 239–40; Alexandra House, 178, 192, 193; Board Meeting, 214; Commonplace Books, *see* Grove, Sir George, principal works; Concert Hall, 193; Council, 211, 228, 238, 241; Festival Concert, 260; Grove Memorial Concert, 268; Junior Orchestra, 211; Orchestra, 199, 200, 214, 227, 255, 267; performances by students, 174, 184, 189, 193, 194, 195 n5, 200, 202, 211, 215, 241; presentation to Grove, 251; scandal at, 238–9; Schubert concert, 249
Royston, 184
Roze, Mme (singer in Liverpool), 164
Rubinstein, Anton, 100, 102, 246; pfte concerto in D minor, 100
Rugby, school, 71, 157, 242; station, 234
Runcorn, 48
Ruskin, John, 110
Russell, Alice Scott, 82, 83 n23
Russell, Anna, 172, 189, 209
Russell, John Francis Stanley, Second Earl, 207 n27
Russell, George, 65
Russell, Lord John, 89
Russell, John Scott, 52, 53, 82, 110, 117
Russell, Luise Scott, 82, 83 n23, 144, 149
Russell, Rachel Scott, 82, 83 n23
Russell, Thomas O'Neill, 255
Rusty (dog), 182
Rutherford, Ernest, 273
Ryan, Desmond, 102
Ryan, Desmond, junior, 128

St Andrews, 231, 256, 283; St Leonard's School, 182 n37, 203, 245
St James's Gazette, 170, 183, 186, 213
Sainton, Prosper, 173